THE RIGGER'S APPRENTICE

THE RIGGER'S APPRENTICE

Brion Toss

INTERNATIONAL MARINE PUBLISHING COMPANY
Camden, Maine 04843

Typeset by The Key Word, Inc., Belchertown, Massachusetts
Printed and bound by The Alpine Press, Stoughton, Massachusetts

Published by International Marine Publishing Company
21 Elm Street, Camden, Maine 04843
(207) 236-4342

Library of Congress Cataloging in Publication Data

Toss, Brion.
    The rigger's apprentice.

    1. Knots and splices.   2. Masts and rigging.
I. Title.
VM533.T58 1984   623.88'82   84-47755
ISBN 0-87742-165-X

Portions of Chapters 3, 4, 5, and 7 appeared in *Sail* magazine.
Portions of Chapters 1, 3, and 5 appeared in *WoodenBoat* magazine.

Cover and book design by Amy Fischer

Contents

·

Foreword

•

I first met Brion Toss at the Port Townsend Wooden-boat Festival in 1979, where he and Nick Benton were giving a hands-on lesson in Liverpool splicing to a large group of enthusiastic sailors. As I watched them I could see the joy they derived from passing on the information and skills they'd learned from other, older riggers. And so goes the haphazard way of passing down practical skills, which is why these skills are so often lost unless some dedicated person will take the time and effort to commit his inherited knowledge to paper. When I learned that Brion was going to do just that I became impatient. His writing has always been scientific but humorous, the accompanying illustrations clear and concise. So I knew his book would allow many sailors, including myself, the creative satisfaction of making gear such as a new headstay, lazyjacks, or a jibnet from wire, rope, and a few thimbles. This handmade gear is a joy to the sailor's eye—strong, simple, and best of all, repairable right on the deck of a sailing vessel. This means no traveling to find a hydraulic swaging machine operator, no running around hoping to find the perfect end fitting for the millimeter wire you bought in Tahiti when you have sailed to another country that uses fittings measured in inches.

Even more interesting to most of us is that if you rig your own boat you will save cruising funds. The cost of the wire and thimbles used for the standing rigging on our 30-foot, 17,500-pound cutter was only $350. If I hadn't spliced this wire myself I'd have had to pay an average of $21 to $25 for each 5/16-inch swage in addition to the cost of the wire. Readers of this book who have nimble fingers and slim pocketbooks will find they can outfit an efficient sailboat at a savings of several thousand dollars.

Beyond recording what the old-timers have taught him, Brion Toss keeps looking for new methods and materials that will combine the best of the old with the practicalities of the new. He has tested the strengths of different wire splices and swages and used this information to develop a smooth-entry Liverpool splice that averages 99 percent of the manufacturers' rated wire strength, a vast improvement over the 85 percent figure we used to use for hand-spliced eyes. When I heard about this fair-entry, high-strength splice, I had to learn how to do it before I made up the standing rigging for our new cruising boat, *Taleisin*. Fortunately, Brion published that section of this new book in *Sail* magazine just when I needed it most.

Now as I read the final manuscript for this book, I feel confident that most of the practical riggers' tricks will remain available to exercise and delight the fingers and eyes of the next generation of sailors.

Larry Pardey
September 1984

Preface

•

Rigging is the art of using knots and lines, either to move things or to keep them from moving. It can be put to such mundane tasks as guying telephone poles or raising the flag at city hall. But it is also expressed in such monuments to engineering as a 12-meter's minimalist rod spiderweb or the awesome hoisting gear of a 300-ton shipyard crane. Somewhere between, there is a branch of the art that seeks to combine technological achievement, human scale, and a minimum of tools and expense. Knowledge of it enables one to sail more efficiently with the help of fewer experts and fewer costly manufactured contrivances, and with the confidence and peace of mind that result from personal resourcefulness. It is called traditional rigging, and it is the subject of this book.

At the beginning I would like to emphasize the distinction between the terms "traditional" and "archaic." No amount of reverence for our maritime heritage will lead us to put tarred-hemp standing rigging on modern craft; time, engineering, and newer materials have rendered that practice obsolete for all but historical reproductions. On the other hand, many procedures and materials from the 19th century and earlier are still in use today, unchanged or only modified to meet new demands. Basic knots such as the Bowline, Anchor Hitch, and Figure Eight are good examples, as are blocks, winches, seizings, lashings—well, the list is continued in the following pages. These items have survived because long, hard experience has shown that they can be counted on to do their jobs with a minimum of fuss and maximum effect. It is up to the individual sailor to decide how much of the old to mix with the new; there is always some mixing, for even an ultramodern vessel carries elements of the past in its design and gear.

An old saying has it that there's "a short splice for every sailor, a long splice for every ship"; I trust the reader will understand that my personal rigging style is reflected in the following pages. Given time and experience, riggers can—indeed, properly ought to—establish their own variations and preferences, making their own unique contributions to the context of tradition. Toward that end, I hope to provide enough procedures, principles, and knowledge of the standard materials to let the reader deduce the *sense* of rigging. That half-intuitive sense, once gained, can guide one's own innovations.

Because this is only a book by a journeyman and not five years with a master, one will find a limited sort of apprenticeship here. It may propel you to work up a new gang of rigging for your boat; it will improve your handling of rope, wire, and rig; and if you ever have to improvise a jury rig, it will stand you in good stead. If you like what you see here and want to continue, then *find a rigger* to teach you more. Watch, badger, cajole, do scut work, even pay for lessons: learn.

If your marlingspike expertise is past the apprentice stage already, consider this a collection of variations on old themes, many little-known, that you might find useful. Tradition involves constant upgrading.

A few comments about the book: In most knot and rigging books, the difference between the table of contents and the index is that the latter is alphabetized; usually there is little said in either about the nature of knots themselves. In the present work, knots are presented in their context in the hope that readers will learn not just the how but the why of things, and so will be better able to apply their knowledge to the infinitely varied demands of marlingspike work. To the rigger, knots are tools, but simply learning to tie a knot doesn't make one a rigger any more than learning to use a socket wrench makes one a mechanic.

The Loft Procedures and Installation and Maintenance chapters contain specialized information telling the story of how one can put together a rig. Take what you need from here and do not be dismayed if your enthusiasm is not initially matched by your dexterity; one big reason store-bought gear predominates on contemporary craft is that the traditional alternatives require a lot of hard work and practice. Persevere, and bear in mind that by taking the manufacture into your own hands, you also take on the responsibility for the quality of the work.

The Fancy Work and Tricks and Puzzles chapters are no less significant than the others; their contents aren't essential to the structural integrity of a rig, but they can do wonders for the sanity of a rigger. The corresponding chapters in *The Ashley Book of Knots* provided welcome relief for me when I had tired of studying the *n*th method of coiling rope or reeving tackle, and I hope that readers will find similar relief and distraction with some new twists here.

The Design and Emergency Procedures chapters are related, inasmuch as attention to the first can go a long way toward preventing the harsh realities of the second. Should things go wrong, the same principles that inform the fabrication and use of a good rig are also our allies in preserving the safety of our vessel and ourselves. It is to be hoped that both chapters provide evidence of the validity of a traditional approach to rigging, even if your boat is a state-of-the-art racer-cruiser.

While writing this book, I have tried always to keep in mind the values of resourcefulness, simplicity, and enduring strength; they seem to have something to do with happiness. So I trust that what follows will be not only a collection of procedures, but an enjoyable way of proceeding.

Brion Toss
Brooklin, Maine
July 1984

Acknowledgments

·

The trouble with writing about a traditional art is that there are millions of people to thank. The list would fill pages even if I limited it to the riggers, sailors, boatbuilders, shopkeepers, truckers, and others from whom I received instruction in the course of my own apprenticeship.

So to pare the list down to those who have had a hand in the production of this book, many thanks to: Jim Bauer, Kathy Brandes, Maynard Bray, Ted Brewer, Nancy Caudle, Jon Eaton, Robin Lincoln, Carl Meinzinger, Freeman Pittman, Peter Spectre, Roger Taylor, Malcolm Wehncke, and Jon Wilson. Several thanks to the staffs of *Sail* and *Woodenboat* magazines, wherein portions of the book first appeared. Millions of thanks to all the rest.

CHAPTER 1

Rigging 101

•

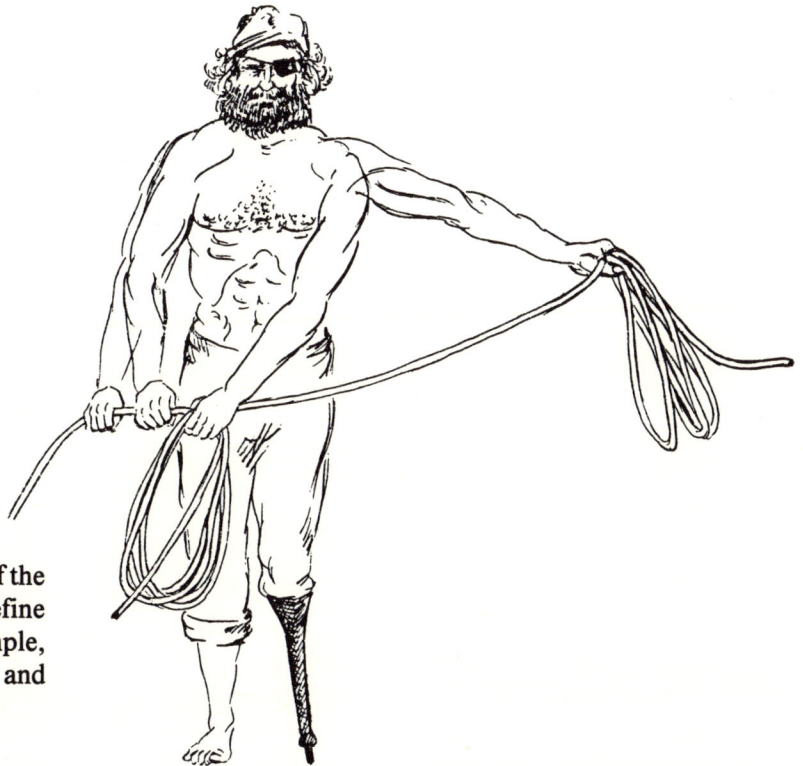

Welcome. This apprenticeship begins with a few of the basic artifacts, principles, and procedures that define and make possible the art of rigging. They're simple, but using them to good effect requires thought and care.

ROPE

Rope is simple, ubiquitous, ancient. A creature of tension, it exists to be stretched between opposing forces. It is a highly evolved tool which, in its myriad sizes, materials, and constructions, can meet every sort of rigging need. Limitations are likely to be on the part of the user; it is for us to develop skill appropriate to the tool.

Start simply by observing rope at work. In shipyards, farmyards, and construction sites it transmits power and performs its many jobs. Look at the size of the rope used, how it is made, how it looks when new and worn, how it is handled by the people who make a living with it.

Before continuing this chapter, go to a chandlery and ask for a ball of marline, a roll of nylon seine twine,

and 50 feet of ⅜-inch-diameter three-strand spun-Dacron rope. Each strand of the rope is made up of short polyester fibers that have been spun together into yarns, much as wool or cotton is. The clerk will measure off 50 feet of rope from a coil or spool, but by cutting it, he or she will transform it into a 50-foot *line*; usually "rope" is a general term and a description of the raw material, while "line" is what you make from rope. Thus a halyard is a line that raises sails, and a sheet is a line that trims them. Both are made from rope. There are exceptions to this terminology, so you can ignore the off-repeated pedantry that "there are no ropes aboard a vessel." Anyone who says that isn't familiar with a tiller rope, manrope, bellrope, or the roping on sails.

1

FIGURE 1. *The turns of a coil will not lie fair without a slight twist put into each.*

Rope as Battery: Coiling and Stowing

Rope in use is in clean, linear tension—an exercise in geometry. Rope that's not in use is a perverse creature, an incipient tangle, a rat's nest waiting to happen. If you let it have its way—and too many people do—you're liable to find yourself in situations that are at best annoying and at worst dangerous. Think of each unused portion of line as a rope battery, upon which you might need to draw at an instant's notice.

When you go to build your battery, it helps to understand the material it's made of. Three-strand rope, for example, is usually right laid—its strands spiral to the right—and given just enough twist in the making to hold the three strands together without rendering the rope too stiff to use. These structural details prove significant when making a coil.

As the title illustration shows, the turns of a coil should be regular and even to discourage the loops from intermingling. When coiling onto your hand, develop rhythm and a sweeping motion for minimum effort, smoothness, and a style conducive to con-

templation. Heavy lines are coiled on deck, then either hung up or turned over so they're ready to run. Leave the end hanging below the coil so that it won't become entangled in the turns. Now notice that as you coil you must impart a slight twist to each loop to lay it neatly against the others (Figure 1); no twist means independent-minded loops. This is the reason for that ancient, seldom explained admonition to "always coil clockwise." When the coil runs out, all those little twists have to go somewhere, and if you coil clockwise (Figure 2-A), right-laid three-strand rope can unlay a bit to absorb them. A counterclockwise coil in right-laid rope can look just as neat, but when it's stretched out, the twists you put in will only tighten an already pretty firm lay, and you're liable to end up with kinks (Figure 2-B). Conversely, in the unlikely event that you come up against left-laid rope, be sure to coil counterclockwise.

In any rope, make the largest loops you conveniently can, or the largest ones that won't drag on the deck if height is limited, so that there will be the fewest total turns and fewer twists to absorb.

2

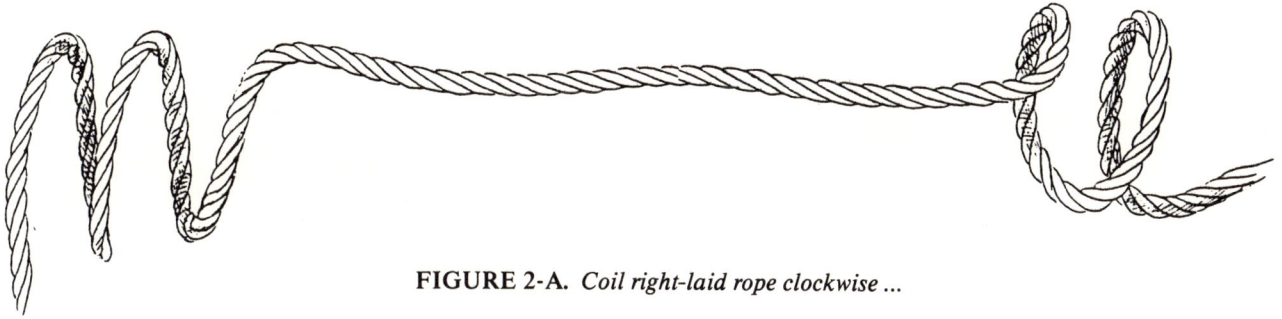

FIGURE 2-A. *Coil right-laid rope clockwise ...*

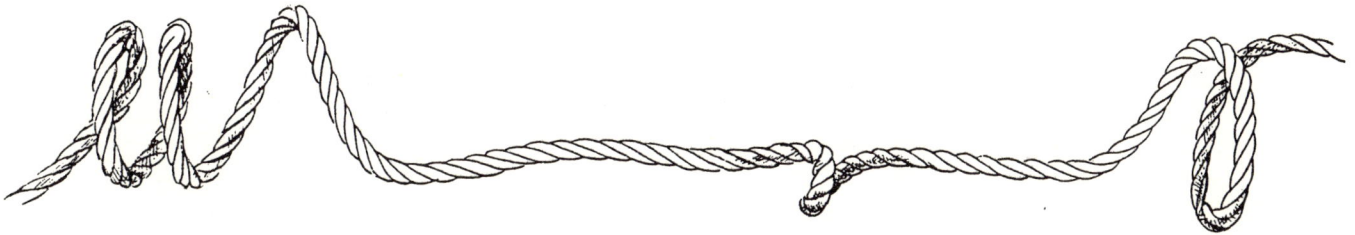

2-B. *...because if you coil it counterclockwise, the lay tightens further when the line is uncoiled, resulting in kinks.*

Alternate Hitch Coiling
Braided rope presents a special problem: Its "lay" runs in both directions, so the twists have nowhere to go no matter which way you coil. This problem has been the source of so many crises that some sailors, finding that a heap on the deck is less liable to foul, don't coil at all. But this approach is not satisfactory either, as a stray wave or stumbling crewmember can reveal. The best solution is Alternate Hitch Coiling, in which regular turns that impart twists in one direction are alternated with hitches that impart twists in the other direction (Figure 3). The twists cancel each other out, resulting in a kinkfree line. Alternate Hitch Coiling is also the method to use for wire rope, garden hoses, electrical cable, and other lay-less lines. But beware: If an end gets accidentally passed through the coil, a string of overhand knots—not just the usual tangle—results (see Tricks and Puzzles chapter).

On belayed lines, another important way to avoid hockles is always to coil *away from the pin or cleat.* That way any twists you do impose will be worked out as you move toward the end.

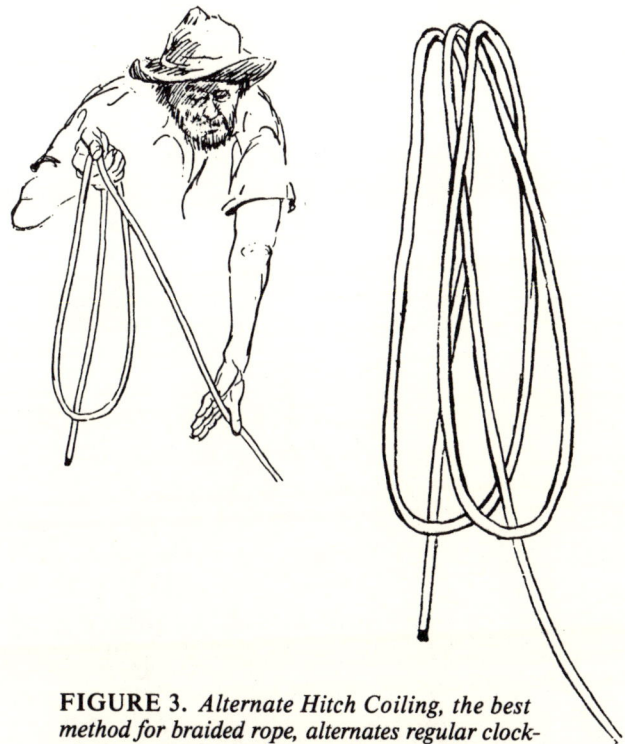

FIGURE 3. *Alternate Hitch Coiling, the best method for braided rope, alternates regular clockwise turns with half hitches. To make the latter, grasp the rope with the back of your hand toward you and turn palm toward you as you bring your hands together.*

3

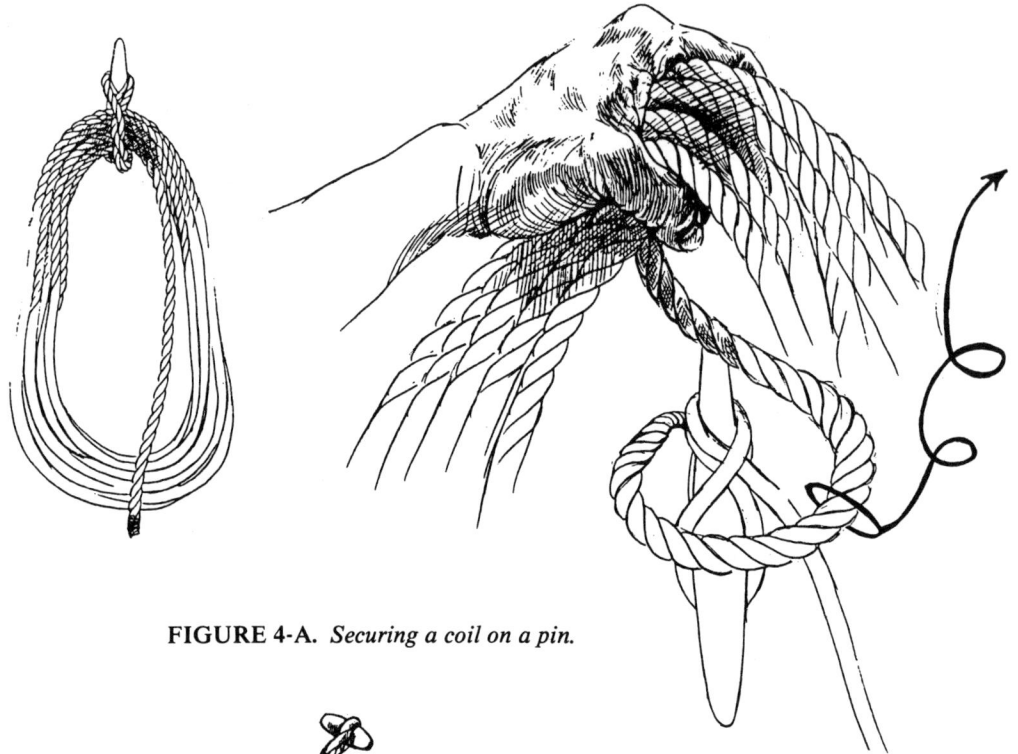

FIGURE 4-A. *Securing a coil on a pin.*

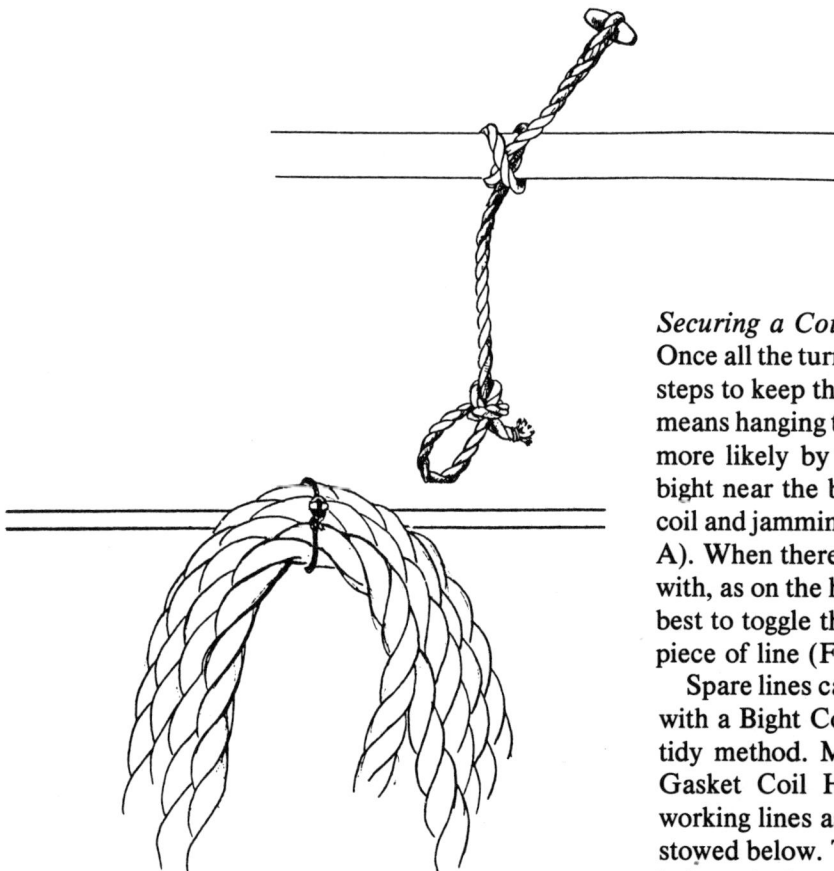

4-B. *To secure a large coil, hang it from a separate, toggled bit of line that is hitched or seized to a sheer pole.*

Securing a Coil

Once all the turns are neat and pretty, you need to take steps to keep them that way. On a vessel, this usually means hanging them on a pin or cleat, either directly or more likely by reaching through the coil, twisting a bight near the belay, then putting that bight over the coil and jamming it down on the pin or cleat (Figure 4-A). When there's a great large amount of line to deal with, as on the halyards of a big gaff-rigged vessel, it's best to toggle the coil to a sheer pole with a separate piece of line (Figure 4-B).

Spare lines can be coiled and hung up out of the way with a Bight Coil Hitch (Figure 5), a very quick and tidy method. More security can be obtained with a Gasket Coil Hitch (Figure 6), which is good for working lines as well as spare ones, either hung up or stowed below. To stow very large lines and wire rope below, the best method is to tie small stuff at regular intervals around the circumference of the coil (Figure 7).

4

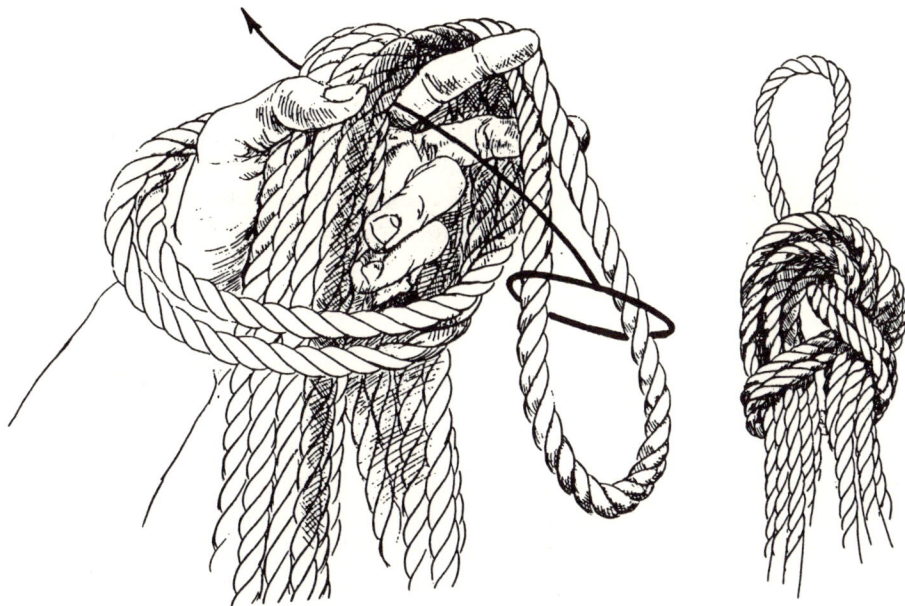

FIGURE 5. *The Bight Coil Hitch. Bring the last turn up counterclockwise to form a long bight. Pass the bight down, around the coil, over its own turn, and finally through the coil.*

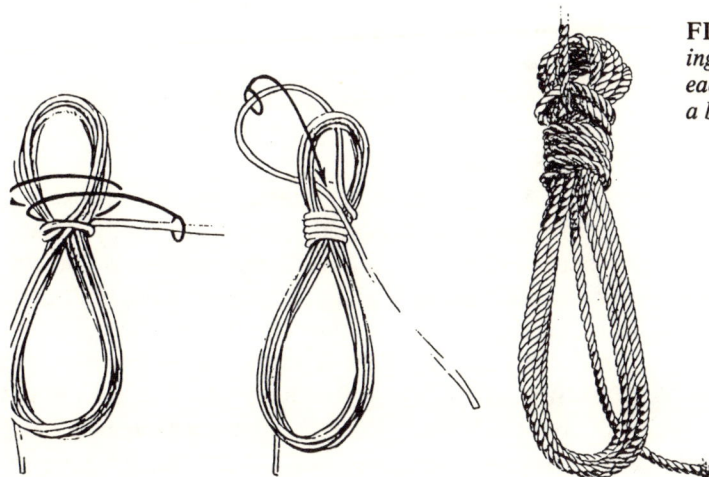

FIGURE 6. *The Gasket Coil Hitch. Using a long working end, make several wraps around the head of the coil, each wrap lying atop the one previous. Finish by passing a bight through the coil, then dropping it over the top.*

FIGURE 7. *To secure large lines and wire rope for long-term storage, coil them and bind with small stuff at regular intervals.*

Letting It Run

When it's time to put a coil to use, lay it face down on deck—that is, with standing part uppermost. When you cast off and let the line run, guide it by letting it run through your hand above the coil. This minimizes the whipping around of the turns as they come out, and gives you some control should a tangle appear. For those gaff halyards or other long lines, it's a good idea to prepare for running by converting the regular coil, which can be hung up but might run foul, into a figure-eight coil (Figure 8), which can't be hung up but will run clear even at high speed. In every instance, even when the line is apparently securely belayed, keep your extremities out of the coil; getting yourself jammed upside-down into a halyard block is a nuisance and an annoyance.

FIGURE 8. *A figure-eight coil will run clear even at high speed. It is always made on deck rather than in hand. Believe it or not it was only coincidence that made Figure 8 a figure eight.*

5

TWO MORE TOOLS

There are many tools associated with ropework, but only three are truly indispensable: rope, the marlingspike, and the rigging knife. The latter two in use reveal characteristics and properties of rope in much the same way that hammer and saw teach a carpenter to understand wood.

The Marlingspike

All of rigging—right up through its most abstract engineering complications—is based on principles and procedures relating to this tool. It is used for pulling seizings and lashings tight, making splices, loosening jammed knots, and tightening shackles. It's also called on to function as a crowbar, wrench, hammer, weapon, and musical instrument (ting!), so it pays to have a good one. By "good" I mean that it:

- Is made of smooth, hard steel, either carbon or stainless;
- has a long taper and small flattened point for easier splicing, prying, and such; and
- has a lanyard hole for tying the tool to your belt or rigging bag so that when you are working aloft, it does not accidentally become a weapon (thud) or a musical instrument (ting! splash!).

Length depends on the job and individual taste; 6 to 10 inches is a good range for shipboard use. Many people like the folding rigger's knife–spike combination, but I don't; a spike is too often needed in a hurry when you don't have both hands free.

The Rigging Knife

This is the spike's complement, a specially designed blade that is equally suited to cutting heavy rope or trimming light seizings. The one shown here is of near-ideal design, incorporating some important features:

FIGURE 9. *The marlingspike, rigging's most essential tool.*

- A heavy, broad-backed blade. The neatest, quickest way to cut rope with a knife is to use a mallet to pound the knife through. Ordinary knives don't stand up well to this treatment, or to heavy shipboard or loft use in general. The back of the blade can be used as a seam-rubbing tool for canvas work and can be rubbed back and forth over the surface of wire rope to remove meathooks.
- The point is fine enough to reach into tight spots or for delicate work, but blunt enough so that you're not liable to poke yourself accidentally some dark and stormy night.
- The blade is slightly curved. Most rigger's knives are flat-bladed, but a little "belly" makes for easier sharpening and slicing, and it lets you cut rope on a flat surface, since the tangent point is aft of the tip, even with the presence of a finger guard.
- Like the spike, a good knife needs a lanyard hole. And again, avoid folding models; as an old caulker once told me, "When you've got your nuts caught in the main sheet, it's a hell of a time to be digging in your pocket for a knife." Female riggers, count your blessings.

FIGURE 10. *The rigging knife is a specialized blade intended for rough use. A sturdy, molded sheath keeps it safe and secure.*

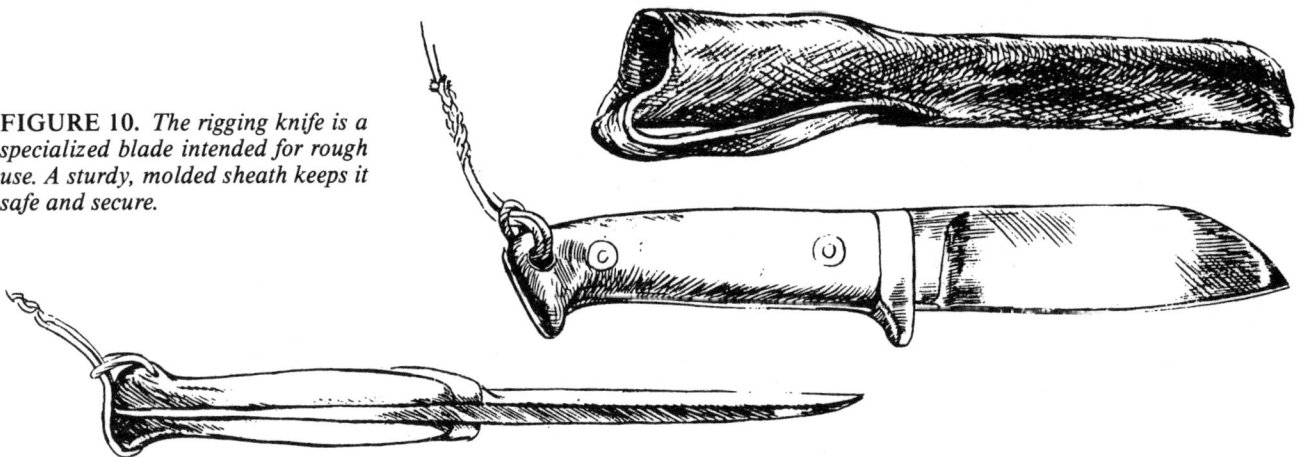

SMALL STUFF—
SPIKE KNOTS, SERVICE, AND SEIZING

It is difficult—even painful—to put much tension on twine or small-diameter rope using only bare hands. But cordage necessarily relies on tension, both for holding things in place and for making knots secure. The handiest solution to this problem is to attach to the twine some other, more comfortable-to-grip object, and then haul on that.

The best knot for this purpose is called the Marlingspike Hitch. It isn't much, just a slipknot made around a spike, but consider this: The Viking longboats of roughly 300 B.C. to 800 A.D., vessels capable of navigating the open ocean, were held together entirely by linen twine lashings. Each lashing was hove taut with this stick-in-hitch procedure, which the Vikings called "marling." Hence "marlingspike" (commonly but with less regard for linguistic antecedents spelled without the "g"), "marline (n)," and incidentally, "mooring." Rivets, nails, glue, and bolts eventually replaced lashings as hull fastenings, but the point remains that flimsy, inexpensive bits of twine can be made structurally significant with tension. The amount one can save in chrome-plated fittings alone can make spike knots worthwhile, and in an emergency, they might be a sailor's only recourse. Good knots to know, even if you're not planning to raid the coast of England.

The Marlingspike Hitch is used to draw up a variety of knots. Some of them are marvels of intricacy, but for starters, snub the end of some twine under two or three turns of its own standing part, around a piece of rope or wire rope. Make your hitch, and exerting even tension wind on a series of tight, tangent turns. That's "service," a means of protecting sails and rigging from chafe. Service is frequently seen over splices; on shrouds, especially where headsails come into contact with them; on mooring lines where they pass through chocks; and on grommets that go around rope-stropped blocks. When sealed with tar, service prevents rot and corrosion in the rigging it covers.

Service is properly applied, as shown, over a bed of twine "worming" and tarred canvas "parceling," usually with a specialized tensioning device called a

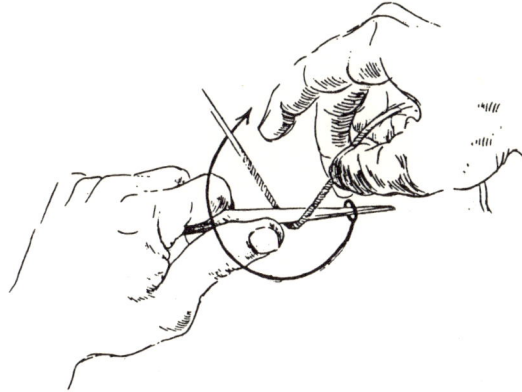

FIGURE 11-A. *Hold line in ring and little ringers of one hand. With other hand, lay spike across line and pivot it in a full circle, ending with the point behind the standing part.*

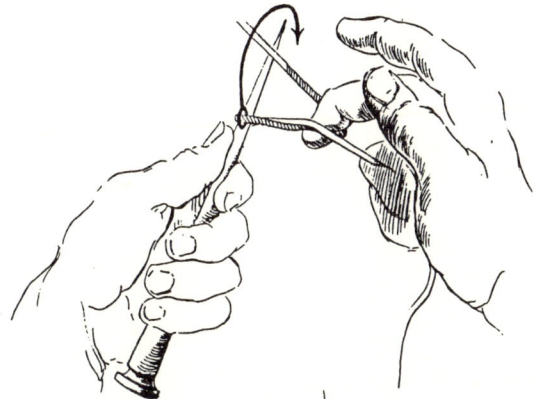

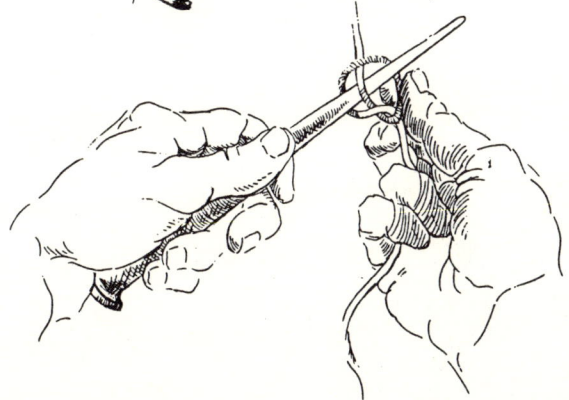

11-B. *In mid-pivot, snag the standing part close to the spike with the tip of your middle finger. This makes it easy to grab (with thumb and forefinger) the bight of line on top of the spike and to pass it over the end of the spike.*

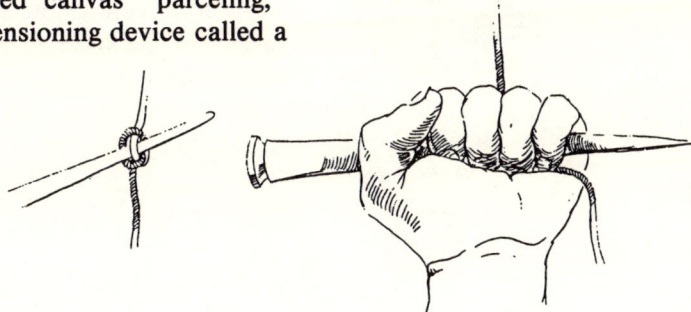

11-C. *The completed knot.*

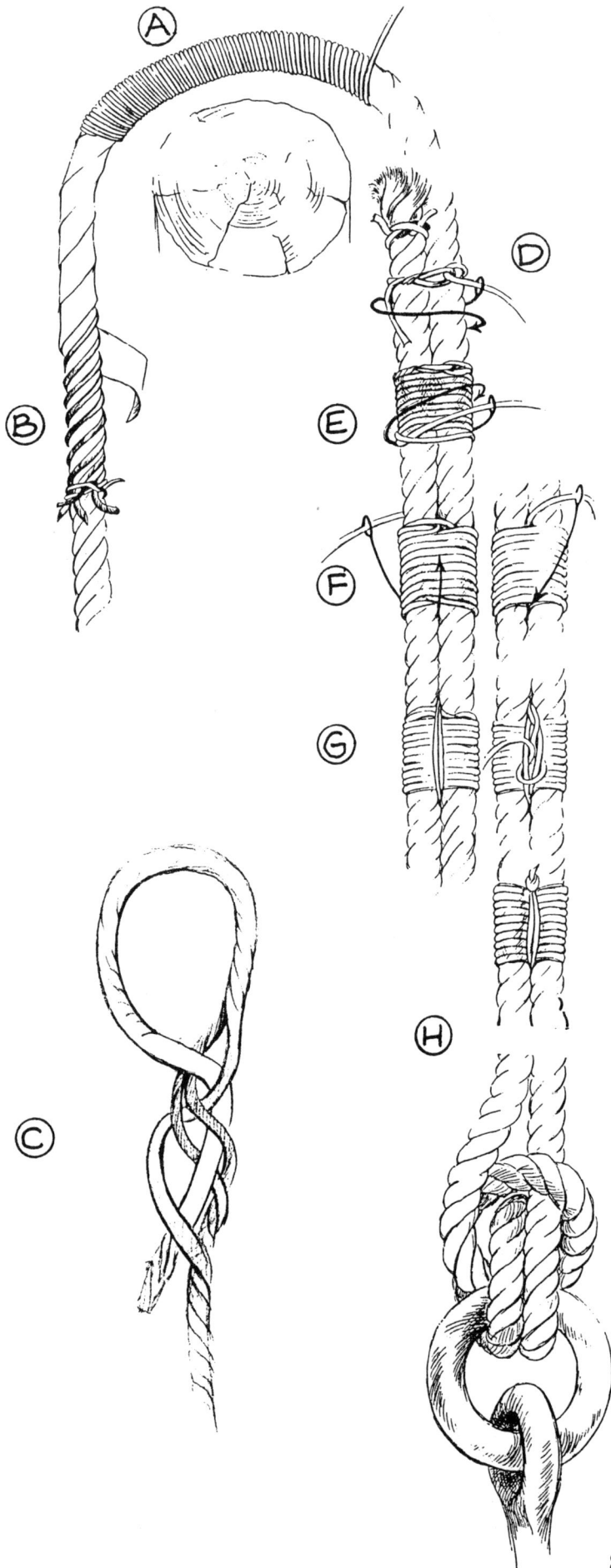

FIGURE 12-A. *Service applied tightly, with the aid of a Marlingspike Hitch, provides waterproofing and protects rope from chafe.*

12-B. Worming is set tightly, filling the spaces where moisture could gather. Parceling of tarred canvas or friction tape provides waterproofing and smooth bedding for service. Worming, parceling, and serving are treated more fully in the Loft Procedures chapter.

12-C. Structure of rope-yarn splice needed to start Throat Seizing.

12-D. Make splice and pass end through eye, forming slipknot around legs of line to be seized.

12-E. Wind on tight turns, as with service, binding legs together. When seizing is roughly square, half-hitch at bottom and proceed to make riding turns over first layer.

12-F. Back at the top, pass the end through the eye of the rope-yarn splice and make two snug crossing or frapping turns.

12-G. Finish with a Flat Knot on the back side of the seizing. Haul the knot tight and cut the end off close.

12-H. A Throat Seizing is used here to supplement an Anchor Hitch.

serving mallet (see Chapter 5), but a marlingspike will do in a pinch. One might say it is used with absence of mallet.

As turns of service are taken, the hauling part shortens. When it becomes too short, the hitch is capsized back into a straight length that in a few more turns becomes part of the service itself. This capsizing calls to notice a hidden characteristic of the Marlingspike Hitch. Notice that the direction from which strain comes on the knot minimizes any tendency for it to jam. To prove this for yourself, make the knot and anchor both ends. When it is pulled on from the wrong direction, it tends to slip around to one side of the spike and jam there. But if pulled the other way, it is more likely to remain stable and to disappear without any fuss once the spike is removed. Be careful, then, to make the hitch as shown.

Now consider seizings, a more sophisticated variety of binding knots than service. Seizing is defined in Steel's *Elements of Mastmaking, Sailmaking, and Rigging* (see Bibliography) as "joining two ropes, or

8

the ends of one rope together, etc., by taking several close turns of small rope, line, or spun yarn around them."

That's right: A seizing is basically a service made around two or more parts. But the function is different, since seizing does not just sit on a line—it must hold separate lines together against lengthwise or lateral strain. There are dozens of specialized seizings, but for general use the preferred knot is the Throat Seizing. It starts with a layer of "round turns," on top of which is laid a protective layer of "riding turns," and finally a tightening finish of "crossing" or "frapping turns." The rigger's way to secure the end is with a Flat Knot.

As with service, each turn of a seizing is hauled tight with the aid of a marlingspike, but the riding turns should not be so tight that they displace the round turns. The importance of strong, even tension will soon become apparent; nothing looks or works worse than a slack seizing.

The Throat Seizing is ideal for ditty bag, water bucket, bosun's chair, deadeye, and many other lanyards, as well as for joining grommet, shell, sheave, and thimble together for a rope-stropped block. What's more, it can be used in combination with other knots for added security. As an example of the latter, consider the Anchor Hitch (see Chapter 3) with the end seized to the standing part. This is neat, strong, and easily cast off to stow the anchor or to shorten the rode if it becomes chafed. If you have a double-braided anchor line, it's also a way to avoid making one of those infernal eyesplices.

There are times when you'll want to make a more temporary seizing. For this, nothing beats the Constrictor Knot, a convenient, relentlessly secure way to bind parcels, keep rope ends from unlaying, or to hold things in place for the application of permanent seizings. To know the knot is constantly to find uses for it (Ashley recommends it for everything from flour sacks to atomizer bulbs). It is at least as valuable as the kingly Bowline.

To tie with the end, make a crossed round turn, then pass the working end under the cross. Two round turns make a Constrictor that is a little harder to draw up but is semipermanent.

When you can drop the knot over the end of the constrictee (sprung oar, garden hose, etc.), tie by the impressively fast in-the-bight method: Arrange the line in your hands as shown in the illustration, then flip both hands over. Done!

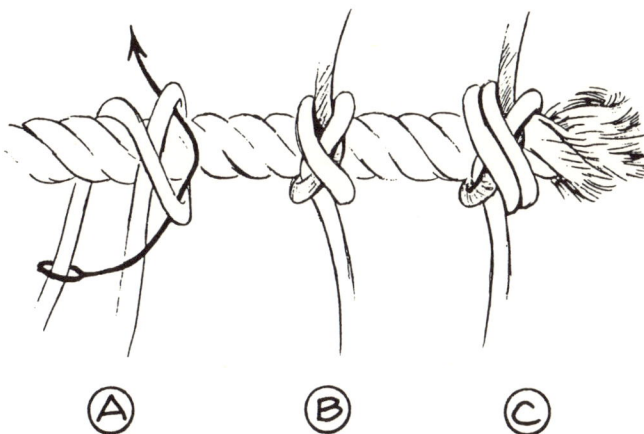

FIGURE 13-A. *To tie a Constrictor Knot with the end, first make a crossed round turn...*

13-B. *...then pass the end under and haul tight.*

13-C. *For a more permanent version, make two round turns before passing the end. Draw up carefully.*

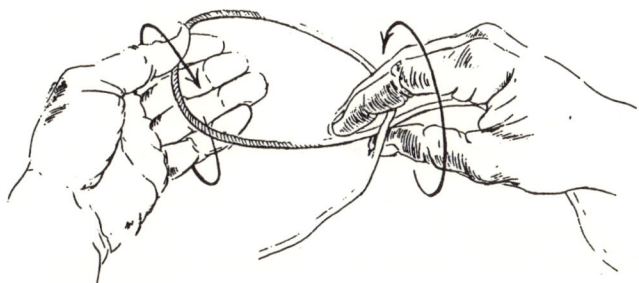

13-D. *To tie a Constrictor Knot in the bight, arrange hands as shown and flip both hands over to get...*

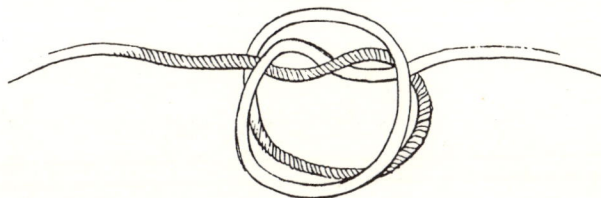

13-E. *...the finished knot.*

The Constrictor Knot can be tightened by hand, but for optimum tension, hitch a spike to each end. For a really stout pull on a really stout cord, sit on the ground with one spike braced between your feet, the other held in both hands. Make a wish.

As a novel example of Constrictor use, note the illustration showing a series of Constrictors made around the butted strands of two rope ends (three-strand). I call this the Quasi-Splice and use it to reeve off new halyards without going aloft. To make it, Constrictor the old and new lines about 8 inches from their ends and cut off one strand at the knots. Cut a second strand from each about 4 inches from the ends. Marry the ends so that all the strands match up, then put Constrictors on either side of where they join. Now use the old line to haul the new through the block(s) aloft. Cut away the Quasi-Splice and whip or eyesplice the new end as conditions require. The procedure is almost the same for wire halyards, except that six strands and a heart are involved instead of just three strands. So cut one heart at the first Constrictor, then proceed as above, but with the ends worked in pairs. Finally, for a double-braid Quasi, cut 6 inches of sheath off one line and 6 inches of core out of the other. Stick core into sheath and Constrictor on either side of the joins.

No maintenance is needed for temporary seizings, but it's an important consideration when you want your work to last. Rope rots, but as with wood or wire, regular inspection and maintenance will prolong its working life. If a stretch of service receives excessive chafe, replace it, then double serve (two layers) or leather that spot to ease the problem. Seizings, too, can suffer from chafe or accidental cuts, but most often they and service are most affected by water, sun, and wind. See the Loft Procedures chapter for preservative mixes to apply to seizings and service.

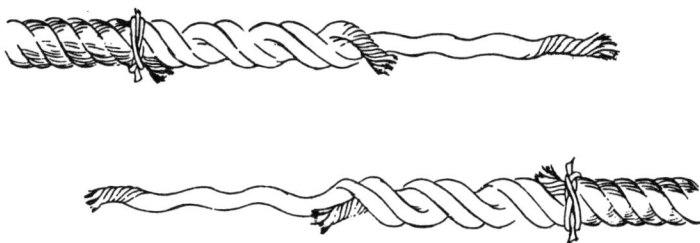

FIGURE 14-A. *A Quasi-Splice for reeving new halyards. Put Constrictors on old and new lines, 8 inches from the ends. Cut one strand from each at the Constrictor, then one from each 4 inches from the end. Marry the two lines, laying them into each other so ends butt.*

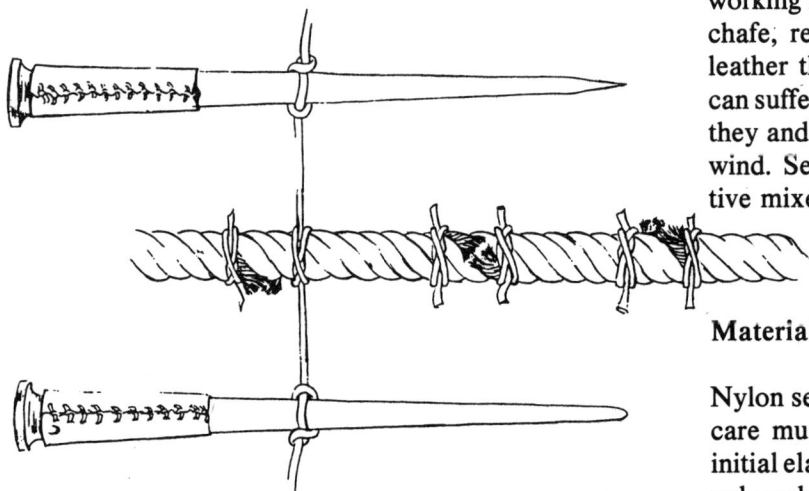

14-B. *Put Constrictors on either side of the joins, pulling them tight with a pair of marlingspikes.*

Materials

Nylon seine twine makes excellent seizings, but extra care must be taken to pull hard enough to remove initial elasticity. Used as service, it holds up well but is vulnerable to sunlight, so regular slushing with a preservative mix is extra important.

Marline is the traditional material for spike knots and is still the preferred one for service *if* it is of good quality. Look for long-fibered hemp. Avoid jute.

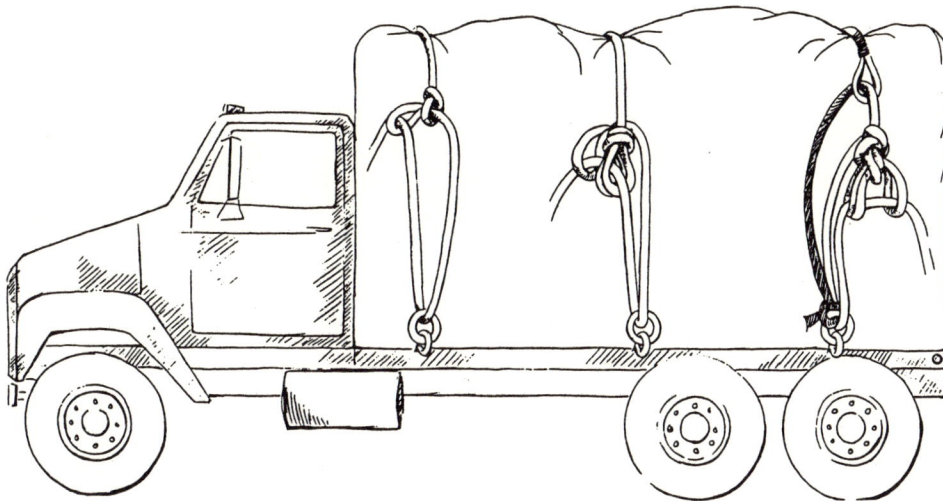

FIGURE 15. *Trucker's Hitches.*

LASHMANSHIP

Viking raiders lashed together seagoing dragonships, but their skill was almost trifling compared to that of their victims in Europe. At that time and through the Renaissance, cathedral builders were lashing whole trees together steeple-high to do their work. Smaller buildings, carts, furniture, tools, and many other items of daily life also relied on rope for their construction. And it's not as if things have changed so much, even here in the technical vastness of the future. Lashings are still used for scaffolds in Oriental shipyards, in the backs of computer cabinets where they keep bundles of wire together and out of the works, for the outriggers that anchor window washers' and masons' suspended scaffoldings, and at the docks of the most modern superferries, where electronically aided pilots still dock by caroming off a bunch of pilings lashed together with wire rope. And every morning you lash your shoes to your feet.

Far from being archaic, lashings still exist in enough profusion to fill a volume of descriptions. No doubt some compulsive cataloger will eventually do just that, but for the practical knotter it's more important to understand the varying demands placed on lashings and the basic techniques used in response. With these "elements of lashmanship," one can tie confidently in a wide variety of circumstances.

Pulley, Frap, and Wedge

Lashings rely on tension to do their work. A few tight turns put on with the aid of a marlingspike will sometimes suffice, but often the object to be lashed is heavy enough so that some form of mechanical advantage must be used to provide adequate security. When something is to be lashed down to a deck, car roof, truck bed, or the like, lines are generally anchored on one side, passed over the cargo, and circled down on the other side with one form of advantage—the pulley. (No, not a sheave turning on a pin, but the principle is the same.) Disregarding friction, the two arrangements on the left in Figure 15 provide a three-fold purchase. That is, the load is shared by three parts so that the part you haul on gets only one third of the load. Put another way, your efforts are multiplied three times; a 100-pound downward pull locks your cargo in place with close to 300 pounds of force. I say "close to" because we can only disregard friction in theory.

The line on the left in Figure 15 is made into a pulley with the aid of a knot called a Trucker's Hitch, of which there are many forms. This one is very fast and easy to tie and is a good knot for light-duty use and emergencies. Unfortunately, it and most other Trucker's Hitches either jam under heavy tension or can spill if tension is removed. What's more, the single loop

11

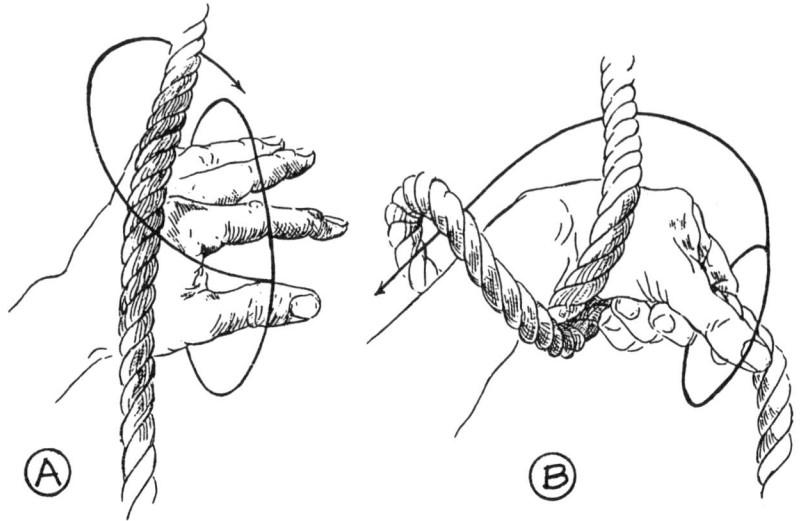

FIGURE 16-A. *Basic Hitch: A slipknot made with one hand. End is led through ring, then through loop. Very handy but has tendency to jam.*

16-B. *Improved Trucker's Hitch: A slipknot made with a bight. Less liable to jam, wider radius for rope to pass over.*

16-C,D,E. *Compound Hitch: Six-part purchase instead of three as in previous knots. Pass end of lashing line through thimble-eye of separate line. Make Improved Hitch, then pass end through ring and then through loops.*

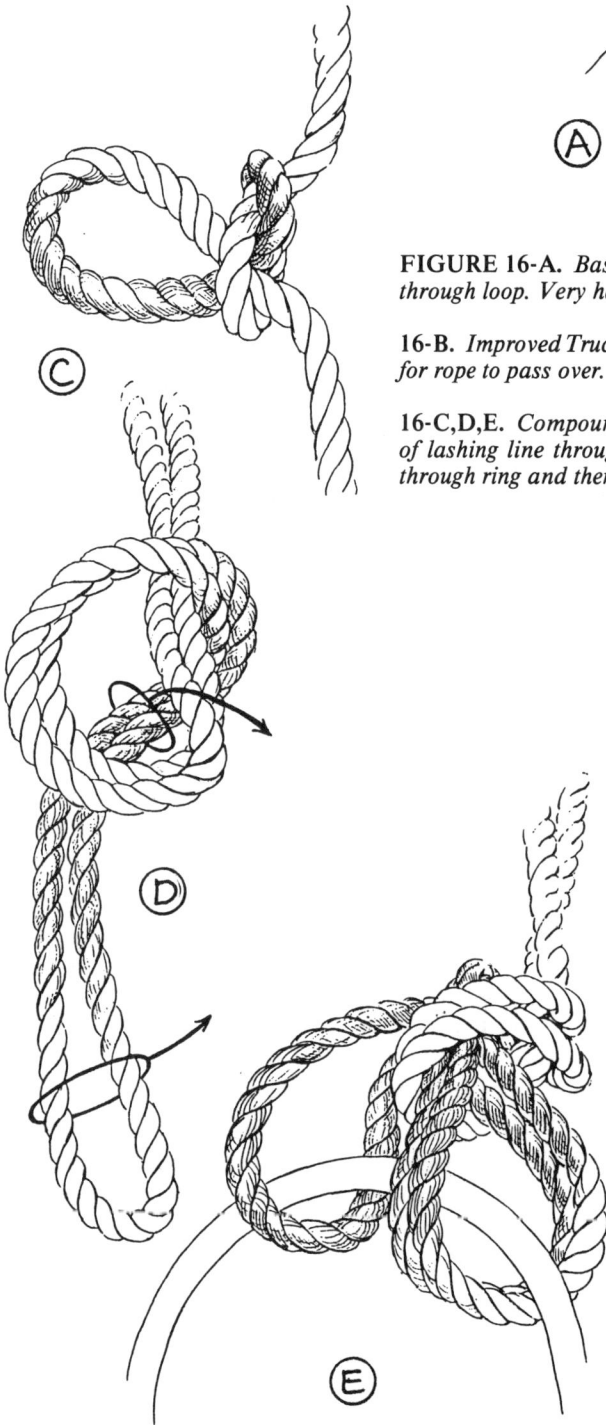

makes a hard bend for the hauling part to go around, resulting in lower breaking strength and shorter rope life. The knot used in the middle of Figure 15 offers some improvement. (It was introduced by Norman Biegner in the August 1980 issue of *Cruising World*.) As the illustration shows, it is a slipknot made with a bight, and the hauling part is rove through all three of the resulting loops. This knot resists jamming and presents a broad bearing surface; use it for medium-to-heavy loads or for any situation when you can take a little time. The most secure and slowest to tie loops are the nonslipping variety, detailed in the Five in a Bight section of Chapter 3. Use them for permanent lashings.

The right-most lashup in Figure 15 is a configuration that is about as involved a Trucker's Hitch as you can get before friction defeats mechanical advantage. Here the line passed over the cargo is cut to an appropriate length and has a thimble spliced in its end. A separate lanyard is anchored by one end below, a bight is passed through the thimble, a Biegner Hitch is made in that bight, and the other end is rove through the hitch. This creates a six-part purchase. If that doesn't do the trick, you probably need a come-along or some chain binders.

Frapping

To compound the tension on a lashing, apply "frapping" turns. These are made at right angles to the basic lashing to snug it a little bit more; they can be so effective as to rip ringbolts out, so use them with discretion. In Figure 17, frapping turns are taken on the head-tensioning strings of a drum, and they tighten the round turns made to "mouse" a hook, reinforcing it for a heavy pick. These two far-removed examples should help illustrate frapping's extraordinary handiness and adaptability. Swaying or sweating up on a halyard is another application of the same principle.

Wedging

When you can't frap, wedge. Figure 18 shows an impromptu clamp made for gluing up some stock. Round turns are made tightly around the work, but there's no place to put frapping turns, so wedges, whose tips are under the lashing to start, are driven in to tighten as well as any clamp. For wide work, like a cutting board, it may be necessary to weight the work to keep it flat.

Before large bar clamps were generally available, wedged chains were used to hold deadwood assemblies in place for boring. It's still an inexpensive alternative.

The Subjects

Consider the things you want to lash. What shapes are they? What materials? How heavy? Under what conditions are they expected to remain together? Is the lashing permanent or temporary? The answers to these questions will determine the configuration, degree of tension, and the kind and size of cordage used for the lashing. Remember that with mechanical advantage, you can often afford to be gentle. Don't crush a light, fragile load. Pad corners and contain it just to the extent the situation demands. On the other hand, don't be afraid to snug right down on a heavy subject; loose deck or freeway loads can be murderous.

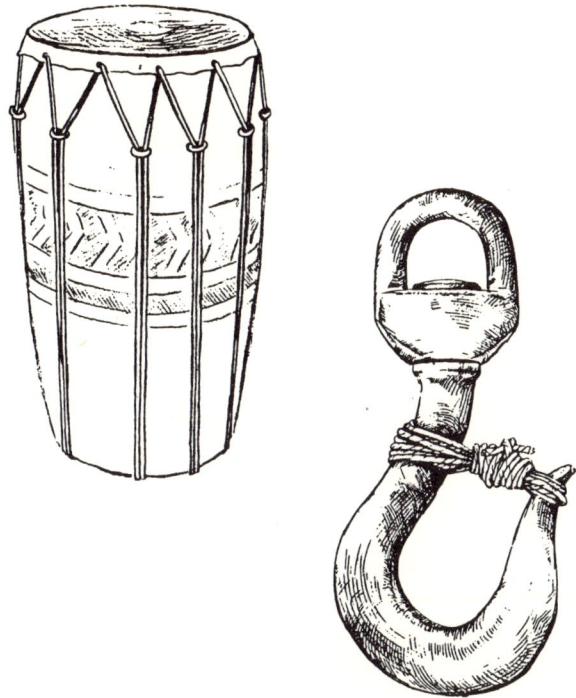

FIGURE 17. *Frapping can be put to such widely divergent uses as lashing drumheads and mousing hooks.*

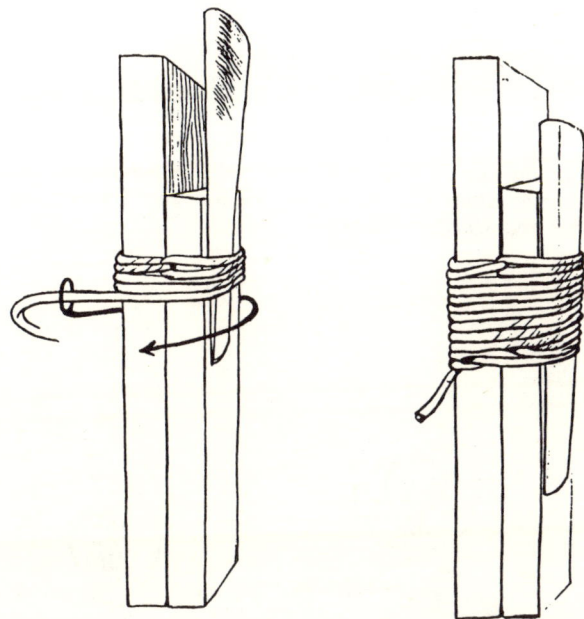

FIGURE 18. *Wedging. Make a series of tight turns around the tip of a wedge whose corners have been rounded. Drive the wedge down to tighten the lashing.*

13

Boom Lacing

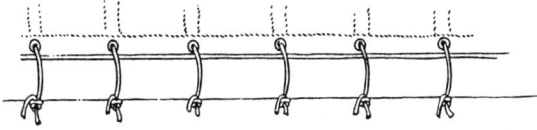

FIGURE 19-A. *Short lines square-knotted around boom. Uses the least line and is fairly snug.*

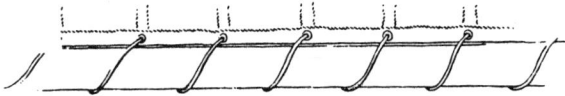

19-B. *Spiral lacing. Quick and easy, but loose.*

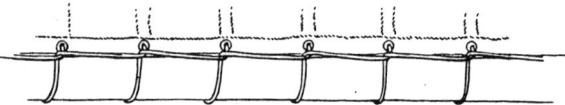

19-C. *Half hitches. More time-consuming, but more snug.*

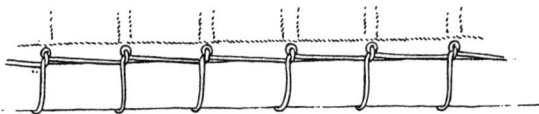

19-D. *Marling Hitches. Still more time-consuming but still more snug. Study Figure 20 to see the difference between half hitches and Marling Hitches.*

The Long and Short of It

Use a minimum of material, especially for heavy work. This promotes economy. Take the shortest distance between points. Avoid figure-eight turns unless nothing else will do—they use more line than round turns and so can generate more slack. Use several short pieces in preference to one long one for optimum fit, minimum slack, and insurance (if one parts, the others might hold). On the other hand, long pieces are sometimes appropriate when the idea is more to contain than to bind, or where only moderate tension is needed.

Sometimes, whether to use long or short lengths of cordage is a matter of judgment, as on the boom in Figure 19 where several techniques for lacing the foot of the sail are shown. The ideal technique would be strong, adjustable, unobtrusive, easy to remove, and would simultaneously snug the foot down and pull it aft. One method, shown at the top, is to have a short line through each eyelet, the ends square-knotted around the boom. This uses a minimum of line and is stout and adjustable, but it is bulky and not very snug. Next comes a simple spiral through successive eyelets, a method employed on the Gloucester fishing schooners. While easy to apply, adjust, and remove, it again sacrifices some tautness. Half hitches, shown next, are less convenient but more snug. They are made in small line, one at a time, and tightened with the aid of a marlingspike. Make the hitch up close to the eyelet so that as it tightens it pulls the sail down and aft (the pulley principle). Better still, "marl" the sail on. The Marling Hitch is a form of overhand knot with the ends led at right angles to the bight. As Figure 20 shows, the line bears more fully against itself than in the Half Hitch, so it is less likely to slip and pass slack along the boom, a handy feature when you want some sections tighter than others for sail shape. Compare these two knots until you are sure of the distinction between them.

Marling is an excellent general purpose lashing for bundles of wood, pipe, etc., and especially for tarp-covered cartop loads, where it keeps the tarp from blowing to noisy shreds as you drive.

FIGURE 20. *Details of the half hitch (left) and Marling Hitch.*

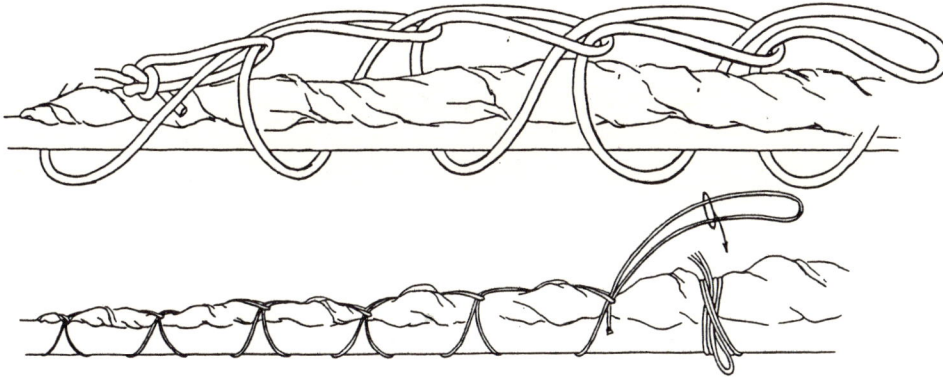

FIGURE 21. *Swedish Furling. Easy to tie, a pleasure to untie.*

Swedish Furling

Moving forward from the main boom, we come to a doused headsail. It only needs to be held in place temporarily. We'll want to break it out with a minimum of fuss, so marling is too time-consuming to use here.

The usual procedure is to tie "stops"—short lengths of rope or webbing—along the sail's bundled length. This works well and uses little material, but short pieces aren't really necessary, since a little slack matters less here than on the mainsail. And the oceans of the world are littered with dropped, blown, or washed overboard sail stops. So take an old halyard instead (or use the sail's downhaul), and get into "Swedish Furling." No, this is not an ethnic joke like "Irish Pennant" or "Spanish Reef." It's a series of slipped hitches, again worked aft (Figure 21).

Start with a Bowline, bring the standing part around the sail, and pass a bight of it through the eye of the Bowline. Pull the bight through until it is 12 to 18 inches long or so, depending on the size of the sail. Now bring the standing part around again, in the opposite direction, and pull another bight through the eye of the first one. Repeat this maneuver, making a zigzag of interlocking bights down the length of the sail. At the end, make a longer bight and half-hitch it around the sail, or belay it to a convenient cleat, post, or crewmember. To undo, cast off the last bight and haul on the standing part. Zip, zip, zip! Ready to hoist. This technique also works on boomed sails, though care must be taken to keep blocks and cleats from snagging the bights.

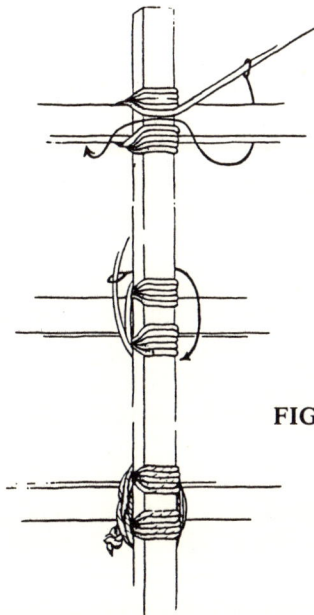

FIGURE 22. *A marline lashing.*

A Marline Lashing

Moving aft, we come to a life-preserver bracket lashed to a lifeline stanchion. This is a permanent seizing of small twine made around a relatively light object. A sufficient number of turns taken in almost any pattern will hold it in place. But it might be nice if it didn't break away when you grabbed it to keep from falling overboard, or at the very least if it didn't shift under your weight when you leaned on it. When considering how strong to make a lashing, it is well to consider more than one intended use. Neatness is no small matter, either, nor is economy of time and materials. Even this quick job is worth doing carefully.

Start with parallel turns around the two pieces, as shown in Figure 22. Haul on each turn with your spike.

15

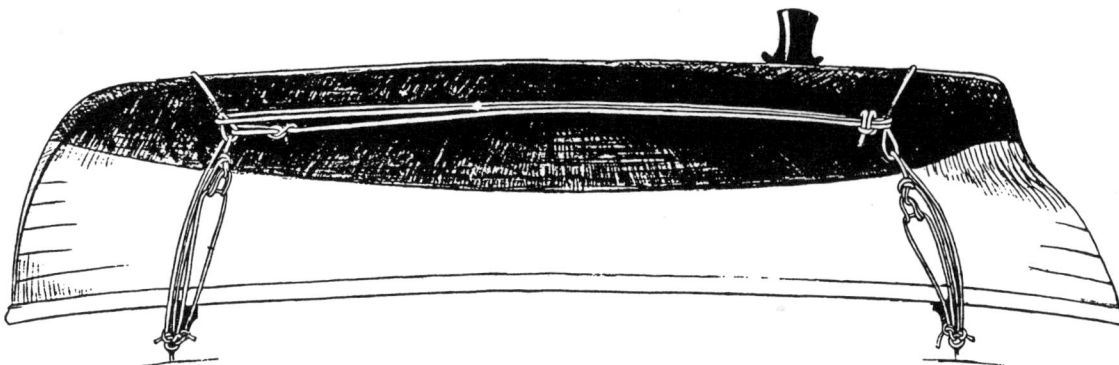

FIGURE 23. *A lashing that will restrain the great Houdinghy.*

Make four or five circuits, being sure that none of them rides over the others, as this would prevent an even distribution of strain. Next, make a not-quite-as-snug layer of riding turns (optional, not shown). These provide extra strength and protect the first layer from chafe. Finally, make three or four frapping turns very tightly. Secure with a Clove Hitch, tying a Figure-Eight Knot in the end as close to the hitch as possible. This is insurance against the end pulling free.

If the bracket is shaped to fit the rail, leaving no room for frapping turns, use wedges. Round their outer corners so they don't cut the twine. Even a sprung tiller can be temporarily repaired by lashing and wedging battens, screwdrivers, driftwood, or what-have-you in place for some distance on either side of the crack.

Escape Artist

Say you want to secure your dinghy for an extended passage. It's not hard to work up a lashing that looks secure, but once at sea with the forces of wind, water, and its own weight to help it, that innocent little boat will be transformed into a master of escape—Houdinghy, if you will—out to defeat your attempts to contain it. As challenger, our first inclination might be to cover the hull with a rat's nest of turns and hitches. The more-is-better school of knots. But this type of job is tedious to tie, difficult to remove, and just plain ugly. Worse still, it provides the escape artist with his greatest ally—slack. Extra turns mean more rope to stretch. Before you know it, things have worked loose and Houdinghy has stepped free to the amazement of the wildly cheering crowd.

So instead, go with the less-is-more lashing in Figure 23. Lay two or three lines from side to side, padding any sharp turns, and snug them down with Trucker's Hitches to chock padeyes, as in Figure 15. By taking the shortest distance across the hull, you simultaneously minimize potential slack and create opposing forces, bracing the lines against each other. Bind everything together with frapping turns of smaller line, hauling the remaining initial elasticity from the larger pieces. For extra security, lead the painter forward and lash it tight, too. There you have it, a handsome, escape-proof setup that is as easy to make, adjust, or remove as it is to describe.

Extemporaneous Work

No matter how carefully you study the above techniques, the odds are strong that you will eventually come up against a situation that seems to defy solution and for which neither this nor any other set of instructions has prepared you. It's like the old Bob Newhart routine about the carefully trained rookie night watchman. His first night on the job is in the Empire State Building, and King Kong shows up. ("There's nothing about this in my manual.")

As it happens, most lashings are extemporaneous. Some things are just too big, but success is usually a matter of simple adaptability. Relax, take an inventory of your materials, and mentally arrange them in different configurations. Invent.

CHAPTER 2

Tension

•

If you can serve, seize, lash, and coil, and if you understand the materials involved, you're well on your way to becoming a rigger; everything from here on is a matter of elaborating on what you already know. You can do much to elaborate on your rigging know-how simply by mastering the concept of "tension." A rig accomplishes its main purpose if it creates, contains, and directs tension efficiently.

Tension is not always as readily apparent as it is in the humming windward shrouds of a sailboat on a hard beat. Riggers learn to recognize its many, more subtle manifestations. In the Lashing section of Chapter 1 we examined several methods of increasing tension to hold an object securely in place. Here we will look at ways of creating greater tension than can be supplied by wedging, frapping, or Trucker's Hitches.

When it's puny you against big, heavy, ornery them, you need an advantage. A mechanical advantage, that is, for all the heavy-duty hoisting, dragging, stretching, and tightening jobs that rigging and sailing entail. For a lot of tension, advantage is usually provided by some form of either block and tackle, lever, winch, or inclined plane, or by two or more of these fundamental tension-gaining tools in combination. Which ones you use for a given situation depends on how fast you want something how tight, with what degree of control, over what distance, and at what expense. Safety and efficiency are determined by the appropriateness of your choices and by the size and health of the gear, so experience and a healthy respect for the forces you are dealing with are important. Choosing the proper pulling gear is a form of design.

FIGURE 24.

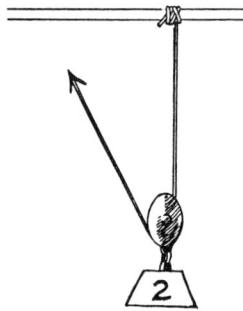

FIGURE 25.

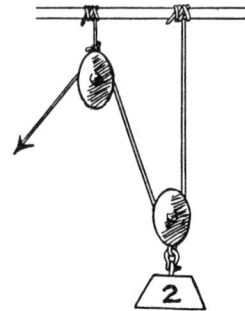

FIGURE 26.

FIGURE 27.

FIGURE 28-A.

28-B.

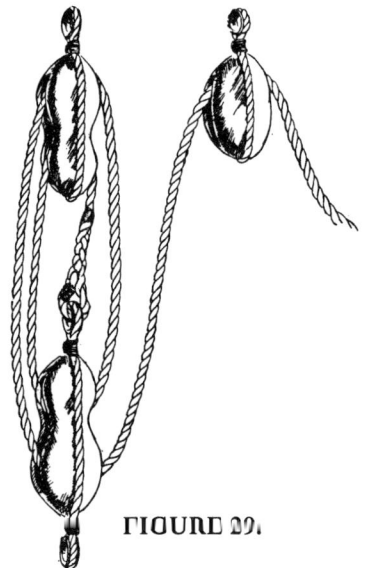

FIGURE 29.

BLOCK AND TACKLE

In Figure 24, a line is led up from the load, through a block, and down to the hauler (force). The only advantage here is convenience—the force is equal to the load, and you can haul something light up over your head.

In Figure 25, the line comes down from an overhead support, through the block, which is attached to the load, and thence to the hauler. Now the hauler shares the load with the overhead support, so the load is halved; you can pick up a much heavier load than before with no more effort, but you can't pick it up far unless you add another block, as in Figure 26. This one, like that first single block, adds no advantage. As we keep adding parts, it will become difficult to figure out when we've added advantage and when the lead is

just being redirected. The basic rule is that you *count the number of parts coming out of the moving block(s)*. In Figure 26, the block that is attached to the load moves as the load is raised. There are two parts coming out of that block, so there is a two-part purchase. The other block doesn't move, so it adds no advantage.

In Figure 27, a small type of tackle (or "block and tackle") called a handy-billy is set up to the load. The lower block shows us that there is a three-part purchase here. Figure 28-A shows the same gear inverted, resulting in a four-part purchase. Again, we have gained height by adding a block aloft, as in Figure 26. We could use two fiddles to the same effect (Figure 28-B), or we could make up a purchase as in Figure 29, simultaneously changing the lead and adding another part to the moving block for a five-part purchase.

18

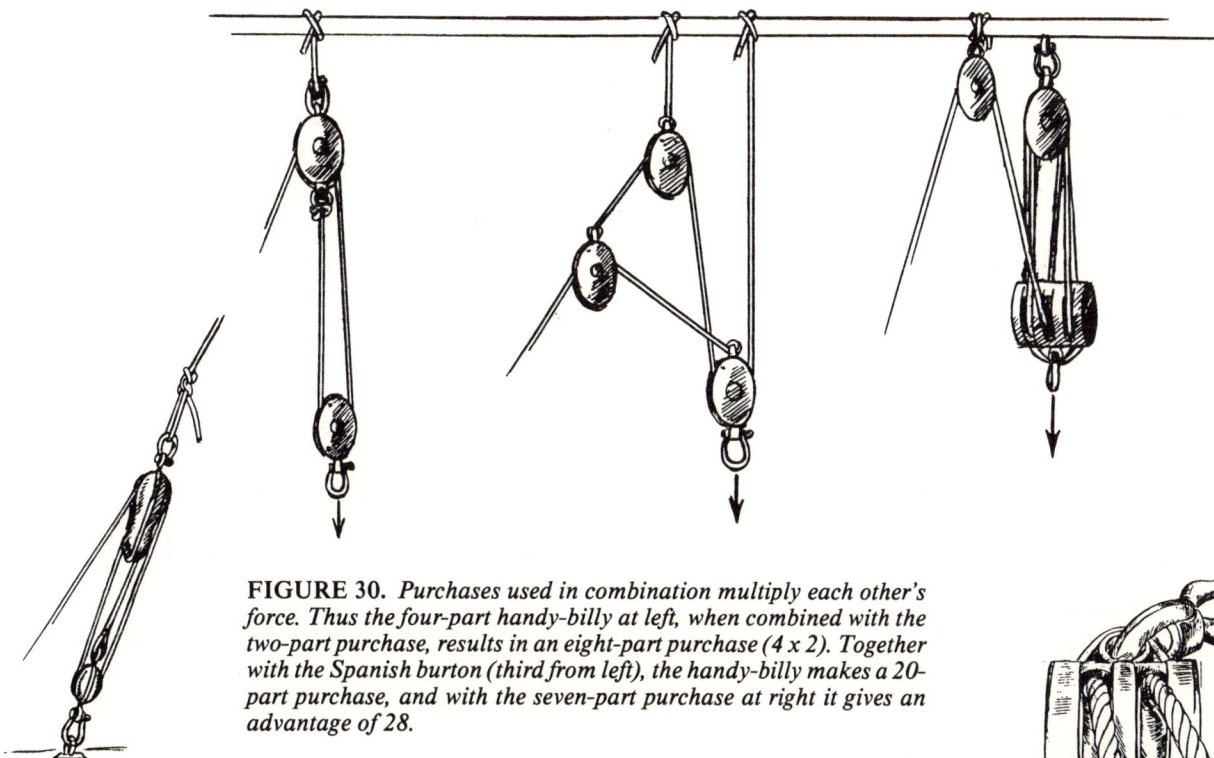

FIGURE 30. *Purchases used in combination multiply each other's force. Thus the four-part handy-billy at left, when combined with the two-part purchase, results in an eight-part purchase (4 x 2). Together with the Spanish burton (third from left), the handy-billy makes a 20-part purchase, and with the seven-part purchase at right it gives an advantage of 28.*

Compound Purchase

It's rare to find a sailboat these days that has any blocks aboard with more than two sheaves. This is because the winch (see below) has largely taken over the high-tension running rigging jobs. But this doesn't mean that you are limited to only a five-part purchase with your tackle collection; the power of any configuration can be not just added to, but literally multiplied by hooking up another configuration to it. Figure 30 shows how combining sets of single and double blocks can produce from 8 to 28 parts of purchase.

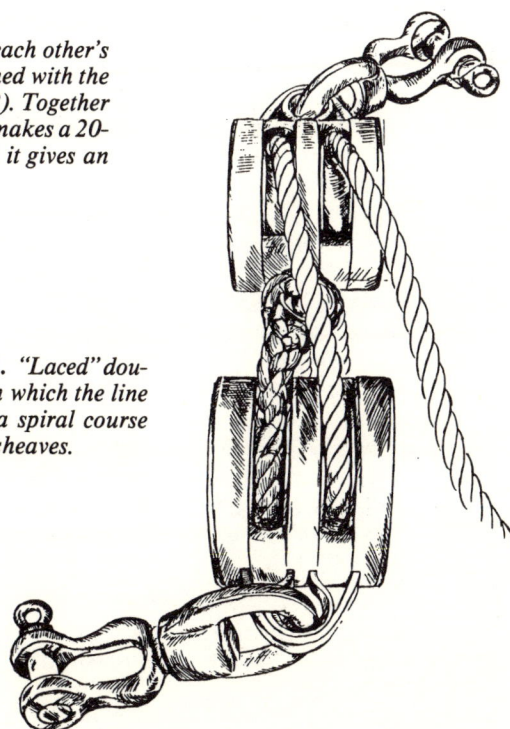

FIGURE 31. *"Laced" double blocks, in which the line proceeds in a spiral course through the sheaves.*

Right-Angle Reeving

With blocks that have their sheaves mounted side by side—most often the case—the manner in which the rope passes from sheave to sheave can make a great difference in hauling efficiency. Figure 31 shows two double blocks reeved in the usual manner, called Lacing. The line travels in a spiral from one side to the other as it passes through the sheaves. This method is simple and easy to remember, but when the blocks are hauled close to one another—"two-blocked"—the

rope on one side bears strongly against the cheeks of the block, causing undue friction just when you need it the least.

The alternative is Right-Angle Reeving (Figure 32), sometimes known as Boat-Fall Reeving, the latter name deriving from its frequent appearance on lifeboat davit gear, which is usually two-blocked when the boat is hoisted. This method requires a little thought at reeving time, but if you've ever had to lift a heavy load the full range of your tackle and felt your power agonizingly diminish as you neared the top, you know

FIGURE 32. *Four examples of Right Angle Reeving. The fairer lead throughout means less chafe and longer rope life. The fall comes from the middle sheave of three-sheave upper blocks, so that the force of hauling does not tip the block.*

Wire Rope Sheave

TREAD DIA. (T. D.)

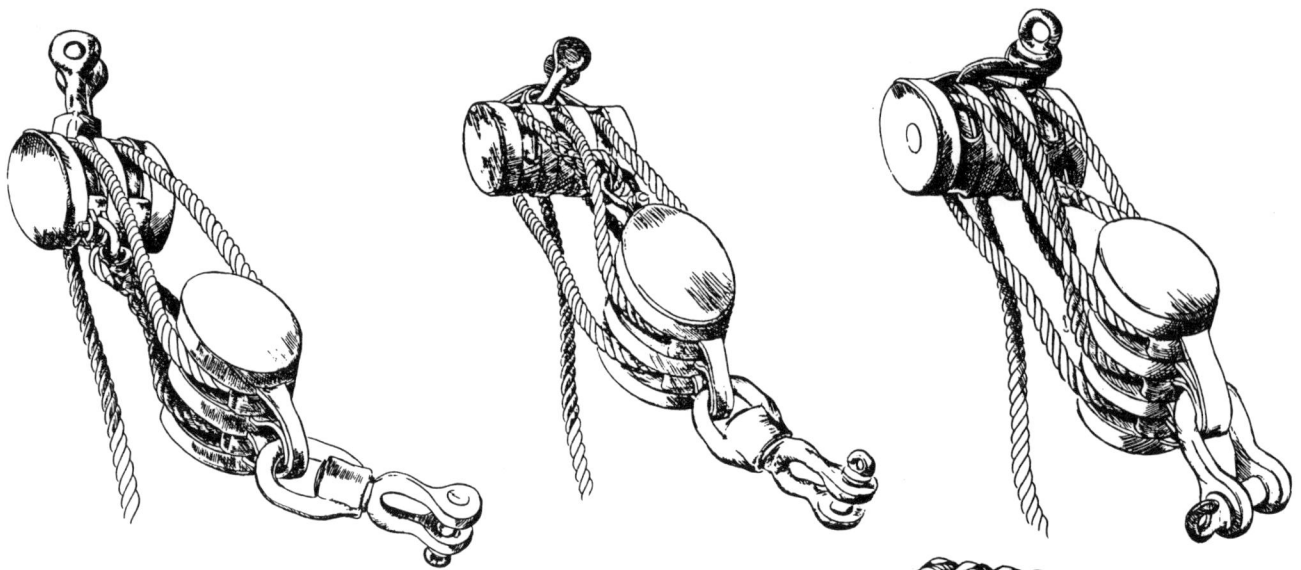

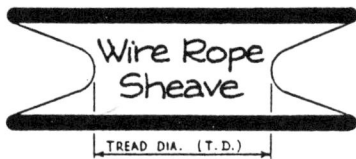

TABLE 1. Recommended Minimum Sheave Diameters and Block Sizes

The "standard" tread diameters shown in this table are sizes that will guarantee the longest wire rope life and highest strength. But if it is not practicable to put a sheave that size into your mast, be aware that as you approach the "critical" diameter the wire's strength and longevity are severely compromised. The accompanying diagram illustrates tread diameter. Block length rather than sheave diameter is the desired standard when working with fiber rope. *(Source of minimum tread diameters: MacWhyte Wire Rope Co.)*

Rope or wire rope diam. (inches)	Sheave tread diameters for 7x19 wire (inches)		Inches of block length for fiber rope
	Std.	Critical	
⅛	5 ¼	2 ¼	1
⁵⁄₃₂	6 ⁹⁄₁₆	2 ⅞	1
³⁄₁₆	7 ⅞	3 ⅜	1 – 1½
⁷⁄₃₂	9 ³⁄₁₆	4	1½
¼	10 ½	4 ½	2
⁵⁄₁₆	13 ⅛	5 ⅝	2½
⅜	15 ¾	6 ¾	3
⁷⁄₁₆	18 ⅜	7 ⅞	3½
½	21	9	4
⅝			5
¾			6
⅞			7
3" circ.			8

that Right-Angle Reeving is worth the effort. Less friction means the rope lasts longer, too.

Speaking of friction, it isn't entirely avoidable in any event; the resistance of each sheave turning on its axis robs from 2 to 5 percent of the tackle's power. In addition, too small a sheave for the rope size used also causes excessive resistance, especially, of course, if the rope rubs against the walls of the block mortise. So see to it that your blocks are of appropriate size (see Table 1) and that you use well-greased roller-bearing sheaves whenever possible. Flaked graphite mixed with lube oil is an excellent non-grit-attracting lubricant.

Tackles provide low to moderate tension, quickly, at prices that range from very low to moderately high depending on complexity and refinement. Used by themselves, they're all you need for small-craft halyards (one-part) and sheets (two- or three-part). Given sufficient crew and numbers of sheaves, they can also serve for gaff- and square-rigged vessels of any size. For peak and throat halyards on medium to large gaffers, a "jigger" on one end of a double-ended halyard compounds the primary purchase for a maximum of luff tension with a minimum of effort and cordage. Block-and-tackle boomed-sail sheets of sufficient purchase are all most craft require, gaff or Bermudian. It's also easy to rig a two-part purchase for boomless staysail sheets, using either bullet blocks or hardwood "lizards" spliced into the ends of sheet pendants (Figure 33).

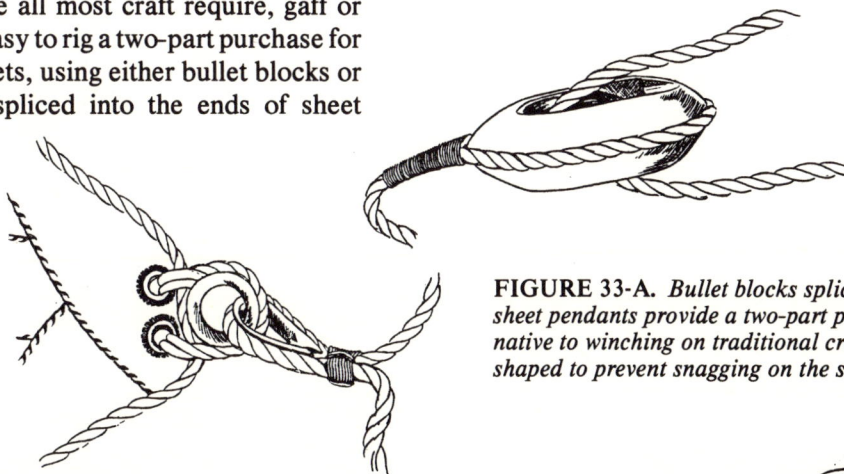

FIGURE 33-A. *Bullet blocks spliced into the ends of sheet pendants provide a two-part purchase, an alternative to winching on traditional craft. The blocks are shaped to prevent snagging on the stay during tacks.*

You should also consider handy-billies, running-backstay gear, and vangs. Aboard *Syrinx* (see the Design chapter) two sets of block and tackle do all three of these jobs; they are ordinarily left attached to the running-back pendants, and on the wind in appreciable air or seas, the weather one is set up to control headstay sag and support the mast. Close-hauled, both sides can be left set up, since the leeward one does not then interfere with boom travel. Off the wind the leeward one can be detached from the pendant and shackled to the boom to act as a vang that both changes sail shape for more efficient draft and prevents accidental jibing. When tacking downwind in a blow, both sets are attached to the boom as vangs; the leeward side is slacked away and the weather side brought in during tacking to bring the boom around handsomely, under complete control. And finally, there are always two sets of handy-billies handy to lift the dinghy aboard, go aloft, set up lanyards, effect shroud repairs, shift gear, etc. A handy-billy is essential to your versatility as a sailor and rigger.

Also to be considered are boat falls, downhauls, gantlines, lazy jacks, topping lifts, and flag halyards. Scale these to the job, checking out other vessels if you're unsure of proportions.

33-B. A hardwood "lizard" is a sheaveless alternative to a single block for small craft or for smaller sails on large craft.

21

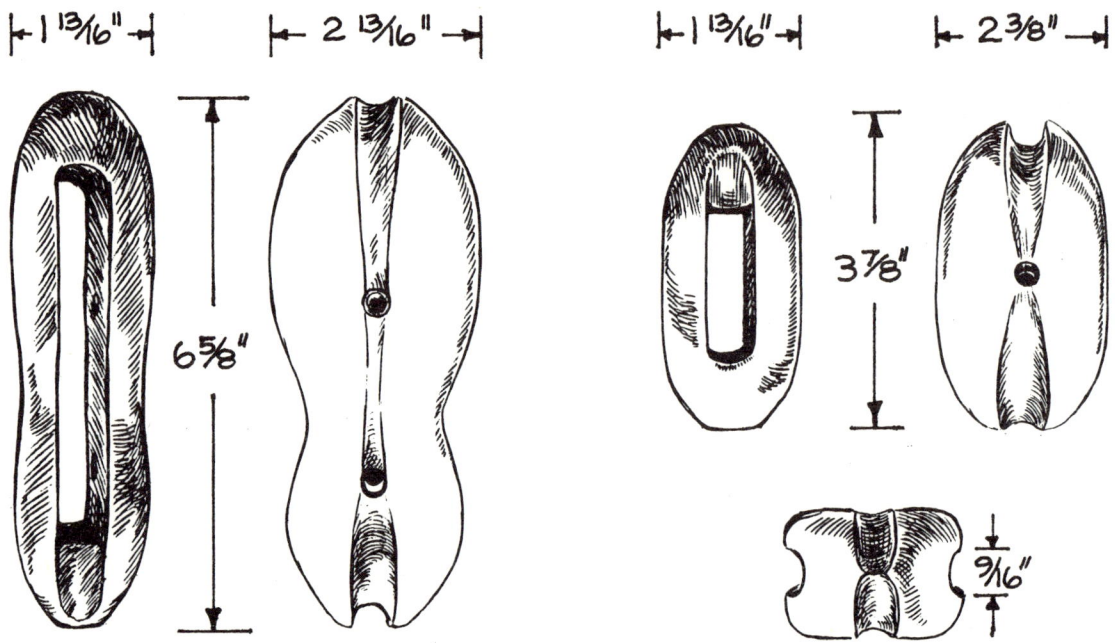

FIGURE 34-A. *Two views of a fiddle (without sheaves) and three views of a single block. Note faired-in strop grooves. The dimensions, which are those of the fiddle and block in the author's handy-billy, are ideal for use with ⁷⁄₁₆-inch line.*

SINGLE BLOCK

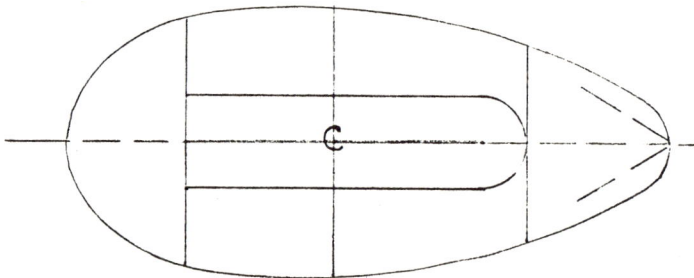

SINGLE BLOCK WITH BECKET

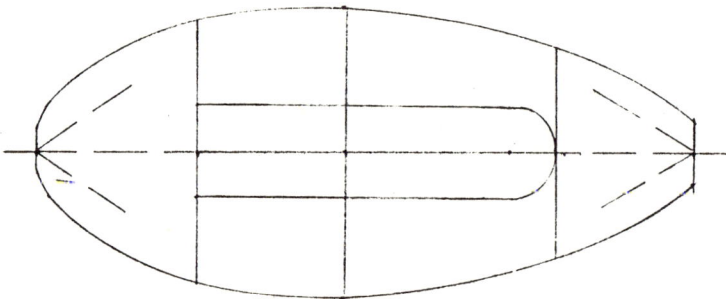

34-B. *Patterns for a single bullet block and a single bullet block with becket. Scale the sizes to the line.*

Construction

Racing craft feature blocks that are extraordinarily light, strong, low-friction, and high-cost. This is appropriate. But racing considerations pervade the sailing craft marketplace to a ridiculous degree, so that the gear of most craft is not appropriate. If you're more interested in a solid, repairable block than a SORC ambience, look for well-made wood shells and bronze roller-bearing sheaves. Ask around about the reputation of the brand or brands you're considering; there are some good-looking lemons out there. The best shells are of lignum vitae or black locust, and the sheave bearings should run smoothly and quietly, ticking instead of clacking.

As the diagrams in Figure 34 show, I have a thing for rope-stropped blocks. Not exactly an off-the-shelf item these days, but they're fairly easy to make; they don't bang up brightwork; they're dirt cheap and undeniably attractive; and they really, really work. There are two elements to stropping a block: the grommet that encircles the block and its thimble (see Chapter 5) and the throat seizing that is applied between block and thimble to hold them in the grommet (see Chapter 1).

22

THE WINCH

Figure 35 illustrates the principle of that magnificent rotating lever, the winch. The winch handle is the lever arm, the barrel axis is the fulcrum, and the load is applied at the barrel face. Divide the distance between fulcrum and face into the length of the handle, and the result is the amount of your advantage. Internal gearing in two- and three-speed winches in effect lengthens or shortens the lever arm so you can winch quickly to take up slack when the load is light, then switch gears for greater leverage as the load increases.

Winches take various forms, depending on the load and application they are designed for, but they all have two requirements in common:

(1) *Good lead.* Several turns with the hauling line around the barrel is the winch equivalent of reeving; their grip allows force to be applied. If the hauling and tailing parts do not intersect the rotating barrel at approximately 90 degrees to its axis, a "wrap" can result—either or both parts becoming bound up in the turns. Very bad news, especially if you need to get the line off the winch in a hurry. When the hauling part's lead isn't fair, a turning block is added between the load and the winch (Figure 36). The tailing part is, well, tailed, either by a crewmember or one of a variety of "self-tailing" gizmos (Figure 37).

(2) *Efficiently applied force.* These things are expensive, so you might as well get some performance out of them. To begin hoisting or sheeting in a sail, leave the handle off for the moment, make your turns (three or four) and begin taking up slack by hand. Pull with your palms away from you to get a full range of motion as you work your arms in alternation (Figure 38). Keep your hands well away from the winch in case a sudden load slips the turns. When the slack is out, the person with the handle plugs it in and begins cranking while you tail, or you can do both jobs yourself, slowly and carefully with a normal winch, slick as you please with a self-tailing model. For maximum cranking efficiency, get your weight over the handle and keep it there. Use both hands when possible. When you're running a capstan use a straight-arm, palms-on-handle technique to take up slack, then switch to the low and slow crooked-arm technique as you take a strain.

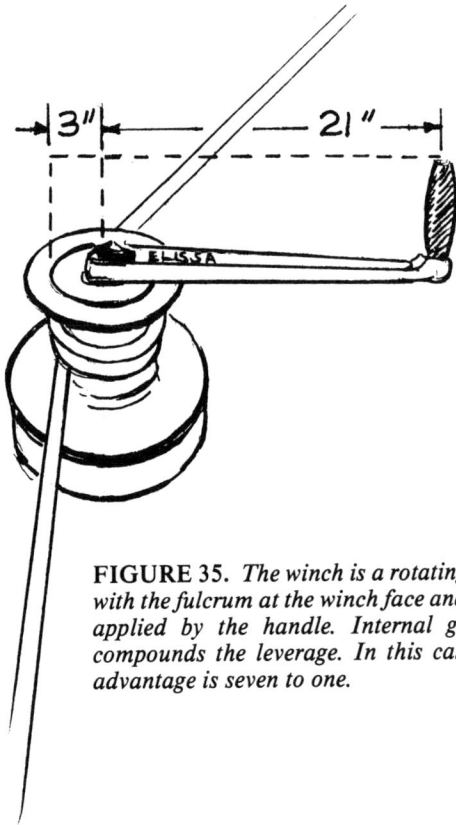

FIGURE 35. *The winch is a rotating lever with the fulcrum at the winch face and force applied by the handle. Internal gearing compounds the leverage. In this case, the advantage is seven to one.*

FIGURE 36. *The turning block next to the stanchion feeds the line to the winch at a good fair angle. Note the shock cord running from the turning block's becket to the lifeline; this arrangement keeps the block from falling down and fouling when the line is slack.*

FIGURE 37. *A self-tailing winch ingeniously eliminates the need for a human tailer at the cost of increased complexity and rope wear. Since they're not failsafe, don't trust yourself to a self-tailer when going aloft.*

FIGURE 38. *Human tailer.*

Winches, unmatched in their combination of speed and power, predominate aboard today's shorthanded high-tension vessels. But winches are also unmatched in their combination of high price and maintenance needs, so use as few of them as you can, and lighten their loads whenever possible by working them in tandem with tackles. Sheets and running backstays are two examples of lines that can either be controlled by blocks alone or blocks compounded by a winch, depending on how much strain the weather is giving. An extra part or two on a purchase means you can go with a smaller winch that will receive less strain than a larger one doing the job all by itself.

Whether your winches have help or work by themselves, protect your investment with regular, careful inspection and maintenance; it's amazing how many people just crank 'em till they freeze up, treating them like convenience items instead of well-bred tools.

24

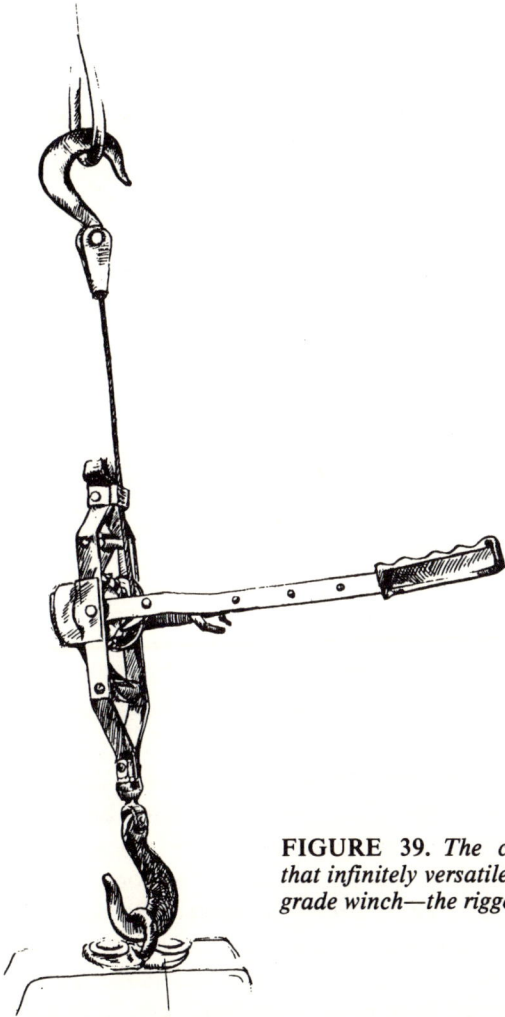

FIGURE 39. *The come-along, that infinitely versatile industrial-grade winch—the rigger's friend.*

FIGURE 40. *Sweating up. A handy technique to know, especially, as here, if you've lost a winch handle.*

THE COME-ALONG

Not exactly part of the rigging, the come-along is an indispensable shop tool and is good to have aboard for installing, shifting, and setting up gear, and for emergencies. It's another winch, but with a wire tackle anchored to the barrel instead of wrapped around it. A ratchet mechanism, not friction, is used to sustain tension, and a relatively small-diameter barrel means a leverage ratio between 20 to 1 and 40 to 1, comparable to the ratios of typical running-rigging winches. With some come-alongs, power is compounded by the use of a block added to the load end of the tackle. Come-alongs are powerful, but they're very, very slow. Because it's fairly easy to put more strain on these tools than they are meant to take, a good feature to look for is a handle designed to bend under excess load. Better that than have the wire break with you standing there, cranking resolutely away.

SWEATING UP

This is a remarkably simple, effective way to get a little extra tension on a purchase. Hauling sharply outward or sideways on an already taut line exerts leverage on the line; if the line is secure at the belay point, the load is forced to shift, giving you a little slack. Following your outward motion with a downward pull feeds that slack to the belay point, where a tailer takes it up (Figure 40). The same principle makes frapping turns effective; the lever is a versatile tool.

25

FIGURE 41-A. *The Inclined Plane, another form of mechanical advantage. In this case, 125 pounds applied by the truck's driving wheels can lift the (very small) 2,000-pound truck.*

41-B. *The threads of a turnbuckle are simply a spiral version of an Inclined Plane.*

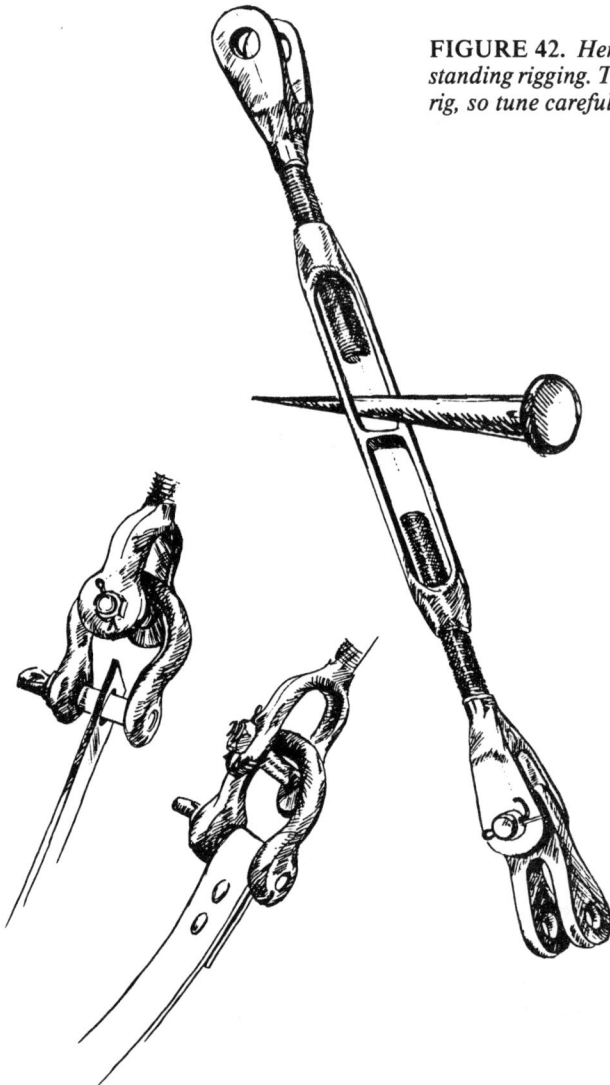

FIGURE 42. *Here a twisting force of 125 pounds could easily put a ton of tension on standing rigging. The device is so efficient that it's very easy to put too much tension into a rig, so tune carefully.*

FIGURE 43. *Galvanized shackles are commonly used as toggles with galvanized turnbuckles, but a standard chainplate (left) provides relatively little bearing surface for the long shackle pin. It would be better in this case to have a chainplate shaped as at right, to prevent an excessive unsupported length.*

TURNBUCKLES (THE INCLINED PLANE)

Step right up folks, and watch as a mere puny 125 pounds picks up a solid ton! Figure 41 shows that this feat is accomplished through the miracle of the Inclined Plane. Once force-resisting friction has been reduced to a minimum (we greased the ways), it's easy to shift the ton up the slight grade, since only a tiny fraction of its weight is directed against the force. Give me a shallow enough ramp and I'll move the world.

Turnbuckles (and bolts and screws) make use of inclined planes that have been bent into a spiral, thereby packing tremendous mechanical advantage into a very small space (Figure 42). Force can be applied by hand or compounded with a lever in the form of spike or wrench. Since the upper and lower threads are oppositely pitched, turning the barrel shortens the turnbuckle, putting tension on the wire.

Because rigs flex and turnbuckles don't, it is extremely important to provide a universal joint in the form of a toggle on each turnbuckle. When using 1 x 19 wire, rod rigging, or mechanical terminals on any material, it's a good idea to have a toggle at either end of the turnbuckle, and maybe one at the upper terminal, too. One often sees galvanized turnbuckles with shackles used as toggles. This doesn't seem like a good idea to me, since shackle pins are designed for broader bearing surfaces than chainplates ordinarily provide (Figure 43). It would be better to fabricate a broad-bearing chainplate, go with bronze turnbuckles and toggles, or have galvanized toggles casted. Anyone out there inclined to do this?

26

A GENERAL ADMONITION TO KEEP THINGS TAUT, OR AT LEAST NOT SLACK

Rope, a creature of tension, does not fare well if it is not kept set up while in use. How firmly set up is determined by vessel, materials, and circumstances, but slack is always to be avoided. Slack allows the large, heavy objects that rope must contain to shift and bang around, inducing "shock loading."

A shock load occurs when a weight fetches up short on a line, as a dog running out of leash. As the gauge in Figure 44 shows, the force exerted at the fetch-up point is considerably higher than the weight of the object imposing the load. Anyone who has seen pile drivers or draft horses at work knows that shock-loading can be turned to useful employment, but it is hell on running and standing rigging, the fittings they make up to, and the masts and hull that *they* make up to. Pretty soon you're shock-loading your bank account.

So take up slack smartly, ease it out smoothly when you jibe, and minimize sail flog with efficient tacks. Keep standing rigging properly tuned (even if you're not concerned with high-level performance) and always be ready to let the sheets run if you're hit by a sudden squall (even if you are interested in high-level performance). Shock load when under tow can be avoided by paying out tow rope until the two vessels rise and fall on the waves simultaneously. Just keep that dog in mind.

FIGURE 44. *Analysis of a cartoon classic. Shock loading is at work with a vengeance in slackly tuned rigs.*

SORTING

We are now possessed of an assortment of highly evolved tightening tools; it remains for us to employ them to greatest advantage, so to speak. They are each suited to one sort of job or another, but it's easy to go wrong, considering the near-infinite range of boat sizes and types, sailing conditions, and owners' preferences, all of this compounded by the range of variations on a theme for each of the tensioning tools. Confronted with the dazzling gear displays at large chandleries, people have been known to go glassy-eyed, emerging from their trance many dollars poorer and with a chestful of pulleys and winches that are hopelessly inappropriate for their boat.

Do not let this befall you! Scale your gear to the job, check out other boats, and shop around.

27

CHAPTER 3
Friction

•

Every knot is an exercise in friction; bends, belays, splices, and seizings all are secure to the extent that they make a line stick against itself when under strain.

If this were all there were to knotting, there'd be no art to it, but rope in use needs to be untied nearly as frequently as it is tied, and we are faced with the conflicting needs of maximum friction when tension is on, for security, and minimum friction when tension is off, so that we can untie. There are exceptions—and there are other desirable qualities—but it is this selective friction which best characterizes good knots.

Many different knots have evolved to meet many different situations and rope types. For example, several of the knots in this chapter are relatively new, invented to deal with modern synthetic rope, which is slicker than Manila or hemp. Rope flexibility also varies widely, as do the sizes, shapes, and consistencies of the objects to which it is attached. And a knot that is good for one situation might prove inappropriate when used in another; use of a Bowline where hitches or an eyesplice are better choices is a classic

example. Given this range of requirements, it is in the rigger's best interest to have a healthy tying vocabulary. In this chapter I have listed several basic types of knots (bends, end of rope, loops, etc.) and detailed the best examples of those types that I know.

Some cautionary words: Since hundreds or even thousands of pounds of pressure might come to bear on the knots you tie, it is well to be sure of the finished product. As Clifford Ashley put it, "A knot is never nearly right; it is either exactly right or it is hopelessly wrong, one or the other; there is nothing in between. This is not the impossibly high standard of the idealist, it is a mere fact for the realist to face. In a knot of eight crossings, which is about the average-size knot, there are 256 'over-and-under' arrangements possible. Make only one change in this 'over-and-under' sequence and either an entirely different knot is made or no knot at all may result."

I might add that some seemingly fussy details can make a significant difference; drawing up in a certain way, or stopping to fair a knot while in the process of tying it, can mean the difference between security and nagging doubts.

28

A TURN AROUND THE COOK'S LEG

I was at a boat show once that was held in a huge circus tent. The entire structure was bucking and vibrating in a September gale, and the only thing that kept me from fleeing in a panic was the calm presence of Spike Africa, widely heralded "President of the Pacific Ocean." He was sitting in the bow of a skiff, chewing tobacco and covering an increasingly empty whiskey bottle with thousands of teensy knots.

"Spike," I said nervously, "a boat in a storm is bad enough, but this tent can't be reefed and there are no cleats to belay to. What are we going to do if it starts to blow away?"

"Do!?" he replied in a conversational bellow, "Why, we'll take a reef in the roof! We'll take a turn around the cook's leg! Do you think they invented belaying just so's they'd have something to do with cleats? Besides," he growled, returning to his hitching, "this thing was put up by pros. Why don't you take a look at their work?"

As it happened, he had every reason to be calm; the tent riggers had sunk plenty of rod anchors deep into the ground and had attached them to the stoutly built tent with heavy rope. And they knew enough about

knots to use a Clove Hitch and Rolling Hitch for a secure belay (Figure 45).

Seeing all this, and thinking about what Spike had said, I realized that the cleats, bitts, and winches I was accustomed to were no guarantee of security in themselves. With or without them, ultimate responsibility has always lain with the sailor (or roustabout)

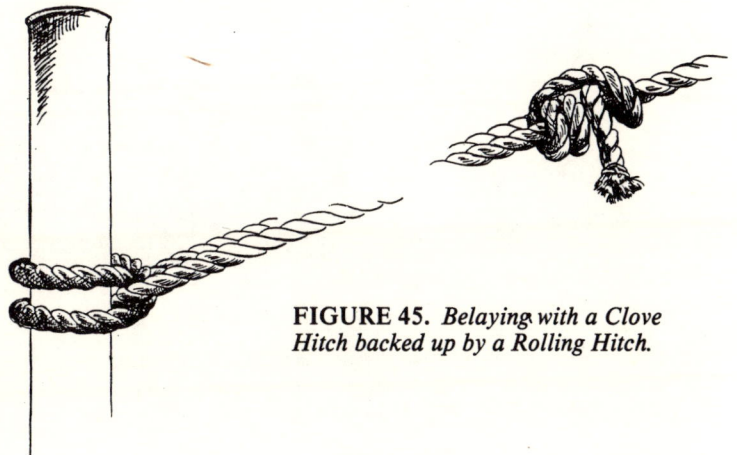

FIGURE 45. *Belaying with a Clove Hitch backed up by a Rolling Hitch.*

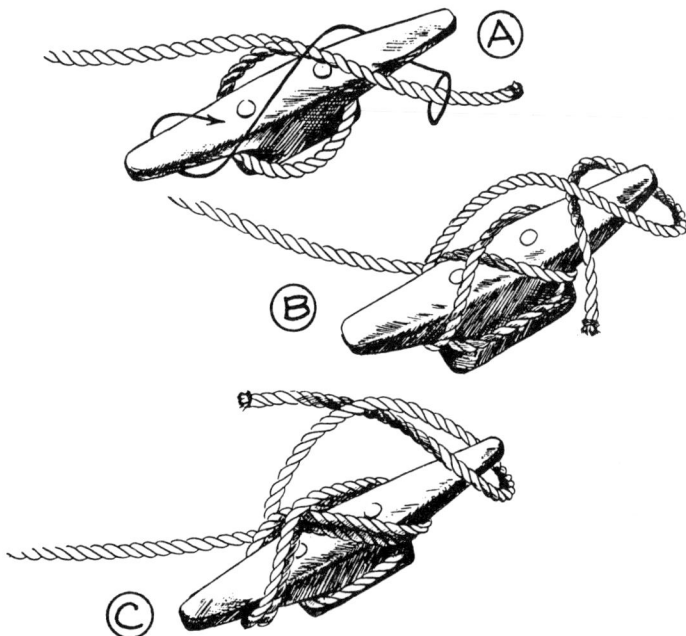

FIGURE 46. *A belay to a horn cleat starts with a full turn around the base* (**A**) *and ends with a half hitch* (**B**). *Avoid turning the finished loop in the wrong direction* (**C**). *Note that the cleat is angled to the lead of the standing part.*

whose job it is to analyze the circumstances and strains involved, take stock of available materials and fittings, and then secure things accordingly. This doesn't mean that you have to learn a special technique for every situation; a few basic elements are present in every good belay, and many of the techniques are interchangeable. All you need to keep in mind are: Control, Security, Ease of Casting Off, and Ability to Surge.

To illustrate, let's look again at those tent guys. The Clove Hitch creates friction, so that only a fraction of the strain comes on the rope end, and it's easier to control the load while making the Rolling Hitch, which provides security. This hitch never jams, so the tent will be easy to strike. And the friction of the Clove Hitch makes surging (gradually paying out slack to a line under strain) an easy and safe operation.

All of this is even easier on a cleat, that most highly evolved belaying tool. In Figure 46, the line takes a turn for control around the base of the cleat before beginning the two or three figure-eight turns that provide security. Note that the cleat is angled away from the lead of the line. This makes it easier to get a turn started, prevents the line from jamming against its own standing part, and more evenly distributes the strain on the bolts that hold the cleat to the deck. When making fast to a bollard (Figure 47), take a turn first around the *nearer* post before commencing figure-eight turns around both. This minimizes the tendency of the farther post to "lever up" under extreme loads.

To keep the turns of a belay from coming loose, make a half hitch to finish. Just pretend you're going to make another figure-eight, then slip a loop under the line and over the horn of the cleat (Figure 46). A hitch made in the opposite direction is perversely inclined either to slip or jam, and looks awful besides.

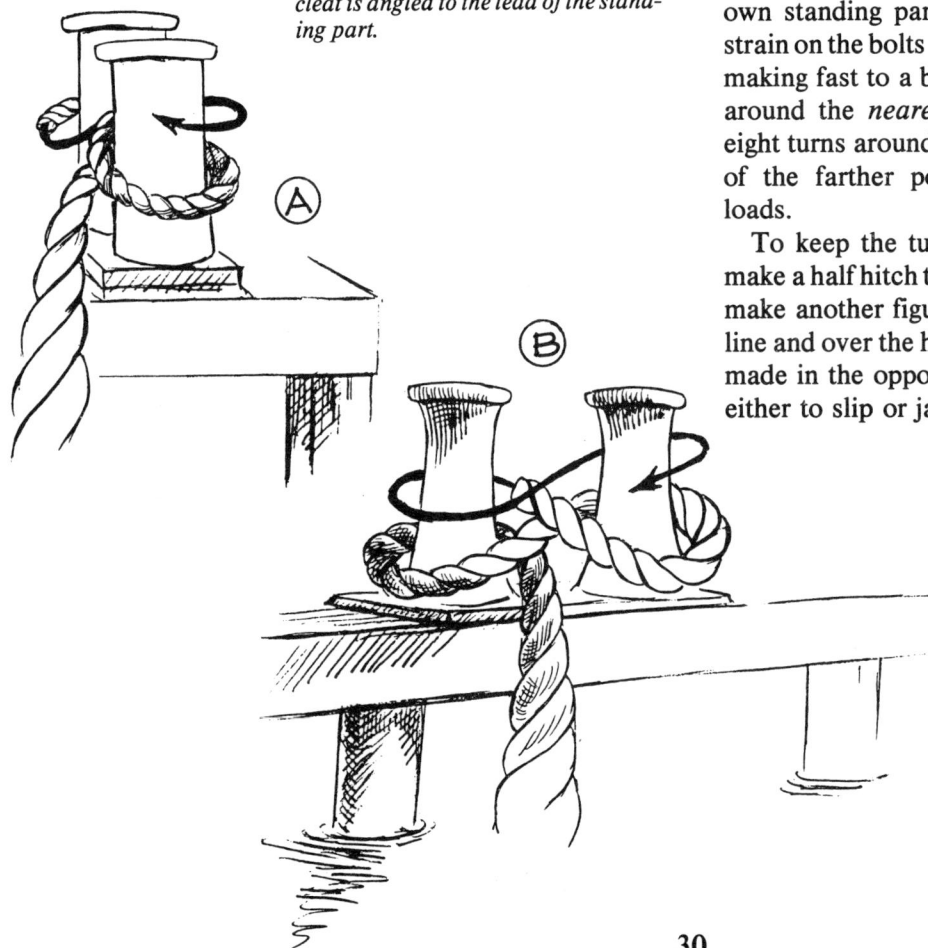

FIGURE 47. *The first turn on a bollard in line with the lead should be around the near post* (**A**). *When the lead is perpendicular to the bollard* (**B**), *either post will do.*

30

FIGURE 48-A. *Belaying to an anchor bitt. Finish with a half hitch around the pin.*

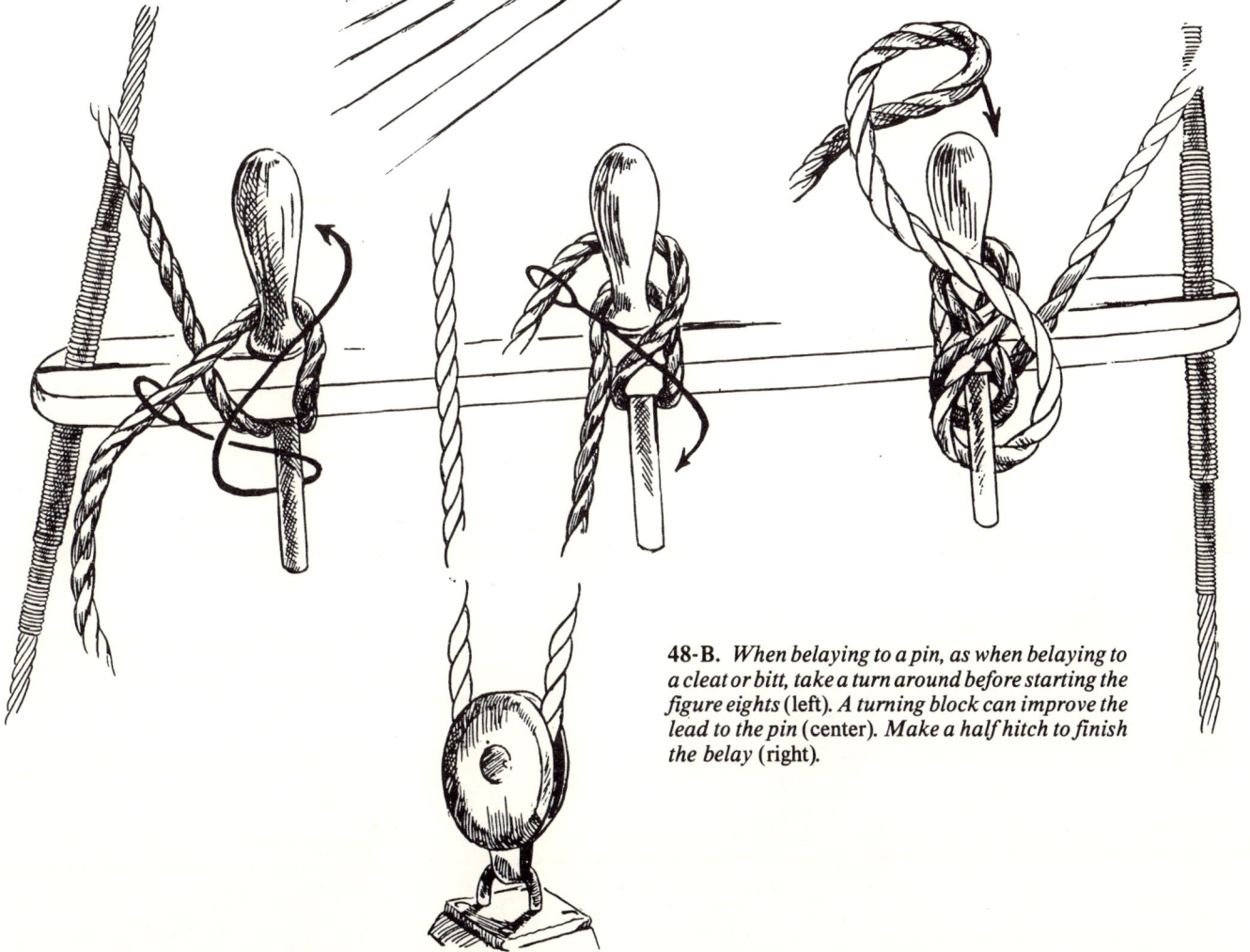

48-B. *When belaying to a pin, as when belaying to a cleat or bitt, take a turn around before starting the figure eights (left). A turning block can improve the lead to the pin (center). Make a half hitch to finish the belay (right).*

Cleating procedures also work on bitts, Samson posts, and belaying pins, though at different orientations (Figure 48). The belaying-pin rail is mounted so as to follow the line of the sheer. This has the advantages mentioned above for cleats and also presents a more pleasing appearance than would a horizontal rail. A fife rail is mounted horizontally at the base of the mast, but the leads themselves come in at an angle whenever possible, often with the aid of turning blocks bolted below the rail. Angled cleats and pins are usually positioned to make things easier for right-handers, but sometimes the angle that a line comes in at gives us left-handers a turn at convenience.

31

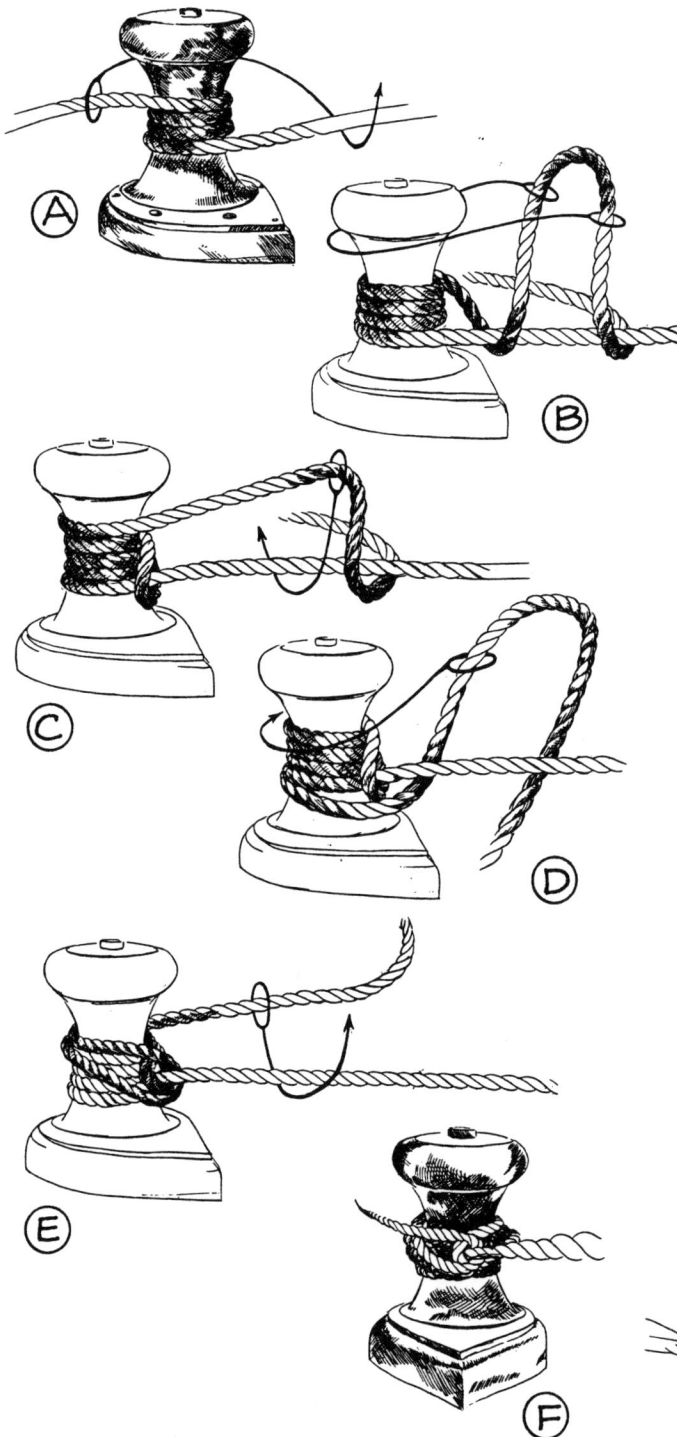

FIGURE 49. *A Capstan Hitch turns a winch into a handy belaying post.*

The Capstan Hitch (Figure 49) is the best method for belaying to a winch, capstan, rail, or post (unless you want an adjustable belay, as on the tent). It's an elegant, ingenious technique that provides absolute control and security around a cylinder without the need to use the end. To tie it, pass a bight of the tail under the standing part and drop the bight over the winch. Then pass a bight from the opposite direction and drop it over. Repeat from both sides and finish with two half hitches made with a bight around the standing part.

When there's no way to drop a bight over, as when belaying to a rail, make the hitch using a long bight as though it were an end or, when convenient, use the end itself. With either method, extra tension can be gained by hauling on the tail after each pass.

When slacking away on a taut line, don't just flip the turns off willy-nilly; the force of the load might suprise you and get out of control. So keep a little tension on the tail as you undo the turns. When you get down to the last turns, the line will start sliding and you'll be able to feel how much tension there is. Pay out the slack, keeping your hands well clear of the cleat, until you can handle the tension with hands only. Then you can remove the last turns. To surge (pay out slack) on a winch or capstan, have someone tail the end while you place your hands on either side of the barrel. Have the tailer give you a little slack, then squeeze your hands against the turns and slide your right hand away from you and your left hand toward you to roll the turns counterclockwise, easing slack into the standing part (Figure 50). Be extremely careful not to get your fingers between the turns and the drum; there are some short-fingered sailors around who can tell you about the consequences.

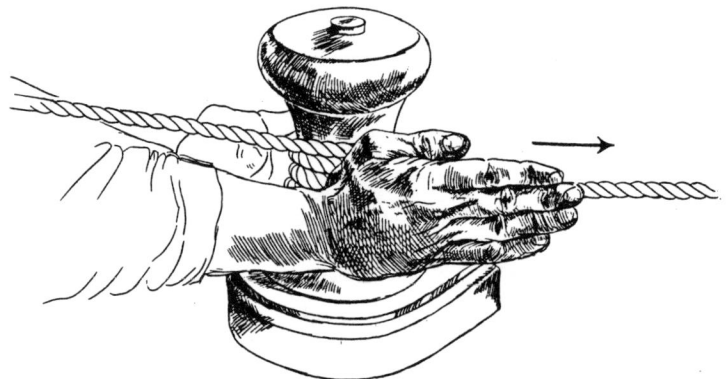

FIGURE 50. *Surging a line on a winch.*

32

The time might come when there is no post, pin, cleat, or seemingly anything else to belay to. Here resourcefulness must take over, even if it means employing procedures that are harder on your gear than you might prefer. Jamming a bight of the fall into the lower block of a tackle is an ancient and effective expedient, as is rotating the load to twist the parts of the tackle together. Just be sure things don't unwind until you're ready. Even pinching the parts together with your hands will keep things from moving if the load isn't too great, and sometimes you can belay to the load itself (Figure 51).

In an emergency, don't be shy about how you gain the friction needed for a belay, just so long as you don't slice the rope on a sharp corner. Tension is what makes rigging work, so do what you must to maintain it....

Hey, Cookie! Come on over here!

FIGURE 51. *When there doesn't appear to be anything to belay to, twisting the tackle or jamming a bight of the fall into the upper block can help control a heavy load* (A). *Belaying the line to the load itself works, too* (B).

33

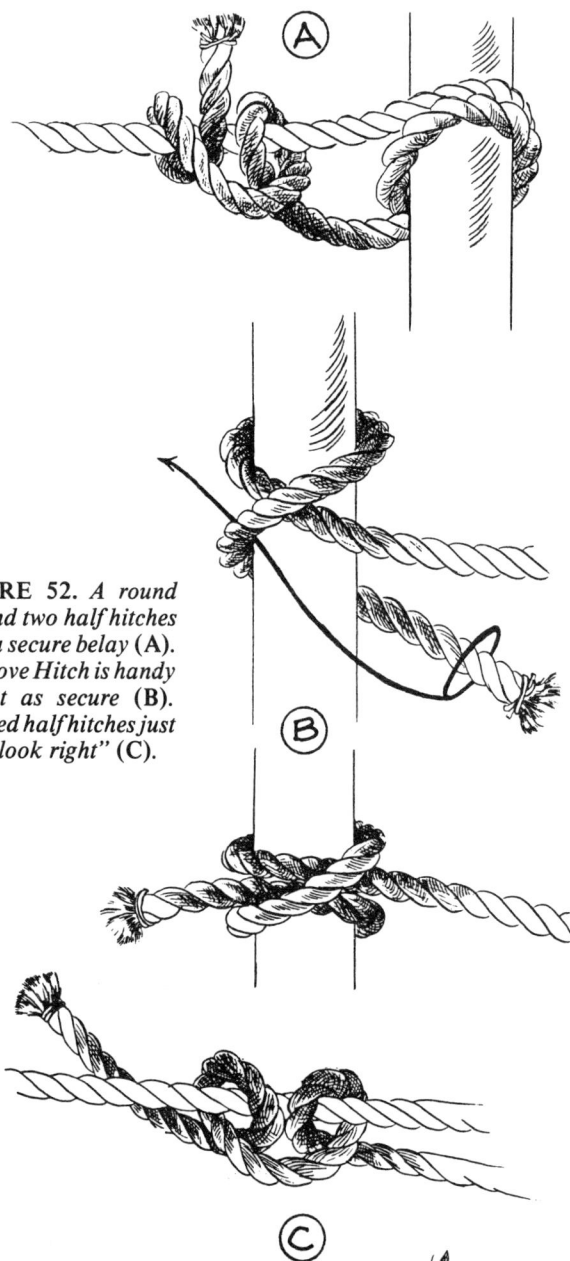

FIGURE 52. *A round turn and two half hitches make a secure belay* (A). *The Clove Hitch is handy but not as secure* (B). *Reversed half hitches just don't "look right"* (C).

FIGURE 53. *The Anchor Hitch also begins with a round turn, then the end is passed behind the standing part and under the turns. Half hitches or a Throat Seizing are frequently added for long-term security.*

FOUR HITCHES

There's a fine line, so to speak, between a belaying hitch and an ordinary one: The former, as we have just seen, is designed to be made around an object while the line is under tension; the latter is most easily applied while the line is slack. Belaying techniques are plenty secure for all purposes, but they're more time- and material-consuming to tie, since they must generate sufficient friction for dynamic control. So it makes sense also to have a few simpler hitches in one's repertoire.

A Round Turn and Two Half Hitches

The old salts say that "a round turn and two half hitches never fail," and it's pretty nearly true. This basic hitch is ideal for starting or finishing off lashings, tying small craft to mooring rings, tethering anything but a camel (see below), making off tool lanyards, etc. The round turn distributes strain and chafe across a greater number of rope fibers than a single turn would, while the two half hitches provide jam-resistant security (Figure 52).

It is widely held that reversed half hitches are the mark of a lubber, but there doesn't seem to be any structural justification for this belief. Perhaps the scorn stems from the can't-make-up-my-mind-which-way-to-hitch appearance of the reversed version. In any event, I recommend same-direction hitches, if only for the sake of confusion-reducing uniformity.

The Anchor Hitch

This one's a little more involved in the making, but worth the effort. The end is passed under a round turn to form, and all is drawn up well (Figure 53). Half hitches are usually added to further secure the end.

This knot's primary virtue is that it holds well on lines that are alternately slack and taut, such as anchor rodes; it doesn't work loose, but doesn't jam either. I didn't fully appreciate this virtue until one summer when I met crews from two boats that had both lost anchors from Bowline-secured rodes. When you want insurance and can take the time, use an Anchor Hitch.

34

The Rolling Hitch and Variations

This knot can be made under tension, which suits it for cleatless belays, but it is by no means limited to that function; of all hitches, it has the widest range of usefulness.

It can be made up close to an object instead of half hitches, or it can be made around rails, rings, spars, or other ropes for slinging or for hanging tackle from. It is adjustable, so tension can be maintained in tidal areas, or in rope that comes and goes when wet, or for temporary staying, when guys must be adjusted relative to one other. It is a ridiculously simple knot suited to either perpendicular or lengthwise pull, but nevertheless ridiculously underused. To form: Make two turns in the direction of the strain, then a hitch on the side of the turns away from the strain (Figure 54). Turns and hitch all travel in the same direction.

If the material is inclined to slip, the Rigger's Hitch, a variation made by jamming the second turn over the first, has a more tenacious grip, though it's also difficult to adjust.

For very slick work, such as hanging a hammock from 1 x 19 wire, try another variation, the Camel Hitch. This is a circus knot, developed specifically for mooring camels, whose copious slobber and head-jerking truculence jams lesser hitches.

For all Rolling Hitch variations, draw up well so that all turns take a strain, and don't push their security by burdening them with extreme loads; get the right rope at the right length.

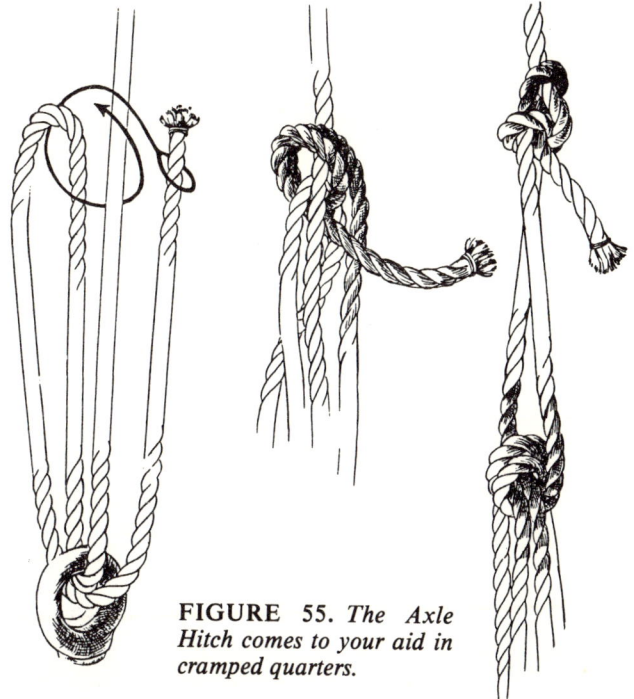

FIGURE 55. *The Axle Hitch comes to your aid in cramped quarters.*

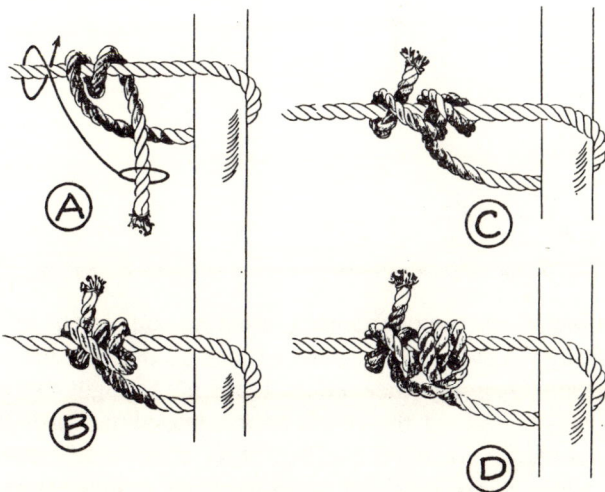

FIGURE 54. *The Rolling Hitch (A and B) is an adjustable knot for lengthwise pull. The Rigger's Hitch (C) is one variation. The Camel Hitch (D) has three round turns and two half hitches.*

The Axle Hitch

Scene: The hold of a ship or the underside of a car or some other god-awful, inaccessible spot. It's hard enough just to crawl or climb in there, and you don't have the time, inclination, or free hand to make a hitch while you're there. Fine—just pass a bight around and bring it back to a more comfortable location (Figure 55). Ah, that's better. Now pass the end around a couple of times as shown, add a Bowline or Rolling Hitch to secure the end, and hoist or tow away.

Because hitching is so basic to the use of rope, and because there are so many sizes and shapes of things to hitch onto, the foregoing must be considered a basic sampler of the class; the four knots shown will cover most situations, but be prepared to improvise. Any hitch that is meant to be more or less permanent will benefit from having its end throat-seized to the standing part (Chapter 1). On the other hand, most hitching jobs suffer from an excess of security; people can't trust a good knot, so they keep adding convolutions that invite jamming and take time to do and undo. Always use the simplest knot—hitch or otherwise—that will properly do the job. William of Occam should have been a rigger.

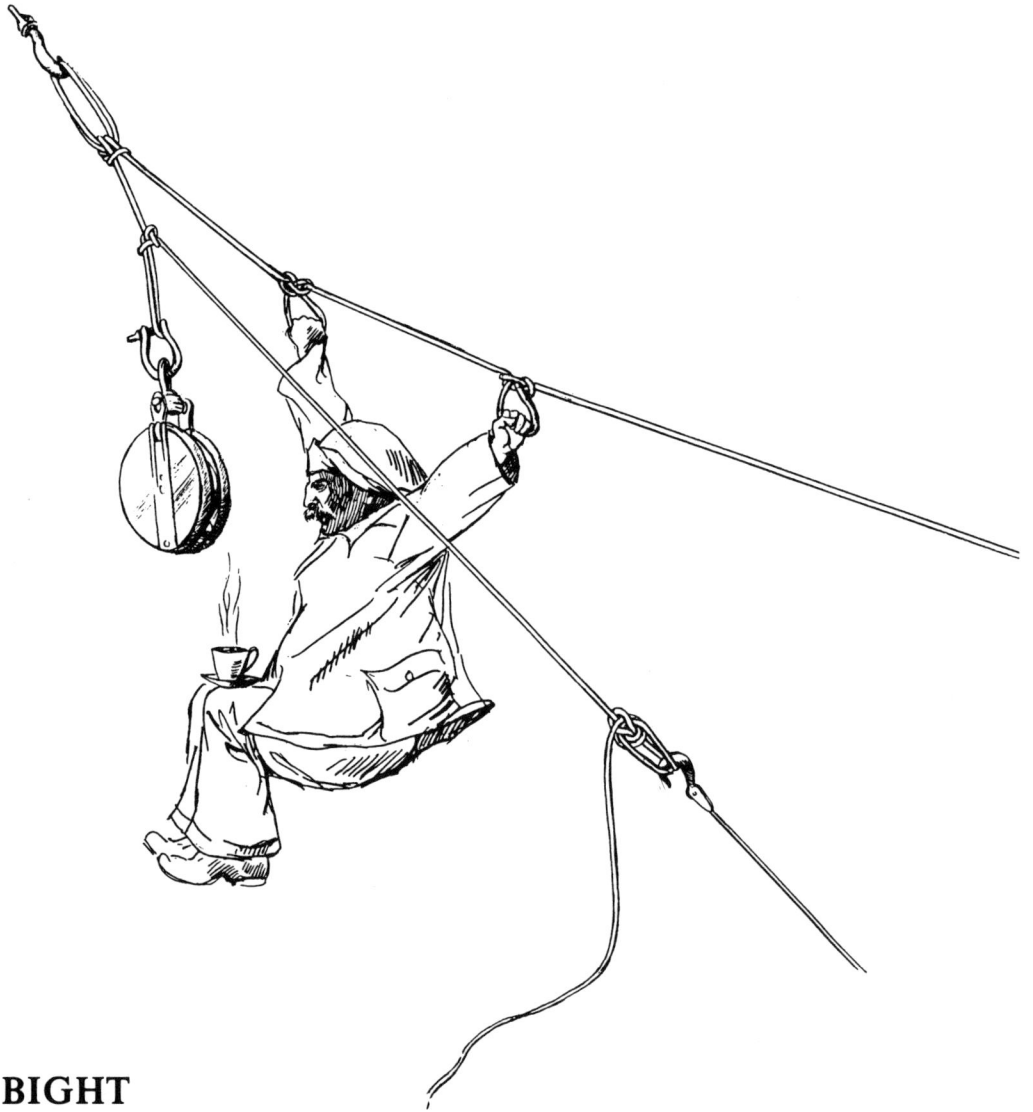

FIVE IN THE BIGHT

Lines don't always end where you want them to. When you need a loop to tail onto, reeve through, or hang something from, but there's no end available to make a knot with, then it's time to do some work in the bight.

There are some elementary examples of this class in the "Lashmanship" section of Chapter 1, specialized knots that depend on a pulley configuration to keep from spilling. But the following examples maintain their integrity unsupported, creating convenient little blurps in the standing part that can be tied and untied easily. Among other things, loops in the bight can be used to extend the reach of a come-along, provide handholds for team hauling, make a place to hang a ladder, plank, block, or container from, or make an eye at the top of a makeshift sling. When you have the time, they're more stable, jamproof lashing loops as well.

FIGURE 56. *The Bowline on a Bight begins with an Overhand Knot. Drop the bight over the Overhand (1) and pull on the uppermost turn of the Overhand (2) to draw in the bight and form the neck of the knot.*

FIGURE 57. *A Bowline on a Bight with a Bowline on it.*

The Bowline on a Bight

This is the best-known member of this class, a two-loop beauty that starts out as an Overhand Knot, becomes an amorphous tangle, and finally resolves itself into elegant utility (Figure 56). This knot is the traditional choice for bight work because of its simplicity and double-bearing surface, but it is not entirely dependable when the strain comes on one part only or when the two standing parts are pulled in opposite directions. In the former instance, make a Bowline on a Bight with a Bowline on it (Figure 57). In the latter instance try a different knot such as the Farmer's Loop or Lineman's Rider.

The Farmer's Loop

This is a fine knot for a number of reasons, not the least of which is that it provides sailors with a non-invective use for the word "farmer." Besides that it is fast to tie, never jams, and has a perfect lead for sidewise pull. And it's fun.

To make it, start with three turns around your hand. Shift the middle turn over the left one, the new middle turn over the right one, the still-newer middle turn over the left one, and pull the newest middle turn straight out while holding on to both standing parts (Figure 58). Done. Because it's so handy, you'll sometimes make a Farmer's Loop at the end of a line instead of a Bowline, especially when a shackle, Backsplice, or Figure-Eight Knot make the end difficult to pass.

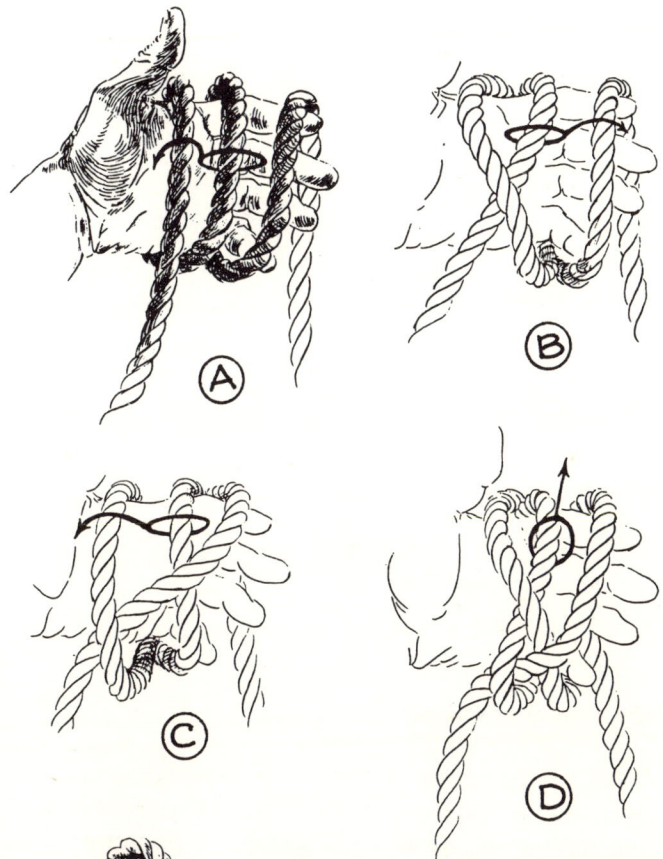

FIGURE 58. *The Farmer's Loop, a good fast knot.*

37

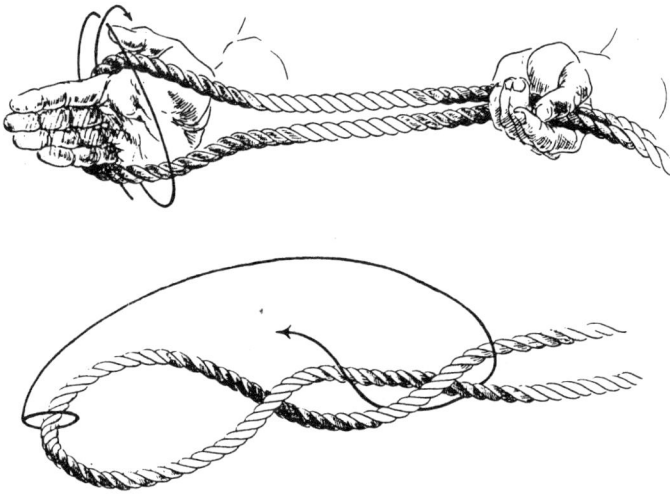

FIGURE 59. *The Lineman's Rider. Draw up carefully.*

FIGURE 60. *The Double Rider.*

The Lineman's Rider

Another important single-loop knot also originated on land: The Lineman's Rider was first used by telephone company crews, giving each member a comfortable loop to haul on for raising poles and tightening wires. It is begun by making a 360-degree twist in a closed bight, forming an eye. The end of the bight is then passed between the legs of the standing part and up through the eye (Figure 59). The Lineman's Rider is strong, secure, compact, and is the foundation of a beautiful double-loop form, the Double Rider.

The Double Rider

This knot (Figure 60) is a little tricky to tie, but its splayed loops make it preferable to the Bowline on a Bight for some slinging applications (ladders, pallets) and for sitting in. Either knot is good as an emergency bosun's chair.

To make a Double Rider, start with a loose single one and drop the two "ears" down into the loop. Pass the loop up to the top of the knot and draw the slack into the ears, which have now become two loops.

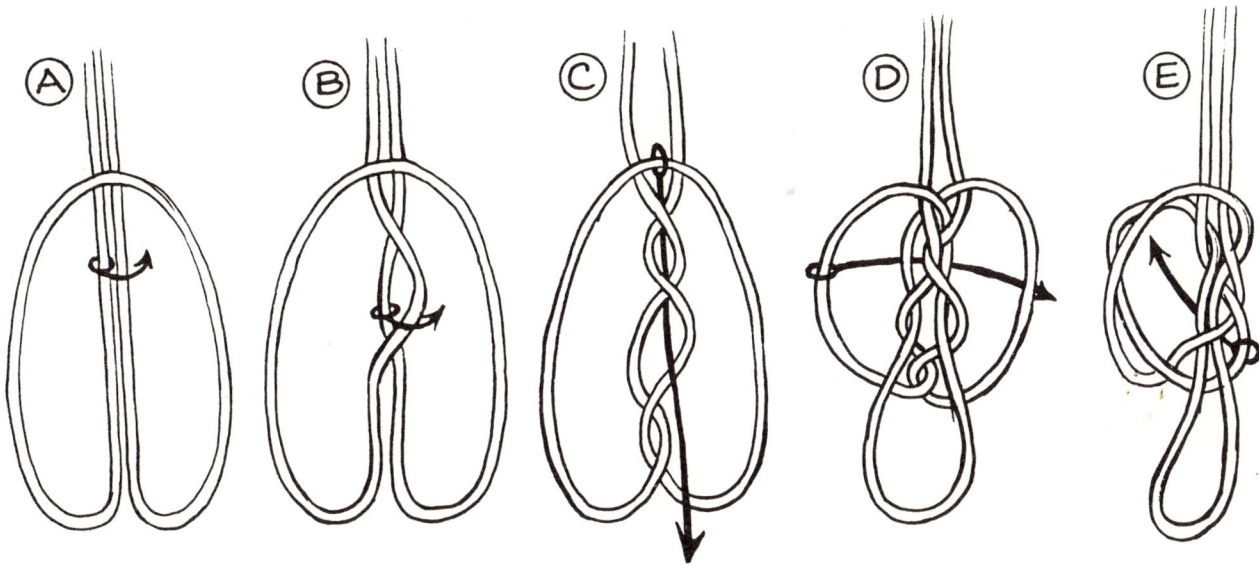

FIGURE 61. The Jug Sling Knot. *Lay a bight back over its standing parts, then twist those parts twice to form an eye. Grasping the knot by its two legs, lift it up slightly, then reach through the eye with the thumb and forefinger to snare the bight between the two legs; pull the bight through the eye (follow the arrow in C), twisting it 180 degrees to arrive at the configuration in D. Now pass the left-hand ear under the knot as in D, then carefully turn the knot over to get the configuration in E. Pass one bight (shown by the arrow in E) under the knot, and arrange the knot to get the configuration in F. Draw up around the neck of your jug.*

The Jug Sling Knot

In a world where plastic and glass containers come with built-in handles, this knot might seem unnecessary and its inclusion here whimsical, but I do have some reasons for showing it. First, it is an excellent example of applied friction. Second, if you've ever had to carry a gallon jug any distance, as from a store to your boat, you know that those convenient little ring handles aren't good for anything but crippling your fingers. Third, this is the best way to secure a wine bottle for a cooling tow astern.

So clear a space and lay down some line as shown in Figure 61. Form an eye by twisting the legs twice. Reach into the eye, palm down. Snag the middle of the

bight and pull it out, turning your hand palm up as you do so, to encourage the mess to take the form shown in 61-D. Pull the leftmost turn back and to the right, turn the knot over, pass one bight under, adjust a bit, and the knot appears. Bend the two ends on one side together through the bight on the other side to form a wrist strap. As long as the line is scaled to the bottle size, this knot will hold on even a hint of a lip with absolute security.

There are many other in-the-bight knots, but these are the cream; compare against them any others that you might want to use, to be certain they also possess the virtues of strength, good lead, ease of tying and untying, and especially security—if a bight knot slips, you can get caught in the middle.

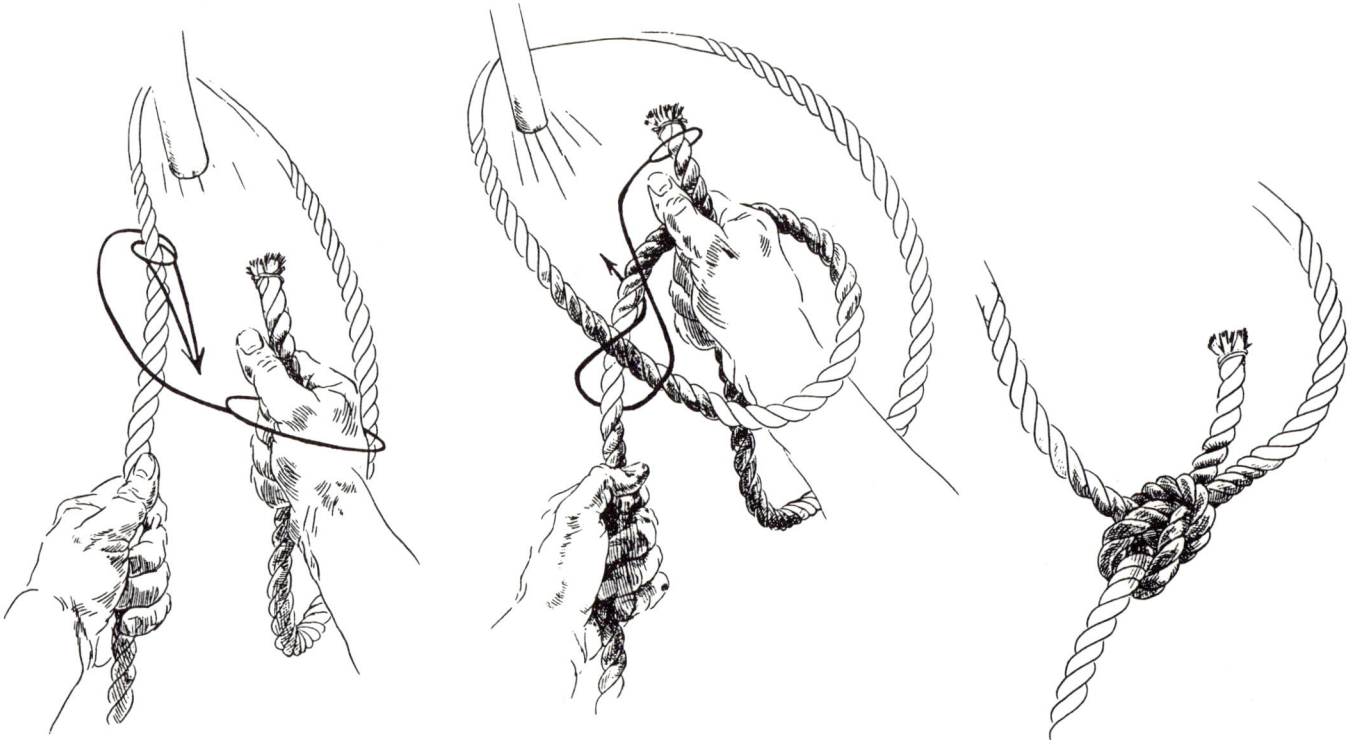

FIGURE 62. Newman Bowline. *Pass the end of the line around a post and hold the standing part in one hand, the end in the other. Reach across the standing part with your end hand (with the end pointing toward the post), and then pivot your hand under the standing part and back toward you. There should now be a loop around your wrist. Pass the end under the standing part and let go of the end momentarily to reach over and grab it from the other side. Finally, pull it and your hand out of the loop to form the knot.*

SEVEN BOWLINES

Paul Newman was up there on the silver screen, swaggering his way through a role as a fiercely independent logger. He swaggered as he climbed a tree, he swaggered as he cut one down, and he swaggered as he put a Bowline into a big hawser.

"Wait a minute! Did you see that?" I said to my companion.

"See what?" she said.

"That Bowline. He tied it without letting go of the end! And fast! How did he do it?"

"Calm down, Brion," she said.

"Shut up!" said people around us. But I was already digging in my pocket for a length of string. The Bowline is the King of Knots because it is strong, secure, and versatile, as kings should be. And simple, as kings generally are. It was rare good fortune to come across a new way to tie it and I wanted to try to duplicate the movements while they were still fresh in my mind.

"You're a log," I said to my friend.

"I beg your pardon?"

"Quiet, you two!"

"The hawser was around a log," I whispered. "Hold up your arm."

So in the crowded theater, with the aid of my bewildered friend, I practiced the method. Quietly. In years to come, in more appropriate circumstances, it would prove itself as the best technique for putting a Bowline into heavy or stiff line. And I could always say, "Here's one Paul Newman showed me."

Newman Bowline

It's an ingenious knot, even an elegant one. Look how that sweeping judo move throws a turn into the line. True, at one point you do let go, but with a little practice, it doesn't look as though you do.

Compare that one continuous motion with the rabbit-comes-out-of-the-hole-and-runs-around-the-tree method of tying a Bowline (mercifully not shown here) that many of us learned. Clumsy and slow. How can we call the Bowline the King of Knots and then make it in a manner that can only be described as low-class? And it's not as if there's only one alternative to the rabbit version.

Spilled-Hitch Bowline

When the line is neither bulky nor stiff, its flexibility will make the Newman Bowline difficult to execute. No matter, the Bowline earned its royal sobriquet not only for its strength, security, and ease of untying—other knots possess those virtues—but also for its versatility. So we have a second alternative, which starts out as an innocent-looking half hitch made with the end around the standing part. A little push and pull spills the hitch into the standing part, the end is tucked, and suddenly you're done. Basically, it is a less flashy version of the Newman method and, like it, is easier in every instance than the usual practice of forming a bight with your hand and threading your way through it.

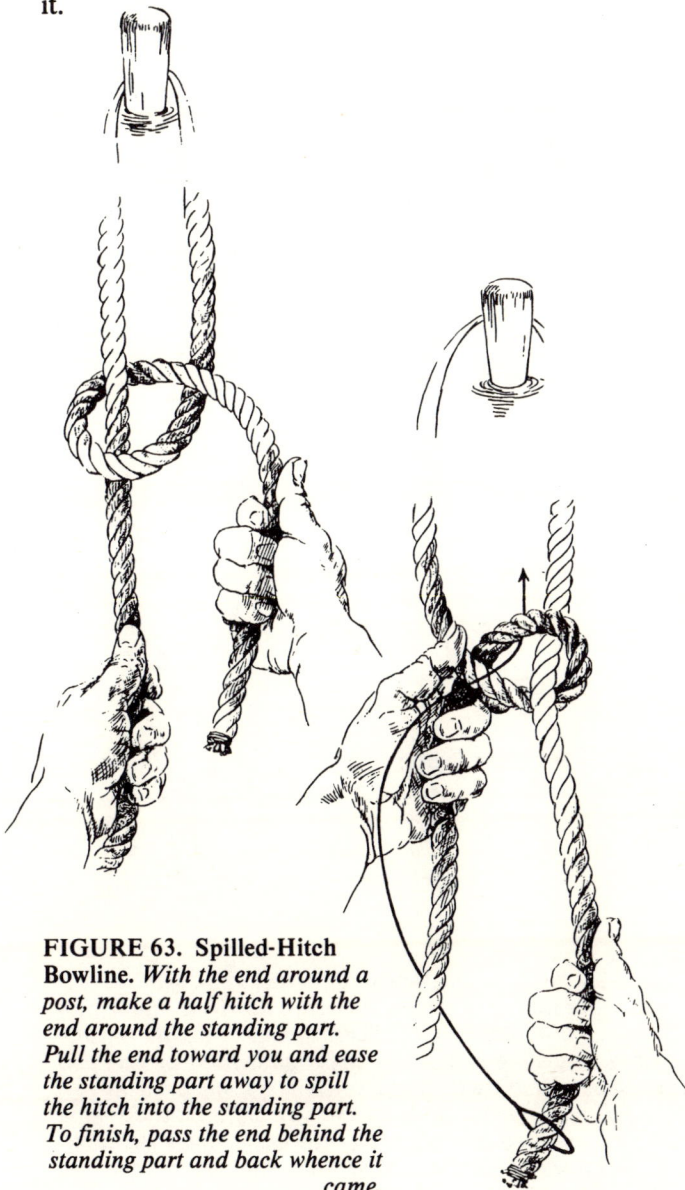

FIGURE 63. Spilled-Hitch Bowline. *With the end around a post, make a half hitch with the end around the standing part. Pull the end toward you and ease the standing part away to spill the hitch into the standing part. To finish, pass the end behind the standing part and back whence it came.*

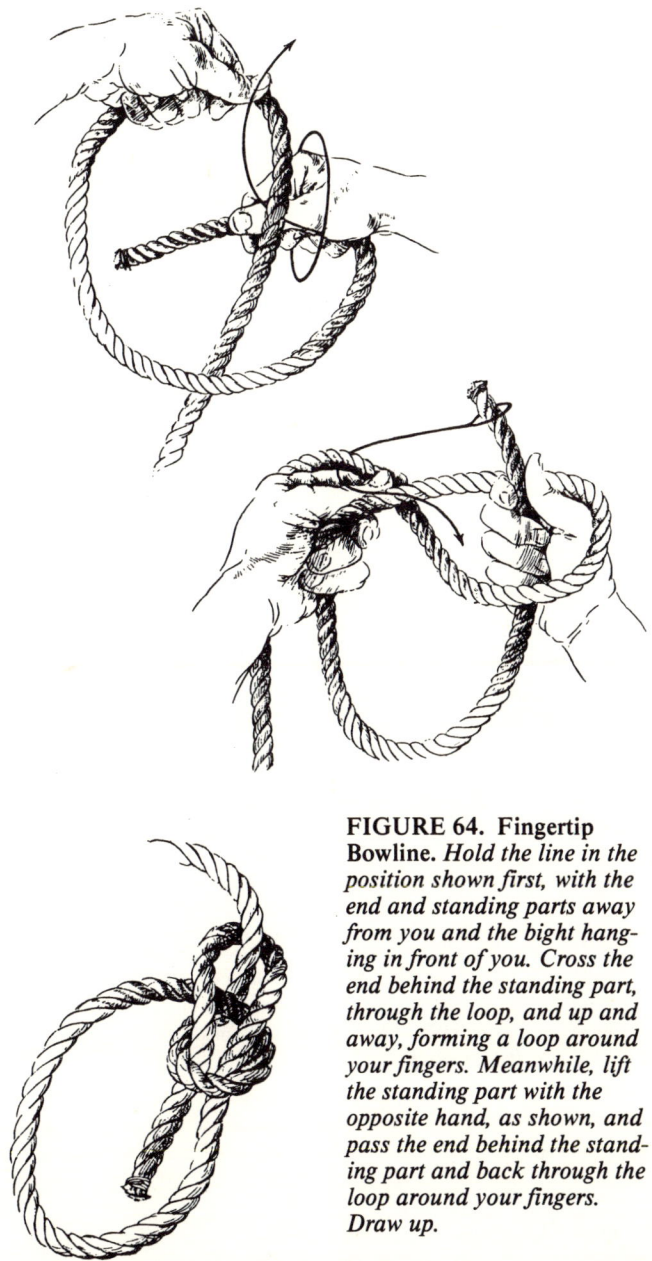

FIGURE 64. Fingertip Bowline. *Hold the line in the position shown first, with the end and standing parts away from you and the bight hanging in front of you. Cross the end behind the standing part, through the loop, and up and away, forming a loop around your fingers. Meanwhile, lift the standing part with the opposite hand, as shown, and pass the end behind the standing part and back through the loop around your fingers. Draw up.*

Fingertip Bowline

Still another variation is used to make a Bowline freehand; there's no piling, cleat, or such to brace against, such as the previous knots require. It's all done with the fingertips and a little wrist motion.

Once you know these first three knots, you can work with the eye of the Bowline toward or away from you and with or without a prop. Never again do you have to hang outboard or hunch sideways to get the line in a familiar orientation.

The Fingertip method is the one to use when you want to impress someone by tying a Bowline behind your back.

FIGURE 65. Two-Bight Bowline. *Start with the Spilled-Hitch Bowline; after spilling the hitch, add an identical hitch and spill it, too. Then pass the end behind the standing part and up through both hitches. This knot is less liable to slip or jam than the regular Bowline.*

Two-Bight Bowline

Even kings have their limitations; the Bowline sometimes slips or jams, especially under extreme stress. If you know that a line will be subjected to some sort of extreme, you might consider using an Eyesplice or other especially strong knot. The Bowline, although stronger than many knots, is still rated at only 60 percent of the breaking strength of the rope in which it is tied, while a splice is closer to 95 percent. But given stout line, short time, and the need for a knot that can be untied when you're through, try the Two-Bight Bowline. To make it, start with the Spilled-Hitch version but with an extra-long end. Make a second, identical spill farther up the standing part, then pass the end back toward the eye, through both bights. Because the load is shared, this knot won't slip or jam.

Slipknot Bowline

And now, for something completely different, a knot startling enough to be performed purely as a trick yet practical enough to save your life, may I introduce the fabulous Slipknot Bowline.

The illustrations tell the story, but it's hard to believe the thing actually works until you've tried it yourself. And then it's just about impossible to resist saying "Voila!" as the knot appears out of nowhere.

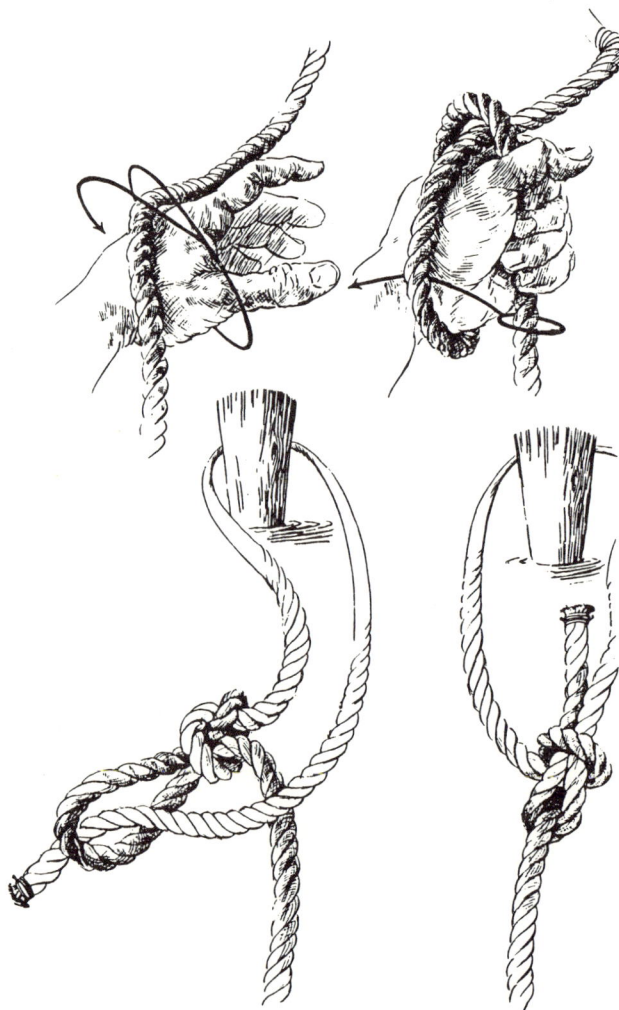

FIGURE 66. Slipknot Bowline. *The tricky part of this knot is making the slipknot. Lay the line over your wrist as shown, with the standing part nearest you. Reach around behind the end and grab the standing part, thumb uppermost. Hang on and pull your hand out of the loop, and you'll have a slipknot. Leave it loose. If you haven't already done so, pass or flip the end around the post, and drop the end into the bight of the slipknot. Haul on the standing part, and a Bowline will spill into existence.*

I once used this knot to make up to a piling at a cleatless section of dock in near-dark in a crowded marina, when a strong tide was running and our engine wasn't. We could have and probably should have anchored out, but we knew the place and the wind was right, so as I stood in the bow with slipknot ready, we luffed up into the current alongside the dock. I threw the long end around the piling and dropped it through the slipknot, and the boat as it drifted back capsized the Bowline into being. Our only misfortune was that no spectators were around to witness this neat trick.

Of course, the Slipknot Bowline's usefulness isn't limited to tight situations; some people use it almost exclusively, since it is easy, minimizes opportunities for fumbling, and is very quickly completed. In fact, the only Bowline that takes less time to make isn't really a Bowline at all.

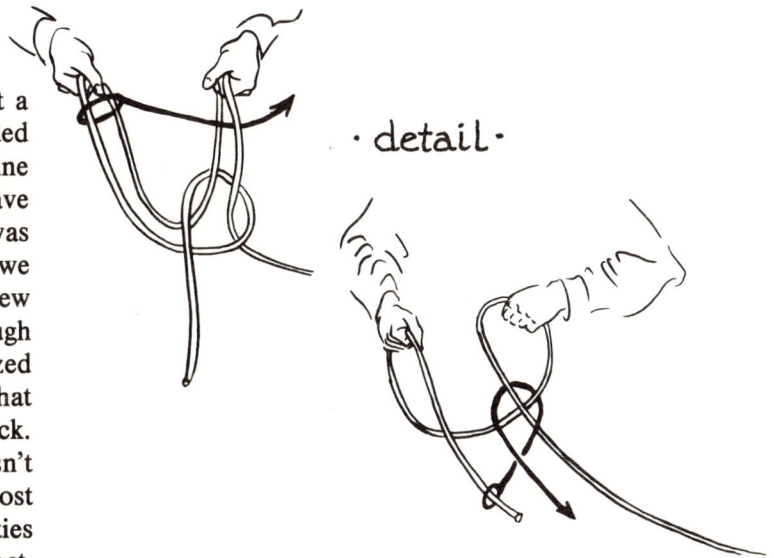

· detail ·

Tugboat (or Flying) Bowline

Call it what you will, this Bowline is really a form of the Angler's Loop *(The Ashley Book of Knots,* #1017), a strong knot with excellent lead but also with a tendency to jam. So if it's not a Bowline, why is it described here? Because sailors at times need a Bowline faster than a Bowline can be made. So they use this knot instead and think so highly of it, despite its shortcomings, that they call it after the King. Think of it as a royal bastard.

It is an action knot; the odds are that when you use it you will be in a hurry, and I've never seen anyone demonstrate it without the prefatory phrase, "So you're running down the deck, see...." In truth, it can be done in a hot New York nanosecond, at a dead run.

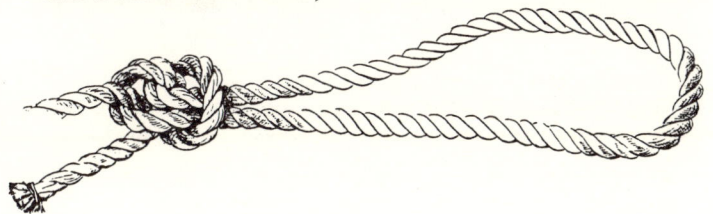

FIGURE 67. Tugboat Bowline. *Start with about 2 feet of end hanging from the thumb side of your right hand, the standing part extending from the thumb side of your left hand, and about 3 feet of line between your hands. By turning your hands inward and toward each other, you form two loops and cause the end to swing over the standing part. As it does so, change its lateral motion to vertical motion by flipping outward with the right wrist and moving your arms sharply away from you (see detail). The idea is to get the end to flip completely around the loop on your left hand and emerge between the two loops. It's a very kinetic knot that requires practice. To finish, reach in through the left loop from the outside with the left hand, and grab the right loop. Grab the standing part with your right hand. Pull your hands apart. Voila! (This knot takes 30 times as long to describe as it does to make.)*

FIGURE 68. *Dragon Bowline.*

Dragon Bowline

Phew! Exertion. There are so many more Bowlines: made on or with a bight, slipped, from half hitches, with round turns, interlocked and sliding, as well as all the national variations (French, Spanish, Portuguese, Chinese), but six at one sitting is plenty, so let's finish up with an ancient, nasty trick. It's best done after an exchange of unusual knots, like some of those just mentioned. At the proper moment casually ask, "Ever see a Dragon Bowline?"

If your audience hasn't read this book, they will probably answer, "No, how do you make that one?"

Look at them carefully for a moment, as if uncertain that they are worthy of the knowledge you are about to impart. Then slowly make an ordinary Bowline and place it very gently on the ground, "with the standing part leading straight out, like this." If they've seen the Slipknot or Flying versions, they'll be staring with rapt attention, waiting for something to happen. Pick up the standing part and walk away, explaining, "Now that's a draggin' Bowline."

Be prepared to duck.

Saying that a bend is a way to tie two ropes together is like saying that Julia Child is someone who cooks food; both definitions are true as far as they go, but they leave out a great deal of information about complex and unpredictable subjects.

For instance, there's the matter of style: Practiced, easy grace can do wonders, whether one is dealing with a recalcitrant mousse or a frozen hawser.

Then there's the need for appropriate use of ingredients: Ms. Child can fashion a religious experience out of a few simple items which, in the hands of a less talented chef, might yield only indigestion. Similarly, a good bend is an elegant, subtle interweaving of the exact same ingredients from which a lubber will fashion that spam of knots, the Granny.

Sometimes the worlds of cuisine and ligature overlap, as in the case of the Butcher's Knots used to bind roasts, corned beef, salt pork, etc., but most often the virtues mentioned above are manifested in quite different particulars. Leaving Julia the Chicken Ballantine, let us turn our attention to bends.

FIGURE 69. *Sheet Bend tied by the Weaver's method. The arrows detail the method of tying. To draw up, hold left standing part and end together while pulling on right standing part. A Left-Handed Sheet Bend (D), in which the ends are diagonally opposite each other, should be avoided.*

The Sheet Bend

This most utilitarian knot, structural cousin to the Bowline, acquires a useful dash of style when made by the Weaver's method (Figure 69). Afloat or ashore, ease and speed of tying are among the most important qualities a bend can have. Note that in the finished knot both ends are above the standing part. It is possible to mistie and finish with the ends diagonally opposite each other, making a "Left-Handed Sheet Bend"—a form that is much more liable to slip than the proper knot.

But then the Sheet Bend is no paragon of virtue, either. It's perfectly adequate for most situations but will jam under very heavy loads and can slip when made in slick material, as Table 2 (page 48) shows. Much modern synthetic cordage is, of course, very slick. So although it is a good basic bend and can be tied in a hurry, the Sheet Bend does have its drawbacks.

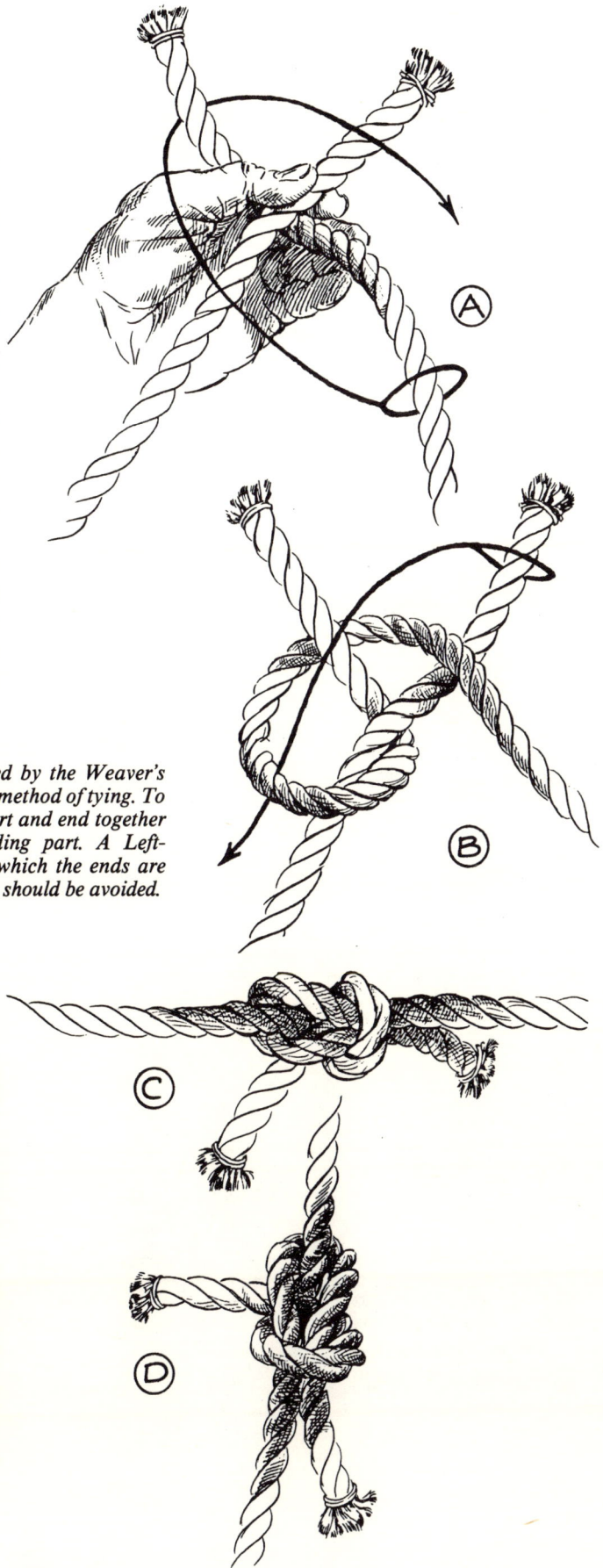

45

FIGURE 70. *Double Sheet Bend, Weaver's method. Make two round turns with the right-hand standing part, the first turn all the way around and the second finishing between the two ends. Tuck the right-hand end into the turns and draw up carefully.*

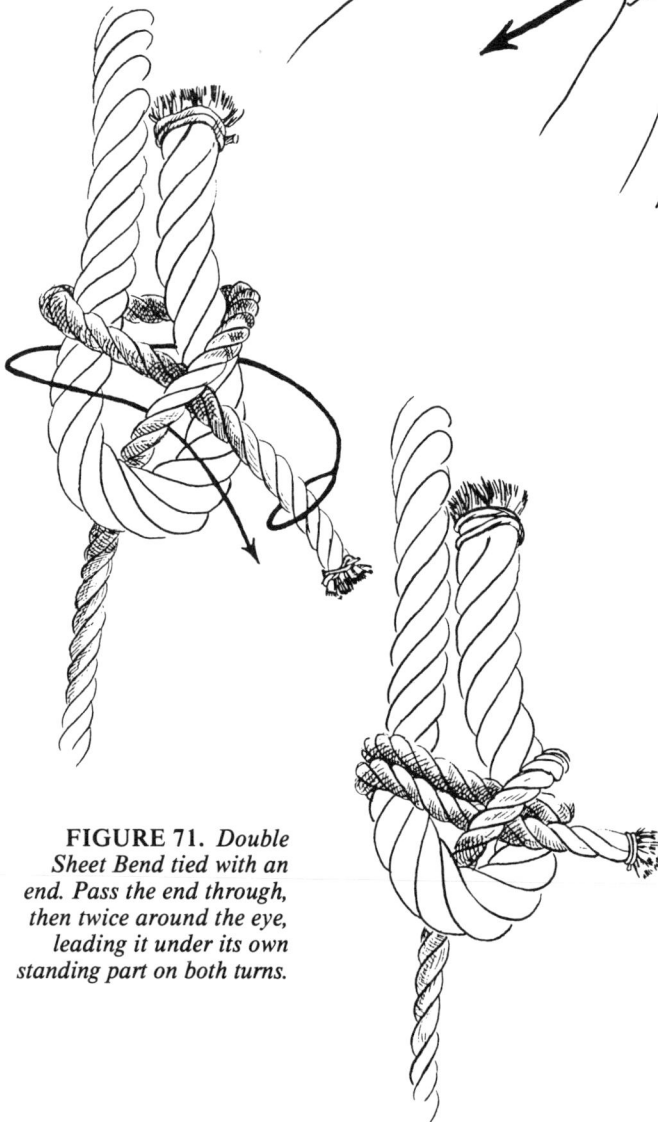

FIGURE 71. *Double Sheet Bend tied with an end. Pass the end through, then twice around the eye, leading it under its own standing part on both turns.*

Double Sheet Bend

Enter the Double Sheet Bend, which has an extra turn in it to prevent slipping. This knot can be made by a variation on the Weaver's method (Figure 70) unless one is bending an end to an Eyesplice, in which case the end must be rove as in Figure 71. By either method, the Double Sheet Bend is the preferred knot for joining lines of different size, consistency, or wetness; the smaller, suppler, or drier line makes the two turns. The Double Sheet Bend is secure but not impervious to jamming, and it needs to be carefully drawn up.

Some texts present these first two knots as the only bends one needs to know, but it is better to think of them as specialized tools, each possessed of important qualities and each afflicted with certain drawbacks. Together they form the foundation of a good bend vocabulary, but we're still only semifluent unless we know some bends that have an additional feature—a good lead.

Both the Sheet Bend and the Double Sheet Bend share the structural defect of poor lead. That is, in each knot an end emerges parallel to the standing part. As

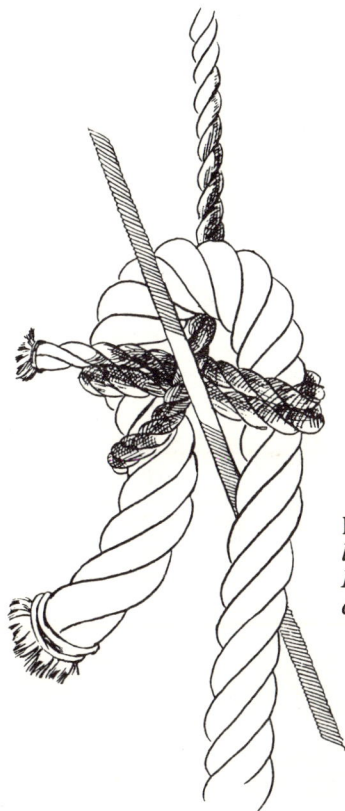

FIGURE 72-A. *The poor lead of a Sheet Bend or Double Sheet Bend can cause snags like this.*

72-B. *The Square Knot combines poor lead with a tendency to spill and fall apart when snagged. Never use it as a bend.*

you can see from Figure 72, the end can snag another object, making the rope hang up in an annoying—perhaps dangerous—fashion. The same illustration shows why the Square Knot is *not* one of our seven bends: abysmal lead is compounded by the likelihood that a snag will "spill" the knot into two half hitches. The same thing can happen even without an end being snagged if the ropes are of different size or consistency. Do not use the Square Knot as a bend.

The Zeppelin Bend

But do use this, one of the very few slip and jamproof knots that also has perfect lead (Figure 73). It takes a teensy bit of dexterity to tie, but that's a small price to pay for the near-ideal knot that results. The story goes that a Capt. Charles Rosenthal of the airship *Los Angeles* wouldn't allow his ground crew to use any other bend for his ship's mooring lines. Since the U.S. Navy never called its airships "Zeppelins," it is likely that this knot came from Germany, but that's all I know of its origin.

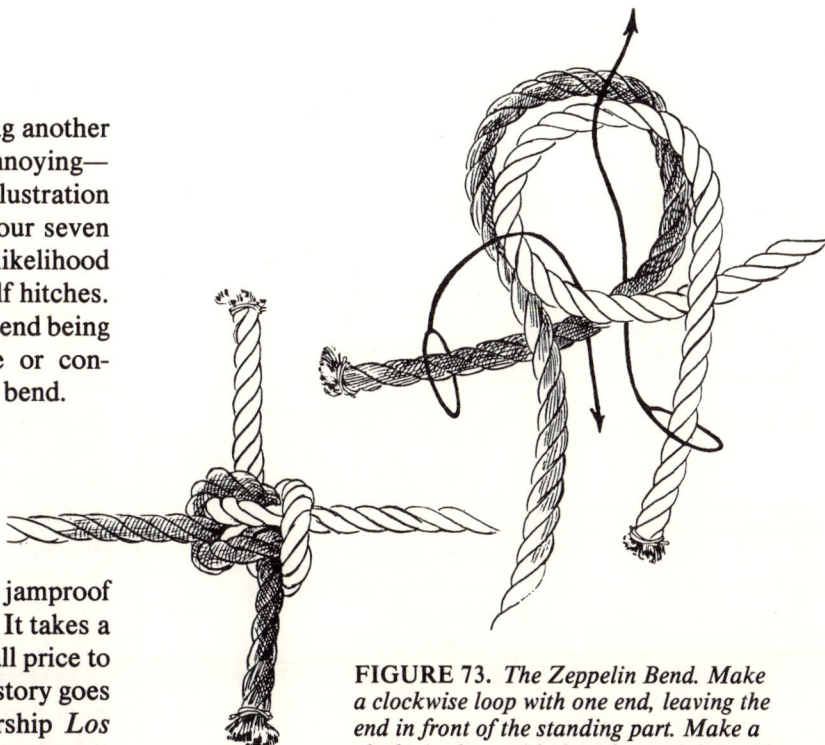

FIGURE 73. *The Zeppelin Bend. Make a clockwise loop with one end, leaving the end in front of the standing part. Make a clockwise loop with the other end, but with the end behind the standing part. Place the first loop on top of the second. Pass the first loop's end up through the two loops and the second loop's end down through the two loops. Draw up snugly.*

47

Since experience had shown him that security was one of the most important attributes of a good bend, Clifford Ashley conducted tests on 20 bends to gauge their resistance to slipping. Each knot (tied in mohair—a very slick, springy material) was given a series of as many as 100 sharp, even tugs and rated by the number of tugs needed to pull it apart. The results were presented on page 273 of *The Ashley Book of Knots*, and are reprinted here with permission.

The figures in the table represent relative security and should be considered a guide only, since most bends will fare better in regular cordage. For example, the Sheet Bend is adequate for use in three-strand Manila, hemp, and spun Dacron, but should not be used in slicker materials such as filament Dacron, nylon, most polypropylene, or any double-braid rope. In the latter cases a more slip-resistant bend such as the Ashley or Strait is called for.

Of the bends described above, the Sheet Bend fared the worst, coming apart after an average of 22.3 pulls. Next came the Double Sheet Bend at 36.2. The Carrick Bend lasted through 70.8 pulls, and the Ashley Bend endured 100 tugs without slipping at all.

The other three recommended bends were not included in the test, but my own experience leads me to rate the Ashley Hawser Bend in a league with the Carrick Bend, the Zeppelin as somewhat more secure than the Carrick, and the Strait Bend on a parity with the Ashley Bend.

Results of Security Tests

Number of tugs to spill knot*	Name of Knot
1.0	Whatnot
2.6	Single Carrick Bend A
3.	Granny Knot
4.5	Single Carrick Bend B
4.6	Single Carrick Bend C
12.2	Thief Knot
14.6	**Left-Hand Sheet Bend
19.	**Reef Knot
19.6	**Carrick Bend, both ends on same side of knot
22.3	**Sheet Bend
22.8	Overhand Bend in left-twisted yarn
25.8	Whatnot, jammed
30.9	Harness Bend, single
33.1	Overhand Bend, left-handed in left-twisted yarn
36.2	**Double Sheet Bend
42.9	Englishman's or Waterman's Knot
70.8	**Carrick Bend with diagonal pull
100.	Ring Knot (slight slip but did not spill)
100.	Barrel Knot (no slip)
100.	**Ashley Bend (no slip)

Maximum 100.
**Knots mentioned in accompanying text.*

FIGURE 74. *The Ashley Bend. Start with a clockwise loop, end behind the standing part, then weave an identical loop into it, passing the second end in a regular under-and-over sequence. Finish by passing both ends into the eye in the middle.*

The Ashley Bend

No doubt about the origin of this knot: It was invented by Clifford Ashley on the 3rd of February 1934 (Figure 74). It has all the advantages of the Zeppelin Bend and is a little easier to tie (both ends are passed simultaneously to finish). Ashley placed a great deal of emphasis on knot security, so he must have been very pleased to find that this was the only nonjamming bend in his security testing (see Table 2) that did not slip at all after 100 tugs.

In spite of these results he was too modest to name it after himself and instead simply listed it as #1452 in his monumental *Ashley Book of Knots*. But so many people found it to be the best bend they'd ever encountered that by 1947, when C.L. Day heartily recommended it in his *Art of Knotting and Splicing*, the inventor's name was firmly linked with his knot.

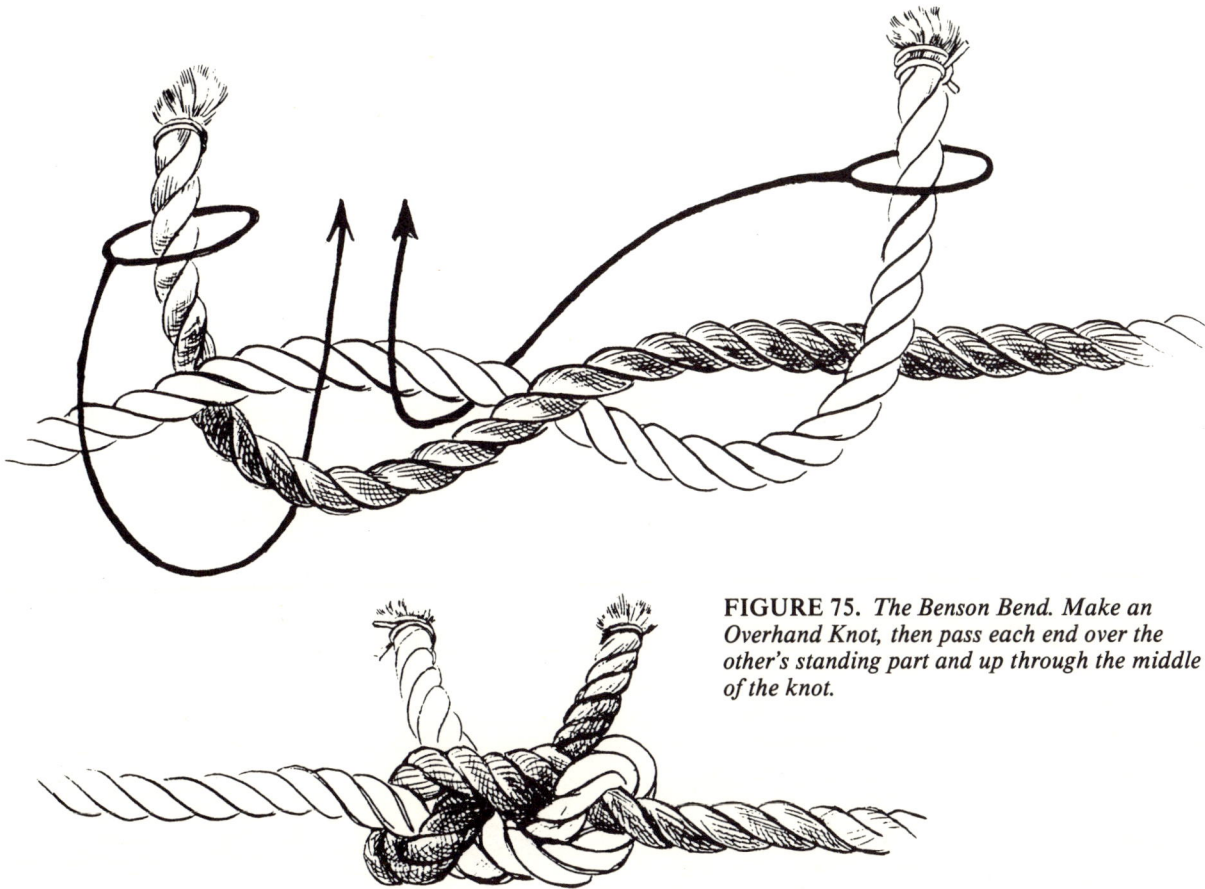

FIGURE 75. *The Benson Bend. Make an Overhand Knot, then pass each end over the other's standing part and up through the middle of the knot.*

The Benson Bend

This one needs a preamble: The appearance of a slightly different version of "Seven Bends" in *WoodenBoat* magazine (July-August 1983) resulted in a flurry of letters suggesting variations, new knots, and different techniques for tying; bends are still fertile ground for innovation. The Weaver's method for tying the Double Sheet Bend, for example, comes to you courtesy of Fred Kenderdine of Billerica, Massachusetts.

It's only because the scope of this book is not encyclopaedic that more suggestions have not been included. But I couldn't leave out the comments of a Mr. John "Fud" Benson who wrote to say, "In tying the Ashley Bend I was struck by its resemblance to a two-strand Crown and Wall Knot...." Indeed, the two knots are analogous, even though they are made and drawn up by completely different methods for completely different purposes. Although the Crown and

Wall Knot (see the Fancy Work chapter) predates this bend by centuries, no one had ever considered using it as anything but a lanyard knot. I'm certain that even Ashley never realized this coincidence of structure, since his knot was the result of trial and error with different configurations.

In a subsequent conversation, Fud pointed out that this situation was something Ashley stressed: The tendency for dormant or underused knots to find new uses as time goes on. In this case the development of slippery synthetic rope brought the Ashley Bend to the fore.

Not content merely to make incisive comments, Fud set about experimenting with two-strand lanyard knots to see if he might surprise another worthwhile bend. Sure enough, the accompanying knot resulted, which I hereby christen the Benson Bend (Figure 75). It is secure, has a perfect lead, and draws up readily; these qualities, combined with its extraordinarily handsome appearance, compensate for a slight tendency to jam— no worse than the Sheet Bend.

The Strait Bend

My own contribution to the world of bends is this one, named after the Strait of Juan de Fuca in the Pacific Northwest.

This knot, structurally analogous to the Lineman's Rider (Figure 59), is the strongest of this series and neither slips nor jams. These and other virtues mentioned in connection with the previous knots are hard to find in combination, but they must be part of any reasonable definition of a general-purpose bend. Which knot you might use comes down in part to personal preference; every knot has a friend somewhere.

It doesn't seem reasonable, but here's one more demand: Make a bend in line that is very large or stiff or both, such as the frozen hawser I mentioned at the beginning, without sacrificing any of a good bend's virtues. This is a specialized challenge that none of the previous knots is well suited for. But here are two that are.

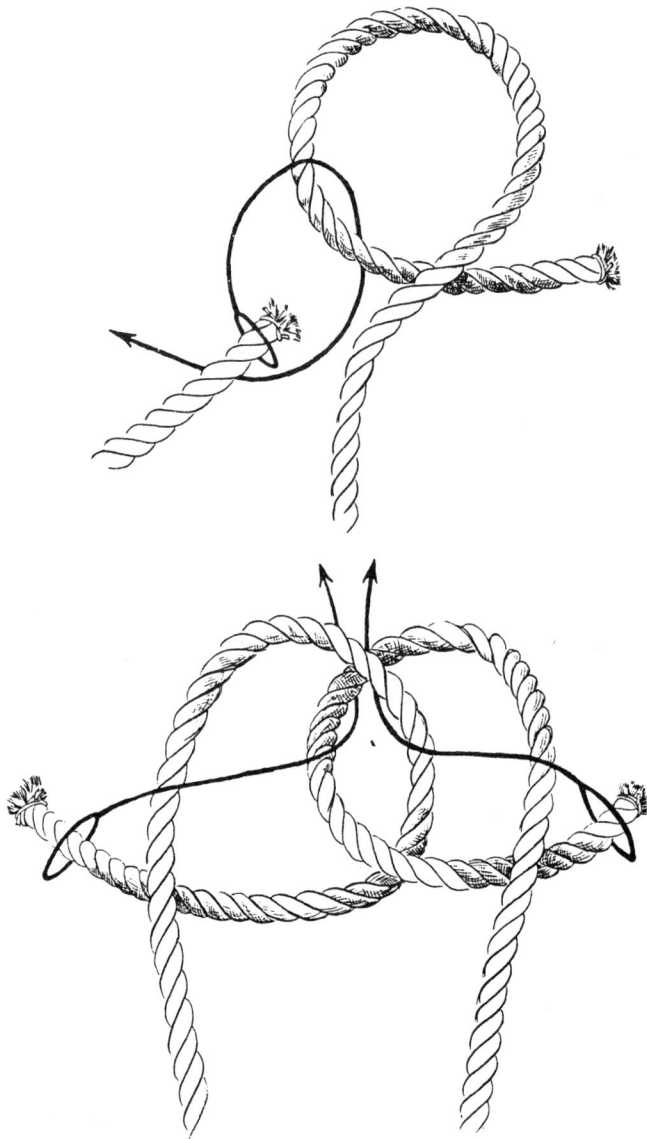

FIGURE 76. *The Strait Bend. Make a counterclockwise loop, end behind standing part. Drop the other end into this loop, then make a clockwise loop with that end, with the end also behind the standing part. Pass both ends into the eye to finish.*

The Carrick Bend

This beautiful knot is the traditional big-rope bend (Figure 77). It's made with an easily remembered over-and-under sequence, and since there are no sharp curves, wrestling with the subject is minimized.

The Carrick Bend will not jam, but owing to the ornery massiveness of the line it is usually formed in, it can be difficult to untie once it is drawn up. Therefore, it is customary to seize the ends to the standing parts with Throat Seizings. These take very little strain, but they keep the knot open, making it much easier to untie. As another look at Table 2 will show, there are several Carrick variations. This, number 17 on the list, is the only one worth tying. Beware of imitations.

50

The Ashley Hawser Bend

Our seventh selection is another hawser bend, one that does not require the use of seizings and is more compact and easily untied than a drawn-up Carrick. It's another Ashley original—with a Zeppelin-like lead—and can always be loosened by nudging the upper bight (Figure 78). Well, nudging might mean hitting it with a sledgehammer, but it will loosen. A seized Carrick is still the preferred knot, but the resourceful big-rope bender will know both.

FIGURE 77. *The Carrick Bend. Make a counterclockwise loop, end in front of standing part. Place the other piece's standing part on the loop, and thread end in regular under-and-over sequence as shown. Drawn up (B), the Carrick Bend is secure but bulky, with a poor lead, and not easily untied. It is usually left loose (C), with ends seized to standing part, for ease of untying.*

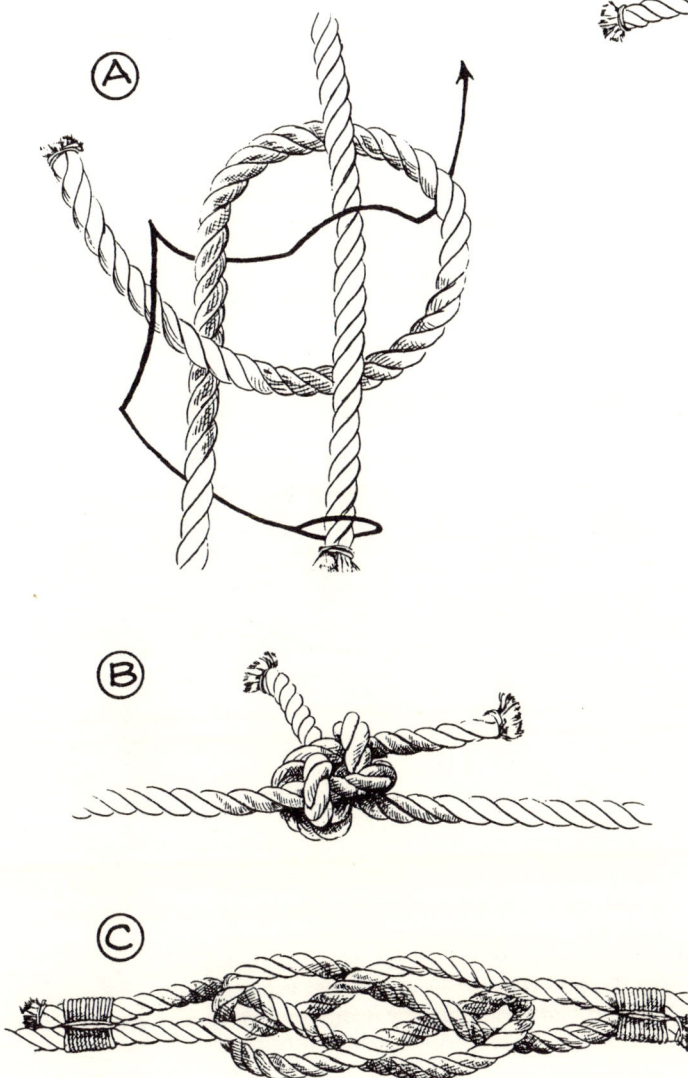

FIGURE 78. *The Ashley Hawser Bend. Cross and recross end over standing part to form two X's. Pass other end under first X, over second, behind standing part, then into middle section. Draw up carefully to reach finished form.*

The Connoisseur's Advantage

Every knot is an exercise in friction, a device to make rope grip itself or another object for a specific purpose and circumstance. As we've seen, even the ostensibly simple task of bending two ropes together can be complicated—even redefined—by basic practical considerations. Some people may prefer a more limited menu of bends, but extreme simplicity can only be had at the expense of effectiveness. Better the pleasures of detail, principle, and resourcefulness—the connoisseur's advantage.

Bend Appetit.

FIGURE 79. *Figure-Eight Knot.*

THE END OF YOUR ROPE

Some years ago I was sitting next to the helmsman in a gaff sloop as we ran before a stiff breeze. The sails were set wing-and-wing, and we were all a little too caught up in the beauty of a blustery Puget Sound day. With the boom way out there wasn't enough of the mainsheet to cleat, and the end dangled from the helmsman's hand. Idly, I reached over and put a Figure-Eight Knot in the end of the line, seconds before our inattention resulted in a vicious jibe. The boom sped across, carrying away a running backstay. It probably would have removed the shrouds too, and maybe the mast, if it hadn't been for that knot jamming in the sheet block. It's the standing part of the line that gets the attention—all that hauling and coiling—but from that day forward I've had a particular interest in how lines end.

FIGURE 80. *Stevedore's Knot. Start as with the Figure-Eight Knot, but make an extra round turn before passing the end.*

FIGURE 81. *Oysterman's Stopper. Make a slipknot so that the standing part slides, then pass the end in front of the standing part and up through the loop from behind. Tighten by drawing up the slipknot, then pulling on the end.*

52

Basic Bulk

The Figure-Eight Knot is the basic stopper knot, so-called from its function. It is preferred to the simpler Overhand Knot because it is bulkier and a little less prone to jam (Figure 79).

When a still bulkier knot is required, as when the block is oversized, tie a Stevedore's Knot or an Oysterman's Stopper (Figures 80 and 81). For the former, commence making a Figure-Eight, but make an extra turn around the standing part before tucking the end through the bight. For the latter, make a slipknot as shown and tuck the end into the bight. To draw up, first tighten the slipknot, then pull the end snug, and finally haul on the standing part. It takes only a moment.

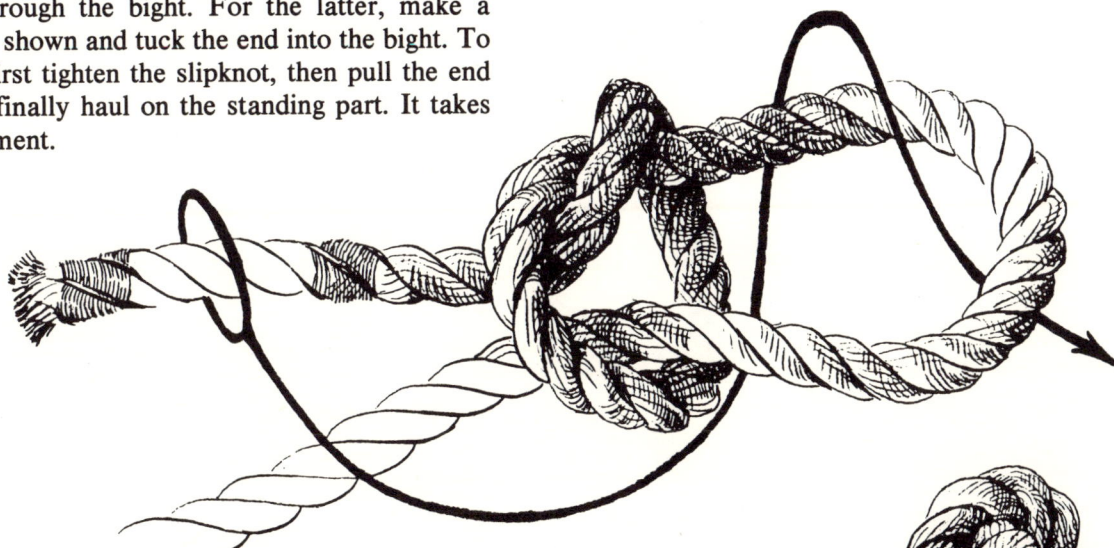

The Oysterman's Stopper is a handsome knot with an instructive story behind it. Its inventor, Clifford Ashley, assumed like most of us that all possible knots had already been invented. Then one day he saw a knot he did not recognize in the end of the foresail halyard of a passing Delaware Bay oyster boat. Being what I can only describe as obsessed with knots, he promptly got a piece of line and set about trying to reconstruct what he had seen, ending up with the knot you see here. But when he later found that same boat and went aboard, he found that his mysterious knot was simply a Figure-Eight tied in extremely gouty rope! He had invented his first knot, and realizing it could be done went on to invent many more. I mention this story to illustrate that there is still room for innovation, even in the simplest forms of knotting.

For example, if you make an extra half-turn with the end before tucking it through the bight (à la Stevedore) you will get a different knot, and one less prone to jam. Because it is both secure and removable, I christened it the Sink Stopper (Figure 82).

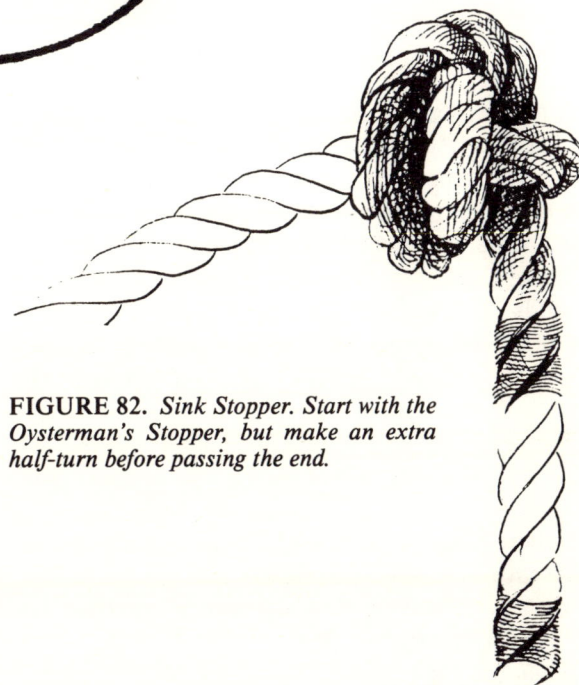

FIGURE 82. *Sink Stopper. Start with the Oysterman's Stopper, but make an extra half-turn before passing the end.*

FIGURE 83. *The Butane Backsplice.*

Non-Bulk

Sometimes stoppers are no advantage or even a disadvantage, as on mooring or lashing lines, where they just get in the way. Yet something is needed at the end to keep the line from raveling. Since the advent of synthetic line, the most prevalent technique has been the Butane Backsplice (Figure 83), made by fusing the fiber ends with a cigarette lighter. This is fast and convenient, but it does have several drawbacks:

1. When melted, synthetics give off highly toxic fumes.

2. The resulting lump is hard and has sharp edges; in use it will slash away at sails, brightwork, and crew.

3. Butane Backsplices crack without warning and let the line ravel. On double-braid the core can pull away from the cover, leaving more tension on one than the other and weakening the line.

4. They are ugly.

So throw your lighters overboard. A Constrictor Knot or two (Figure 11) is just as handy. The classical method, the Palm and Needle Whipping, is more time consuming but is without doubt the best knot for the job (Figures 84 and 85). As you can see, the round turns contain the rope strands while the diagonal turns, being pulled down into the cuntlines, tighten the whipping and prevent it from coming undone even if some of the round turns chafe through. One has advance warning of the need for replacement.

Those of you who already know how to make whippings might want to examine the illustrations anyway; there are some particulars of technique that you may not have seen before, which result in a firmer, more symmetrical knot. If you have not been introduced to this knot before, be assured that the hardest thing about it is coming up with the money for a good palm and set of needles.

Notice in the final drawing that there are two whippings on the line, the second about three rope diameters up from the first. This is safety and neatness insurance in case the first whipping chafes through. Otherwise you might find yourself with an Irish Pennant—a raveled rope—something worth taking a little extra effort to avoid, especially with yacht-diameter rope retailing at up to $2 per foot.

54

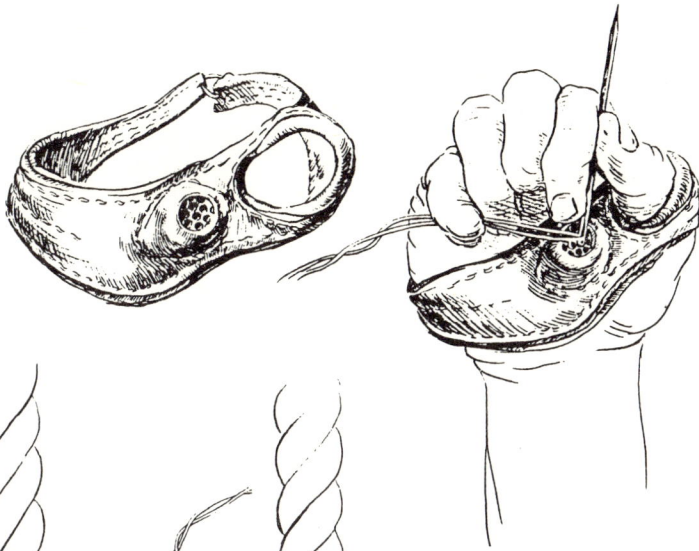

FIGURE 84. *A palm, shown at right on the hand with needle in place.*

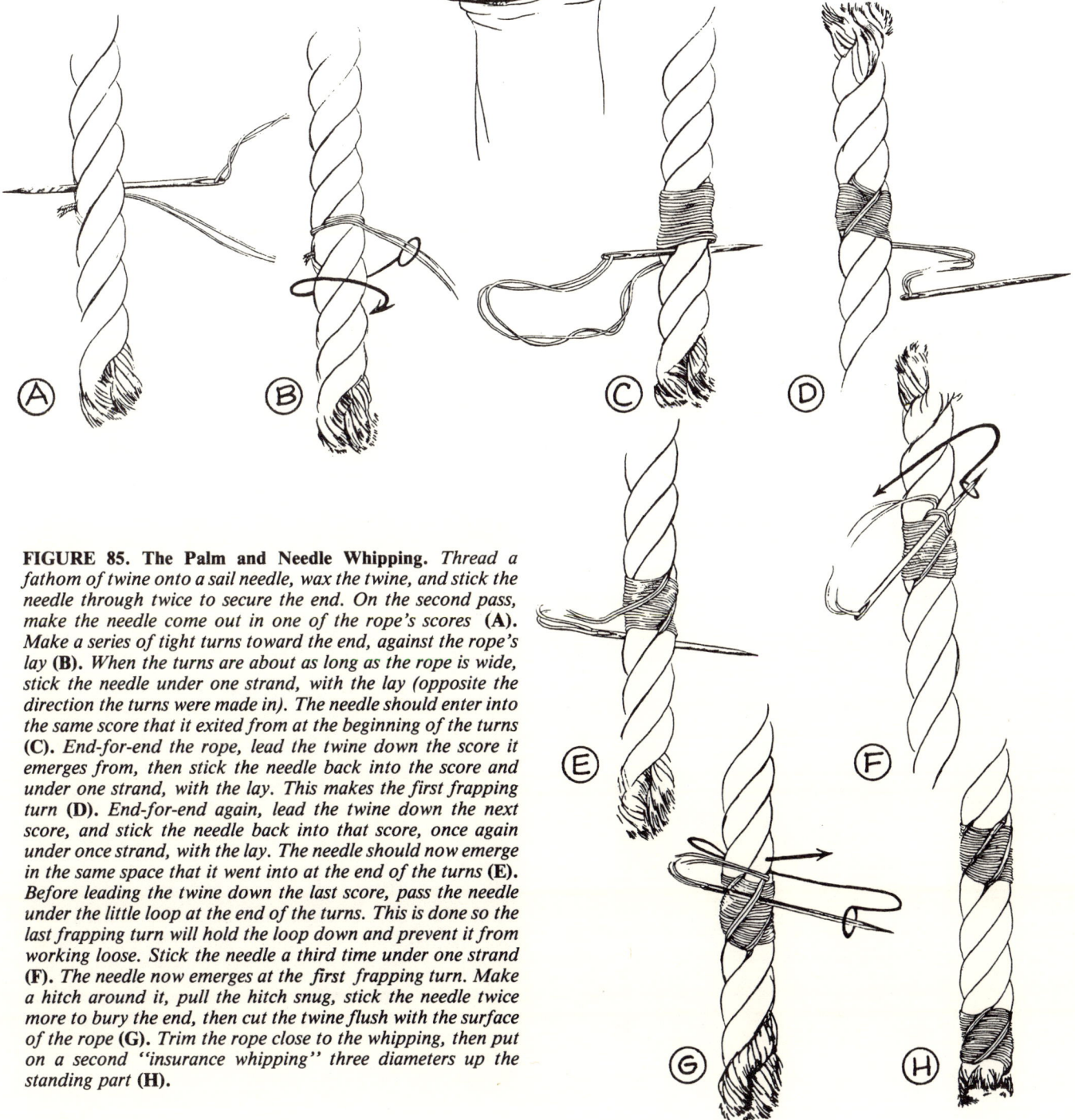

FIGURE 85. The Palm and Needle Whipping. *Thread a fathom of twine onto a sail needle, wax the twine, and stick the needle through twice to secure the end. On the second pass, make the needle come out in one of the rope's scores* **(A).** *Make a series of tight turns toward the end, against the rope's lay* **(B).** *When the turns are about as long as the rope is wide, stick the needle under one strand, with the lay (opposite the direction the turns were made in). The needle should enter into the same score that it exited from at the beginning of the turns* **(C).** *End-for-end the rope, lead the twine down the score it emerges from, then stick the needle back into the score and under one strand, with the lay. This makes the first frapping turn* **(D).** *End-for-end again, lead the twine down the next score, and stick the needle back into that score, once again under once strand, with the lay. The needle should now emerge in the same space that it went into at the end of the turns* **(E).** *Before leading the twine down the last score, pass the needle under the little loop at the end of the turns. This is done so the last frapping turn will hold the loop down and prevent it from working loose. Stick the needle a third time under one strand* **(F).** *The needle now emerges at the first frapping turn. Make a hitch around it, pull the hitch snug, stick the needle twice more to bury the end, then cut the twine flush with the surface of the rope* **(G).** *Trim the rope close to the whipping, then put on a second "insurance whipping" three diameters up the standing part* **(H).**

FIGURE 86. British Admiralty Whipping.
*Unlay the strands a short distance. Double a
fathom of waxed twine and loop it over one strand
of the rope. The bight end of the twine need only
extend about 4 inches. Lay the rope back up (A).
Pull the twine a short distance away from the
strand it is looped around and commence making turns against the lay with the long end, as
with the Palm and Needle Whipping (B). When
the turns are completed, pass the bight over the
end of the strand it was looped around. Pull on
the bight end to snug it down (C). Reef-knot the
end and bight end together across the middle of
the knot. Cut the twine ends off and trim the rope
short (D).*

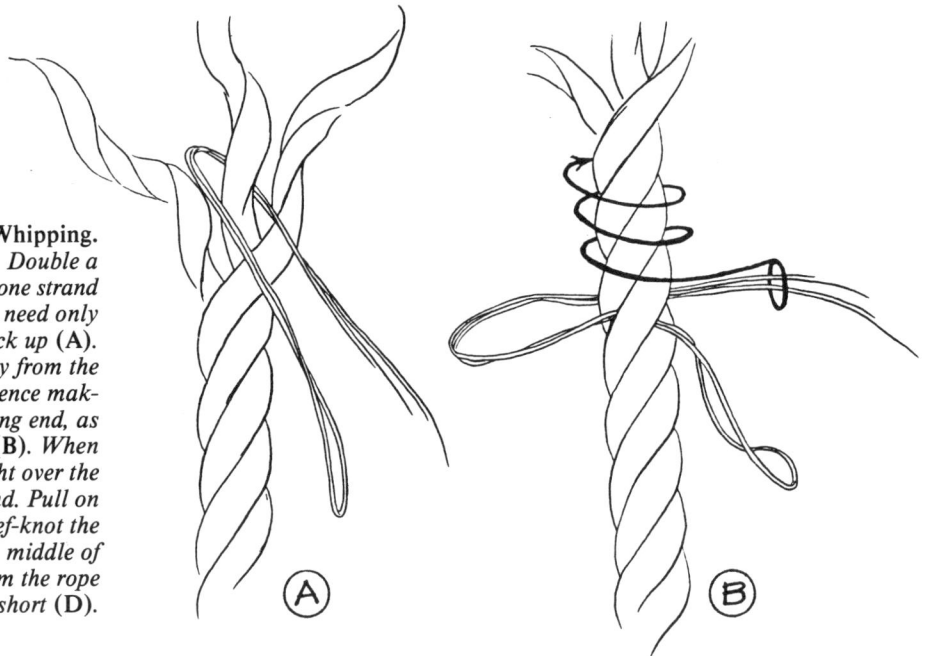

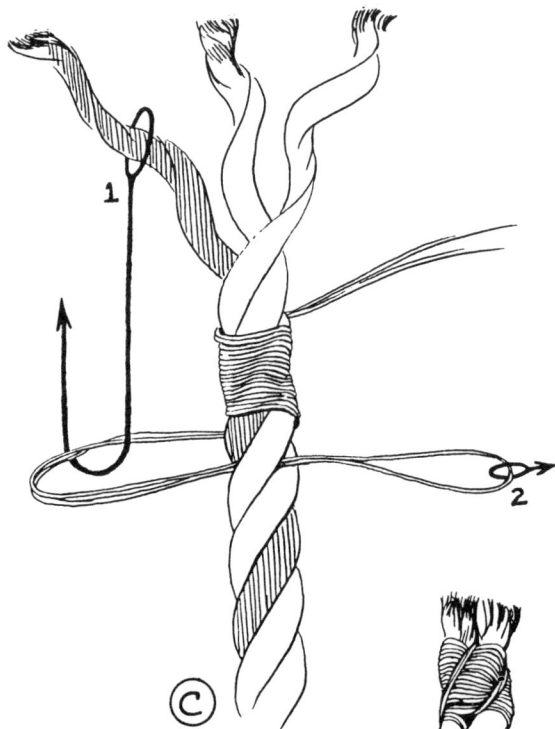

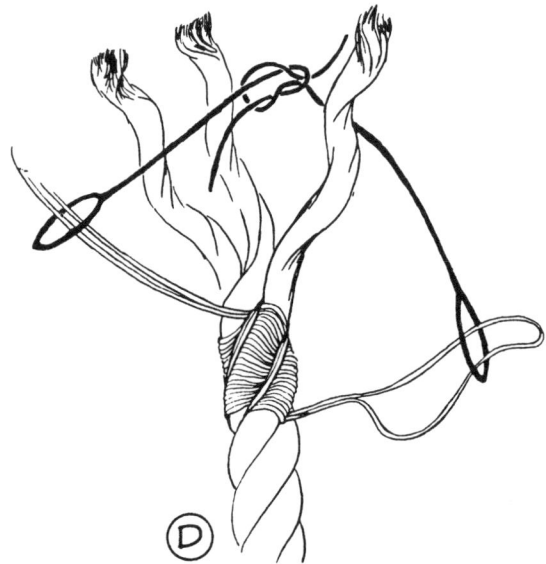

If, as sometimes happens, you are without palm and
needle but still want something more permanent than a
Constrictor Knot, try this remarkable barehanded
whipping (Figure 86) from the British Admiralty's
Manual of Seamanship for Boys' Training Ships
(Vol. I-II, London, 1932). It looks just like the real
thing and is at the very least useful to impress your
friends.

56

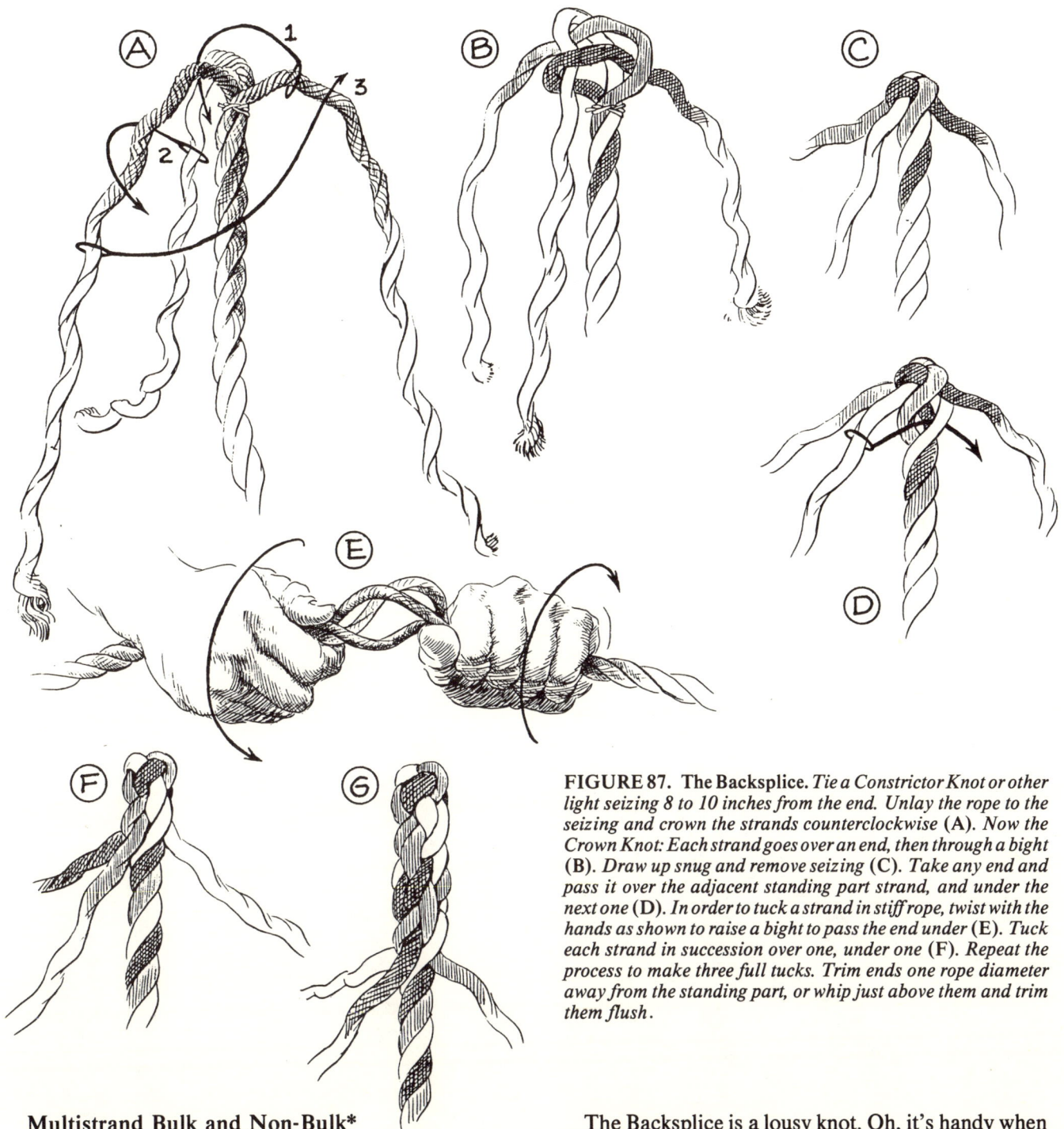

FIGURE 87. The Backsplice. *Tie a Constrictor Knot or other light seizing 8 to 10 inches from the end. Unlay the rope to the seizing and crown the strands counterclockwise (A). Now the Crown Knot: Each strand goes over an end, then through a bight (B). Draw up snug and remove seizing (C). Take any end and pass it over the adjacent standing part strand, and under the next one (D). In order to tuck a strand in stiff rope, twist with the hands as shown to raise a bight to pass the end under (E). Tuck each strand in succession over one, under one (F). Repeat the process to make three full tucks. Trim ends one rope diameter away from the standing part, or whip just above them and trim them flush.*

Multistrand Bulk and Non-Bulk*

The most complex end-of-the-line work is done with the line's component strands. To start with there's the Backsplice (the real thing, no butane). To make, unlay the strands 8 to 10 inches, make a snug, counterclockwise crown, then tuck each end in sequence under one and over one, against the lay (Figure 87). Make three or four rows of tucks.

*Unlike those in the preceding sections, the knots listed here are not suited to braided line.

The Backsplice is a lousy knot. Oh, it's handy when there's no twine or knife, but basically it's a quick fix for raveling, too narrow to be an effective stopper but too bulky for reeving through chocks or for passing lashings. About the only place it's much good is as a comfortable handhold, say at the end of a deck bucket's lanyard. But there are a couple of very useful variations.

A Tree Surgeon's Backsplice (Figure 88) is identi-

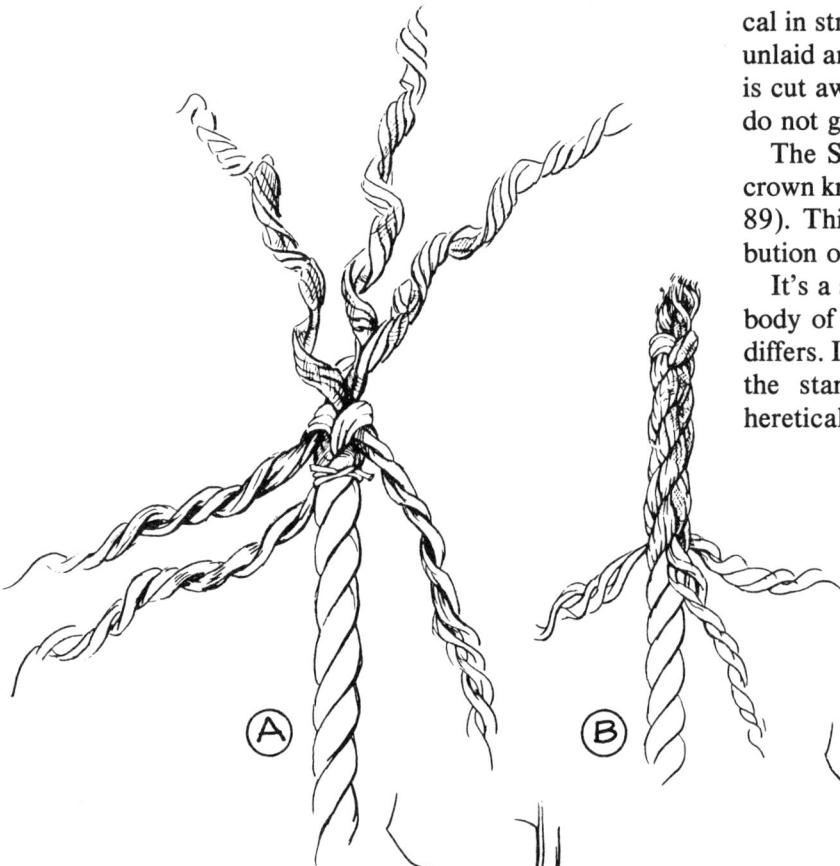

cal in structure to the above, but after the strands are unlaid and before crowning, two-thirds of each strand is cut away. When tucked, the one-third-size strands do not greatly increase rope diameter.

The Snap Shackle Splice is a Backsplice with the crown knot made through the *eye of a shackle* (Figure 89). This can't be beat for compactness and distribution of strain.

It's a simple step from a Back to an Eyesplice; the body of the knot is the same, and only the entrance differs. I should mention that my preferred entry is not the standard one—some might even consider it heretical—but it snugs up to a thimble better and is

FIGURE 88. Tree Surgeon's Backsplice. *Start as with the Backsplice, but lay out two-thirds of each strand before crowning (A). Tuck three full times and trim all ends short (B).*

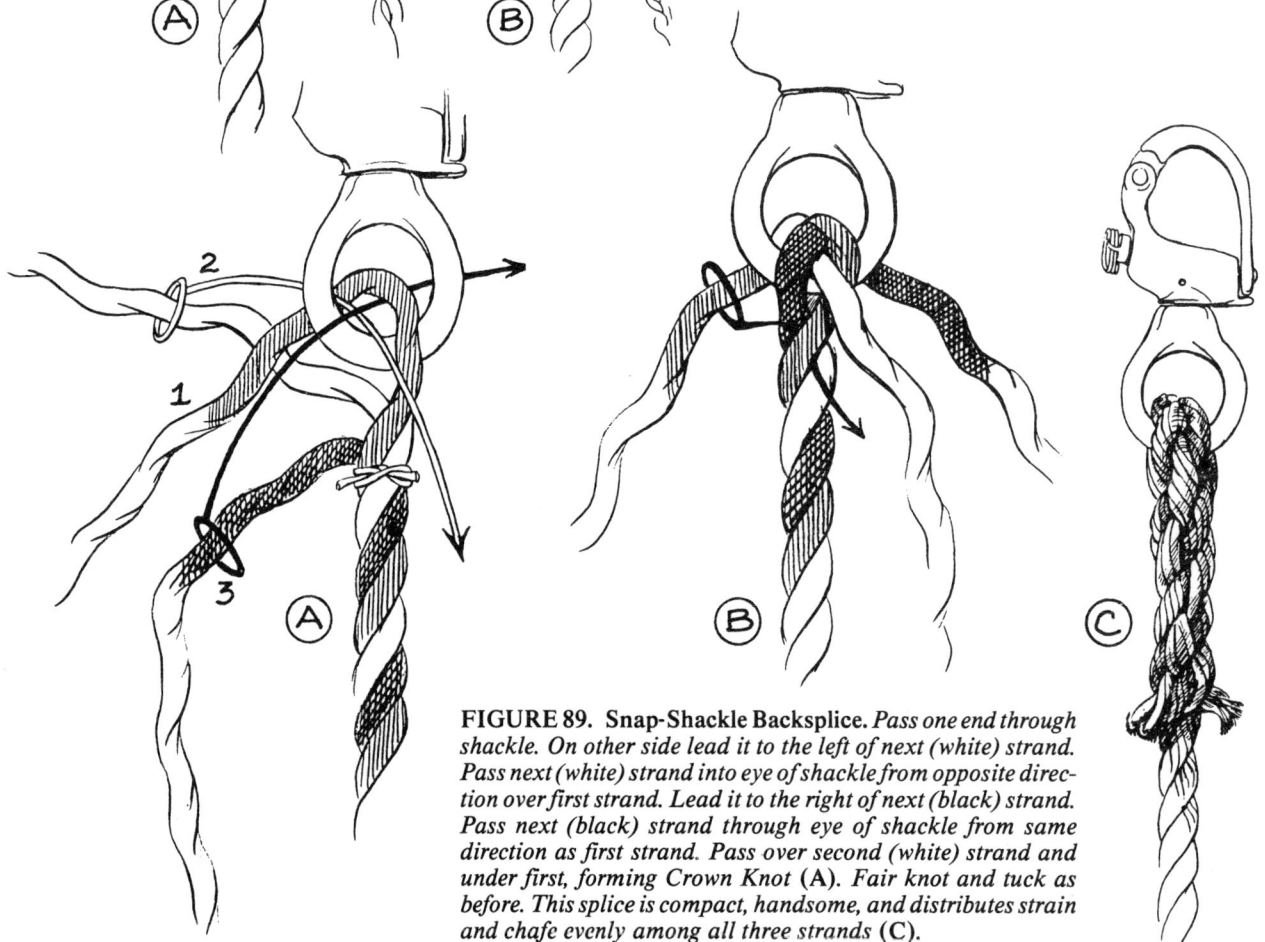

FIGURE 89. Snap-Shackle Backsplice. *Pass one end through shackle. On other side lead it to the left of next (white) strand. Pass next (white) strand into eye of shackle from opposite direction over first strand. Lead it to the right of next (black) strand. Pass next (black) strand through eye of shackle from same direction as first strand. Pass over second (white) strand and under first, forming Crown Knot (A). Fair knot and tuck as before. This splice is compact, handsome, and distributes strain and chafe evenly among all three strands (C).*

58

smooth on both sides (see the comparison in Figure 90). It is sometimes known as Lever's Eyesplice, but if anyone gives you guff about it, it's more effective to call it by the name towboaters do: the Pro Splice.

Start by unlaying the rope a sufficient distance for tucking, preferably to a Constrictor Knot or whipping, which keeps the three strands evenly aligned while you work. Bend the end around to form the desired-size eye and tuck the leftmost strand under, over, and under again, against the lay. Tuck the middle strand under where the first strand went over, then turn the work over and tuck the third strand under the last remaining uninvolved standing-part strand. It's right there in the middle.

FIGURE 90-A–E.
The Pro Splice.

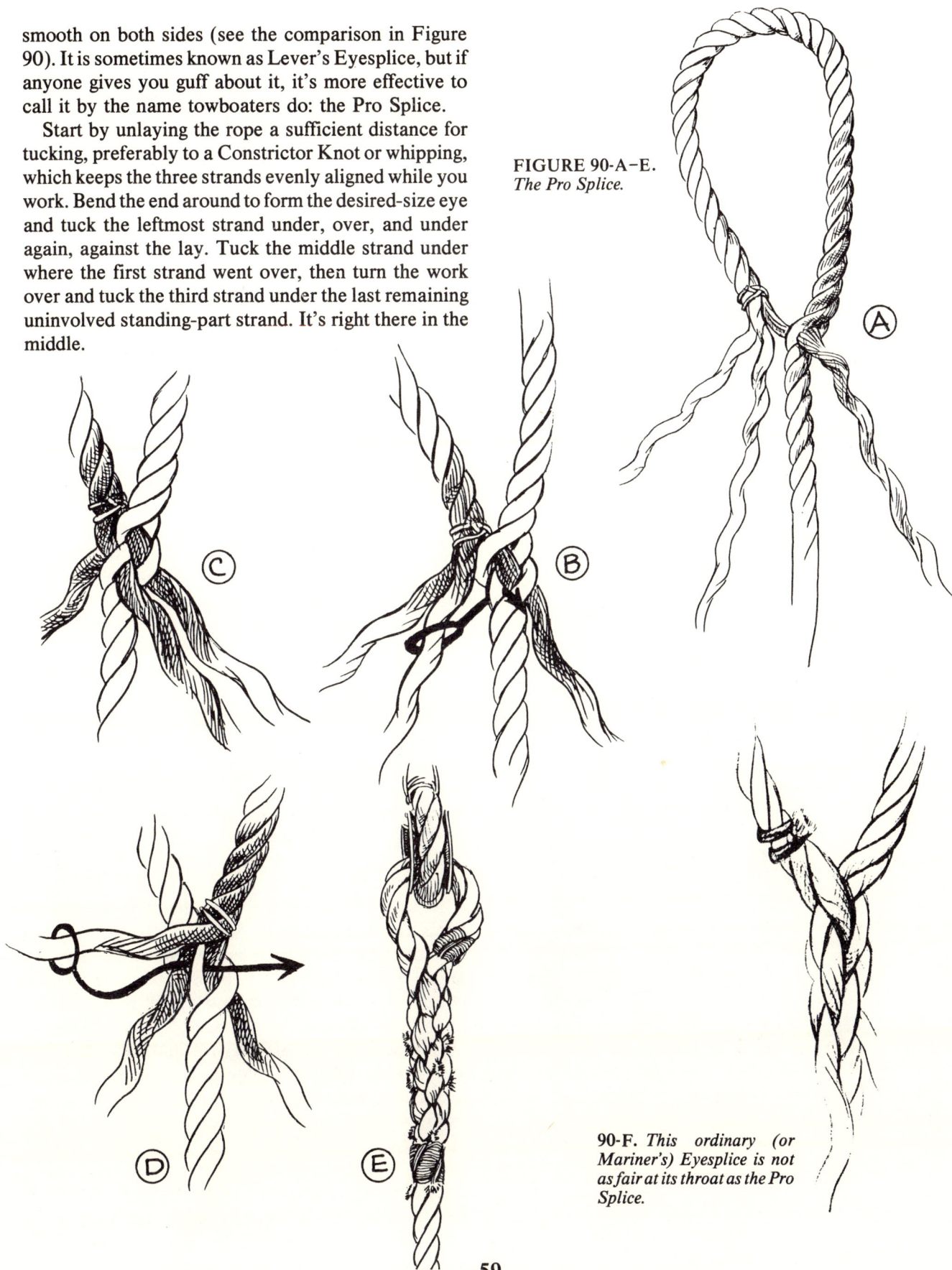

90-F. *This ordinary (or Mariner's) Eyesplice is not as fair at its throat as the Pro Splice.*

59

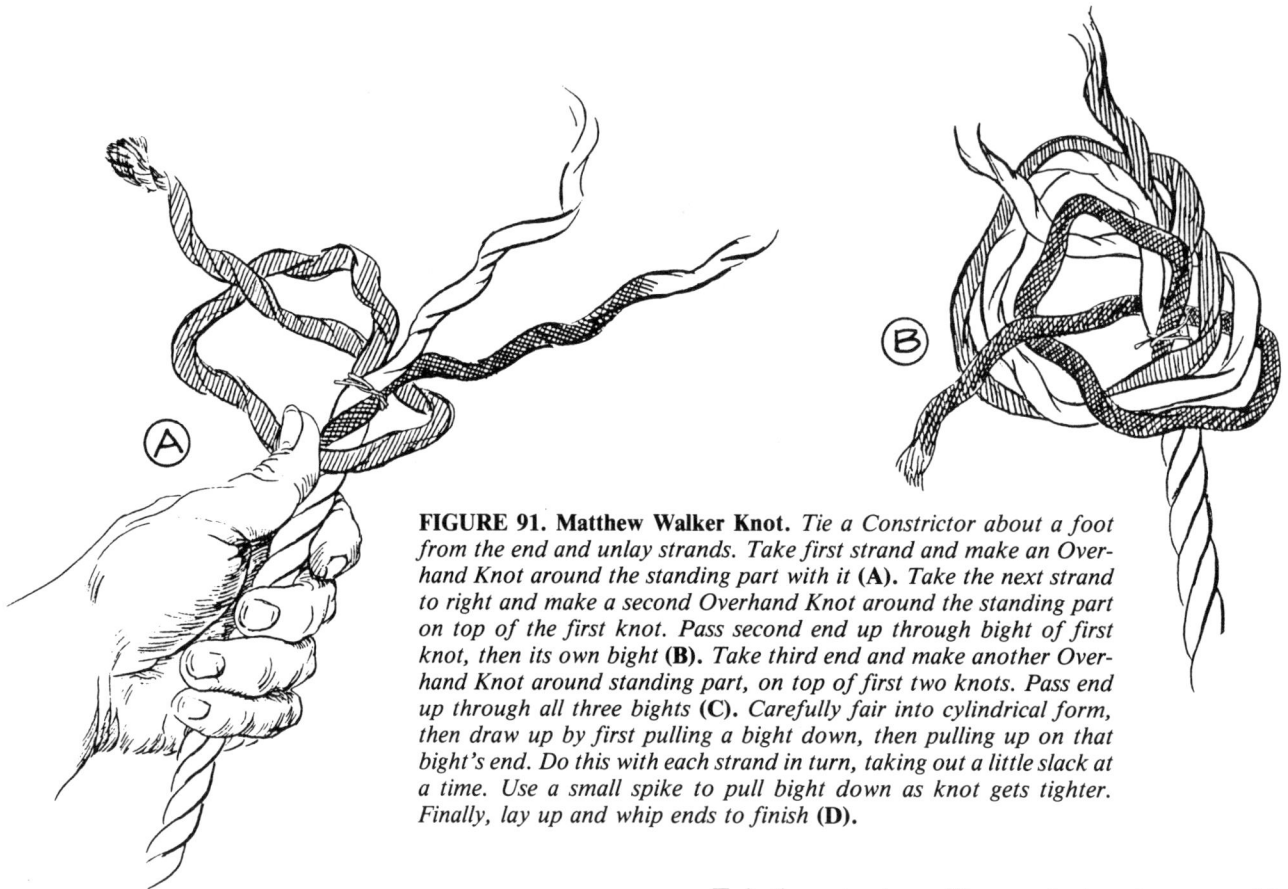

FIGURE 91. Matthew Walker Knot. *Tie a Constrictor about a foot from the end and unlay strands. Take first strand and make an Overhand Knot around the standing part with it* **(A).** *Take the next strand to right and make a second Overhand Knot around the standing part on top of the first knot. Pass second end up through bight of first knot, then its own bight* **(B).** *Take third end and make another Overhand Knot around standing part, on top of first two knots. Pass end up through all three bights* **(C).** *Carefully fair into cylindrical form, then draw up by first pulling a bight down, then pulling up on that bight's end. Do this with each strand in turn, taking out a little slack at a time. Use a small spike to pull bight down as knot gets tighter. Finally, lay up and whip ends to finish* **(D).**

Fair the entry by pulling each strand snug, making sure that they all enter against the lay and come out at the same level, then commence regular under-and-over tucking to finish, as with the Backsplice.

If it's multistrand bulk you're after, the traditional knot is the Matthew Walker, structurally a series of interlocked Overhand Knots (Figure 91). The real challenge comes not in tying it but in drawing it up, a procedure that is for some reason always left out of knot books. The trick is to take out a little bit of slack at a time, first by hand, then with a spike, first pulling down on the bight, then up on the end. For a neat finish, lay the strands up again for a short distance (1 to 1½ inches) and whip them.

Buttons can serve the same function as stopper knots like the Matthew Walker, but differ from them in that the ends are buried in the knot, obviating the laying-up-and-whipping step. But don't think that buttons save labor; they are more intricate and harder to draw up. Their big selling point is that they are not only functional but also stylish and rare. The one shown here (#880 in Ashley) is my favorite for three- and four-strand rope. Like most buttons, it is built up from two basic knots, the Wall and Crown. We've already used the Crown in the Backsplice, and the Wall is just an upside-down Crown.

To make this button, tie a Constrictor Knot about a foot from the end, unlay the strands to it, and make a

FIGURE 92. Ashley's Button Knot #880. *Constrictor the rope about a foot from its end, unlay the strands, and "wall" them counterclockwise by passing each strand under its neighbor to the right. A Wall is an upside-down Crown (**A**). Fair the Wall and make a Crown Knot on top of it, also counterclockwise. Fair the Crown, then pass each end under the bight to its right, ahead of the end to its right (**B**). Open the middle of the knot up a bit so you can see the three strands where they exit the Constrictor. Drop each end in turn into the second space to its right. Draw up slowly and carefully, working out a little slack at a time (**C**). Trim the ends off flush with the bottom to get the finished knot (**D**).*

Wall Knot as shown in Figure 92. Fair this knot to make it even but not tight, then make a Crown on top of it. Now fair the Crown so that the combined knots look exactly like the drawing. Take a deep breath. Do you see the three bights (scallops or arcs) around the outside of the knot, with an end across the middle of each bight? Take each end and pass it up through the bight to its right, ahead of that bight's end. Looks like a real mess, huh? Fair it into some semblance of order and take a look at the very center, down inside where the three strands fan out from the Constrictor. There are three spaces there, and you are going to drop each strand into the second space to its right. Got it? Good, that's all there is to it.

Draw up with a blunted spike or awl, making several passes along each strand, until the knot is hard. Carefully trim the ends off flush with the bottom of the knot. This button, the Matthew Walker, and related knots are most often used as stoppers on deadeye and other lanyards, as well as hand- and footrope ends, gaskets, beckets, and for decoration.

As you can see, stopping has a lot going for it, providing a boat's gear with extra security and versatility. And because these knots are so handsome and comfortable, they give a whole new meaning to being at the end of your rope.

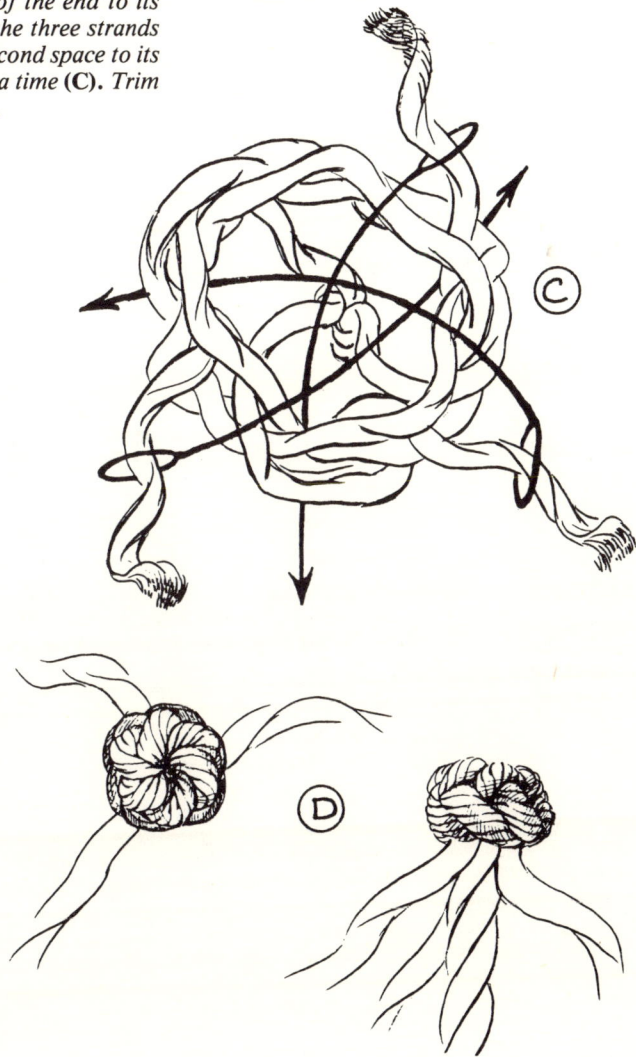

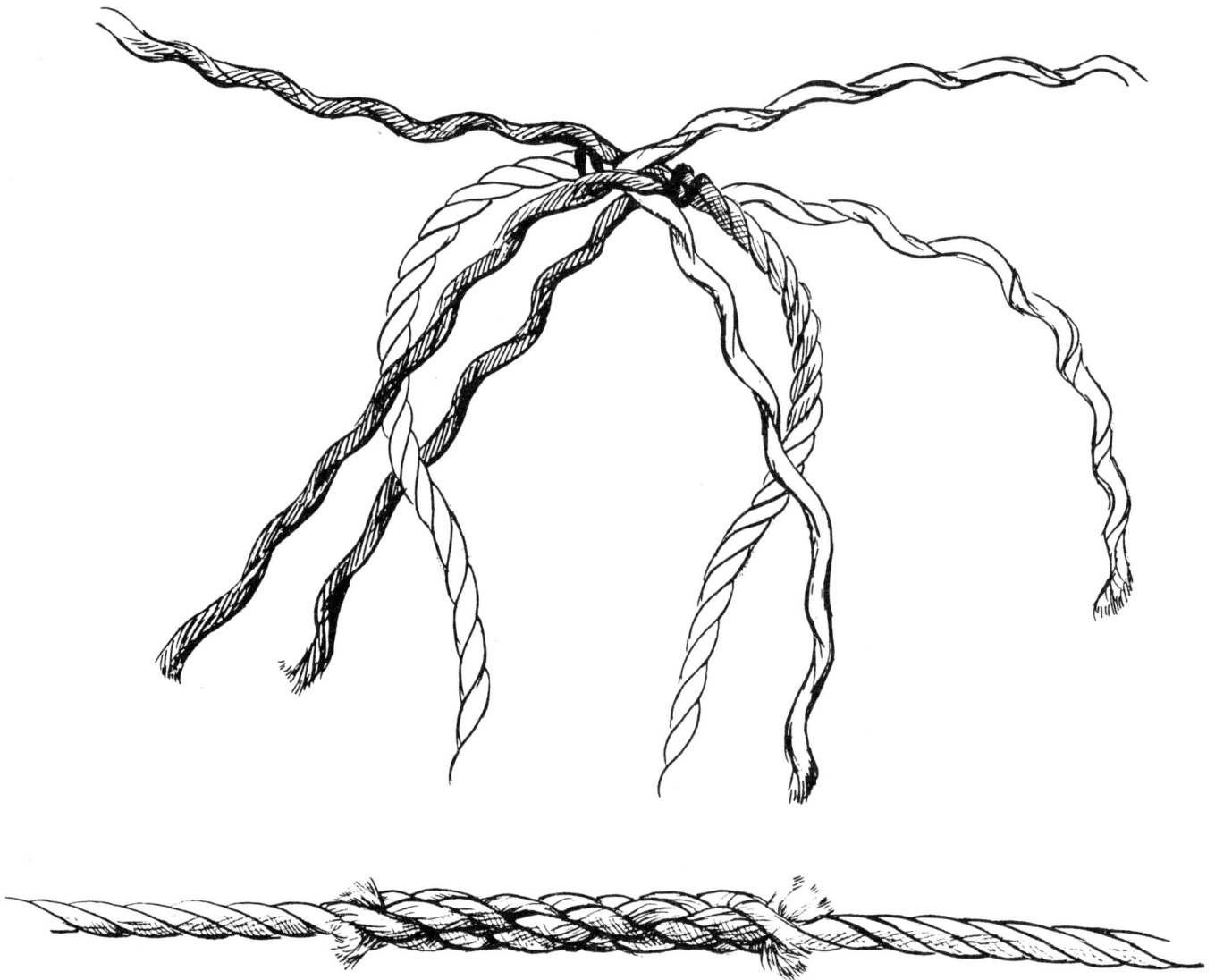

FIGURE 93. *The Short Splice is a very strong multistrand bend. Unlay the two ropes far enough for three tucks (minimum) in Manila, five in synthetics. Marry the two and tuck each set of strands over and under as for the previous splices.*

NOT THE END OF YOUR ROPE

This book wouldn't be right without a Short Splice, the strongest way to lengthen a rope whose end you're not ready to come to.

To make one, unlay two ropes of the same size to Constrictor Knots, as for the Backsplice. "Marry" them and tuck each strand over one and under one, against the lay. Remove the Constrictors, snug things up, then continue tucking as with the other splices. Carefully done, this knot can't be beat for towlines, pendants, and all sorts of temporary repairs, particularly in emergencies. Its one drawback is that it bulks too much to pass through a block.

Short Splice, short explanation.

CHAPTER 4
Design and Materials

•

Rig design usually is something the rigger is given. Although we can often suggest modifications, the basic layout and configuration are already established, so that our primary responsibility is proper design execution. But this is not to say that we are excused from technical considerations; we owe it to the vessel and ourselves to understand the characteristics of hull and rig type, the sort of sailing intended, and thus what types and degrees of strain will be imposed on the rig.

No need to second-guess the designer, just to equip ourselves with the ability to make informed decisions. It would be easier to just do the handwork and let other people worry about design, but getting involved in the abstract side of rigging gives us two very important benefits:

(1) Understanding the whole, we see the reasons for using certain materials and procedures; we are not so likely to alter or substitute as we would be if the reasons for each particular were not technically justified. Knowledge keeps us honest and provides motivation for honing our skills.

(2) Much of a rigger's work is extemporaneous— replacing failed pieces, inspecting, tuning, shifting leads, lashing, hoisting, lowering, and jury-rigging. Experience and practice are our greatest allies here, but there's nothing so reassuring as having one's judgment borne out by calculations.

Since this book is about traditional rigging, its bias is toward long-proven practices. "We pay attention to tradition," a boatbuilder friend once said, "so we don't have to make two hundred years of mistakes." By studying design, we benefit from the experiences of others. One of the clearest lessons is that good designs always evidence a firm grasp of basic mechanical principles.

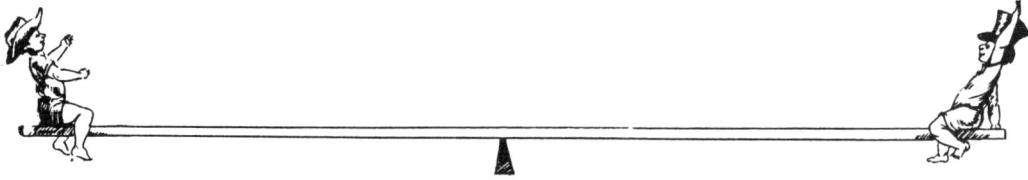

FIGURE 94. *The seesaw, a familiar form of lever.*

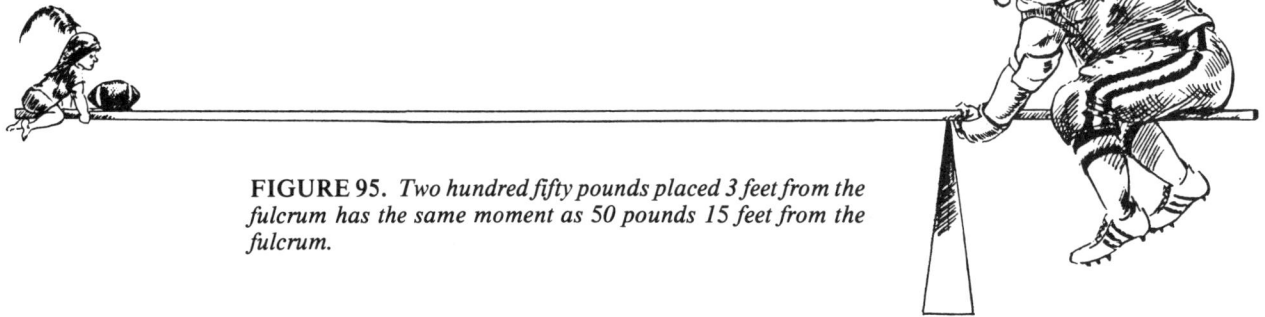

FIGURE 95. *Two hundred fifty pounds placed 3 feet from the fulcrum has the same moment as 50 pounds 15 feet from the fulcrum.*

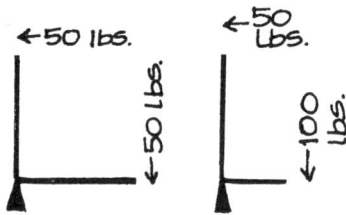

FIGURE 96. *A lever with a right-angle turn.*

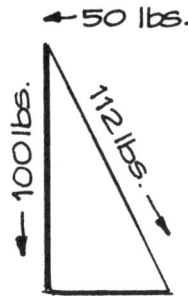

FIGURE 97. *Take away the horizontal arm, replace it with a wire, and you've started rigging. The principle of moments still applies, but now there's also a compression load on the mast.*

DESIGN PRINCIPLES

Standing rigging is an exercise in leverage, so to explain its mechanics we'll begin with the lever. Figure 94 shows a familiar form of lever, the seesaw. The children are seated 9 feet on either side of the support, or fulcrum. Each child weighs 50 pounds, but as far as the seesaw is concerned they each produce a *moment* of 450 foot-pounds. That is, leverage is a matter of weight (50 pounds) times distance from the fulcrum (9 feet). The children balance not merely because they weigh the same, but because they exert the same number of foot-pounds.

To prove this, let's shift the position of the fulcrum to the right 6 feet (Figure 95). Now the child on the left is 15 feet from the fulcrum, which means she produces a moment of 750 foot-pounds (15 feet times 50 pounds). The seesaw now extends only 3 feet on the other side of the fulcrum. As you can see, it takes a 250-pound football player (3 feet times 250 pounds) to balance the seesaw.

Now let's make a lever that takes a 90-degree turn at the fulcrum (Figure 96). It's not a seesaw anymore, but the same principles apply. A 50-pound push against the top of the vertical arm, 9 feet from the fulcrum, is balanced by 50 pounds on the horizontal arm, 9 feet from the fulcrum. The same push against the same height vertical arm is balanced by 100 pounds placed 4½ feet from the fulcrum: 9 ft. x 50 lbs. = 450 foot-pounds, and so does 4½ ft. x 100 lbs.

Hang on, we're about to start rigging. If you took away the horizontal arm and in its place set up a wire that ran to the top of the vertical arm, you would be exerting leverage on that wire (Figure 97). This is how stayed masts work. An important change, other than the wire, is that there is now a *compression load* on the vertical member or mast; the wire exerts a downward pull of, in this case, 111.8 pounds. The closer the lower end of the wire is to the mast, the greater the proportion of effort it expends in a downward pull, and the more tension is exerted on it (Figure 98). In every instance, the wire must be strong enough to deal with

64

FIGURE 99. *The curve shows tension on a shroud induced by a 50-pound lateral load at the masthead, given various shroud-to-mast angles.*

FIGURE 98. *The closer the lower end of the wire is to the mast, the higher the compression load on the mast and the tension on the wire.*

FIGURE 100.

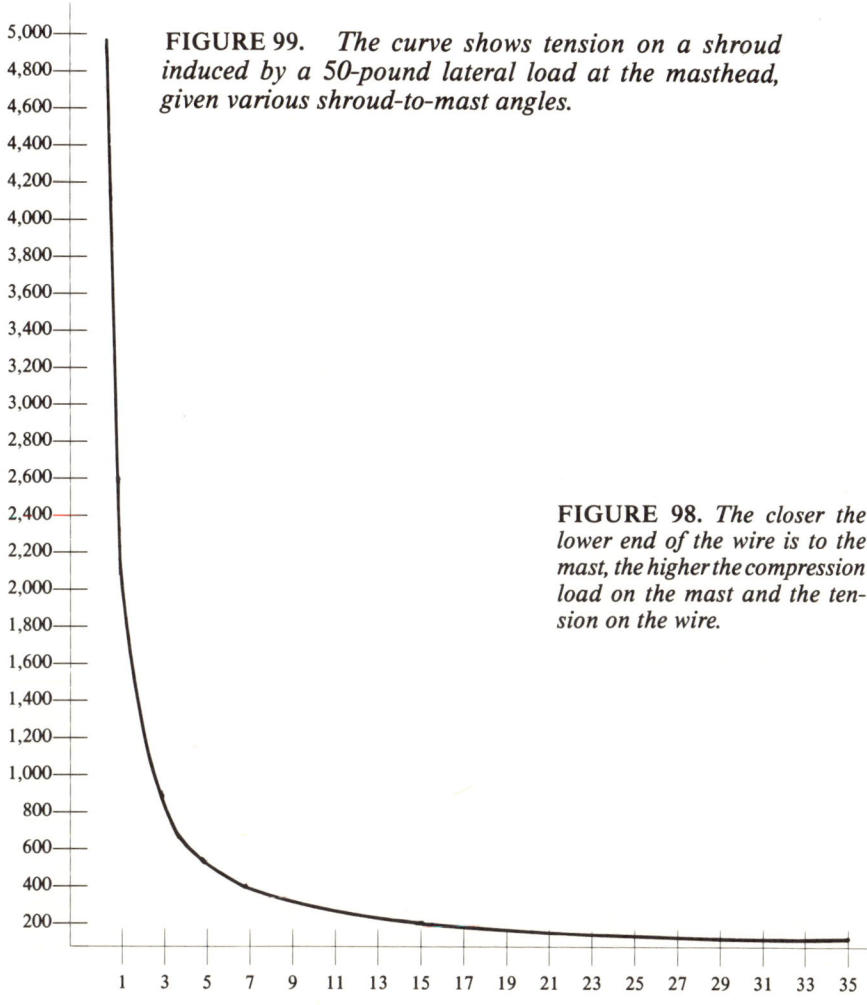

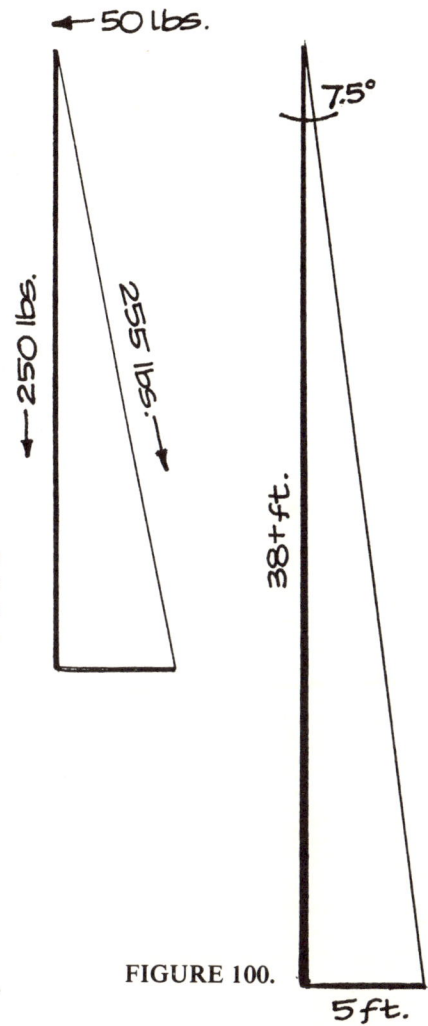

the moment produced by a force exerted at the top of the mast, and the mast must be strong enough not to buckle under the imposed compression load. A very great thing is that all these forces can be resolved into components having defined direction and magnitude relative to one another. Using lines of proportionate angles and lengths or the corresponding formulas, you can calculate moments without having to set up a real mast and attach tension gauges.

Figure 99 is a graph that represents the results of calculations to determine wire strain at a variety of staying angles (the angle of the wire relative to the mast). As you can see, the amount of tension accelerates as the angle narrows, approaching infinity as it approaches vertical. Since sailboats are usually narrow things with tall masts, and since neither wires nor masts can take loads approaching infinity, the angle-to-load relationship is central to rig design.

Notice that the greatest acceleration of tension comes in the 0 to 12 degrees range. If the shroud angle is 12 degrees or greater, it can more easily resist the

pressure of wind on sails without generating undue strain. But can this be done? Rigs are tall and narrow to allow the greatest length of luff and closest headsail sheeting angles. For example, when Lyle Hess designed the 30-foot cutter *Syrinx*, he drew in a mast extending 38-plus feet above deck, but the half-beam was only about 5 feet (Figure 100). Given those dimensions, a wire to the top of the mast would describe an angle of less than 7.5 degrees, which is too narrow. Given that we want neither to widen the boat nor shorten the mast, the only way to obtain an adequate staying angle is to install a spreader, a strut extending outward from the mast, in this case 20 feet above deck (Figure 101). This spreader is 4½ feet long, and the length of the mast above it is about 19 feet. With the aid of that traditional rigger's tool, the electronic calculator, we can determine that the angle at the top of the mast is now a healthy 13.3 degrees (see the Loft Procedures chapter for the how-to of trigonometric functions).

If we now construct a stress diagram that includes

65

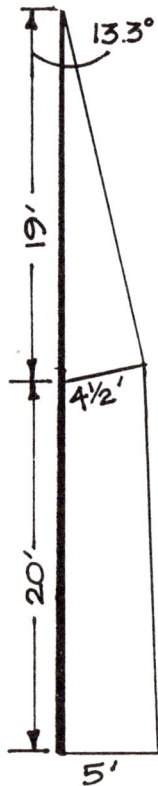

FIGURE 101.

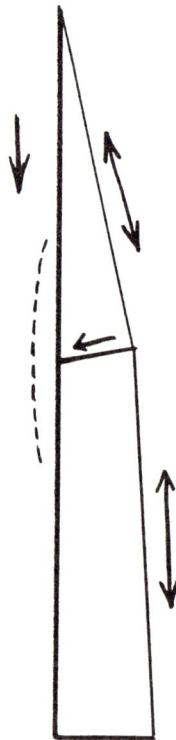

FIGURE 102.

FIGURE 103.

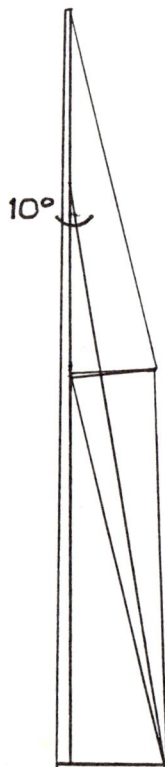

FIGURE 104.

the spreader, which functions as a compression member (Figure 102), we see that the wire's condition has been eased at the expense of the mast, which now must withstand not only a downward force from the wire without buckling, but also a sideways thrust from the spreader. The solution to this problem is the addition of another wire, running from the base of the spreader to the rail, where the first wire is also attached. The new, more equitable diagram that results is Figure 103.

Next, since there remains a long length of unsupported mast above the spreaders, we'll add a third, intermediate wire to take the strain there (Figure 104). The staying angle without a spreader is only 10 degrees, about as narrow as we can safely go. Have to do something to improve this before we're done.

Meanwhile, things are sufficiently evolved to see that the mast and all the wires have become interdependent, creating a system for delivering strain to the hull: The upper shroud takes a portion of the sail's lateral load at the masthead and delivers some of it to its base, but also "drops" some of it off at the spreader. The lower shroud picks up the spreader's lateral compression load, some of the mast's compression load that was imposed by the uppers, and the lateral load imposed by the sail, as well as imposing a compression load of its own. At the deck, the mast partners provide one last lateral support before the mast compression load is finally delivered to the keel. Every time you add a wire, you must balance it against all the other wires and the mast so that no one part of the system receives a disproportionate amount of strain.

So far we've assumed that the sail's load will only be imposed laterally, as in the original staying diagram. If this were the case, we could now proceed to calculate actual pounds of strain for a given vessel, choose appropriate materials, and begin construction. But sailing imposes strains from all directions, so the rig must be elaborated to suit.

Starting again at the top, the lateral guying of the upper shroud is complemented by the fore-and-aft guying of the jibstay and backstay. The intermediate shroud can be made to guy both laterally and aft by moving its point of attachment to the hull aft. Happily, this also results in its staying angle increasing from 10 to 10.5 degrees. The forestay leads from the same point on the mast as the intermediate, and since its forward pull is more than the intermediate can handle under some conditions, additional aft guying is provided by a running backstay. One could accomplish the same result by angling the intermediate farther aft, but this would interfere with the travel of the boom off the wind. Splitting the lower shroud into two pieces and leading one forward and one aft will nicely contain motion of the middle of the mast.

As you can see from Figure 105, we now have a well-formed rig, except for the jibstay and backstay, which are hanging in midair. The boat is too short. We could bring these two stays in (dotted lines) so that they would fit on the hull's 30-foot length, but only at the sacrifice of considerable sail area. The alternative is to extend the length forward with a bowsprit and aft with a boomkin (Figure 106). These pieces, like the mast and spreaders, are under compression from their standing rigging, but their location near the waterline presents special problems.

First, the bowsprit. The jibstay at its end, with a staying angle of 64 degrees relative to the bowsprit, has an advantage in leverage over the bobstay, which has an angle of only 25 degrees relative to the bowsprit. It's like pitting a long crowbar against a short one. As the dotted line shows, we could increase the bobstay's angle by attaching its lower end at a point just tangent with the hull, but this would make the stay much more vulnerable to corrosion and to damage from striking objects in the water, as well as contributing to drag. Better to keep its lower end above the surface and deal with the leverage inequality with a larger wire and stronger end-fittings.

Lateral staying for the bowsprit is effected by bowsprit shrouds. No asymmetry here, but once again staying angle is at a premium, and once again, this time in order to keep the wires short and out of harm's way, we won't use the maximum angle available.

At the other end of the boat, the boomkin extends outward to pick up the backstay. The presence of the rudder precludes a staying arrangement like the bowsprit's, so the two boomkin shrouds extend diagonally out and down to provide guying in both vertical and lateral planes. Because the stern is relatively beamy, a healthy staying angle isn't hard to come by.

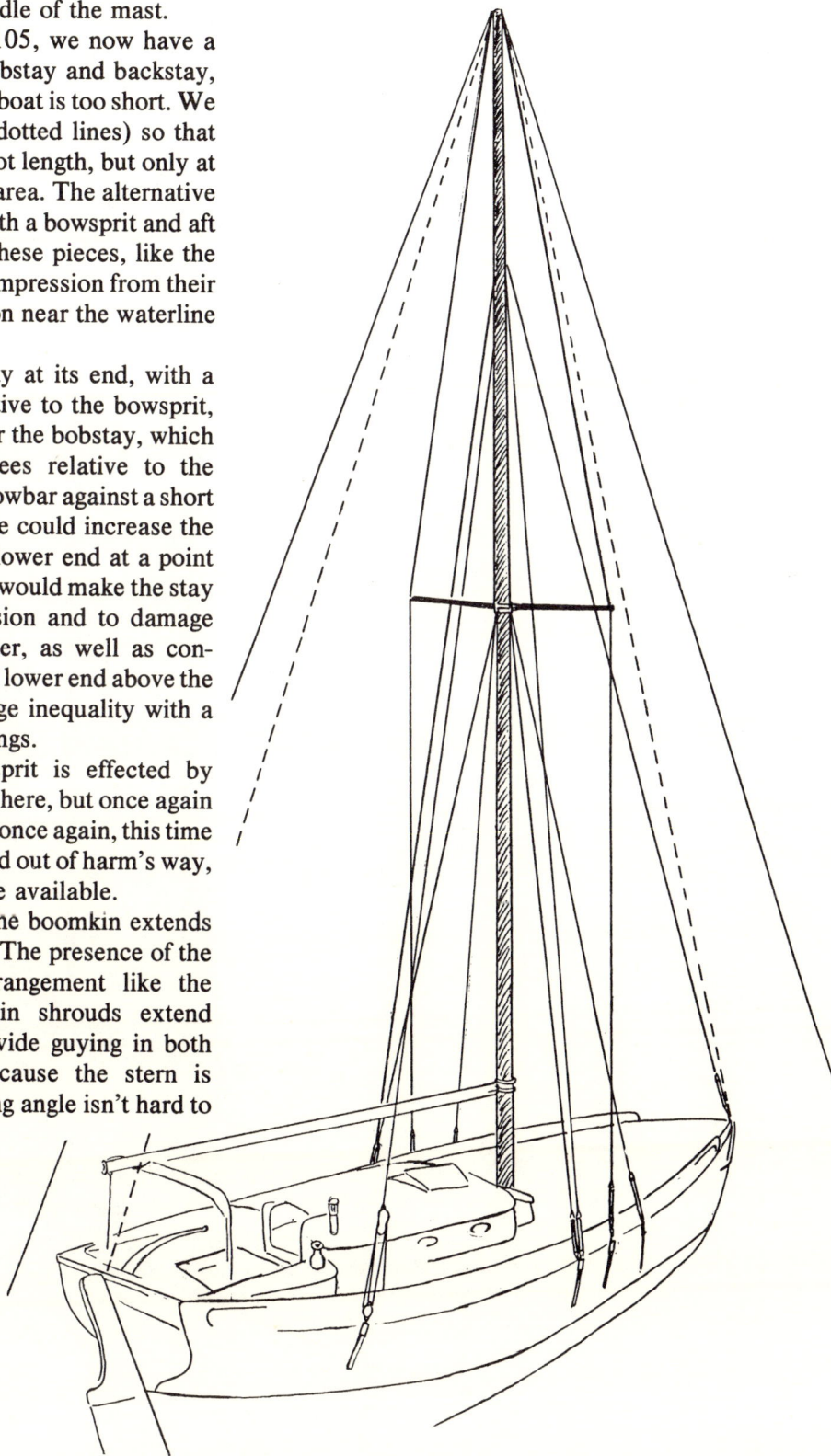

FIGURE 105. *A perfectly balanced rig for* Syrinx—*except that the backstay and jibstay are hanging in midair. Bringing them inboard (dotted lines) would too greatly reduce sail area.*

LOAD CALCULATIONS

Figure 106 shows the completed rig, one of an infinite number of ways to turn the mast into a pure compression member, almost entirely restrained from bending, leaning, or buckling in any direction. We must provide of course that the materials used in the mast, rig, and hull are equal to the loads imposed. One can do the same thing with a taller mast or a shorter one, with more or fewer wires, or with the same number of wires in different configurations. The exact layout of any rig is part mechanical necessity, part intended vessel use, and part designer preference. But no matter what form the design takes, the time comes to translate it into reality, and that means figuring out how much strain comes where. The trouble is, nobody knows with precision. By observing and keeping track of enough successes and failures, we can develop an empirical data base. By conducting strain-gauge tests while sailing particular boats under a variety of conditions, we can check our general data and more closely determine what happens on those particular boats. But different weather and sea conditions, the habits and skills of those on the helm, the quality of rig tune, hull design variations, and many other considerations mean that our figures can only be approximate. So we come as close as possible and try always to err on the safe side.

FIGURE 106. *A bowsprit and boomkin extend outward to pick up the jibstay and backstay. A bobstay and bowsprit shrouds forward and boomkin shrouds aft serve as guys. The bobstay's narrow staying angle can be improved by attaching it lower on the hull or by adding a spreader-like "dolphin striker." Alternatively, we can leave the angle narrow and use larger wire to compensate.*

To calculate *Syrinx*'s rigging loads, we start with her righting moment at 30 degrees: the number of foot-pounds necessary to cause a 30-degree heel. This number varies with vessel size and the distribution of displacement, and can be arrived at with precision only through tedious and complicated calculations. On the other hand, most cruising auxiliaries of the same waterline length have *approximately* the same righting moment at 30 degrees. Figure 107 is a graph from *Skene's Elements of Yacht Design*. It shows figures for typical 20- to 50-foot boats. If the vessel you're working on is an untypical one, such as a multihull, bugeye, or brig, consult a designer.

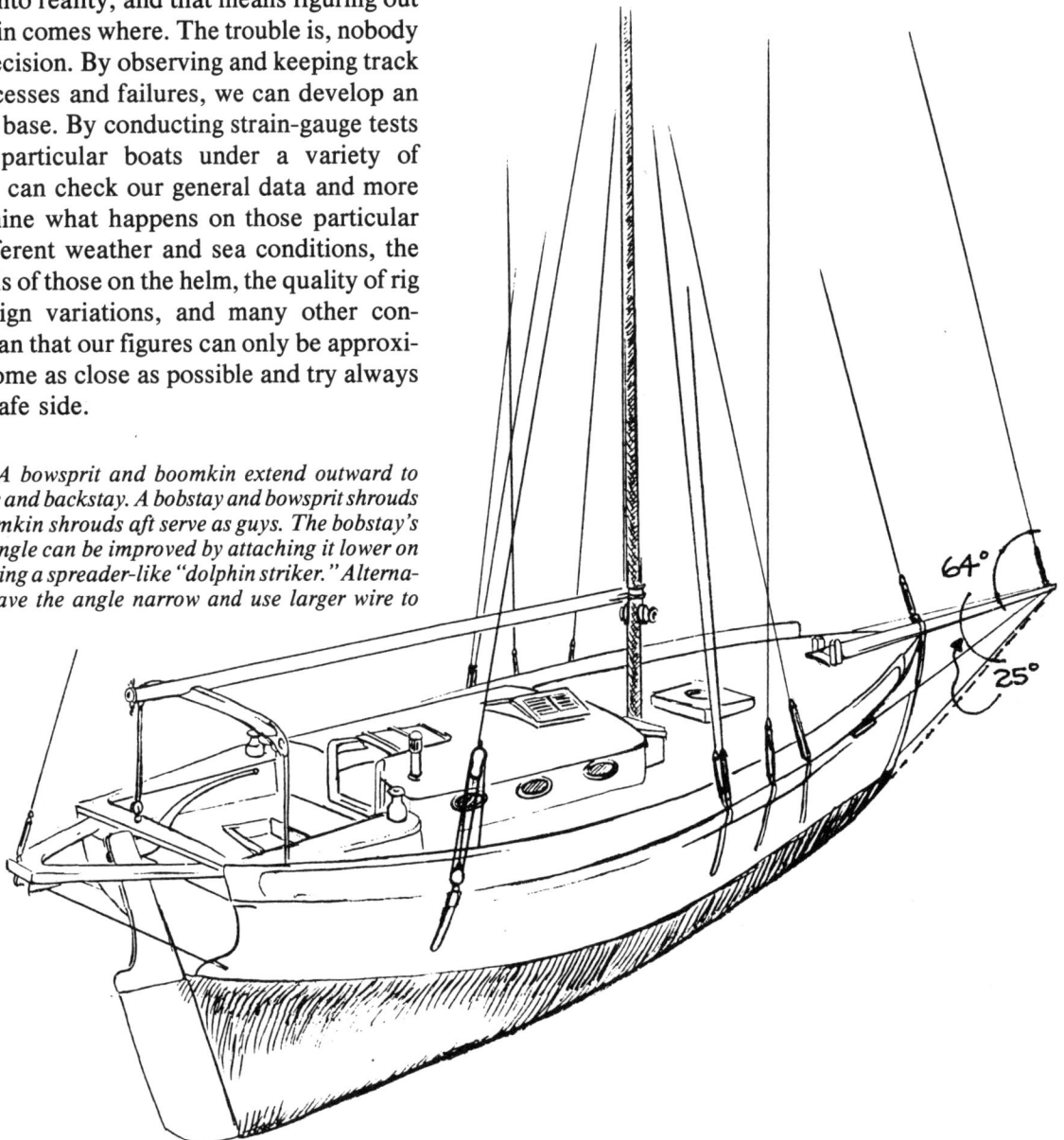

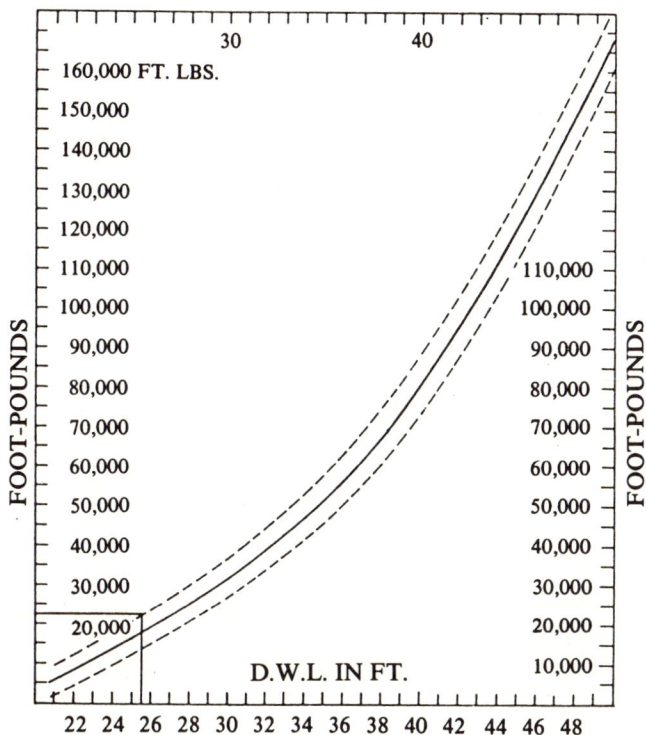

FIGURE 107. *A graph of righting moments at 30 degrees. Note that a small increase in vessel length results in a large increase in righting moment. (From Skene's Elements of Yacht Design, Dodd, Mead and Co. Reprinted by permission.)*

For *Syrinx*, at 30 feet, our working figure is 30,000 foot-pounds. Notice that a 32-foot boat jumps to 37,000 foot-pounds and that a 40-footer is over 80,000 foot-pounds; a little length adds a lot to the moment, something to consider if you plan to load the boat heavily or if you're wondering why a slightly larger boat needs substantially larger rigging. The trick is to convert moment into actual pounds of tension on the standing rigging. This is done by the use of the following formula developed by Sparkman & Stephens:

Transverse Rigging Load = R.M. x 2.78 ÷ ½ beam

This formula can be found on page 167 of *Skene's Elements of Yacht Design* under the heading "Mast Compression Loads." On page 169, under "Transverse Rigging Loads," there is a similar formula, but with the factor 1.5 instead of 2.78. As originally written the smaller figure referred to strains on both mast and rigging at 30 degrees of heel, while the larger figure represented corresponding strains under a knockdown load. Since most designers still use Skene's as a standard reference, many rigs today are undersized by the standards that Sparkman & Stephens developed from empirical data. In spite of this, you don't see masts falling over frequently—just often enough that you might be interested in using the larger figure to determine loads on your own rig, in the interest of safety. If low windage and weight are overriding concerns or if the vessel is a lightly worked daysailer, it is appropriate to use the 1.5 figure instead. With the help of a designer and sparmaker you can get an even lighter rig, and Grand Prix racers do, but such practice is outside the realm of traditional rigging.

In the case of *Syrinx*, 30,000 x 2.78 ÷ 5 = 16,680, our expected maximum transverse load.

The next step is to crank in a healthy safety factor to guarantee that, even with materials flaws or degradation, shock-loading, or formula insufficiency, we can go forth with a reasonable expectation of keeping the mast in the boat. Safety factors vary according to the amount of abuse the gear will receive and the seriousness of the consequences should it fail. Elevator cables, you will be glad to know, are 10 or more times stronger than they need be for the loads they carry. Industrial standards for slings, which pick up expensive stuff and see a lot of abuse in the process, prescribe a safety factor of 8. For sailboat standing rigging, ostensibly well maintained, replaced in good time, and not abused, a safety factor of 2.5 to 3 is considered adequate. I like to use 3 as the standard, compromising it grudgingly only when there are closely reasoned arguments to do so.

So, 3 x 16,680 (transverse load) = 50,040 pounds, a figure to be distributed equitably among the shrouds, which take that load. On *Syrinx* the lowers will take about half the strain and the intermediates and uppers will share the rest, so the load can be divided four ways to make a 12,510-pound pull on each of the four wires to a side. This pull comes very close to the rated strength of ⅜-inch 7 x 7, ⅜-inch 7 x 19, or ⁵⁄₁₆-inch 1 x 19 wire rope, either galvanized or stainless steel. The distribution of strain would be different if the rig configuration were different; for other examples, refer to Skene's rigging chapter or to a designer. On *Syrinx* the actual shroud strength per side is 44,000 pounds; the safety factor was lowered from 3 to 2.6 for reasons we'll discuss later in the chapter.

With shroud size established, we can move on to the

dimensions of the other wires. On most vessels the forestay should be at least as strong as the strongest shroud while the jibstay (if there is one) and standing backstay can be one size lighter. In practice, for cruising vessels, it makes a lot of sense to make all the shrouds and stays the same size so you're only dealing with one size turnbuckle, tang, toggle, and cotter pin, and you only have to stow one size of spare wire. An exception to this might be a jibstay running to a short, light topmast, but apart from that, a rig that truly must have an assortment of wire sizes is likely highly bred and not suited to cruising in the first place. Aboard *Syrinx*, all wires except the running backstay pendants and the bobstay are the same size, and the running backs were a judgment call, slightly smaller than the other wires. The bobstay is a different matter, undergoing, as we noted earlier, a heavy strain owing to its angle relative to the jibstay.

Figure 108 shows a diagram for determining just how much more strain the bobstay must endure than the jibstay. By scaling off distances, we find a leverage advantage of 2.8 to 1, so the bobstay needs to be 2.8 times stronger than the jibstay. The bobstay is the most corrosion and collision-prone wire on a vessel, and much of the rig depends on its integrity.

For initial analysis of most vessel rigs, there is a shortcut method that bypasses all those calculations:

The shrouds on one side should have a total rated strength of 1.5 to 3.5 times the vessel's displacement, depending on how heavily it is sailed. Daysailers and racers are nearer the low end of the spectrum, while cruising sail, working sail, and trimarans (due to their high initial stability) are nearer the high end. With a 16,000-pound displacement and a total shroud strength per side of 44,000 pounds, *Syrinx* comes in with a ratio of 2.75. If this were to be a more lightly sailed boat, we might cut the ratio down to 2 or even lower. This is the equivalent of reducing the safety factor well below 2.5 in our previous calculations. Both methods require that one exercise judgment in determining just how hard a boat will be used. A final backup check is to collect displacement-to-wire-size data for several boats similar to yours. You should also consider the properties of rig materials relative to prevailing climatic conditions; as we shall see, the expected interaction between materials and climate can have a pronounced effect on rig design.

FIGURE 108. *Jibstay strain relative to bobstay strain. Measure up the jibstay 1 inch, then draw a line parallel to the bobstay to intersect the bowsprit, and one parallel to the jibstay to intersect the bobstay. The resulting bobstay segment is 2.8 times as long as the jibstay segment, thus the bobstay must be 2.8 times as strong as the jibstay. A dolphin striker will reduce this disparity.*

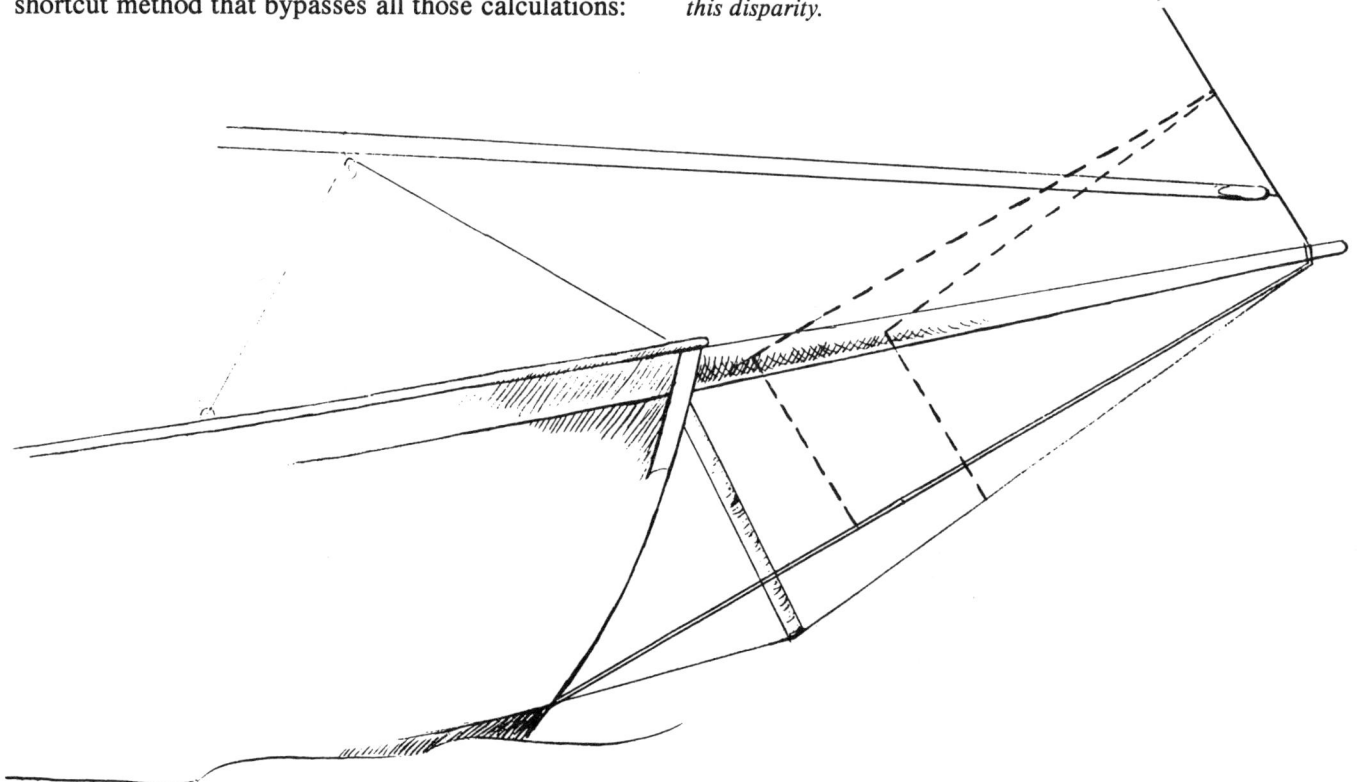

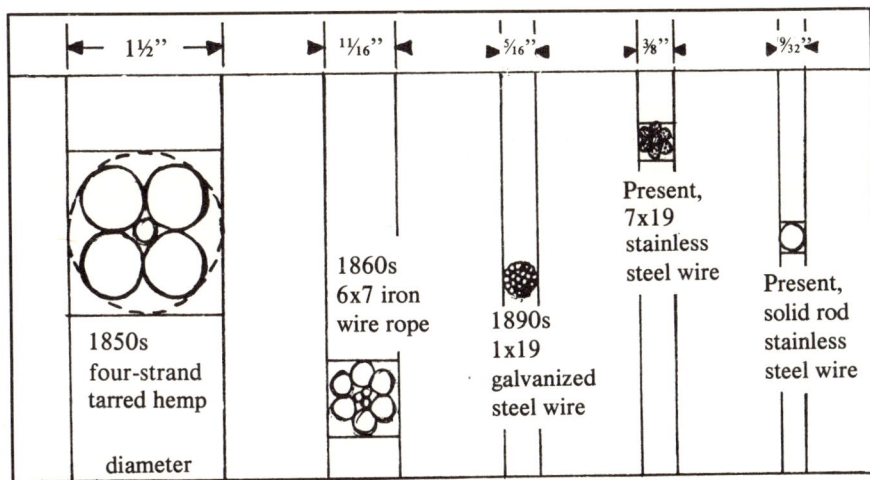

FIGURE 109. *A chronology of materials. All of the examples shown are of equal strength, rated for loads of about 12,000 pounds. Over the decades, diameter has shown a downward trend due to better materials and constructions.*

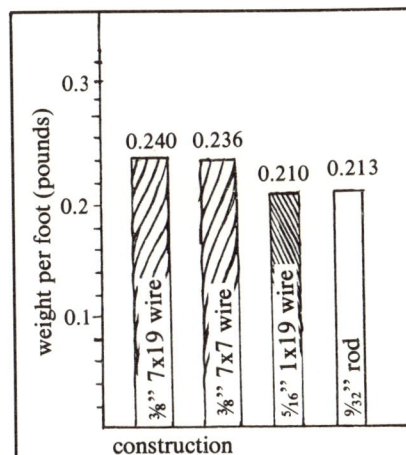

FIGURE 110. *Weight per foot for four stainless steel stay constructions. All are rated for 12,000- to 12,500-pound loads.*

THE MATERIAL DIFFERENCE (STANDING RIGGING)

In theory you can make a rig out of anything that is strong enough to take the strain; clothesline of sufficient diameter would do. In practice, you're more likely to choose from among a very few wire-rope types developed and tested by generations of sailors and engineers. This does not mean your choices are made for you. Although there are few wire or rod types, they are of specialized material and construction with variations to suit a broad range of functions, sailing conditions, boat types, cost and maintenance considerations, and even the sailor's personal style; understanding and balancing specific requirements is the key to choosing the most appropriate wire rope for a given job.

Windage

Figure 109 shows, in order of their development, standing-rigging materials that have been in use over the last 130 years. The most obvious trend has been an increase of strength relative to diameter. This benefits sailing performance because the smaller a wire is, the less resistance or windage it causes as it passes through the air.

At first, strength-to-size gains were the result of the introduction of different materials: Hemp gave way to iron, and iron to steel. By the early years of this century, gains based on materials improvements were diminishing, so designers turned their attention to construction. The more cross-sectional area of metal you can cram into a wire of a given diameter, the stronger that wire will be. So 6 x 7 and 7 x 7 constructions were superseded for the most part by the current standard, 1 x 19. Of course, a solid cylinder has the greatest cross-sectional area and thus the greatest strength of all, but until recently, engineering problems made rod rigging too short-lived to be of use to any but the most extreme racing craft. With the advent of improved alloys and cold-drawing techniques, rod rigging has begun to enter the cruising and charter market.

Weight

Another trend has been the reduction of rig weight. One extra pound of weight 30 feet up adds 30 foot-pounds to a vessel's heeling moment, making the vessel that much less stable and putting that much more strain on the mast and rig. Lightness is a virtue. But again, recent developments have produced a diminishing-returns catch: Increasing the cross-sectional area of metal in wire of a given diameter in order to increase wire strength means increasing weight relative to diameter. Figure 110 shows in graph form the relationships between weight per foot, diameter, and strength for 7 x 19, 7 x 7, 1 x 19, and rod rigging of comparable materials.

Elasticity

Construction		F
rod rigging,	stainless	4.45 x 10^{-6}
1 x 19	carbon	6.98 x 10^{-6}
	stainless	7.79 x 10^{-6}
7 x 7	carbon	1.07 x 10^{-5}
	stainless	1.20 x 10^{-5}
7 x 19	carbon	1.40 x 10^{-5}
	stainless	1.62 x 10^{-5}

Induced mast bend can alter sail shape to improve performance; unwanted mast bend due to rig elasticity can impair it. It's odd to think of wire rope as something that stretches, and it's true that we're dealing with tiny increments here, even in the most elastic wire, but this is a situation in which tiny increments can make a difference. To the extent that wire stretches, the mast will bend or "go out of column." Stayed masts are designed to function as nearly pure compression members, so it is important that they stay straight.

There are two forms of stretch at rated loads that are of interest to sailors: constructional and elastic. Constructional stretch is a permanent elongation that results from the strands in a new piece of wire settling into place when the wire is put to use. This does not affect sailing efficiency unless it is not allowed for when the wire is cut for rig fabrication; with long pieces of the more elastic constructions, one can use up a lot of turnbuckle thread taking out this stretch and thus have too little adjustment left for tuning.

More important is elastic stretch, a function of rope or rod load and diameter relative to cross-sectional metallic area and the inherent elastic properties of the metal used in making the rope. A formula for the approximate percentage of stretch for a given length of wire rope is as follows:

$$e = [P/D^2] \times F, \text{ where}$$

e = elastic stretch as percentage of length
P = load on rope in pounds
D = nominal rope diameter
F = the reciprocal of (A x E x 100)

The factor "F" is the tricky part of the equation because it is the result of a fairly complex equation itself. "A" is the cross-sectional area of metal in a wire rope of given diameter, and "E" stands for the modulus of elasticity, which is to say how much a substance stretches per pound of tension applied. Carbon steel, for example, has a lower modulus of elasticity than stainless steel. Ropes with the greatest cross-sectional area made of metals with the lowest modulus of elasticity will stretch the least. Values of the factor "F" for the materials and constructions commonly used in rigging are as follows:

Don't let those numbers intimidate you; Figure 111 renders them into some real-life examples. Theoretical 50-foot lengths subjected to a load of 25 percent of their rated strength would stretch by the amounts shown. A load of 25 percent reflects moderate rig strain for most vessels. From the 1.05-inch stretch of the rod rigging sample to the 2.07-inch stretch of the stainless 7 x 19 sample, one sees an increase of elasticity with increase of numbers of strands. But once more, the returns diminish as we approach minimum elasticity, with only a 0.44-inch difference separating 1 x 19 stainless and rod rigging.

Whether this difference is worth bothering with depends on the boat. The wider spreader angles on cruisers lessen shroud strain and the distance that the masthead travels to leeward for a given amount of stretch. A lower-aspect rig accomplishes the same thing. But the fastest boats have the tallest, narrowest rigs, with shroud chainplates set well inboard so they can sheet in those huge genoas; utter inelasticity is required, so rod rigging makes sense.

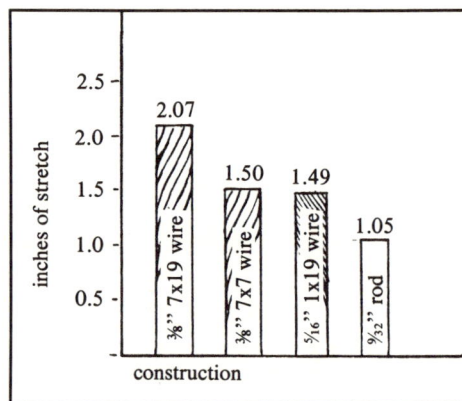

FIGURE 111. *Inches of stretch per 50 feet, at 25 percent load, for the stay constructions in Figure 110.*

72

Flexibility

The only formula you need to know here is that more strands equal more flexibility. So rod is the least flexible and 7 x 19 wire the most flexible of the constructions we're considering. Greatest flexibility is required for halyards, so 7 x 19 is the only construction to use if you want wire halyards. Running back pendants, span wires, straps, and bowsprit shrouds are good in 7 x 7 or 7 x 19, because these constructions are less prone to damage by kinking in these applications than 1 x 19 is. And if structural considerations can be satisfied, 7 x 7 is a good choice for spliced standing rigging because it is relatively docile and easily worked, while 1 x 19 is a perverse, vicious beast.

Cost

So much for engineering; now we get to the important question, "What's it gonna cost me?" The answers can be found in Figure 112, a cost-per-foot chart.

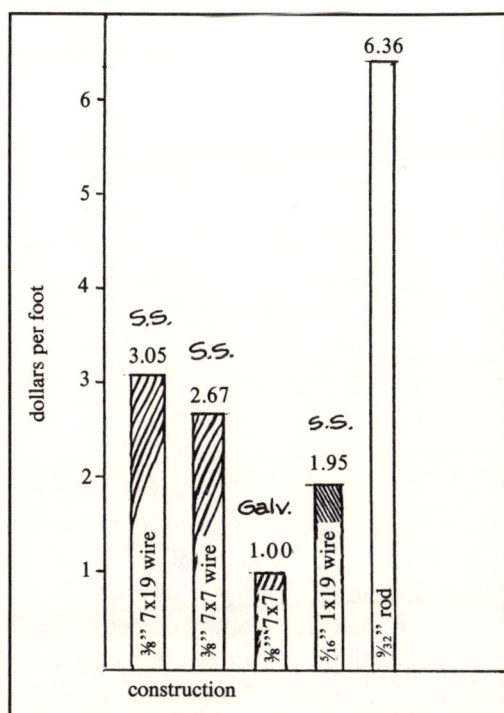

FIGURE 112. *Typical retail prices per foot in 1984 for the stay constructions shown in Figure 110.*

Compare this to Figures 110 and 111, and you can see what you get for your money.

It's easy to see why 1 x 19 wire is the overwhelming first choice for most contemporary craft: the combination of good weight, windage, and elasticity characteristics, and a low price. For cruisers, it and 7 x 7 are appealing in that they are more likely than rod to give advance warning of failure. Even if you do spot a flaw in rod rigging ahead of time, where can you safely stow the spare's 6-foot-diameter coil? If you want to race, and have the money, it can make sense to indulge in rod rigging, assuming your hull is bred to benefit from the slightly increased efficiency; a cruiser, or even a racer cruiser, being inherently slower than a pure racer, may not have its performance measurably improved. And some traditional craft that roar along nicely with 7 x 7 wire would be silly with anything else. No doubt there exists somewhere a Norwegian lifeboat with rod rigging and hydraulic backstay, but this sort of design behavior is, as sailing writer David Kasanof once put it, "like paring the hooves of a Clydesdale before entering it in the Kentucky Derby."

Cost Effectiveness

Now to consider cost-over-time, a sort of budgetary moment of forces. Aside from proper tuning, scantlings, terminals, and staying angles, the biggest determinants of rig longevity are what the wire is made of and how well it is maintained. A long-lived rig is a good return on investment and also provides a sort of insurance: If it's healthy enough to last, it's healthy enough to withstand occasional rough going.

In spite of the obvious advantages of durability, the world of contemporary sailing is filled with tales of spectacular dismastings in moderate conditions. Many of these stories concern racers who shaved a teensy bit too much weight out of their rigging or mast, but many others are about sailors who either started out with poor materials or let good ones degrade. Some unfortunate real-life scenarios:

An owner chooses good stainless 1 x 19 wire for a corrosive environment, knowing that the small number of strands presents a small total surface area for corrosion to work on. But then he gets some not-so-good swages applied, and the small number of strands works against him—if just one strand is broken, or not sharing the load, the wire loses more than 5 percent of its strength.

Someone else gets properly applied terminals but accelerates metal fatigue by neglecting to use toggles. If the wire is alloy it will harden up and break if it isn't replaced in time.

Another party gets a beautifully spliced 7 x 7 rig but uses truly lousy wire because it was available cheap. The mast goes over the side and people blame the splices.

Having the right wire in the wrong place can also reduce cost-effectiveness. An alloy at home in California might not want to spend too much time in Hawaii; charter boat skippers there change rigs every three to five years. Private vessels, sailed less, can expect longer service—maybe 10 years with maintenance. The best thing to do in Hawaii is invest in a highly corrosion-resistant alloy and take good care of it. The tropics are one place where rod rigging is gaining in popularity. Minimum surface area and excellent metal beat the heat.

Maintenance and regular inspection are crucial even for stainless steel; "stainless" is a relative term, applied to a whole family of alloys with widely differing levels of corrosion and fatigue resistance. Rinsing the rig with fresh water whenever you hose down the deck can greatly prolong rig life, but if the vessel is in a particularly hostile-to-wire environment or if you simply want the rig to last the longest possible time, it's a good idea to give some thought to the alloy it's made of.

For example, Carolina Wire and Rope recommends their Type 302, a high-carbon alloy with good fatigue and corrosion resistance. This wire has low initial cost, high strength, and will outlast many other alloys. It is best suited to temperate climates.

The MacWhyte company has recently introduced "Sailbrite," a new alloy with high corrosion resistance, strength on a par with other alloys, and only slightly higher initial cost. MacWhyte is keeping mum about exactly what the alloy is, which makes analysis difficult, but it holds up well even in the tropics.

Universal's "Super Stainless" is another corrosion-resistant wire, known in engineering circles as Type 2213-5. Navtec uses the same alloy in its rod rigging, partly because it doesn't rust or fatigue readily, partly because it can be drawn with the high uniformity that rod rigging must have.

Finally, I would urge you to consider galvanized wire rope. My enthusiasm for it tends to be met with incredulity by most sailors, yet it is possessed of virtues that make it ideal for the running or standing rigging of many vessels. Specifically, it is less elastic and more fatigue-resistant than any alloy, at one-third

the cost. The first two reasons make it attractive to go-fast boats, for consistent luff and sheet tension. And stainless is not only stretchier, but likely to become brittle and break sooner than well-maintained galvanized will rust. Twelve-meters use galvanized headsail sheets and halyards. The sole drawback of this material is that it requires a lot of maintenance, which for a boat owner can be like saying that it was a pleasant trip except for the hurricane. But I've seen enough 20-, 40-, 50- or more year-old rigs in perfect condition to know that galvanized wire is underrated.

Who Makes It

Enough traditionalist propaganda; now for a little chauvinism. Besides wire size, construction, and material, you need to decide who to buy it from. Officially speaking, all wire sold in this country must meet federally established standards, notably for breaking strength. These are minimum standards—you meet them, you can sell your wire. But it's been my experience that reputable domestic manufacturers make a wire that is stronger and longer-lived than the imported stuff. Production standards have something to do with this, as does America's "no minus tolerance" requirement for domestically produced wire. That is, while importers can sell a wire that is, say, 9 millimeters, plus 4 percent or minus 1 percent, our corresponding ⅜-inch size must be ⅜ inch and *no smaller*, but it can be up to 5 percent larger. I think of this standard as a federally provided factor of safety.

Regardless of whom you buy your wire from, learn all you can about it beforehand from manufacturers' reps, riggers, and sailors who've had experience with it, good and bad.

Deciding

Take a good, hard look at your boat and at yourself. What kind of sailing do you want to do? In what climate? For how long? Will you often be far from land, or will there always be a boatyard nearby? List as many rig considerations as you can think of, and rate them in order of their importance to you. Compare cost benefits of different rigging materials.

Most sailors just go with whatever the boat comes with, and may not even realize that there are alternatives. But rigging materials are specialized in order to suit any sailing style; you might as well get what suits you.

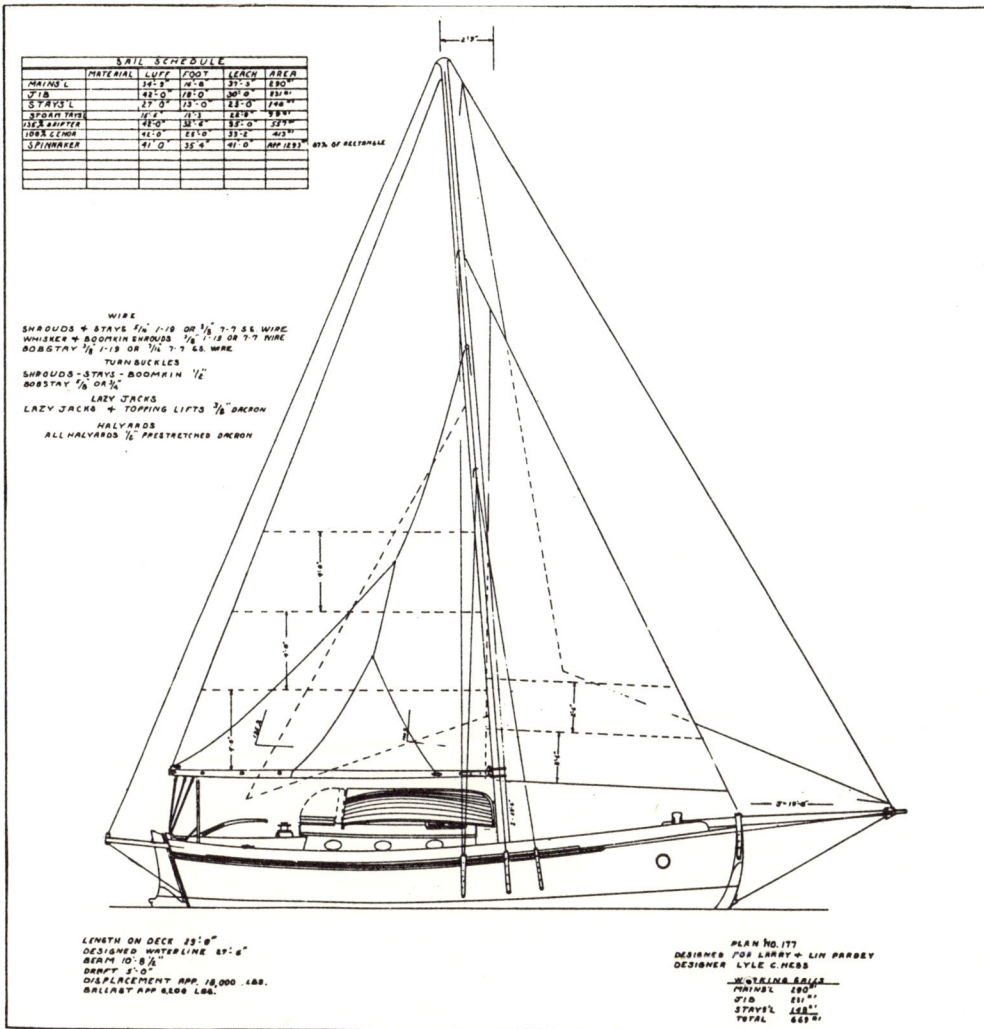

FIGURE 113.
*The 29-foot 6-inch
Lyle Hess cutter* Syrinx.

SOME SAMPLE EVALUATIONS

Here's decision-making in action—three boats built, rigged, and sailed to suit widely differing tastes.

Syrinx's 7 x 19 standing rigging is a highly fatigue- and corrosion-resistant Type 316 wire—yet another alloy—with the drawback of being 10 to 15 percent weaker than other blends. It was chosen in spite of this drawback for three main reasons:

(1) Because it will degrade more slowly, 316 will keep its initial strength while other, initially stronger alloys grow weak and brittle. The rigging-load formula for *Syrinx* indicated shrouds of about 12,000 pounds' rated strength, which is what a ⅜-inch-diameter standard-alloy 7 x 7 or 7 x 19 is rated at. The 11,000-pound strength of ⅜-inch Type 316 7 x 19 is less than we'd originally specified for this boat (see page 69), but is ample in light of materials longevity, the wide staying angles, and our having started with a generous safety factor.

(2) The owner got a great deal on this very well-made domestic wire, which usually costs considerably more than other alloys. With tight finances, 316's long-term cost effectiveness might otherwise have been outweighed by high initial cost.

(3) Low maintenance was a requisite. Galvanized wire would have been cheaper still, but you have to keep after it.

A 1 x 19 stainless would also have been cheaper than the 7 x but would have been much more difficult to splice well; the owner definitely wanted splices and wanted to learn to do them himself.

With a good, wide staying angle and a relatively low proportion of working load to rated strength, the difference in elasticity between 7 x 19 and 1 x 19 is minimized, so good sail shape is maintained.

Overall, the rig is low-cost, low-maintenance, very dependable without being overbuilt for its purpose, and quite handsome.

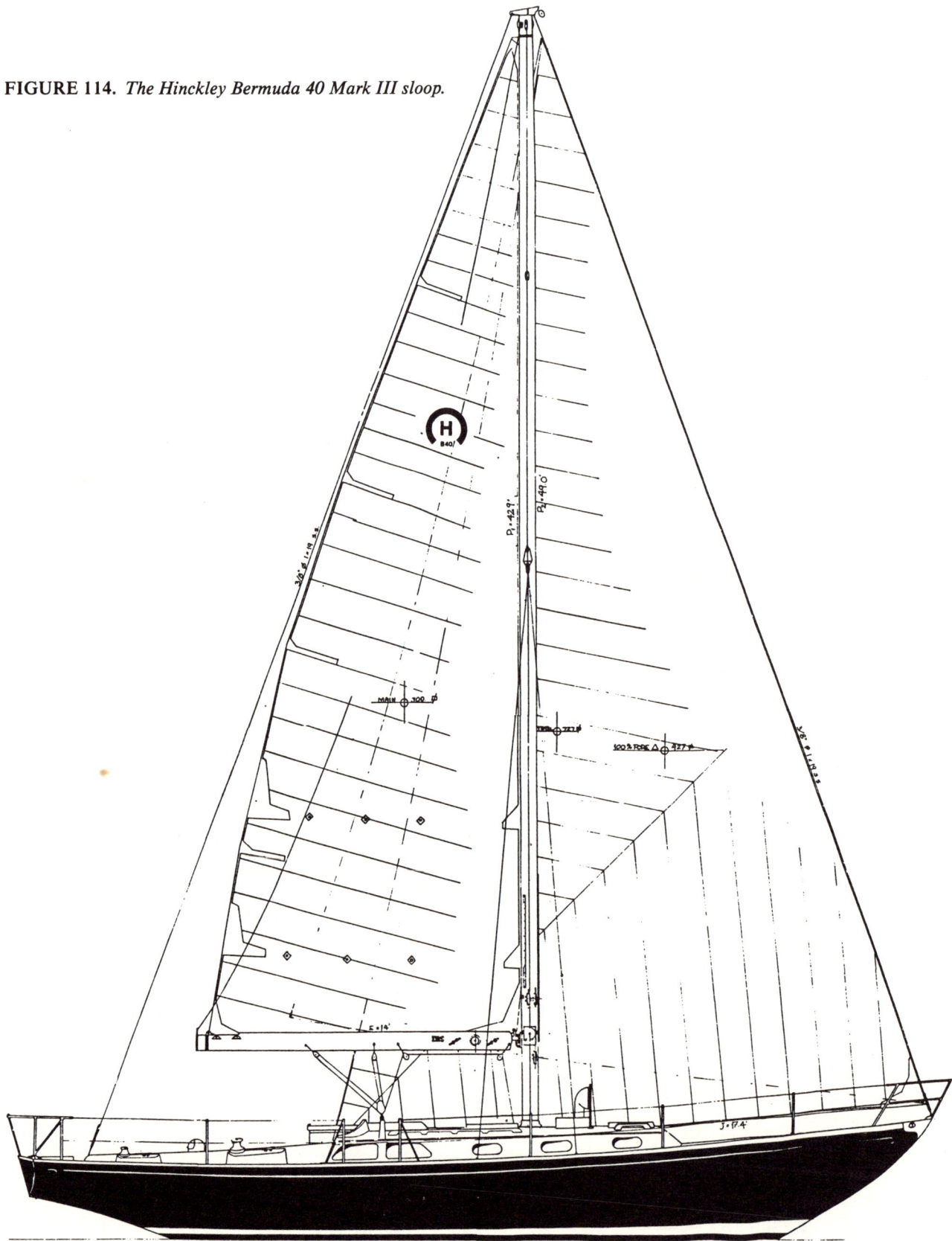

FIGURE 114. *The Hinckley Bermuda 40 Mark III sloop.*

For something to suit the contemporary cruising sailor with a taste for fairly high performance, consider the Hinckley Bermuda 40 Mark III sloop, a highly regarded production boat made in Maine.

Low maintenance and longevity are still desirable, so owners choose alloys to suit the climates their boats spend the most time in. Cost is not so much an object and spliceability is usually not considered at all, since mechanical fittings are standard. Swages are most often seen on this and other modern production boats, but Norsemans, Sta-Loks, and the like are preferable owing to their lower failure rate and more consistent high strength.

The Hinckley's straightforward sloop rig includes two 5/16-inch 1 x 19 lower shrouds per side. A 3/8-inch 1 x 19 shroud runs from deck to spreader tip on either side, and above the spreader this shroud bifurcates into a 3/16-inch 1 x 19 intermediate and a 5/16-inch 1 x 19 upper. This configuration is very light with low windage, but for long-distance cruising it would be better to run intermediates and uppers all the way to the deck, rather than letting the entire mast above the spreaders rely on that lone lower spreader shroud and the spreader-end fitting.

With 21,000 pounds of displacement for the rig as illustrated, we get a wire-strength-to-weight ratio of 2.02, plenty stout enough for coastwise cruising yet light enough for competitive speed. If you were to bring the intermediates and uppers to deck for cruising security, you might want to make both of them 5/16-inch diameter to up that ratio a bit more.

Finally there's the *Sophia Christina*, a 46-foot Ted Brewer–designed pilot-style schooner. Her traditional lines have been enhanced by modern design concepts, but she's not intended to race, except perhaps against others of her type. The owners wanted a supremely comfortable, handsome, and safe vessel, but one that could also be exciting when they felt like roaring along. The well-designed gaff schooner rig is versatile enough to meet these requirements, and the traditional rig materials that best suit it have some considerable benefits.

To start with, the 7 x 19 galvanized wire employed throughout is very inexpensive. It is fully served and so should last indefinitely with the regular maintenance that the owners are not loath to do. All terminals are spliced, again providing durability at low cost, and the traditional appearance, enhanced by deadeyes and lanyards used instead of turnbuckles, attracts the

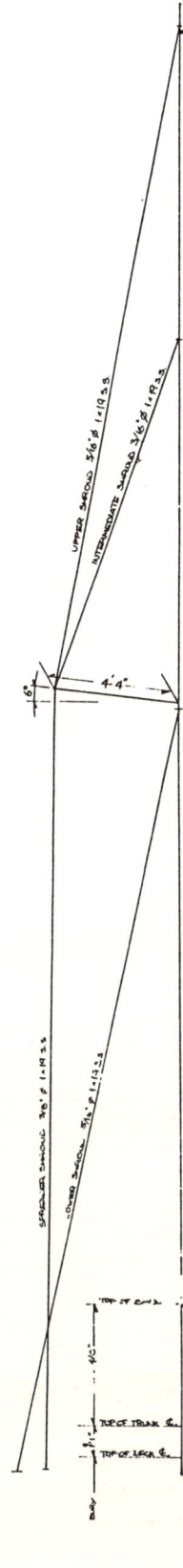

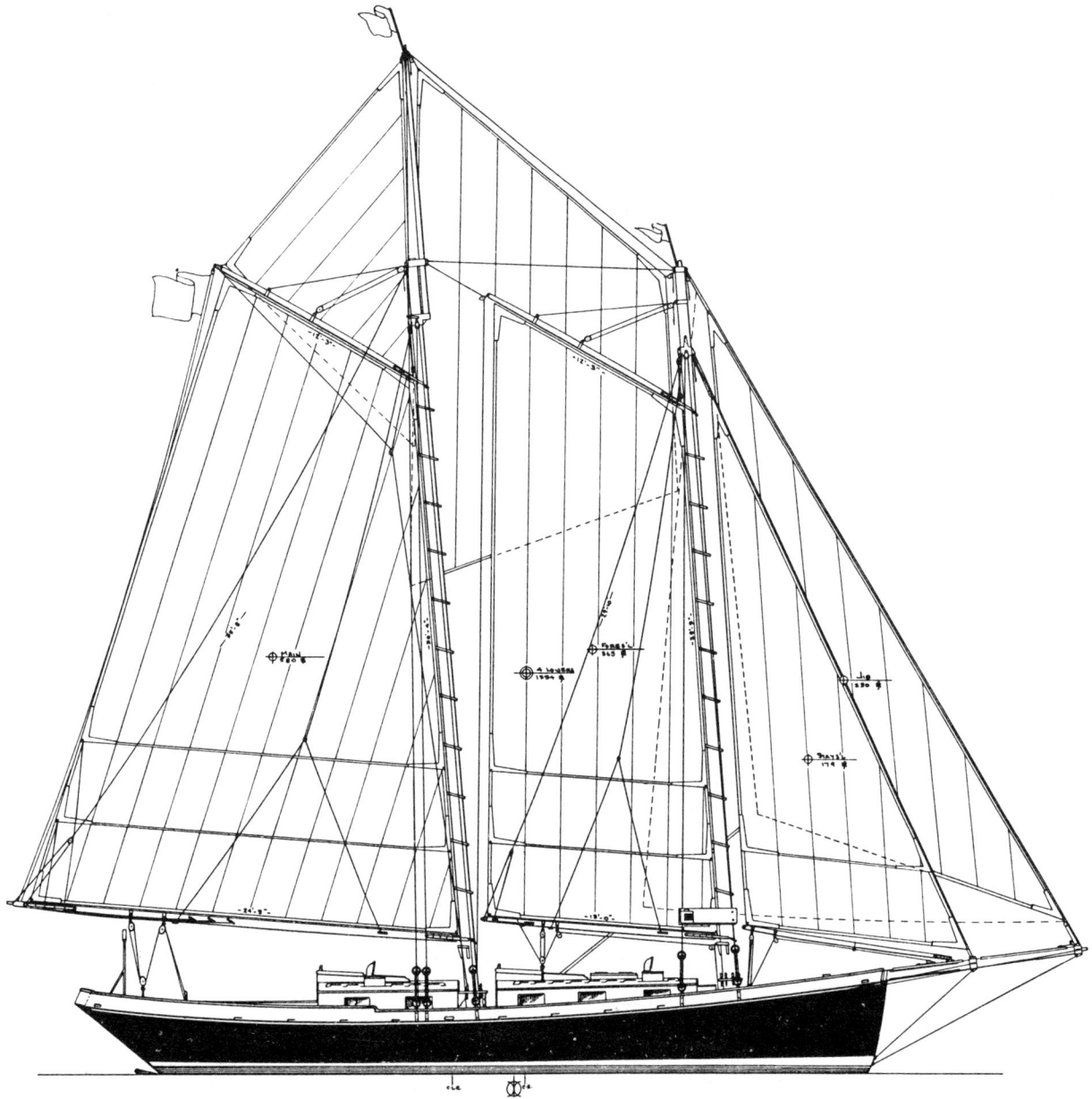

FIGURE 115. Sophia Christina, *a 47-foot length-on-deck Ted Brewer–designed schooner.*

charter customers with which this vessel earns her keep.

The lower shrouds on the mainmast and the shroud pair on the foremast are 7/16-inch diameter; the topmast backstays on the main are ⅜-inch diameter. The 1.75 wire strength-to-displacement ratio is fairly low, but so is the aspect of the rig. This, combined with big, solid Douglas fir spars that take a great deal of the lateral load themselves, makes for a rig capable of holding to sea in any weather without the overbuilt quality one frequently finds on gaffers.

Once you've properly evaluated standing rig requirements, it's easier to choose the rest of your gear; just keep in mind the standards you've decided on for a particular vessel, and match the equipment to those standards.

CORDAGE

Always choose the least elastic, longest-lived, cheapest running rigging that suits your vessel. Always choose an elastic, long-lived, cheap-as-you-can-find-it material for ground tackle and docklines.

Running rigging is subject to the same considerations that standing rigging is (including economic ones); and again, inelasticity and longevity come dear. Ground tackle is different only in that you *want* it to stretch as well as to be strong. Weight and windage don't matter as much as with standing rigging; rope is relatively light, and those who worry about its windage just run their halyards up the inside of the mast. And because synthetic rope is so strong, you're likely to scale its size for a comfortable grip as much as for structural requirements on small craft. The accompanying graph and tables give recommended sizes for sheets and halyards and sizes and lengths for docklines and anchor rodes for vessels of up to 70 feet. If you're heading out to sea for a serious cruise, make everything a size bigger.

Constructions

There are two basic constructions to choose from: three-strand and double-braid. The former is cheaper, easier to splice, comes in very elastic to fairly inelastic materials, and, at least to me, is more comfortable to hold. The latter is expensive, stronger for its size, a bizarre and difficult splicee, and comes in fairly elastic to startlingly inelastic materials. It also best resists hockling and kinking when led around winches. I like three-strand but wouldn't recommend it for halyards or headsail sheets that go to a winch; the heavy loads for which winches are designed imply a need for the strongest, least elastic rope you can wrap around them, which is to say double-braid. Use or at least try three-strand wherever high-tech, high-strain isn't a big issue; double-braid is overrated and overused for many applications: as mainsail sheets, boomed forestaysail sheets, staysail halyards, and dock- and anchor lines. And if you're running a gaffer, double-braid is downright silly. Again, evaluate your craft and sailing style, then choose accordingly.

TABLE 3. **Recommended Sizes for Dacron or Polypropylene Sheets and for Nylon Docklines and Anchor Lines**
(Used by permission of Merriman Holbrook, Inc.)

Dock Lines

Boat Length	Diameter	Bow Line Length	Stern Line Length	Spring Line Length
up to 20'	⅜"	20'	10'	15'
20–30'	½"	25'	15'	20'
30–40'	½"	30'	20'	25'
40–70'	⅝"	35'	25'	30'

Anchor Lines

	Power		Sail	
Boat Length	Line Length	Line Size	Line Length	Line Size
up to 20'	75'	⅜"	100'	⅜"
20–25'	150'	⅜"	150'	⅜"
25–30'	200'	½"	200'	½"
30–40'	200'	½"	200'	½"
40–50'	250'	⅝"	300'	⅝"
50–70'	300'	¾"	350'	¾"

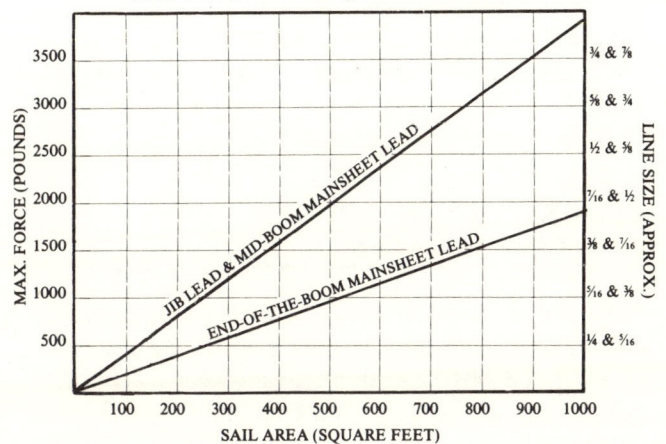

Maximum Force on Sheeting Gear versus Sail Area

79

Materials

For running rigging, you could say that Manila, made from the leaves of the abaca tree, is the traditional material. But given the low, low quality in which it is generally available today, I would not recommend it. Besides, Dacron, the standard contemporary choice for either three-strand or double-braid rope, is far stronger, lasts much longer, and doesn't stiffen or shrink when the weather turns wet.

"Spun" three-strand Dacron, in which the yarns are spun from a series of short fibers, is a preferred construction because of its comfortable feel. "Filament" Dacron, with the yarns made up of continuous fibers or filaments, is slicker but slightly stronger and is generally used on the racier boats. There are some very exotic Kevlar-cored ropes for those who want no stretch whatever, but owing to the expense and the tendency toward fatigue of those extreme plastics, I recommend good wire halyards with rope tails instead.

One other running-rigging choice, especially appropriate for traditional craft, is Roblon, a Danish product originally developed as a substitute for hemp aboard training ships. Roblon is an ultraviolet-stabilized split-fiber polypropylene—a multisyllabic way of saying that it won't break down in sunlight or chafe to pieces as fast as ordinary polypropylene does. Scandinavian farmers and fishermen discovered these attributes and adopted Roblon as a utility cordage. You still need to be very conscious of chafe with the stuff, using large blocks and making sure all leads are fair, but it is inexpensive, has a delightful feel to it, holds its lay, is easily spliced, and even floats. It's the rope I use on my boat.

BLOCKS, TANGS, HOUNDS, AND CHAINPLATES

Now we're really cookin'. Running and standing rigging are settled, and this means we have a clear idea of what the boat's character, and thus mechanical details, will be. If the standing rigging is fully served galvanized wire spliced around deadeyes, and the running rigging is Roblon, it follows that you'll set soft eyes around the mast rather than installing tangs. Your blocks might be stropped but will definitely be of wood, and chainplates will be hefty, maybe bent outward to clear a high bulwark rail.

On the other hand, you might, for some reason I'll never understand, have opted for rod rigging and gee-whiz cordage that stretches half an inch in a mile of length. Your attendant gear will almost certainly include superlight, superstrong plastic-and-alloy blocks, a multitude of two- or three-speed winches, streamlined upper terminals, and chainplates coming out of the deck frighteningly far inboard for close headsail sheeting.

Regardless of your preferences, it is important to follow through your design decisions. Don't put fiberglass gear on a wood boat, or vice versa, since not only aesthetics but structural qualities might clash. A good example is soft eyes for shrouds—a strong, simple, economical alternative to tangs. On tall rigs, however, the slight shifting of the eyes around the mast from tack to tack can result in appreciable mast bend that could endanger the mast and will certainly impair sailing performance. Then there are bronze turn-buckles: very nice, very strong. But if you spliced your 7 x 7 shrouds around heavy-duty thimbles, you will find that the thimbles will not fit into turnbuckles of corresponding strength. Bronze turnbuckles are made to fit swaged 1 x 19 these days.

For your mast's standing rigging, there's nothing wrong with using galvanized steel turnbuckles with either stainless or galvanized wire, but don't mix the two metals where electrolysis is likely to be severe, as on the lower ends of boomkin shrouds, bowsprit shrouds, and bobstays. For further discussion of electrolysis as it affects rigs, see Ross Norgrove's *Cruising Rigs and Rigging.*

So compatibility is the key to gear selection for a good working rig. Make lists, check catalogs, compare specs, think things through. Do you need to have every line leading to the cockpit? Are there enough of them to make color-coded rope worth the bother? Will people laugh at a sheer pole with belaying pins in it? Will the boat work well without it? Are you going to regret having a spinnaker, or not having one? Should it have a pole or not? Sop up all the data you can, let it slosh around inside for a while, and then *solve by association.* You understand the boat pretty well by now, so just pay attention to the engineering and use what suits—the gear that fits naturally with all the other gear. Don't let the sales rep from TurboWinch convince you that halyard jiggers went out with the mastodons, and don't let me convince you that roller-furling is the work of the devil. Although it is. You can match great, trustworthy systems to any rig style you can think of. Listen to counsel, compare opinions, but go with the gear that fits.

Traditional rigging involves not only the ability to turn up a good splice but to do it in the right materials in the right size, for the right boat. And to understand why.

CHAPTER 5
Loft Procedures

•

My loft is a factory, library, warehouse, office, laboratory, store, and museum. There I can contemplate and execute in a place made just for making rigs.

To hear me talk, you'd think this was some sort of intricately detailed, gizmo-filled fantasy shop, but it's really just a room in an old Odd Fellows Hall where I've bolted down some tools, filled the shelves with other tools and materials, and gone to work. There isn't anything I do in there that I couldn't and haven't done while up a mast, but I'd much rather work where everything is ready to hand. A rigging loft makes difficult work easy.

This chapter covers some of traditional rigging's most involved procedures: advanced ropework and ways to make a gang of rigging fit. You will find that the most difficult part of mastering these procedures lies not in comprehending their intricacies, but in training your hands and eyes; you must develop skill. Make your loft conducive to this. Make it quiet, uncluttered, orderly, and well lit. See to it that your tools are of appropriate size and good quality. Collect reference books. Leave a space where you can sit and think. Rigging work might take up only a small corner of your life in a small corner of your shop or garage, but it is sufficiently involved, in itself and in its relationship with other arts, that it requires no slight accommodation on your part before you can expect to do it well.

MEASUREMENT

Will it fit? God, what a headache of a question. Will it *fit*? Complete standing-rigging fabrication in the loft is the most efficient method, but you're in there, the boat's out there, and every time you turn up an end you ask yourself once again, "Will it fit?" Sometimes you can't stand the worry or can't get sufficiently precise measurements for confident cutting. Then you can splice the upper end in the loft, leave lots of extra length, and splice the lower end in place. It sounds convenient but seldom is; your working platform is crowded or moving or both, and it is wet, or cold, or hot, and you can't keep track of your tools, and there are too many people looking over your shoulder, and believe it or not there's still a very good chance you'll make a mistake in measurement. Better to work it all out at the loft, using measurement routines that are sufficiently precise and redundant to muffle that recurrent question, if not silence it.

Replacing An Old Rig

We'll start with a piece of cake, a little sloop whose gang has gone brittle. You want to replace it all with the same diameter and construction of wire. Get a notebook and pen and study the boat while the old gang is still in it, to see whether the last rigger measured right; no sense duplicating someone else's mistakes.

First of all, check the turnbuckles:

(1) Are they overextended or two-blocked (both threads drawn as close together as possible)? List each piece and note how much longer or shorter the new one will need to be.

(2) Are they toggled? Frequently not. Make a note to subtract the length of a toggle from the new piece.

(3) Are they the right size? Heavier turnbuckles are longer, lighter ones, shorter. Consult Table 4 to see whether wire and turnbuckle sizes match. If not, measure from the existing thimble's clevis-pin centerline to the chainplate's clevis-pin centerline and note the distance (Figure 116). Determine whether the new turnbuckle exceeds or falls short of that length, and adjust the new wire length accordingly. If the distance is 1 foot but the current turnbuckle is ridiculously heavy, the new turnbuckle might be, say, 8 inches long. The new wire will be 4 inches longer than the old one.

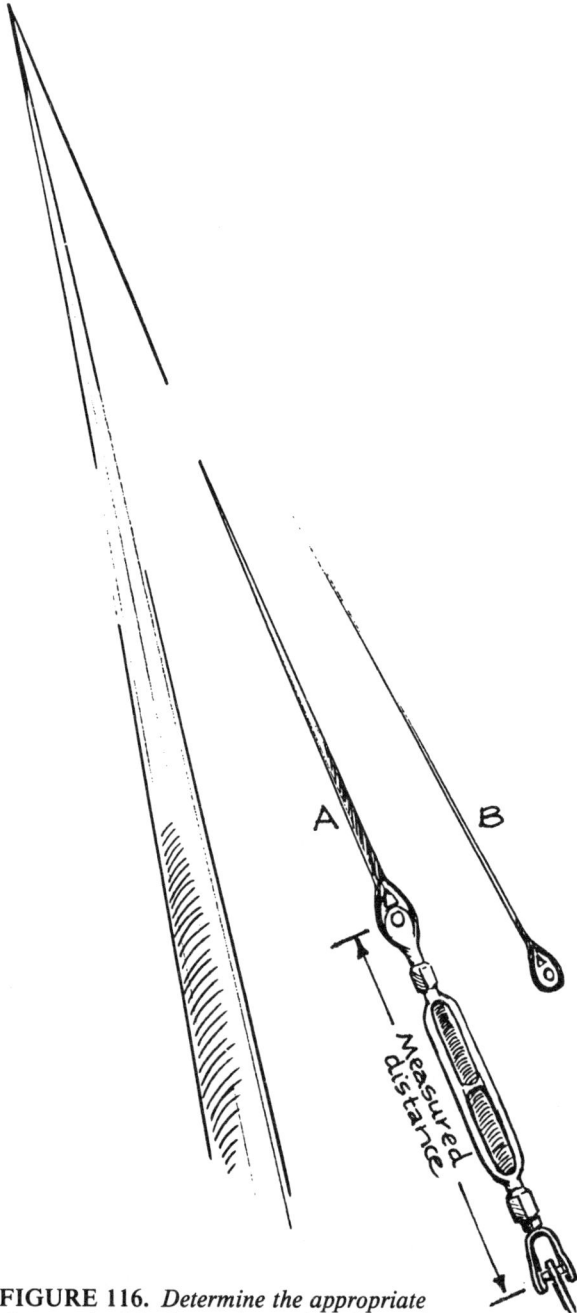

FIGURE 116. *Determine the appropriate size turnbuckle for a given wire size and construction, then measure the distance between the chainplate and thimble on the old rig (A). In this instance, the old turnbuckle is too large and two-blocked. If the distance is longer or shorter than the half-extended proper turnbuckle with toggle, add or subtract accordingly for the new wire length (B).*

TABLE 4. Matching Wire and Turnbuckle Sizes

Turnbuckle tensile strength figures vary depending upon manufacturers; for practical purposes it is safe to assume that bronze and galvanized steel turnbuckles of the same thread diameter have the same strength. Appropriate wire sizes are given in parentheses after each bronze or galvanized jaw width. Note that although 7x7 or 7x19 wire ropes can be made to fit bronze turnbuckles of corresponding strength, the narrow jaws of these turnbuckles, designed for 1x19 wire, make this difficult.

Turnbuckle Size Thread diameter (in.)	Tensile Strength (lbs.)		Jaw Width (in.)	
	Bronze	Galv. steel	Bronze (wire size 1x19)	Galv. steel (wire size 7x7 or 7x19)
¼	2,750	2,500	¼ (⅛)	13/32 (5/32)
5/16	4,300	4,000	5/16 (5/32)	15/32 (3/16)
⅜	6,500	6,000	⅜ (3/16)	½ (7/32-¼)
7/16	9,000	9,300	7/16 (7/32)	9/16 (5/16)
½	10,300	11,000	½ (¼-9/32)	⅝ (⅜)
⅝	17,000	17,500	⅝ (5/16-⅜)	¾ (7/16)
¾	29,000	26,000	¾ (7/16)	15/16 (½)
⅞	43,500	36,000	⅞ (½)	1⅛ (⅝)
1	56,500	50,000	1 (⅝)	1 3/16 (¾)

Next, check to see whether shackles have been added aloft or alow to extend the wire; note their length. See that chainplate, tang, and stem fittings are in good condition and lead properly, and find out whether the owner (if you are not the owner) intends to alter or replace any of them. If the upper terminals are spliced or seized soft eyes, see if they are of sufficiently large circumference to lead fairly from the mast (Figure 117). Try to think of any other variables peculiar to the particular boat and rig. When you can't think of anything else to note, remove the mast, tag all the pieces, and bring them back to your shop.

On a stretch of floor longer than the longest piece of the rig, lay out a tape measure; drive all but 2 or 3 inches of a large nail in at point "0," making sure "0" is not in the middle of a doorway or other traveled area. For long-term convenience, you might want to mark and number 1-foot intervals on the floor and use a short tape or measuring stick to measure smaller increments from these marks for each piece.

Now go off to the stationer, get an accounting pad, and fill it in as in Figure 118. In this case we have a pair of lower shrouds and one upper shroud on each side, plus forestay and jibstay. The "Diameter/Construc-tion" is a uniform 3/16-inch 7 x 7. "Configuration" is thimbled splice ("Th.") at both ends, and the combined turnbuckle and toggle length for all pieces is 11 inches.

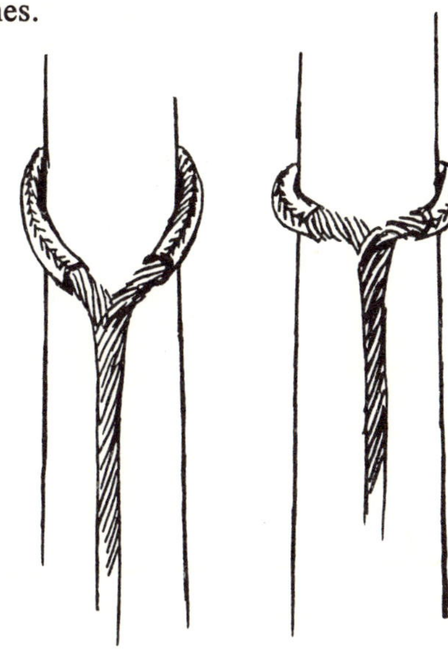

FIGURE 117. *Soft eyes should lead fairly from the mast* (left); *avoid a soft eye so small that considerable lateral strain comes on it* (right).

FIGURE 118. *To expedite layout organization, list rigging pieces, their pertinent dimensions, and any notes on an accounting pad.*

Schooner "Galatea"

	Piece	Diam/Constr.	Conf. Top/Bottom	Cut Length	Fin. Length	Thimble Circ./Length	Soft Eye Circ./Length	NOTES
1 Stbd	Main lower shroud	7/16"/7x7	S.Eye/Th.	29'	23'6"	7"/2"	2'6"	Jibstay eye has wire throat seizing
2 Pt.	Main lower shroud			29'2"	23'6"		2'6"	to form 7'4' eye.
3 Stbd	Main int. shroud			39'6"	34'		2'4"	
4 Pt.	Main int. shroud			40'	34'6"		2'4"	Marline serve shrouds 2' above thimbles
5 Stbd	Lower R.B. pend.			39'8"	24'		2'4"	
6 Pt.	Lower R.B. pend.			39'8"	24'		2'4"	Seize ring to each main int. shroud
7	Spare strop	5/16"/7x7	Grommet				3'	11" above thimble eye. Seize ring with
8	Triatic strop						2'6"	shackle to thimble of port forward
9	Triatic Stay	3/8"/7x7	Th./Th.	14'6"	11'6"	8"/3"		foremast shroud.
10	Fisherman Peak haly. strop	5/16"/7x7	Grommet				2'3"	
11	Springstay		S.Eye/Th.	22'2"	20'6"		1'2"	Eliminate chain from forestay. Use 1/2"
12 Stbd	Upper R.B. Pend.	5/16"/7x9	Th./Th.	51'6"	48'3"		1'2"	turnbuckle instead of 3/8" provided. Use 1/2"
13 Pt.	Upper R.B. pend			51'6"	48'3"		1'2"	std. thimbles with marline service under.
14 Stbd	Main upper shr.	3/8"/7x7	S.Eye/Th.	58'1"	48'		1'4"	
15 Pt.	Main upper shr.			58'1"	48'		1'4"	Eliminate turnbuckle on springstay?
16	Main topping lift strop	1/4"/7x7	Grommet				2'3"	
17 Stbd	Forward foremast shroud	3/8"/7x7	S.Eye/Th.	36'2"	31'6"		1'5"	Triatic strop has 22" eye, seized
18 Pt.	Forward foremast shroud			36'2"	31'6"		1'5"	around thimble. Use 1/2" shackle.
19 Stbd	Aft foremast shroud			30'	25'6"		2'4"	
20 Pt.	Aft foremast shroud			30'	25'6"		2'4"	
21	Forestay strop	5/16"/7x7	Grommet					
22	Forestay		Th. Th.	30'7"	27'			
23	Throat halyard strop		S.Eye/Th.	5'6"			2'1"	
24	Jib halyard strop			4'6"			1'5"	
25	Jibstay	7/16"/7x7		40'5"	34'6"	8"/2 1/2"	1'8"	

83

Skipping over to "Notes," we might enter something like:

> All shroud turnbuckles correct diameter ($^5/_{16}$") and at consistent ½ extension [ideal] but lack toggles. Subtract 1½" from all shroud lengths to fit toggles.
> Forestay has overextended ⅜" turnbuckle and two shackles. Stay too short. Space between thimble head and stem fitting: 16". Add 5" to new forestay length to leave 11" space for $^5/_{16}$" turnbuckle and toggle.
> $^5/_{16}$" jibstay turnbuckle two-blocked, no toggle. Space between thimble bottom and stem fitting: 7¾". No slack in jibstay w/ two-blocked turnb., so subtract 3½" from length to fit ½-extended turnbuckle and toggle.

Use abbreviations on your notes if you wish; just be sure you'll know what you're talking about when you come back.

Get out the starboard after lower shroud, set one thimble over the nail, stretch the wire, and check its length to the bottom of the other thimble. According to our notes we want to subtract 1½ inches from this length to add a toggle. If the old piece is 12 feet, enter 11 feet 10½ inches under "Finished Length" opposite "starboard after lower shroud."

Now stretch out the port after lower shroud, which is not necessarily the same length as its starboard-side counterpart. Slight irregularities in mast or hull can easily make a significant difference. In this case the lengths match, and 11 feet 10½ inches is entered for this wire, too.

Repeat this procedure for the starboard and port forward lowers, then lay out the starboard upper. Its length is, say, 20 feet. In wire this length we begin to worry about "constructional stretch," the initial elongation of new wire as its individual strands settle into place under load. The short length of the lowers would result in negligible stretch, and it wouldn't amount to much in a 20-foot length either, but to be cautious, refer to Table 5 showing approximate constructional stretch in percentage of length for various kinds of wire rope. Our 7 x 7 preformed carbon steel will stretch 0.06 percent of its length. This works out to a little over ⅛ inch, not enough to bother deducting from the length of the new wire, so for both uppers we'll just subtract 1½ inches for the toggle.

If we were instead using 7 x 19 stainless wire for the rig, constructional stretch over the same length would have amounted to over ¾ inch, enough to use up an excessive amount of turnbuckle slack; it would have been better to deduct this plus the toggle length from the original length for the new piece.

TABLE 5. **Wire Rope Constructional Stretch as Percentage of Length**
(Courtesy MacWhyte Co.)

	7x19	7x7	1x19
Galv. steel	0.25	0.06	0.018
Stainless steel	0.33	0.07	0.021

Moving to the jib- and forestays, subtract 3½ inches from the former and add 5 inches to the latter, as per notes, to obtain finished lengths.

Thimble Length and Circumference

It is one thing to measure thimble head to thimble head for a finished length, quite another to cut a piece of wire that, when spliced, will have the required length. There are several complications. First, in order to reach the thimble head the wire must detour around the thimble's contours; there is thus a considerable difference between thimble length and eye circumference. We need to know how much extra wire to add for a given thimble length. Second, as you'll see in the "Service" section of this chapter, some thimble eyes are oversized to allow for replacing damaged thimbles. With this configuration, one must allow for thimble circumference plus twice the length (the two legs of the eye) from splice crotch to thimble foot. Some anatomy. Third, since the measuring point is inside the thimble and not at the wire surface, deduction must be made for the thickness of each thimble size and type.

The easiest way to solve these problems is to set up a sample eye using the same size wire and thimble that will be used in the actual rig. With the eye clamped in place, measure the distance from thimble head to splice crotch. Then mark this latter point on both sides, remove the wire from the vise, straighten it, and measure the distance between the two points. This gives you the thimble-eye circumference. In our case, the thimble length is 1¾ inches and the circumference is 4½ inches. (To find thimble circumference when precise eye length is not important (as when making slings or pendants), use the technique in Figure 119.)

To put this information to work, start again with the

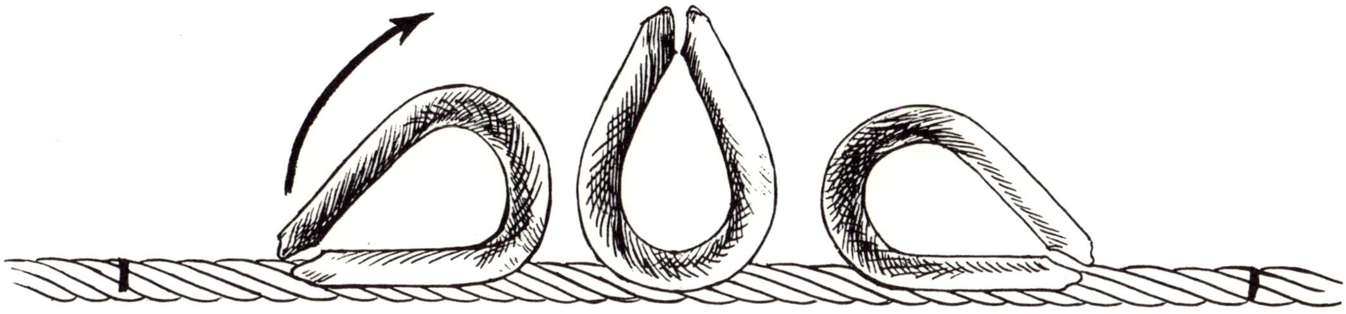

FIGURE 119. *Rolling a thimble along the wire is one way to determine approximate thimble circumference. Add a bit extra for an oversized eye.*

starboard after lower shroud (Figure 120). Subtracting a thimble length (1¾ inches) from each end leaves 11 feet 7 inches. Proper length is restored by adding a thimble circumference (4½ inches) to each end. Finally, add enough length to splice with, in this case 12 inches to each end (see Liverpool Splice, this chapter). After these assorted additions and subtractions we end up with 14 feet 4 inches to enter under "Cut Length." If you take a wire that length and use 2 feet of it to make two splices with 4½-inch-circumference eyes around thimbles, you will most assuredly get a shroud that is 11 feet 10½ inches long.

Repeat this procedure with the other wires to obtain the rest of the cut lengths.

Measuring Soft Eyes

The above procedure also works for eyes made around deadeyes, lizards, or other thimble-like objects, but a soft eye—an eye made around a mast—poses a couple of extra problems. First, soft eyes might travel at various angles across a mast, ranging from horizontal to a steep diagonal, depending on the rig. How can we determine eye length and circumference for an eye at any angle? Second, what portion of the finished length of the wire does the eye constitute?

For a nearly horizontal lead, the simplest though seldom-seen case, the eye rests on a "stop," a shoulder formed by a reduction of mast diameter at the desired height. An obvious and simple procedure is to measure the circumference of the mast above the shoulder and make an eye of this circumference. Unfortunately, this results in an eye that is far too small, since there's no allowance for the thickness of the wire (Figure 121). One response is to add wire diameter (including its layers of service and leather) to mast diameter, giving

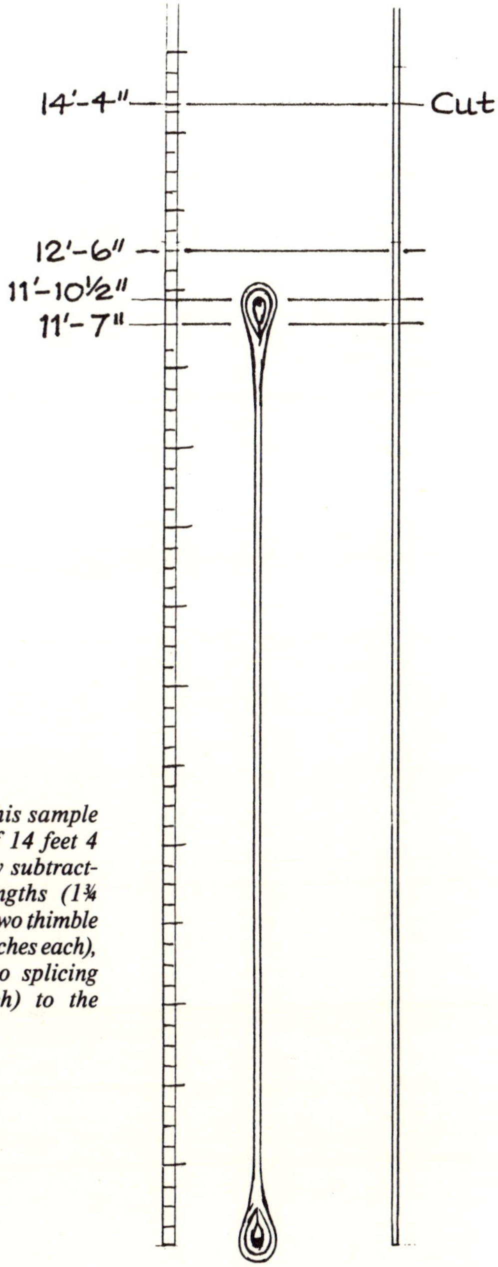

FIGURE 120. *In this sample case, a cut length of 14 feet 4 inches is obtained by subtracting two thimble lengths (1¾ inches each), adding two thimble circumferences (4½ inches each), and also adding two splicing lengths (1 foot each) to the finished length.*

85

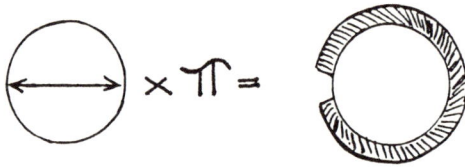

FIGURE 121. *Making an eye exactly the mast circumference doesn't work, because wire thickness isn't allowed for.*

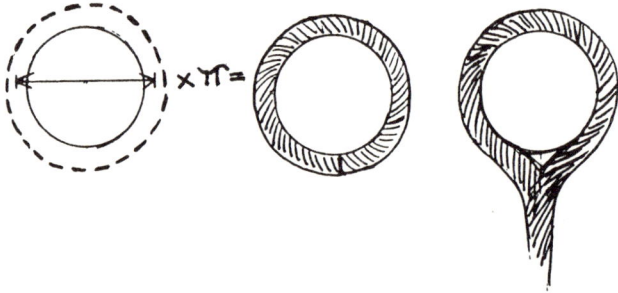

FIGURE 122. *Adding wire diameter to mast diameter and multiplying the sum by pi gives a true working circumference, but this would still result in too tight an eye, even for eyes that fit on "stops"; add just enough length so the eye will fit easily on the mast.*

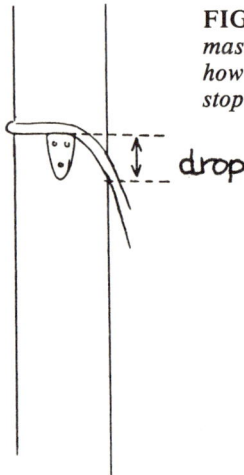

FIGURE 123. *A sample eye on the mast, or on a dummy mast, will show how much an eye will "drop" from a stop or bolster.*

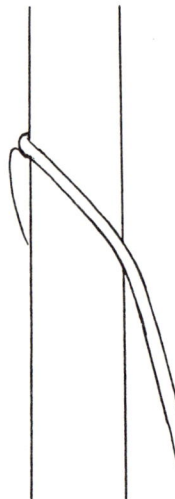

FIGURE 124. *Thumb cleats and long, fair leads characterize soft eyes on Bermudian-rigged craft.*

a "working diameter" that extends to the center of the wire on either side (Figure 122). Pi x Working Diameter = Eye Circumference. The eye can still be too tight to be practical, however; the wire has to bend at nearly a right angle where it exits the seizing. Wire rope is reluctant to do this, and the seizing would in any event be put under extreme lateral strain. Add another 2 inches or so to the eye circumference and you'll have an eye that goes on more easily and has a better lead out of the seizing, but is still tight enough to stay securely on its shoulder. To determine what the resulting sag adds to the finished length, put a sample eye on the actual mast, or a dummy section, and measure the drop (Figure 123).

Eyes sometimes rest not on stops but on "bolsters" affixed to trestletrees at a mast top. These eyes can be considerably larger than those that go to stops, one-and-one-quarter times mast circumference being a standard size that provides a good lead and allows the seizing to clear the bolster. Again, sag is measured on the actual or a dummy mast.

When stacking successive eyes on a stop or top, add the thickness of each eye to the finished length of the next eye.

The lightest, strongest soft-eye configuration—what you want for a Bermudian or high-efficiency gaff-rigged vessel—features an arrangement in which thumb-cleat–like bolsters are affixed to the side of the mast opposite the strain (Figure 124). This allows for the fairest lead and thus the greatest strength of any soft-eye configuration; the wire follows a gradual curve from the bolster to the splice or seizing, the two legs meeting at an angle that, ideally, does not exceed 90 degrees, and can be as low as 60 degrees. The smaller the angle, the less strain each leg bears.

Since Bermudian and efficient gaff rigs are light and precisely designed, approximate measures will result in poor fit, ill appearance, and impaired efficiency. So for a properly engineered soft eye, fire up your traditional electronic calculator with basic trigonometric functions and prepare to lay out the Ideal Soft Eye.

Start by establishing Working Circumference—Pi x (Mast Diameter + Wire Diameter)—and divide this figure by two. This gives you enough wire to get halfway around the mast (Figure 125). We next need to calculate how long the "legs" must be if they are to intersect at the seizing at an angle of, say, 70 degrees. To do this divide one-half the Working Diameter (Mast Diameter + Wire Diameter) by sin 35°. The result will be the length of one of the legs. Double this figure and add the result to one-half the Working Circumference, and you have the circumference of the desired eye.

Why does this work? In Figure 125-B, one line is drawn from the center of the mast to the intersection of the legs, a second line is drawn from the center of the mast, at right angles to the first line, for a distance equal to one-half the Working Diameter, and a third line is drawn connecting the free ends of the first two. This process forms a right triangle, the relationships among whose proportions were long ago worked out in exquisite detail. These relationships are in the program of any calculator equipped with trigonometric functions. Among other things, these functions enable one to start with the length of any one side and the value of one of the two acute angles and determine the length of the other two sides. In Figure 125-B, we have the length of one side of our triangle—6 inches is one-half the Working Diameter—and we know the angle 35 degrees—one-half the desired convergence angle of 70 degrees. What you want to know right now is how long that hypotenuse is. Turn on your calculator. Punch in "35" and hit the "sine" button; you should get "0.5735764." This is the ratio between the side we know (the side opposite the angle 35 degrees) and the side we want; to put it in mathematical form, $\dfrac{6}{X} = 0.5735764$. Transposing these numbers to isolate X, we get $X = \dfrac{6}{0.5735764}$, so X, the length of the side we want, is 10.46 or approximately 10½ inches.

The legs are 10½ inches each—21 inches taken together—and the half-circumference is 10⅜ inches, so the total soft-eye circumference in this case is 31⅜ inches (Figure 125-C). Put an eye this size on the mast or dummy mast to see how far it drops, and calculate the rest of the shroud length from the point where the seizing or splice touches the mast. If this wire is a shroud, its mate will fit over it, thereby losing a little length. To compensate for this, make the second eye circumference longer than the first by twice the wire diameter, including service and leather.

Measuring for a New Rig

If you skipped over all that trigonometric hoo-haw, figuring you'd just eyeball eye size, you're in big

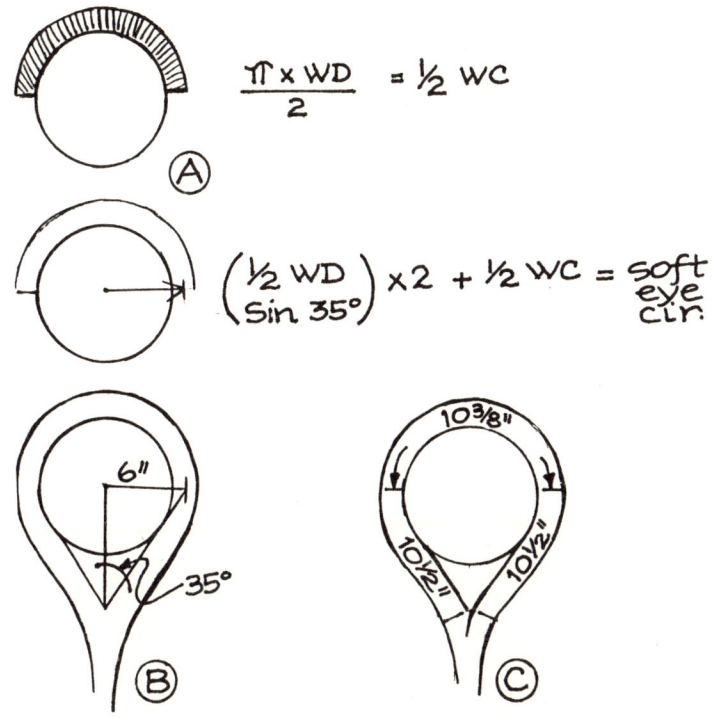

$$\frac{\pi \times WD}{2} = \tfrac{1}{2}\,WC$$

$$\left(\frac{\tfrac{1}{2}\,WD}{\sin 35°}\right) \times 2 + \tfrac{1}{2}\,WC = \text{soft eye cir.}$$

FIGURE 125. *Arriving at the Ideal Soft Eye circumference.*

trouble now. That was a way of showing you a useful procedure while introducing some mathematics that are central to what follows. When you don't have an old rig to base measurements on but you still want to turn up both ends in the loft, trigonometry can be a very good friend to know.

The measurements we'll make in this section are for a new gang of rigging for *Katy,* my 16-foot catboat, designed by Sam Crocker about 1933. The old rig design wasn't quite what I wanted, so sailor and aristocrat David Ryder-Turner came up with the sliding-gunter arrangement shown in Figure 126.

The first thing I want to do is check David's work. Ahem. What I mean is that I'm interested in finding out what angles the shrouds and forestay make relative to the mast. For most vessels this angle should be 10 to 12 degrees, but in this case the rig is intended more to check the motion of the mast than to turn it into a compression member, and low stresses are involved.

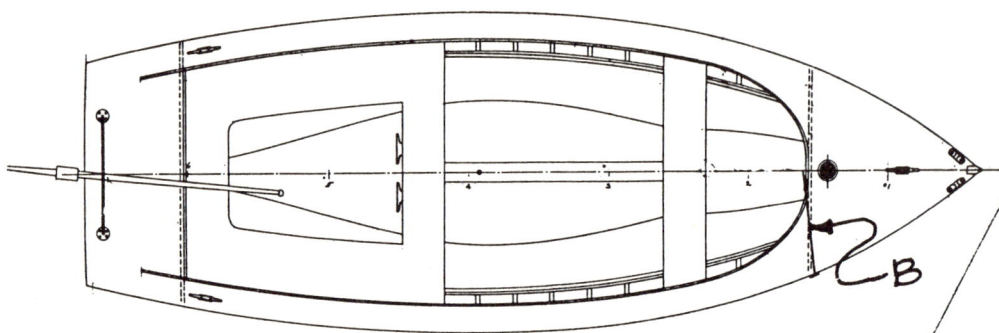

FIGURE 126. *The sail and deck plans of Katy. The dotted line in the sail plan represents the vertical leg of a right triangle (A). The line crossing to the chainplate on the deck plan is the base of the triangle (B). The proper shroud length is represented by the hypotenuse of the right triangle (C). To determine the shroud angle relative to the mast, find the arctangent of the ratio between base and height. In this case, the angle is 8.58 degrees.*

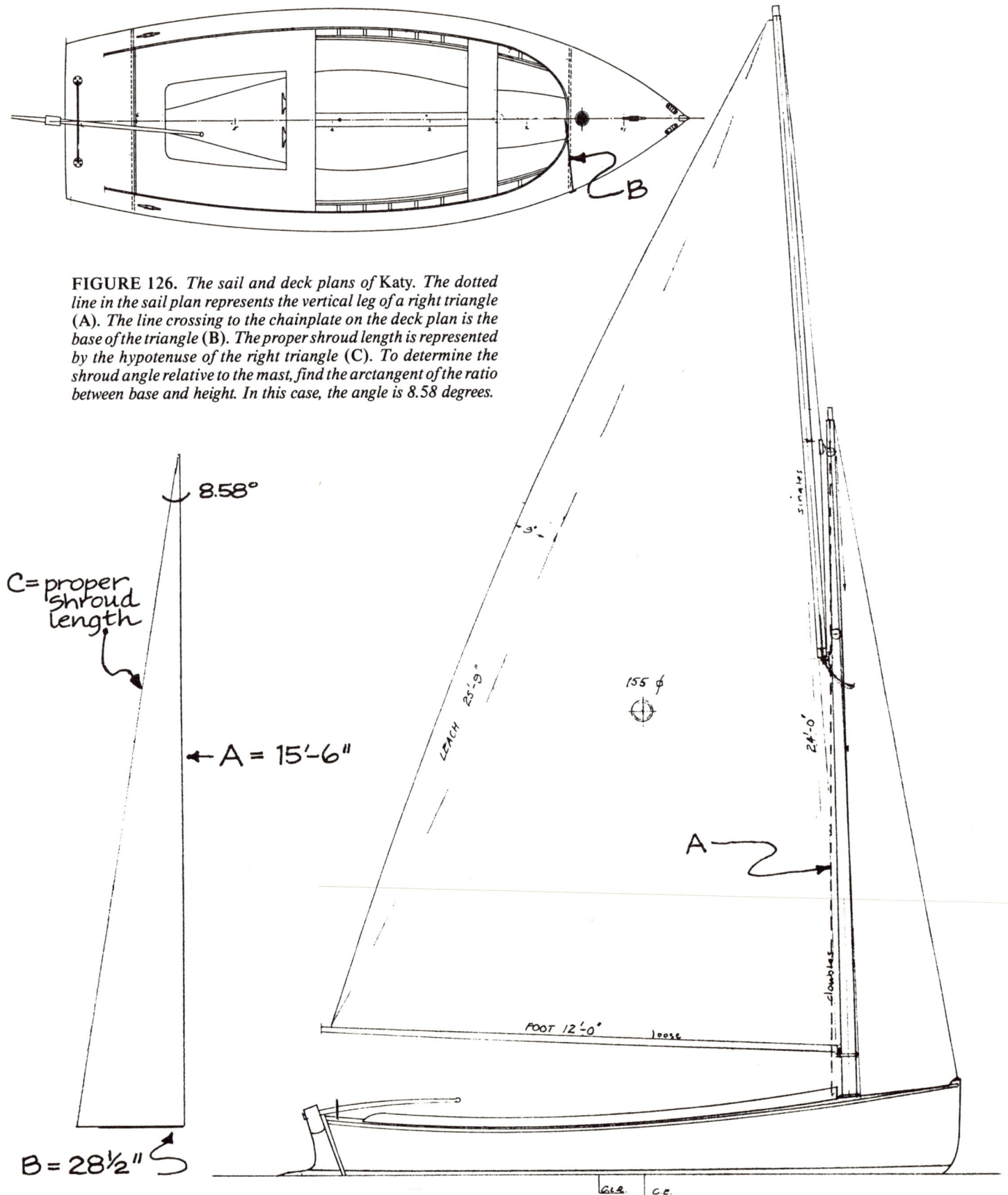

8.58°

C = proper shroud length

← A = 15'-6"

LEACH 25'-9"

155 φ

24'-0'

A

FOOT 12'-0"   loose

B = 28½"

A somewhat lesser staying angle ought to suffice. In order to find out what the designed angle is, I'll construct a right triangle for the shrouds based on the sail and deck plans shown in Figure 126. The base is 28½ inches and the length is 15 feet 6 inches. In a right triangle, the ratio of base/height is the "tangent" of the angle opposite the base. (For a fuller explanation of trigonometric functions, see *Understanding Calculator Math*, available from Radio Shack.) In this case, the tangent is 0.1507936, and a tangent of 0.1507936 means that the angle at the top (represented by the symbol θ) is 8.58 degrees. How do I know? Because my calculator tells me so. It has a key on it marked "tan^{-1}," a function sometimes written out as "arctangent." If 0.1507936 is the tangent of angle θ, then θ is the arctangent of 0.1507936. If you enter 0.1507936 on your calculator and then hit "tan^{-1}," you'll get 8.58 degrees, the angle of the shrouds relative to *Katy*'s mast. A glance at the staying angle–stress curve (Figure 98) reassures me that this angle should be sufficient for *Katy*.

Another example: The right triangle for the forestay has a base of 2 feet 6 inches and a height of 15 feet 6 inches. The tangent of the angle in question is given by $\dfrac{\text{base}}{\text{height}} = \dfrac{2.5}{15.5} = 0.1612903$, and the arctangent $= 9.162347$. The forestay angle relative to the mast is 9.2 degrees. Because staying angles are inversely proportional to standing-rigging loads, the tangent and arctangent functions are of particular value to the rigger.

Hypotenuse and Wire Length

> Of all the words of rigger's wit,
> The saddest are these: "It doesn't fit!"

Thimbles and soft eyes affect finished length, but of course the major determinant of rig fit is length between terminals. Because the sail plan appears to show wire length, many people scale their lengths from it. Their rigs are too short. "Ahh," say others, "but that's why we have the rigging plan" (Figure 127), and they scale their lengths from it. Their rigs are too short. The sail plan has no depth, so does not show length-consuming thwartships shroud travel, although it is accurate for fore-and-aft wires, which have no thwartships travel. The rigging plan has no depth, so does not show length-consuming fore-and-aft travel, although it

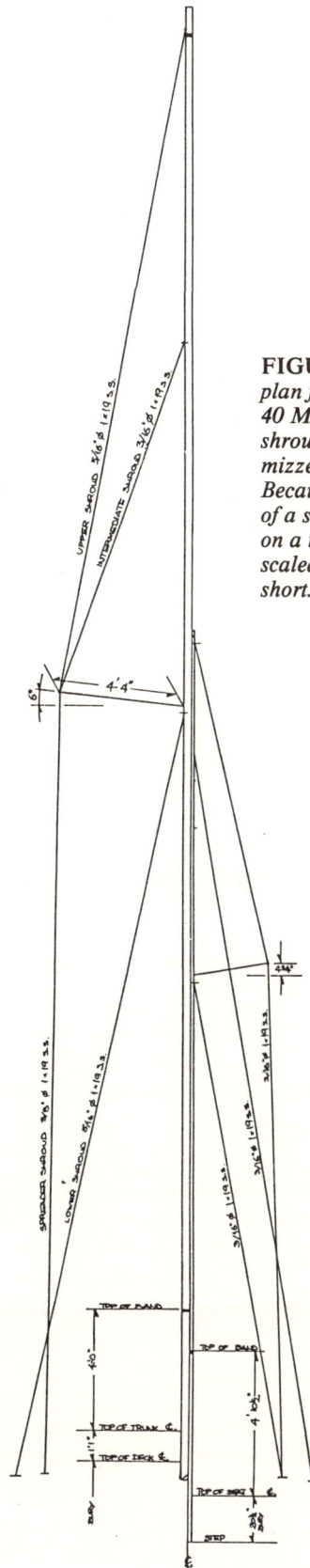

FIGURE 127. *The rigging plan for a Hinckley Bermuda 40 Mark III yawl. Mainmast shrouds are shown on the left, mizzen shrouds, on the right. Because the fore-and-aft angle of a shroud does not show up on a rigging plan, shrouds scaled from one will be too short.*

FIGURE 128. *To obtain a base length when a house or other obstacle intrudes, measure straight out, make a 90-degree turn, and measure straight to the chainplate. The square root of the sum of the squares of these two lengths is the desired base length.*

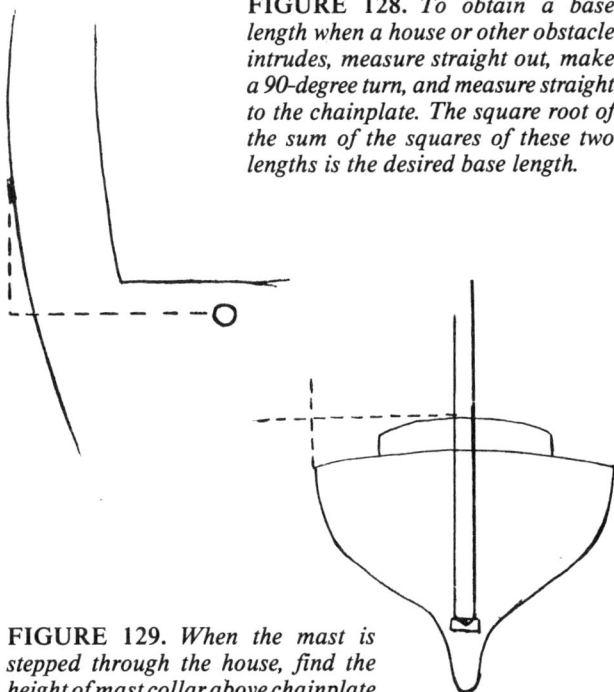

FIGURE 129. *When the mast is stepped through the house, find the height of mast collar above chainplate by measuring horizontally out to a plumb-bob line at the chainplate (assuming the vessel is level in both planes). Proceed as in Figure 128.*

figures plus the square of the height is also the square of the hypotenuse. If the mast is stepped through a house, or if some other impediment makes a direct horizontal measurement from mast to chainplate impossible, use plumb bobs and level to establish the distance (Figure 129). Add the distance from chainplate to intersection "A" to the height of the mast. If the chainplates do not project far above the rail, deck camber alone can necessitate this procedure.

To measure the length of wires that pass over spreaders, proceed in two steps. First, find the point on deck directly below the spreader tip. To do this draw a vertical line on the sail plan from the spreader tip to intersect the deck, then measure how far aft of the stem this intersection is. Turn to the deck plan and measure from the stem aft the same distance, then measure out from the hull centerline the length of the spreader plus one-half the diameter of the mast at spreader height (Figure 130). Measure and square the distance from this point to the chainplate on the deck plan, square the height of the spreader above the chainplate on the sail plan, add the two figures, hit the square root key, and you'll have the distance from chainplate to spreader.

The second step is a lot simpler: Square the spreader length plus one-half the mast diameter at the spreaders, add the square of the vertical distance between the spreader and the shroud's upper end, and find this square root for the length of the shroud above the spreaders. If rake is negligible, you can scale this length directly from the rigging plan. Add the two figures to get the total wire length.

Spreader wires are the most difficult to measure accurately and present the greatest opportunity for error, so don't be tempted by shortcuts. Be picky.

For a tang rig, measure from the mast attachment of the tang down to the chainplate. When you've established total length, subtract tang length from the upper end and turnbuckle-and-toggle or lanyard length from the lower end.

Given that builders do not always build what designers design, first-hand measurements should be made whenever possible, even if you have all the plans. Track down and take into account any discrepancies between the plans and the real thing. If, for instance, you get a measurement of 40 feet from the actual mast but the sail plan says 40 feet 3 inches, don't automatically assume that the mast height is shorter than designed; the boatbuilder might have decided that the mast step was too thin, installed one that was 3 inches thicker, taken 3 inches off the mast to compensate, and forgotten to tell you. But this

is accurate for the rare shroud that has no fore-and-aft travel. Each plan shows a dimension that the other does not; our problem is how to get the vertical, thwartships, and fore-and-aft dimensions in one place. That's why I used the sail and *deck* plan to construct the right triangle for *Katy's* shroud. Height was taken off the sail plan and fore-and-aft and thwartships travel off the deck plan. We could now measure wire length from our diagram, but for greater precision let's return to trigonometry, which tells us that "the square of the hypotenuse is equal to the sum of the squares of the other two sides." For *Katy's* forestay, the sum of the squares is 35,496 inches. The square root of this is 15 feet 8½ inches, the length of the stay.

Some fine points:

If the mast rakes, do not use it for the vertical leg of the triangle. Draw a true vertical line from the upper point of attachment to the deck.

If plans are unavailable, measure directly from the actual mast and deck. Be sure to account for rake. If a house or other obstruction prevents you from measuring a straight line from mast base to chainplate, first measure out to the rail, then aft or forward to the chainplate (Figure 128). The squares of these two

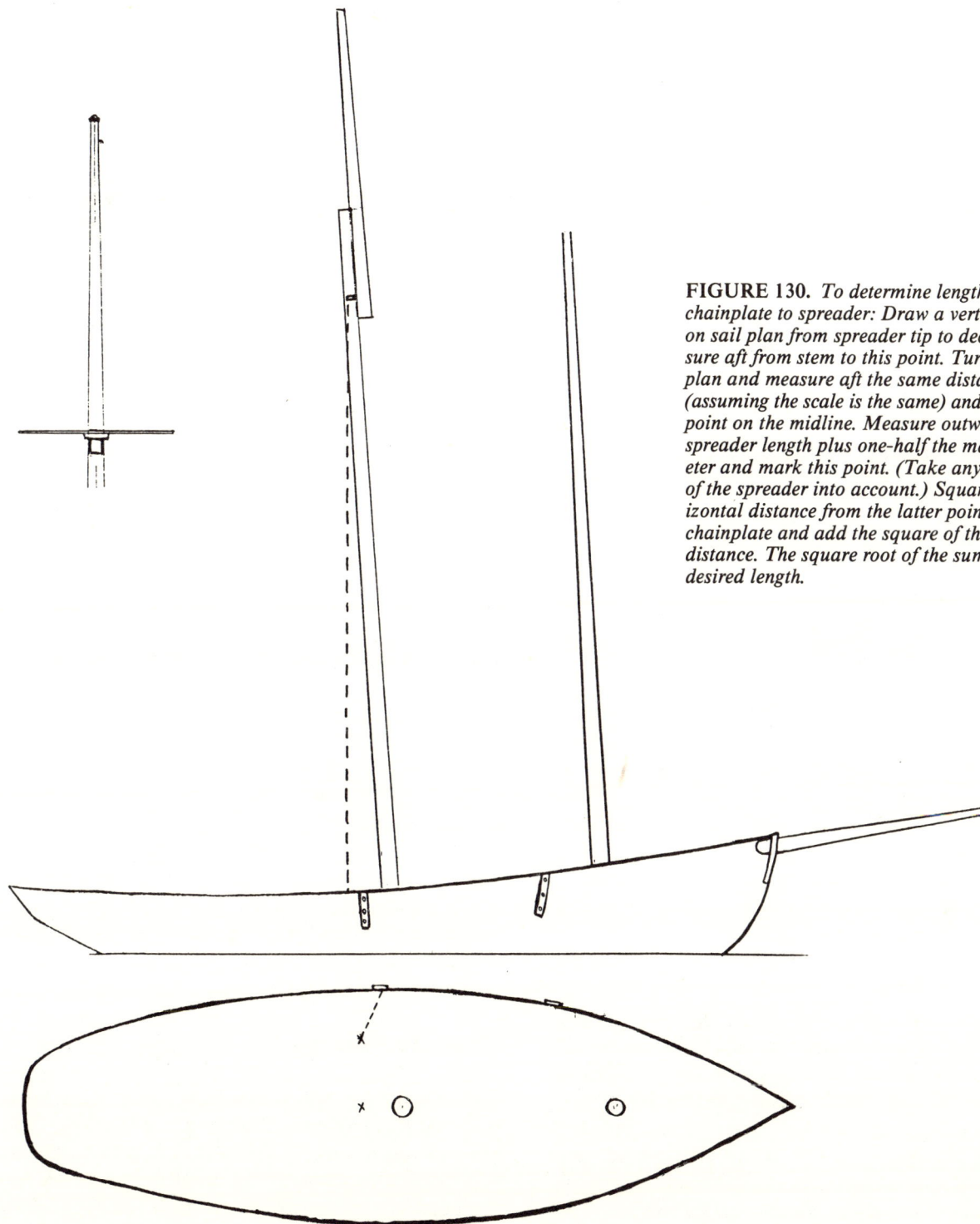

FIGURE 130. *To determine length from chainplate to spreader: Draw a vertical line on sail plan from spreader tip to deck. Measure aft from stem to this point. Turn to deck plan and measure aft the same distance (assuming the scale is the same) and mark this point on the midline. Measure outward one spreader length plus one-half the mast diameter and mark this point. (Take any aft swing of the spreader into account.) Square the horizontal distance from the latter point to the chainplate and add the square of the vertical distance. The square root of the sum is the desired length.*

discrepancy will show up, if no other changes have been made, in the distance from step to partners.

Lofting

An alternative method of rig measurement involves making base and height measurements, plotting them on the floor and one wall of a large room, and directly measuring the shroud or stay length with a tape measure. This is full-scale lofting, analogous to the system boatbuilders use to lay out hull shapes. It requires a level floor, a straight wall at right angles to that floor, and the careful transfer of measurements taken from vessel or plans or both to obtain an accurate result. Trigonometry is quicker.

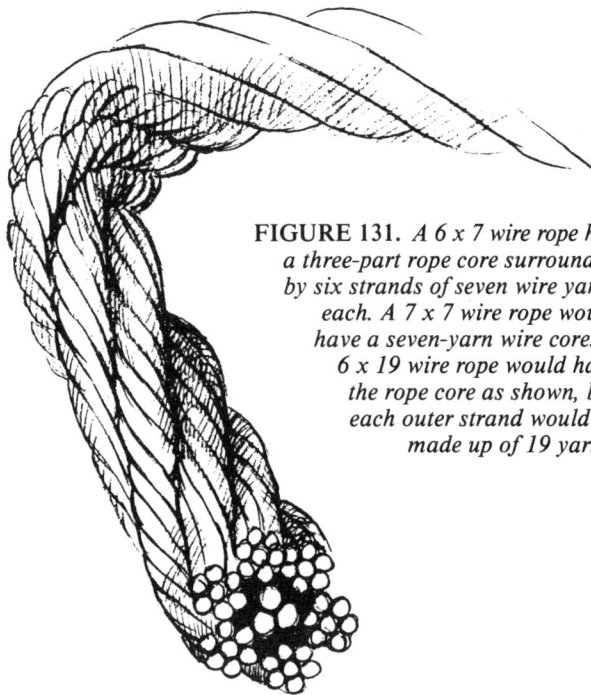

FIGURE 131. *A 6 x 7 wire rope has a three-part rope core surrounded by six strands of seven wire yarns each. A 7 x 7 wire rope would have a seven-yarn wire core. A 6 x 19 wire rope would have the rope core as shown, but each outer strand would be made up of 19 yarns.*

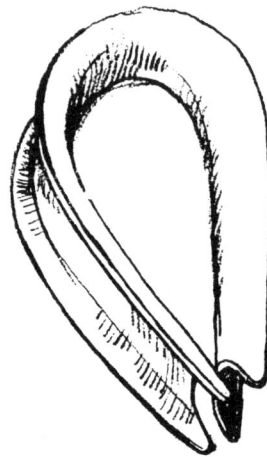

FIGURE 132. *A wire rope thimble.*

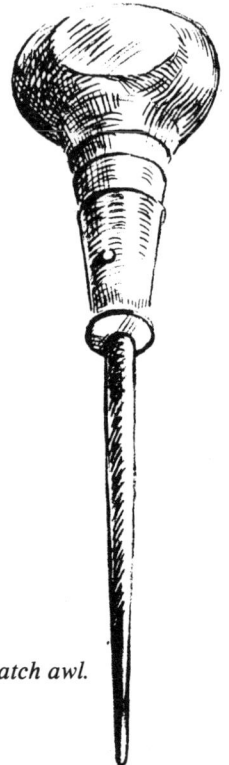

FIGURE 133. *A spike made from a scratch awl.*

THE LIVERPOOL EYESPLICE MADE DIFFICULT

"Life is too short to splice wire rope."
- Bernard Moitessier, circumnavigator and author

"Any idiot can do it."
- Nick Benton, master rigger

Braiding a tremendously strong steel squid into itself is a formidable task. But that is exactly what faces any would-be wire splicer, and it is one reason why there are so few of them. Score one for Moitessier.

On the other hand, a little study, preparation, and care will enable even the most slow-witted and clumsy-fingered among us to produce a sound, relatively painless splice. Score one for Benton, who never tires of telling me that I am living proof of this view.

The truth lies somewhere in between: The job is neither easy nor onerous, just difficult. It is up to the individual to decide if learning the Liverpool Eyesplice is worth the effort.

The variation described here is loaded with details that add strength and longevity. And difficulty. But if you practice enough, you should be able to produce a splice that is as good as any the professional lofts can offer. If you are not interested in taking spike in hand yourself, the instructions here will acquaint you with the details of a good splice, so that you can make an informed decision when the time comes to hire a professional.

Tools and Materials

Part of splicing is knowing what to splice: Each job has different requirements. For the job of learning, use an easy-to-splice wire: oilfree 5/16-inch galvanized wire rope with a fiber heart. The construction to ask for is 6 x 7 or 6 x 19 (Figure 131); both are readily available at hardware or marine-supply stores. This type of wire is low-cost, supple, and easy to handle.

Speaking of ease, use a rigging vise. Manufacturers advertise in the boating magazine classified sections. As in branding or diaper changing, the trick with wire work is to keep a firm grip on the subject. A vise won't help you with calves and babies, but even the occasional splicer will find it worthwhile for greatly reducing setup time and effort while improving splice quality.

92

① ② ③ ④

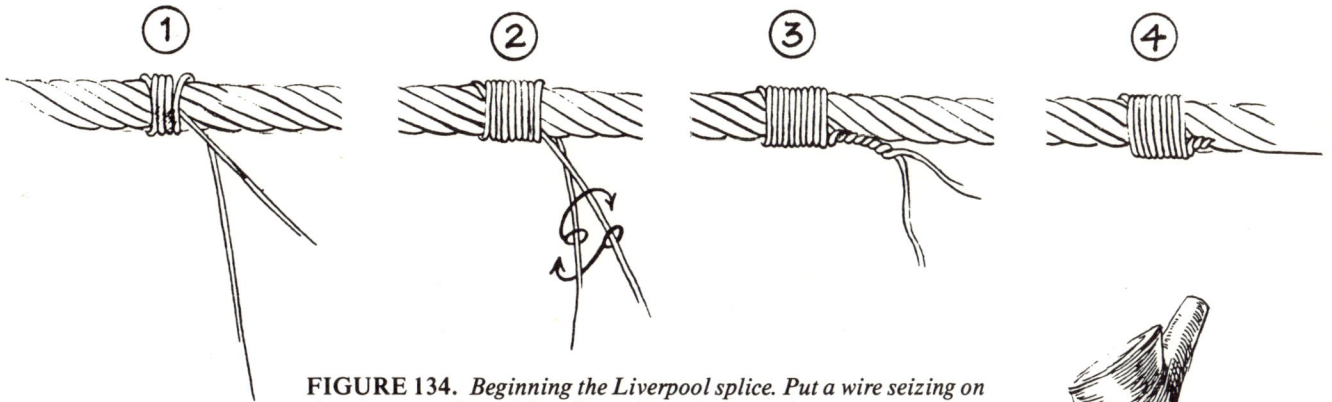

FIGURE 134. *Beginning the Liverpool splice. Put a wire seizing on the wire rope about 1 foot from the end of the wire...*

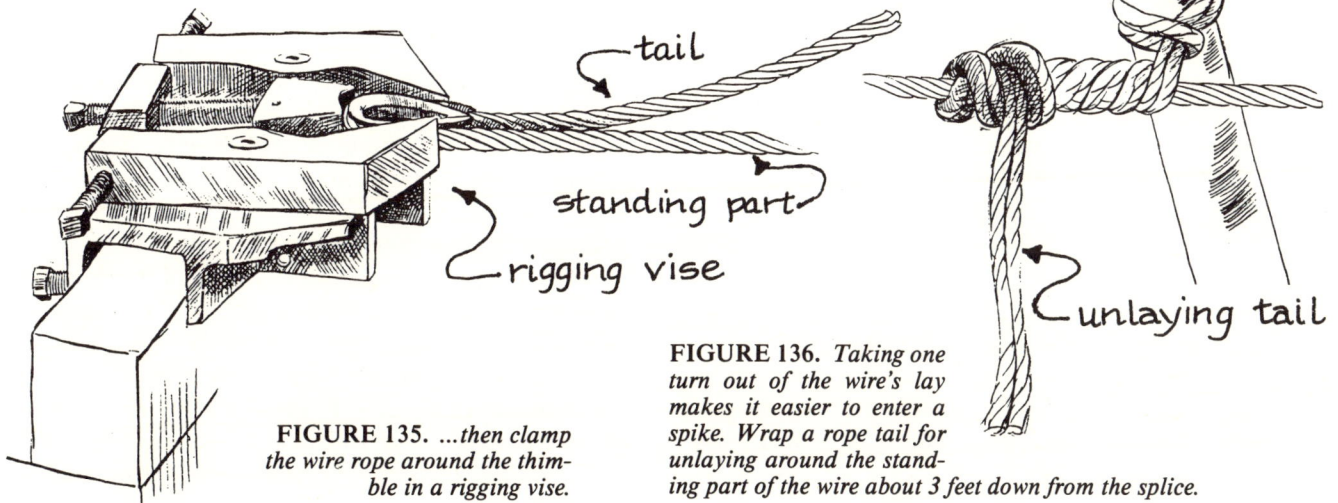

tail

standing part

rigging vise

FIGURE 135. *...then clamp the wire rope around the thimble in a rigging vise.*

unlaying tail

FIGURE 136. *Taking one turn out of the wire's lay makes it easier to enter a spike. Wrap a rope tail for unlaying around the standing part of the wire about 3 feet down from the splice.*

The third basic ingredient is a spike. For this size wire, a large scratch awl (Stanley 7A or equivalent) is perfect, once you file a flat, rounded tip on it.

You'll also need some nippers to trim the splice, a mallet—preferably of hardwood, brass, or lead—to fair it, a bit of seizing wire, and safety goggles. An optional item is an unlaying line, a stick with a braided rope tail that is used to untwist the wire slightly, making it easier to enter the spike into the wire.

Setting Up

The first step in making a splice is to put a wire seizing on the wire rope near the rope's end (Figure 134). It will keep the wire from unlaying too far and will make it easier for you to put an even strain on all strands. The formula for the seizing position is: Allow 1 foot of splicing length for every inch of wire circumference. The ⁵⁄₁₆-inch wire you are using for practice is about 1 inch in circumference, so put the seizing on 1 foot from

the end. Half-inch wire, to use another example, is 1½ inches in circumference, so its seizing would be 1½ feet from the end.

Clamp your vise in place at elbow height, and clamp the wire in the vise around a ⁵⁄₁₆-inch thimble with the seizing at the end of the thimble and just outside the jaws. Be sure that the tail is on the far side of the standing part, as shown in Figure 135. Tighten the vise jaws to hold the thimble snugly against the wire, and then lead the standing part out horizontally. (Splices can be made either horizontally or vertically; which way is better is a subject of frequent and earnest debate among riggers—one of those Ford-versus-Chevy questions that comes down to personal taste. Like any sane, intelligent individual, I always splice horizontally.) Tie or clamp the wire in place with moderate tension on the standing part, as if it were slack rigging.

If you're using the unlaying line, wrap it on tightly, against the wire lay, about 3 feet from the vise. Pass the stick around once and brace it. You're ready.

93

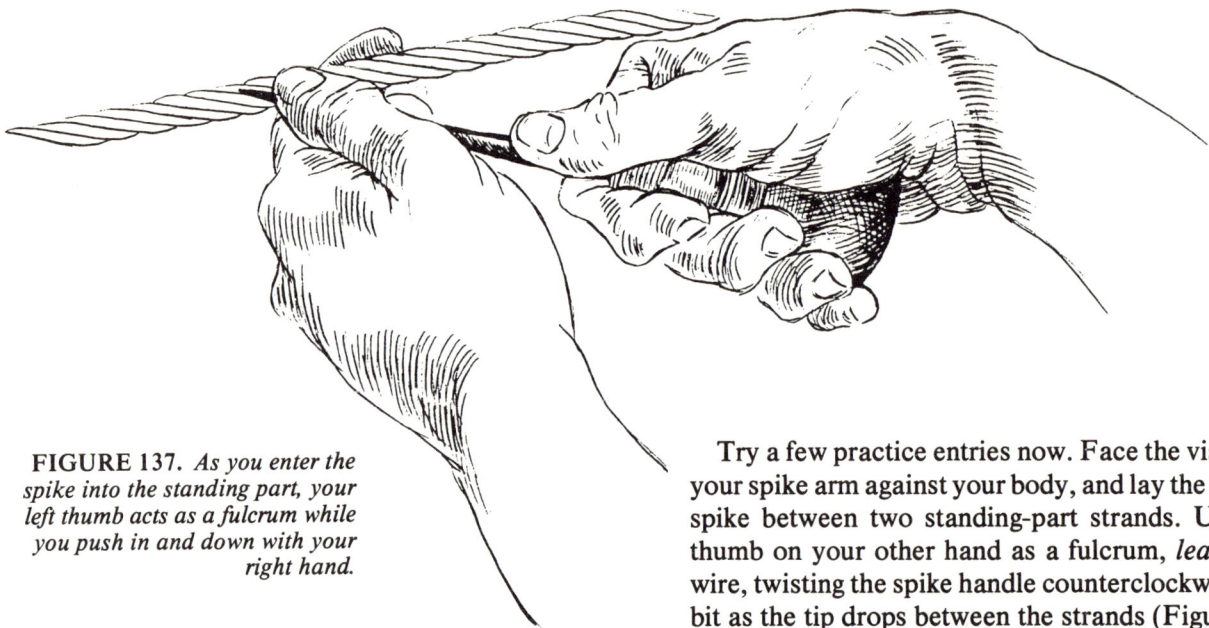

FIGURE 137. *As you enter the spike into the standing part, your left thumb acts as a fulcrum while you push in and down with your right hand.*

A Little Presplice Theorizing and Practice

The idea in splicing wire, as with cordage, is to lift one or more standing-part strands just enough to pass a strand end underneath. Do this with all strands in succession, several times, and the ends become woven into the standing part very securely and very evenly. Only in splices can the strain be thus distributed among all of a rope's component strands. That is why splices are the strongest knots. When you work wire, capitalize on this virtue by trying for perfect smoothness. To minimize distortion, use the smallest spike that will make a space big enough to tuck in the strands.

Try a few practice entries now. Face the vise, brace your spike arm against your body, and lay the tip of the spike between two standing-part strands. Using the thumb on your other hand as a fulcrum, *lean* on the wire, twisting the spike handle counterclockwise just a bit as the tip drops between the strands (Figure 137). That's it; you've just picked up a strand. Take the spike out and try it again, but this time go under two strands; then do it again, under three. Outwit the wire, guiding the tip under the strands without snagging the heart.

Remember that wire is too stiff to be tucked directly where you want it to go. It kinks. Therefore you have to tuck it in well down the standing part and then "roll" it home. This is the spike's other duty, to shuttle back and forth, conveying the strands to their destinations. Practice the shuttling motion illustrated in Figure 138, keeping the spike parallel with the lay for the least wire distortion. Note that as you move toward the vise you have to push on the handle to keep the tip in. Likewise, traveling away from the vise causes the spike to get swallowed up unless you pull it out a little as you go.

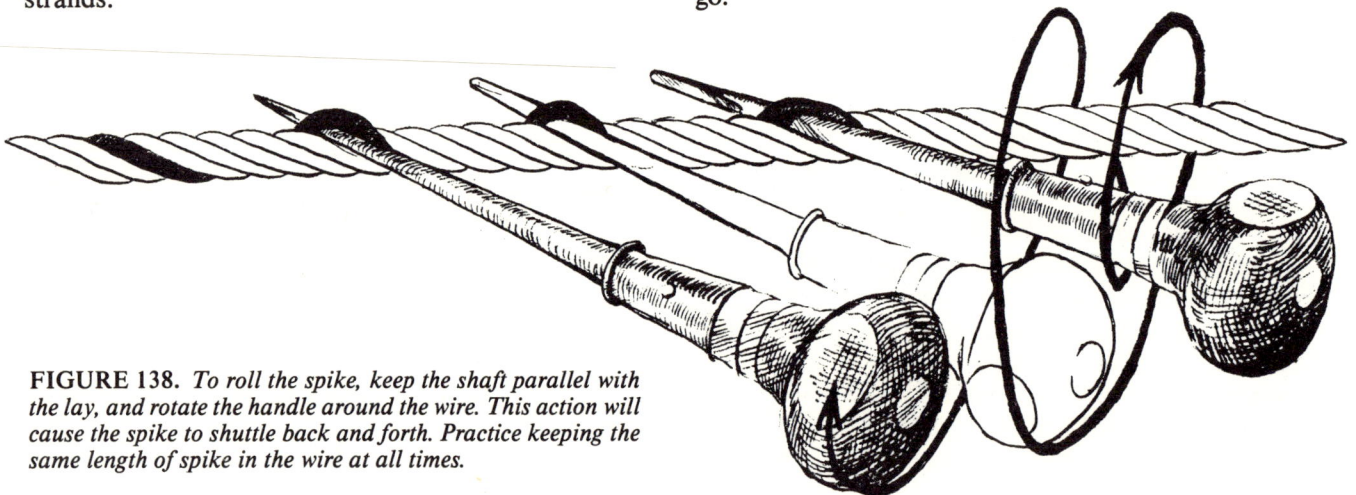

FIGURE 138. *To roll the spike, keep the shaft parallel with the lay, and rotate the handle around the wire. This action will cause the spike to shuttle back and forth. Practice keeping the same length of spike in the wire at all times.*

94

strand #6
tail side
standing side

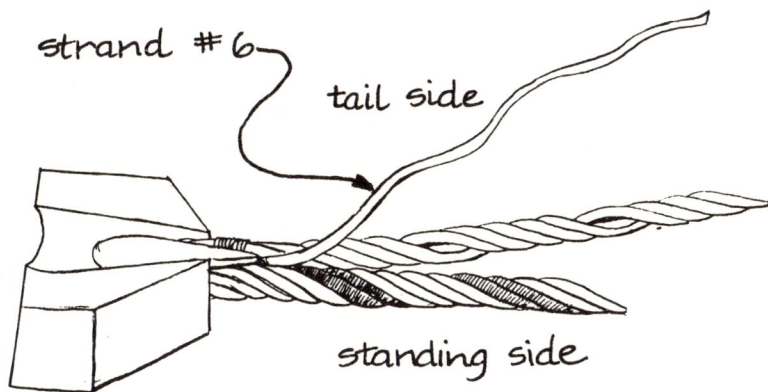

FIGURE 139. *After separating strand #6, the innermost of the tail strands at the base of the thimble as seen from above, pick out the two strands that correspond to those shaded, and enter the spike under both.*

The Splice

Preliminaries over. Look at Figure 139, at the one strand that is separated. That's the first one to be tucked. It's the innermost tail strand you can see from above at the thimble. By the way, most riggers just unlay the whole bundle immediately, but doing one strand at a time is considerably easier; you'll be dealing with a squid soon enough.

The strands are numbered 1 through 6, and the strand you have just unlaid is #6. I can't explain now why you're starting with the last strand, except to say that how the splice starts is important and that this start is unusually smooth. You'll see why later.

Look again at Figure 139, at the two shaded strands on the standing part. Like #6, they intersect the thimble at its base, but the one on the right will not be visible from above the thimble, and the one on the left will barely be visible. Enter your spike under these two and roll it down a full revolution. Take #6 and pass it once counterclockwise around the standing part, and then tuck it under those two strands from the *near side* to the *far side* (Figure 140). Turning the spike at right angles to the wire will make a bigger space through which to tuck the end.

Remove the spike, put it back into the same space from the opposite direction, and roll the strand home, toward the vise. Pull on the strand as you roll, to

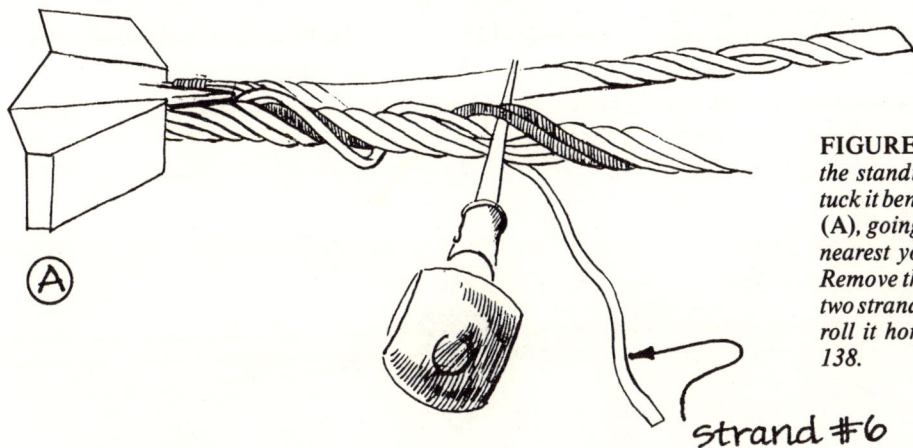

FIGURE 140. *Pass the end completely around the standing part, counterclockwise, and then tuck it beneath the two strands the spike is under (A), going from the standing-part side (the side nearest you) to the tail side (away from you). Remove the spike, put it back in under the same two strands from the opposite direction (B), and roll it home, rotating the handle as in Figure 138.*

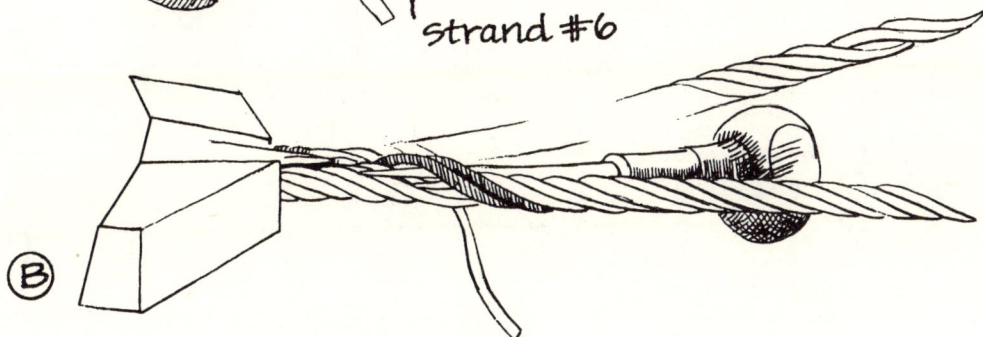

strand #6

95

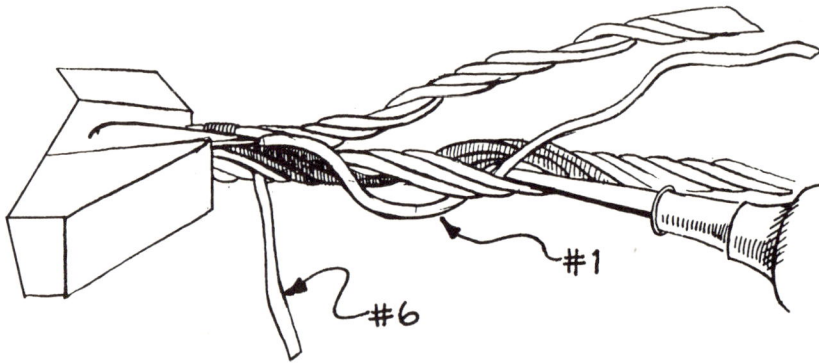

FIGURE 141. *Separate strand #1; it's the one on the right side of the space vacated by #6. Enter the spike under the three shaded strands. Pass strand #1 around the standing part once, counterclockwise, and pass it under the three strands from the tail side to the standing side. Roll home. All subsequent tucks are also made in this direction.*

prevent slack and to keep the strand in front of the spike, but do not pull the strand toward the vise; let the spike push the strand ahead of it. The counterclockwise turn you made will come out as you approach the vise, where the strand should snuggle into place naturally. Don't force it.

You will return to #6 soon. For now, enter the spike under the three strands on your wire that correspond to the three shaded strands in Figure 141. They are the three that are immediately to the left of where #6 went in. It's awkward in this case to make the entry at the vise, so you can trace the strands around with your finger for one revolution, entering the spike where shown. Roll home to make sure you have the correct strands (the point of the spike should come out where #6 went in), and then roll back. Separate strand #1 from the bundle—it's to the right of the space vacated by #6. Pass it once counterclockwise around the standing part as before, but this time tuck from the tail, or *far side*, to the *near side* of the standing part. All subsequent strands are also tucked from tail side to

standing side. Strand #6 was an oddity in more than one way.

Pull the slack out of #1, and leaving the spike in the way it was entered, roll the strand home as in Figure 140. Again, keep tension on the strand, keep the strand in front of the spike, and let the spike push the strand ahead.

Now enter the spike under the two strands that correspond to the shaded strands in Figure 142. Be sure that the point comes out in the same space that it did for #1. Separate end #2, the next one to the right in the bundle; pass it around once counterclockwise; and tuck it under the two strands from tail side to standing side. Roll it home.

Enter under one strand, as in Figure 143. The point still comes out in the same place that it did for strands #1 and #2. Separate strand #3 from the tail, tuck it in, and roll it home. All three strands should now be going cleanly into the same space and coming out under separate, adjacent strands in the standing part.

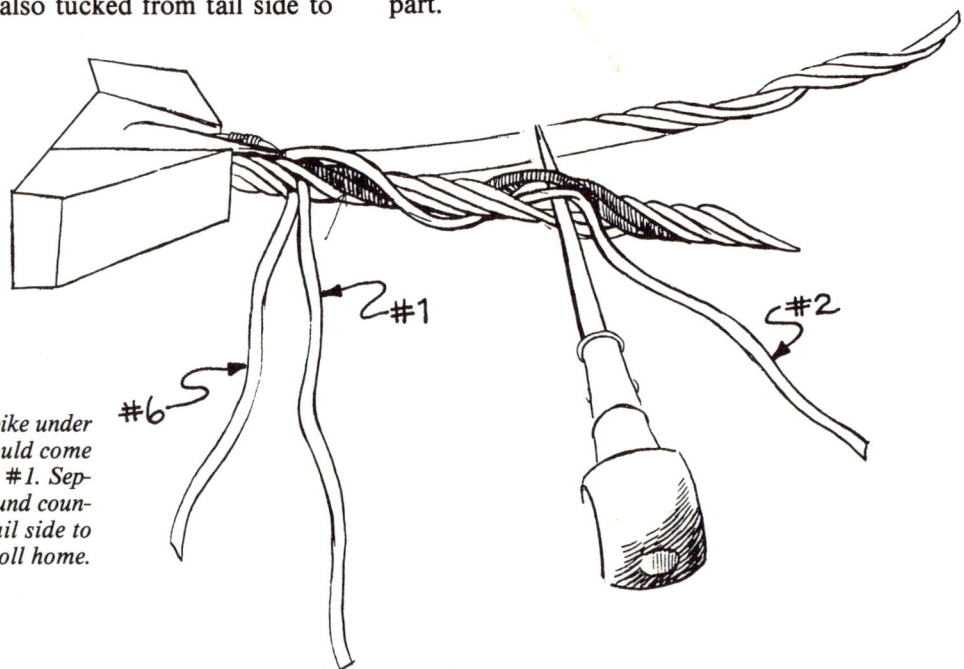

FIGURE 142. *Enter the spike under two strands. The point should come out in the same place as for #1. Separate strand #2, pass it around counterclockwise, tuck from tail side to standing side, and roll home.*

FIGURE 143. *Enter the spike under one strand only, so that the point again comes out in the same space as it did for strands #1 and #2. Separate out strand #3, pass it around, tuck, and roll home.*

The Heart

You're probably warming up to the tuck-and-roll procedure, so I hate to interrupt, but we must now deal with the heart. You can see it exposed in the tail and in the middle of the standing part. The common procedure is to cut the heart out of the tail at the outset, but you are going to lay it alongside the heart in the standing part. The idea here is this: When you introduce six strands into a configuration that already has six strands very nicely arranged around a heart, hollow spaces result. By fattening up the interior with an extra heart, you get a firmer splice that won't distort under extremes of loading.

Separate the tail's fiber heart from the remaining two strands and unlay it into its three components. If you're working with a wire heart—not shown—divide it into four or five parts. You are unlaying the heart's tail components to be able to wrap it more easily around the heart in the standing part. Enter the spike into the same space that #6 went into, but put the spike under only one strand (Figure 144). Roll the spike ahead as far as it will easily go—and then a little farther. This action will pull the strand the spike is under slightly away from its fellows, leaving a little space. Pull the heart (all its loose parts) down firmly into this space, so that it is behind the spike. Keep pulling while rolling the spike toward you so the heart will be pushed into the middle of the standing part. Keep the heart behind the spike, keep the spike parallel with the lay, and use as little spike as possible. After being rolled in, the heart will show a little, but a hernia (which happens when the heart completely protrudes from the standing part) will not do—there's too much distortion. If a hernia results, you probably have too little tension on the standing part or too much spike.

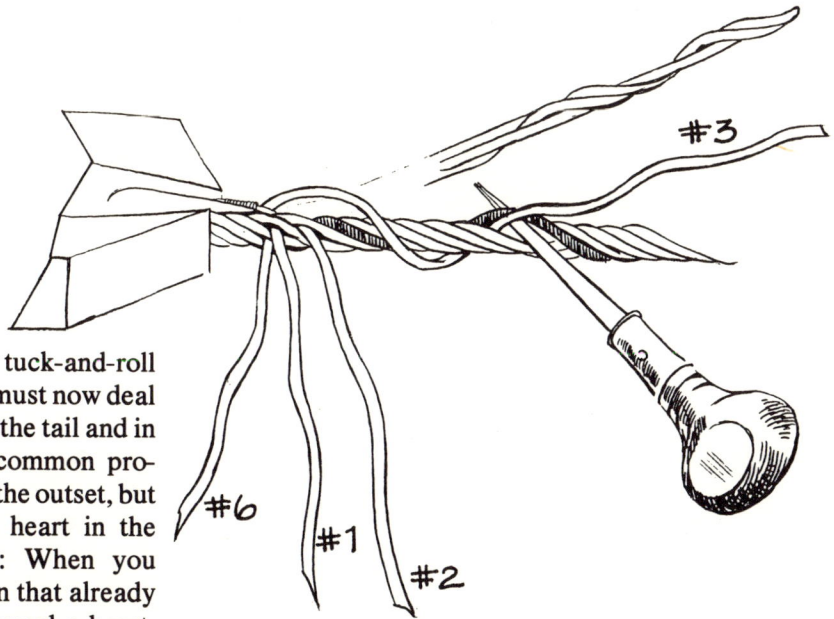

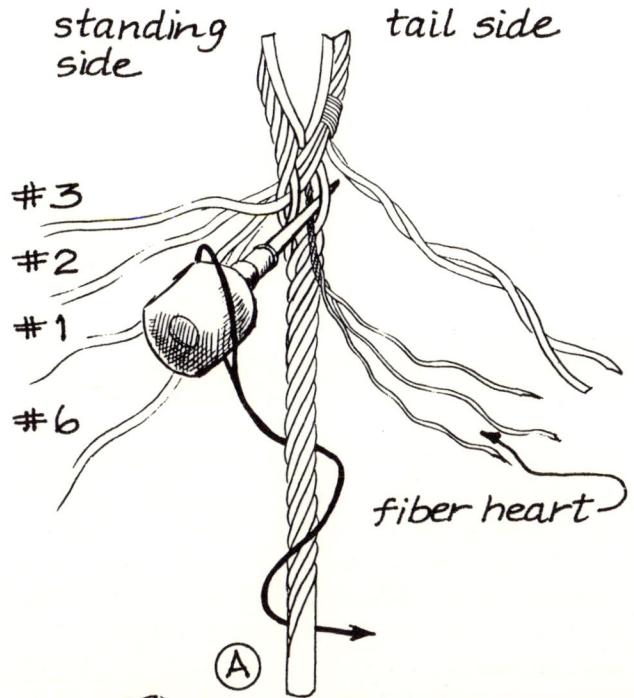

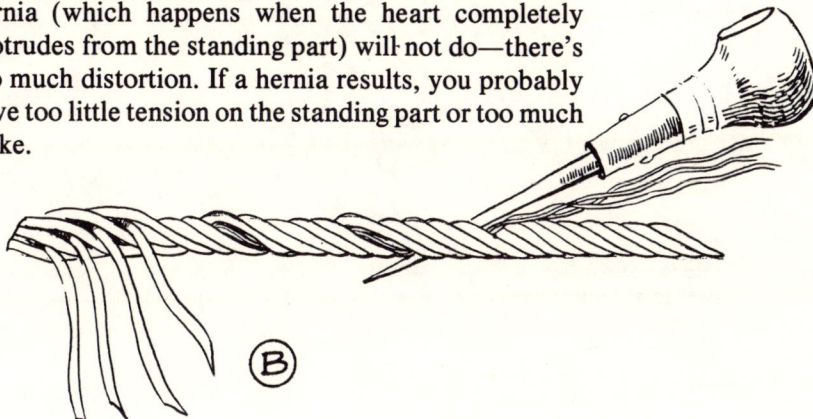

FIGURE 144. *Enter the spike into the space #6 went into, but under only one strand. This strand is immediately to the right of the one that #3 is under. Roll the spike as far home as it will go easily—and then a little more (A). Pull the unlaid heart down into the space thus formed; then roll the spike back down the wire (B), pushing this extra heart into the middle of the standing part as you go.*

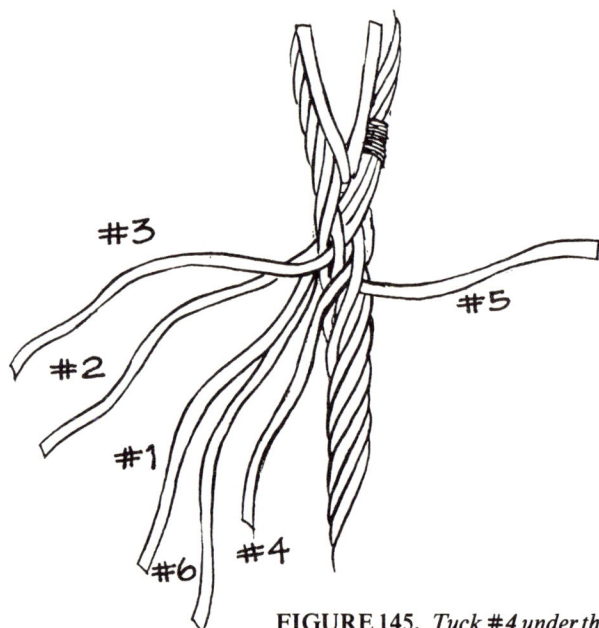

FIGURE 145. *Tuck #4 under the same strand you lifted to roll the heart in. Tuck #5 under the next strand to the right. The splice should now look as shown.*

Back to Roll-and-Tuck

With the two hearts beating as one, you may proceed. Enter the spike under the same strand that you lifted for rolling in the heart. Roll down one revolution, tuck in strand #4, and roll home. Enter under the next strand to the right, tuck in #5, the last untucked strand, and roll home. A light tapping with the mallet will ensure that these two strands are seated well. The splice thus far should look like that in Figure 145.

Return now to the mysterious strand #6. Enter the spike under the next strand to the right and prepare to tuck. Ready? Wait.

Breaking the Lay

The strands you've tucked so far have entered almost straight into the wire. But from now on, they'll each describe a tight spiral down the length of the splice. If you allow the strands to keep a round cross section, the yarns (the individual wires that make up each strand) on the outside of the spiral will have to travel farther than the yarns on the inside; when a load comes on the splice, the outside yarns will take a disproportionate amount of strain. Since a splice relies on even distribution of strain, you need to flatten the strands into a ribbon shape by "breaking the lay."

Make a small bight, close to the splice, by arcing the end of a strand around counterclockwise (Figure 146). As the bight tightens, you will see the strand yarns open up. Relax the tension and they spring back. But if you apply a little more tension they will lose some of their elastic memory and stay open when the tension is eased. The trick is to break the lay without completely dissociating the yarns or, worse yet, kinking them, so be very gentle. As you proceed with the splice, you will find that the act of passing the strands around to be tucked also helps open up the yarns.

So, to return to the splice, break the lay of #6, tuck it again, and roll it home; it will settle smoothly into place, wrapped flat around its strand.

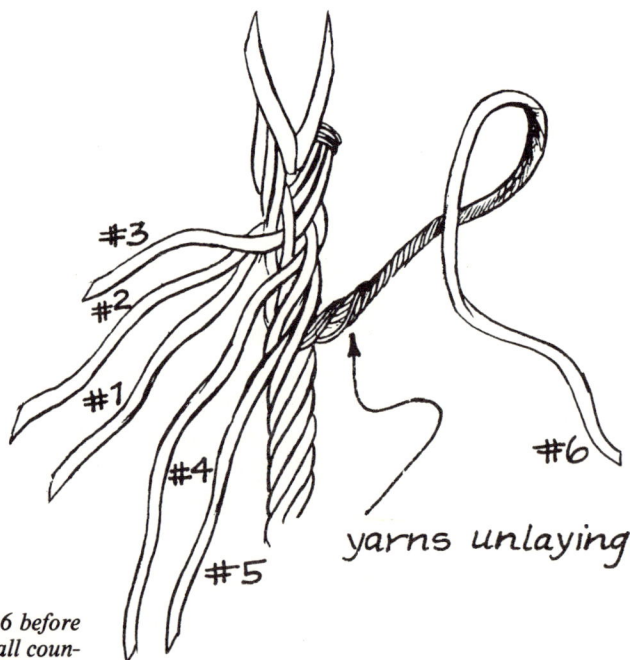

FIGURE 146. *Break the lay of #6 before tucking a second time by making a small counterclockwise loop, or bight, and twisting it just enough so that the yarns do not completely spring back when tension is released.*

That Odd First Tuck Finally Explained

Figure 147-A shows from the underside how the splice would look had you begun in the conventional manner and not made that first tuck under two strands with #6 (see Figures 139 and 140). Without that tuck, the strand would have had to travel a considerable distance from the seizing to its entry point, so far that it would be difficult to make it lie fair and take an even strain. But now it emerges directly to the right of strand #5 (Figure 147-B), exactly where it needs to be for all consequent normal tucks. (Steven Hyman and Will Gates, fellow riggers of the barque *Elissa*, introduced me to this technique.)

Roll-and-Tuck Again

Now you have tucked strands #1 through #5 once and #6 twice. But pretend you are even and have tucked them all just once. It's easier, because from here on you will be treating them all the same. So, for the second row of tucks, start with #1. It's closest to the vise and comes out from under three strands. Enter the spike where #1 emerges, but pick up only one strand. Roll back (away from the vise), break the lay, tuck, and roll home. Take each of the strands in

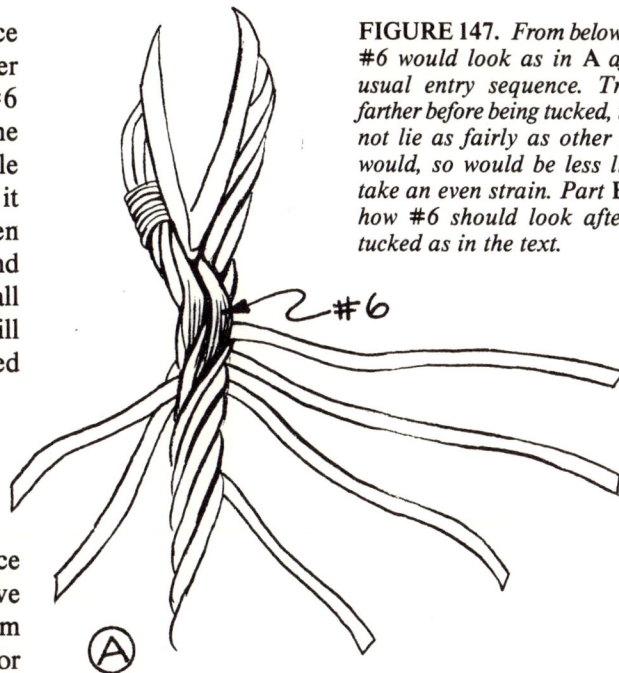

FIGURE 147. *From below, strand #6 would look as in A after the usual entry sequence. Traveling farther before being tucked, it would not lie as fairly as other strands would, so would be less likely to take an even strain. Part B shows how #6 should look after being tucked as in the text.*

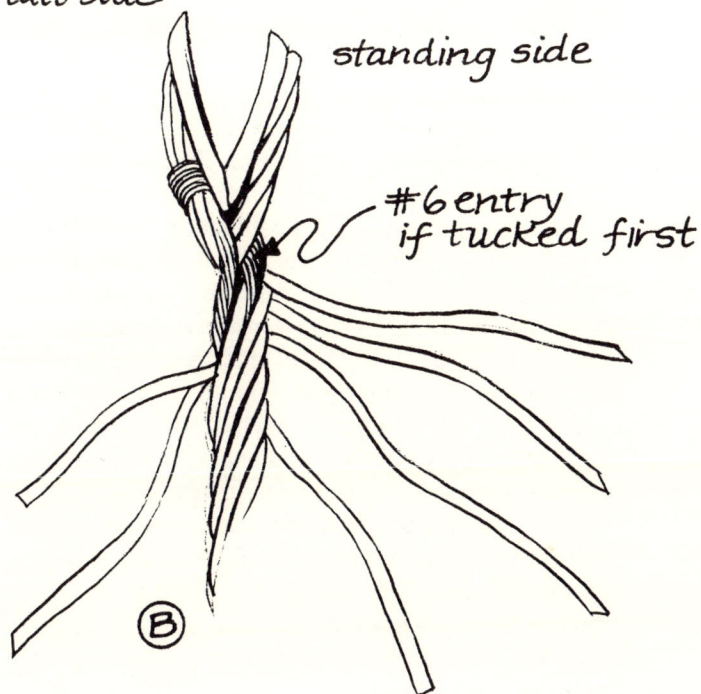

99

FIGURE 148. *Proceeding with the second row of tucks. Always enter the spike under the strand from which the end to be tucked emerges. Continue in sequence until all strands have been tucked four times.*

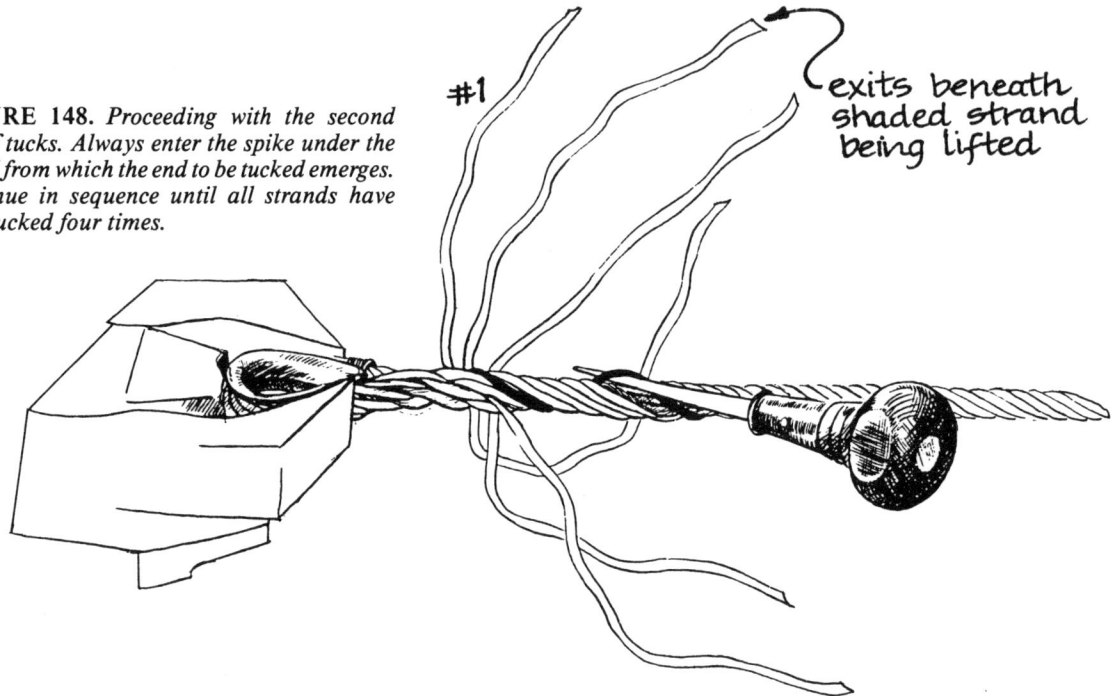

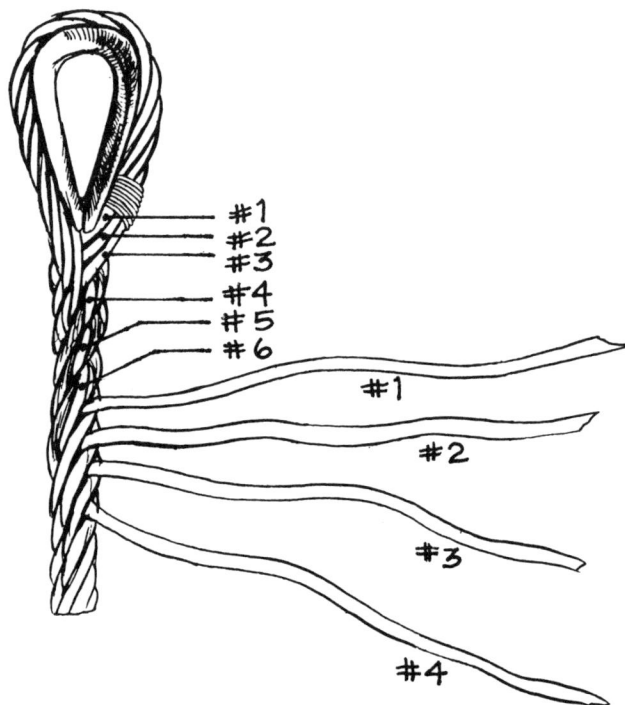

#1

exits beneath shaded strand being lifted

#1
#2
#3
#4
#5
#6

#1
#2
#3
#4

FIGURE 149. *Locating strand #4 gives a point from which to count if you lose track. The other strands lie in relation to #4 as shown.*

succession, working away from the vise, always entering the spike under the same strand beneath which each end being tucked emerges (Figure 148).

Count the ends aloud as you go so you'll always know where you are in the sequence (for example, "Row two, 3; row two, 4; row two, 5"; and so on). If you get distracted or called away, find your place again by going back to the top of the splice and finding where #4 enters. It's visually distinctive (Figure 149). Count strands down from there until you get to the bottom-most (last-tucked) strand. The number you say when you reach it is the number of that strand.

Sooner or later you will probably tuck a strand in the wrong place. Any time things don't look right as you roll home, stop and check. Remember that each strand goes under to the tail side, over to the standing side, then back under to the tail side, always spiraling around its own standing-part strand. To correct a mistuck, put everything in reverse, rolling the spike back and pushing on the strand end until it comes out, and then retucking in the proper place.

Keep tucking until you have made four full rows of tucks (not counting the extra one for #6). Five rows of tucks is the standard for a Liverpool Eye—that is, each strand is tucked five times. But since you've done so much work already, you might as well learn the proper finishing touch.

100

separated yarns

lump resulting from
improperly laid out
strand

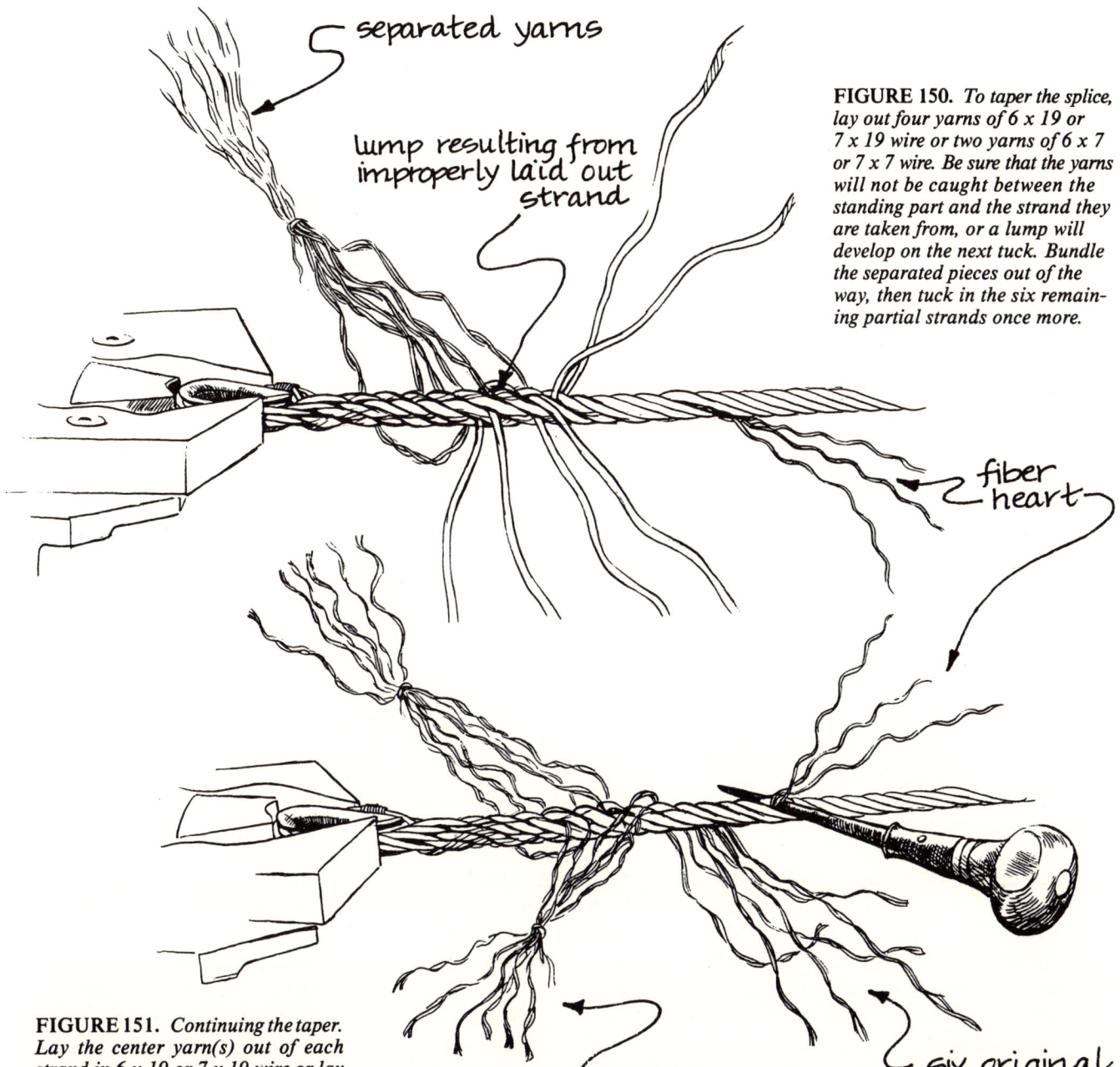

FIGURE 150. *To taper the splice,
lay out four yarns of 6 x 19 or
7 x 19 wire or two yarns of 6 x 7
or 7 x 7 wire. Be sure that the yarns
will not be caught between the
standing part and the strand they
are taken from, or a lump will
develop on the next tuck. Bundle
the separated pieces out of the
way, then tuck in the six remaining partial strands once more.*

fiber
heart

FIGURE 151. *Continuing the taper.
Lay the center yarn(s) out of each
strand in 6 x 19 or 7 x 19 wire or lay
out two more yarns of 6 x 7 or 7 x 7
wire. Tuck each remainder once more.
Back out the fiber heart of the wire
rope as far as the end of the splice.*

second set of
separated yarns

six original
strands

The Taper

The taper provides a gradual transition from splice to
standing part, blurring the distinction between the two.
A tapered splice is more appealing to the eye and less
liable to snag running rigging and sails than an
untapered one—or a mechanical fitting. More important, the taper makes a splice more flexible and thus
less subject to fatigue.

After making four full rows of tucks, peel four or five
adjacent surface yarns off each strand for 6 x 19 or
7 x 19 wire, or two adjacent surface yarns off each
strand for 6 x 7 or 7 x 7 wire. Separate them all the way
to the splice; simply make sure they don't stop on the
right of the strand they were peeled from—you'll be
tucking to the right and don't want separated yarns to
be in the way, preventing the tucked strand from lying
fair (Figure 150). When all the strands have been

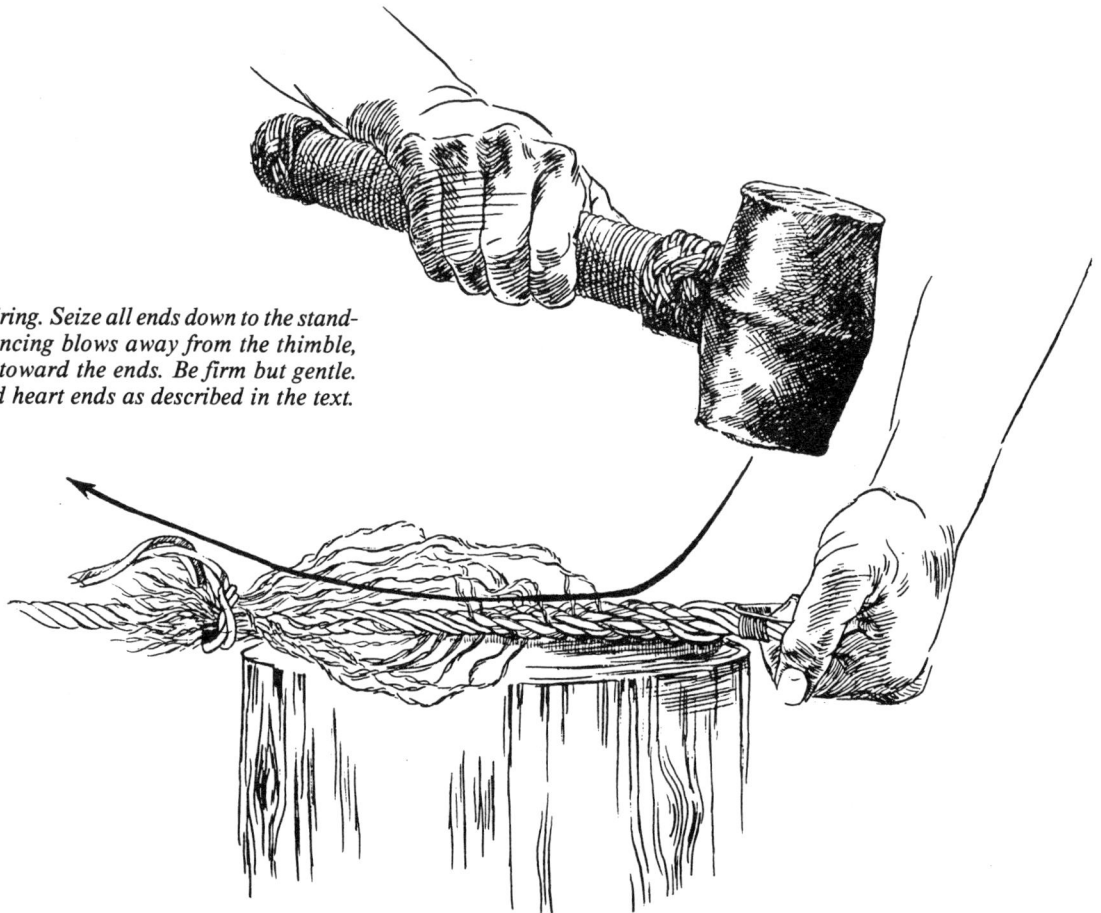

FIGURE 152. *Fairing. Seize all ends down to the standing part. Strike glancing blows away from the thimble, working any slack toward the ends. Be firm but gentle. Trim all strand and heart ends as described in the text.*

reduced in size, tuck all six large remainders once more.

Next, separate the center yarn(s) out of each strand for 6 x 19 or 7 x 19 wire or two more adjacent surface yarns out of 6 x 7 or 7 x 7 wire, and then once again tuck the large remainders of all six strands. Those are all the tucks you really need to make, but the taper can be further elongated by tucking once more, with or without splitting the strands again.

Finally, unroll the fiber heart that you rolled in previously back to the splice by entering the spike behind it and rolling the spike toward the vise (Figure 151). Just ease it up to strand #4's last tuck and leave it there; then tie all the loose yarns and strands to the standing part.

Fairing

"Svensken splejser daaligt, men han banker godt."
– Frank Rosenow, *The Ditty Bag Book*

That's a Norwegian saying that means, "The Swedes are lousy splicers, but they're good at pounding."*

This bit of slander refers to the temptation to rely heavily on this step, which involves pounding the finished splice with a hardwood or soft metal mallet to smooth out any irregularities (Figure 152). You can't beat a poor splice into a good one, but any splice will benefit from a proper fairing. Using a stump or the like as a base, strike glancing blows toward the standing part with the mallet, constantly turning the work, trying to get any slack worked out. Go over the work two or three times.

It is difficult to describe in print exactly how hard one should strike to fair different-sized wires, but the matter is important, so as an aid I will tell you a little story. A sailmaker and I once had a loft on the top floor of City Hall in Anacortes, Washington. Ours was the only unrenovated room in the old building—below, city employees typed and filed away in carpeted, fluorescent-lit comfort. Trying to work quietly, I discovered how little muscle was actually needed to fair a splice. Since gentleness is a good thing for wire, imagine, as you fair, a nest of bureaucrats below. For wire up to 5/16 inch in diameter, the noise will not bother them at all; pounding 3/8-inch wire is noticeable but reasonable; 7/16 inch can be tolerated anytime except

FIGURE 153. *A finished Liverpool Eyesplice.*

first thing Monday morning; ½ inch should be done only during lunch or after hours; and ⅝ inch and up will drop plaster into the typewriters, so should be done in the parking lot.

Trimming

One more chance to ruin the whole thing. Ends cut too long are "meathooks" that will work their way through service and then through your hide. Ends cut too short will untuck themselves. So hold the work still (you can put it back in the vise with some tension on the standing part) and gently pull the last-tucked bundle toward the thimble, breaking the lay. Nip the wire just above the splice—1/16 to ⅛ inch above—and the ends should fall back until they're nearly flush. If the wire is too thick to cut all at once, take successive bites, working toward the thimble. Be extra careful at the ends of the splice, where the strands are most likely to slip out.

With 7 x 7 wire, a very neat finish can be made by completely unlaying each strand and breaking the individual yarns with your bare hands. There's no karate involved—it's more like judo actually. Bend each yarn sharply left and then right, creating a weak point at its base. Then twist the yarn clockwise two or three turns and the end will break off completely out of the way.

When you trim the heart—fiber or wire—taper it, too, by pulling some of its strands closer to the vise before trimming.

Trimming completed, give the splice a few light taps with the mallet for a final fairing. Your job is done and ready to be cut off and thrown away.

"Thrown away! Are you crazy!?"

I know, I know. You've spent hours on your first splice, cursed the wire, probably cursed the instructions; you've finally finished, and you're not about to junk the thing. Well, keep it as a memento if you like; just don't use it. Practice until you develop a consistent proficiency, and then take some samples to a testing machine and break them. It's the only way to prove your work.

Many sailors prefer eyespliced wire rigging to rigging with mechanical terminals, even though a wide variety of the mechanical terminals are available. Why? Splices are flexible and resilient and thus long-lived. They are also easy to maintain and inspect, have no abrupt shoulders to snag other objects or jam in sheaves, and are cost effective even if you pay someone else to make them for you. Do-it-yourselfers spend nothing but time on their terminals. And if you plan a leisurely cruise across the Pacific, your rigging vise and ditty bag contents are all you need to be a self-sufficient rigger.

But despite these and other virtues, Eyesplices have always faced a major stumbling block: tensile strength. Standard references[*] list splices as being 10 to 15 percent weaker in sailboat-size wire than swages and fittings such as the Sta-Lok, Norseman, Cast-Lok, and so on. For traditional vessels and some industrial applications, compensating for this deficiency is simply a matter of using slightly oversize wire, thus gaining ample strength along with the splice's other virtues. But on most vessels today, with weight and windage at a premium, this practice is unacceptable. The only alternative is to make a more efficient splice, a knot more nearly as strong as the wire rope in which it is tied.

I've always thought that this was possible given proper technique and a fair level of skill. To prove or disprove it, I arranged tests at the Monson, Massachusetts shop of Daniel O'Connor and Sons, Inc., using wire rope made by the MacWhyte and Carolina companies. O'Connor, a third-generation rigger specializing in ski-lift equipment, is the proud owner of a 200,000-pound capacity hydraulic testing machine. In January 1983 we fed this device 17 sample wires with Eyesplice terminals. Eleven of the samples were my idea of "proper" splices: smooth, with fair entries and tapers (for the sake of experiment, different tapers were used). Two of the samples were made, after about 40 hours of practice, by a student of mine. The wire used was ⅜-inch diameter in 7 x 7, 7 x 19, and 1 x 19 constructions, both stainless and galvanized, plus one 5/16-inch 7 x 19 galvanized sample. Although the number of pieces tested was small, I believe that the

Rossnagel's Handbook of Rigging, page 61; MacWhyte Catalog G-18, page 214; Broderick and Bascom's Rigger's Handbook, page 163.

TABLE 6. Splice Strength as Percent Rated Strength of Wire Rope

All splices were variations on the Liverpool Eyesplice, with differing entrances and tapers. These destruction tests were arranged with the help of the MacWhyte Wire Rope Co., Phillip Rand Co., and *Sail* magazine.

	Piece	Diam. (in.)	Rated Str. (lbs.)	Broke at (lbs.)	% of Rated Strength
other taper	7x7 galv.	3/8	13,300	13,350	100.00
	7x7 galv.	3/8	13,300	13,350	100.00
taper described in text	7x7 galv.	3/8	13,300	14,300	107.50
	7x7 galv.	3/8	13,300	13,850	104.00
	7x7 s.s. 302	3/8	12,000	12,150	101.00
	7x19 s.s. 302	3/8	12,000	12,000	100.00
	7x19 galv.	3/8	14,400	14,900	103.50
	7x19 galv.	5/16	9,800	11,600	118.00
diff. taper for 1x19 diff. entry too	1x19 s.s. 302	3/8	17,500	17,850	102.00
	1x19 s.s. 302	3/8	17,500	17,950	102.50
Tony's early	7x19 s.s. 316	3/8	11,000	10,100	91.82
Tony's later	7x19 s.s. 316	3/8	11,000	11,350	103.00
untapered, std. thimbles	1x19 s.s. 302	1/4	8,200	7,200	88.00
	1x19 s.s. 302	1/4	8,200	5,800	70.50
very short	7x19 galv.	5/16	9,800	9,400	96.00
old piece (12 yrs.)	7x7 s.s. 302	9/32	6,100	5,300	83.00
old piece (12 yrs.)	7x7 s.s. 302	1/4	7,600	7,400	97.00

consistency of the results puts well-made splices in a league with any other terminal.

The results, as shown in Table 6, averaged 103.8 percent of the manufacturers' *rated* strength for the rope. None broke at below 100 percent; the highest mark was 118 percent. In case these numbers seem impossible, understand that manufacturers rate their wire rope at a little less than *ultimate* strength, by margins of a few percent to well over 10 percent, depending on the brand. In terms of ultimate strength, the average for the splices was 95 percent for the 3/8-inch samples and 99 percent for the best 5/16-inch sample. The important thing is that the splices were within a few percentage points of the very best mechanical terminals and better than most swages. Compare these results with those obtained by the staff of *Practical Sailor*. In their test, the results of which were presented in the November 1, 1982 issue, fittings were measured against the wire's rated strength. Cast-Lok and Sta-Lok fittings tested at 110 percent and 106 percent, while the swaged wire broke at 95 and 105 percent of rated strength.

The other six samples tested by O'Connor were "improper" splices: an early splice of my student's (made after only a few hours' practice); 1 x 19 splices with standard thimbles instead of the solid or heavy-duty thimbles that should be used with this construction; splices in old wire; and one sample made very short, so that the splices backed into each other at the middle. This group averaged 87.7 percent of the rated wire strength; technique and proper materials do make a difference.

GROMMETING

You find them occasionally, littering decks, washed ashore, or hidden away in forepeaks, those pitiful, twisted, lumpy, often bloodstained approximations of rope rings that poor, misguided souls have abandoned in disgust.

And then there are those hapless individuals who curse their way to the last tuck, call the resulting grotesquerie a grommet, put it to use, and so must live daily with the evidence of their failure.

Why do people torture themselves so? Why do they sit there, knot book open on their laps, tangle of line in their hands, desperately trying to come up with something that vaguely resembles the final diagram? Because they are fired up with a notion: Save Money by Replacing Expensive Fittings with Grommets. It's a commendable, reasonable, sensible idea that runs up against two difficulties:

(1) It takes skill and patience. This is a big reason why manufacturers can Make Money by Replacing Grommets with Expensive Fittings; most people don't have the time or inclination to master yet another skill. ("Fer cryin' out loud, I learned to navigate, learned to trim the genoa, even learned to varnish the damn brightwork! Why should I go blind and crazy trying to make those stupid little hoops?!") But grommets don't need to be that hard to make. Given time, the

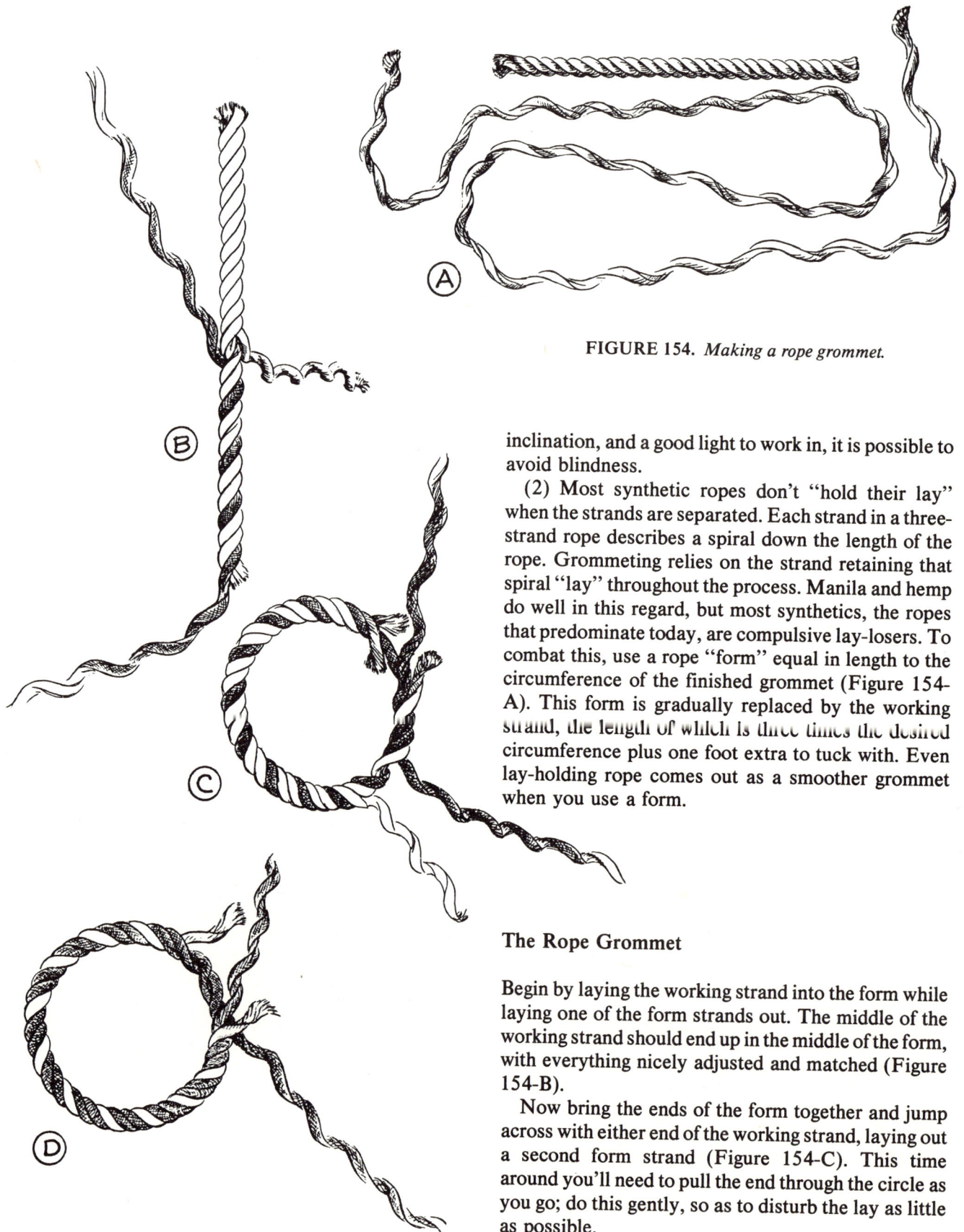

FIGURE 154. *Making a rope grommet.*

inclination, and a good light to work in, it is possible to avoid blindness.

(2) Most synthetic ropes don't "hold their lay" when the strands are separated. Each strand in a three-strand rope describes a spiral down the length of the rope. Grommeting relies on the strand retaining that spiral "lay" throughout the process. Manila and hemp do well in this regard, but most synthetics, the ropes that predominate today, are compulsive lay-losers. To combat this, use a rope "form" equal in length to the circumference of the finished grommet (Figure 154-A). This form is gradually replaced by the working strand, the length of which is three times the desired circumference plus one foot extra to tuck with. Even lay-holding rope comes out as a smoother grommet when you use a form.

The Rope Grommet

Begin by laying the working strand into the form while laying one of the form strands out. The middle of the working strand should end up in the middle of the form, with everything nicely adjusted and matched (Figure 154-B).

Now bring the ends of the form together and jump across with either end of the working strand, laying out a second form strand (Figure 154-C). This time around you'll need to pull the end through the circle as you go; do this gently, so as to disturb the lay as little as possible.

(E)

(F)

(G)

(H)

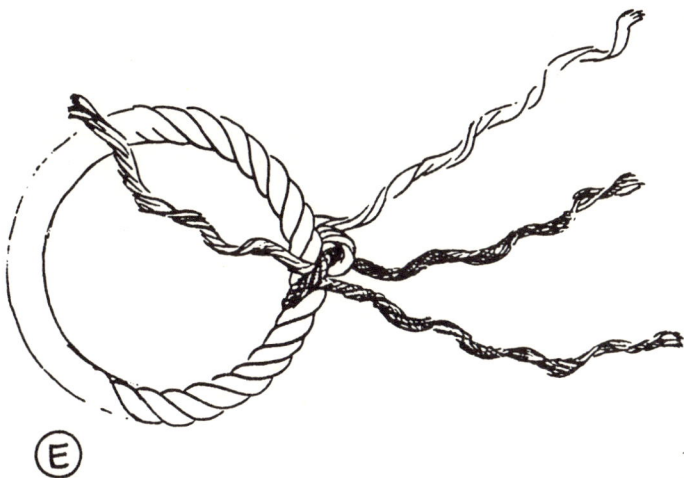

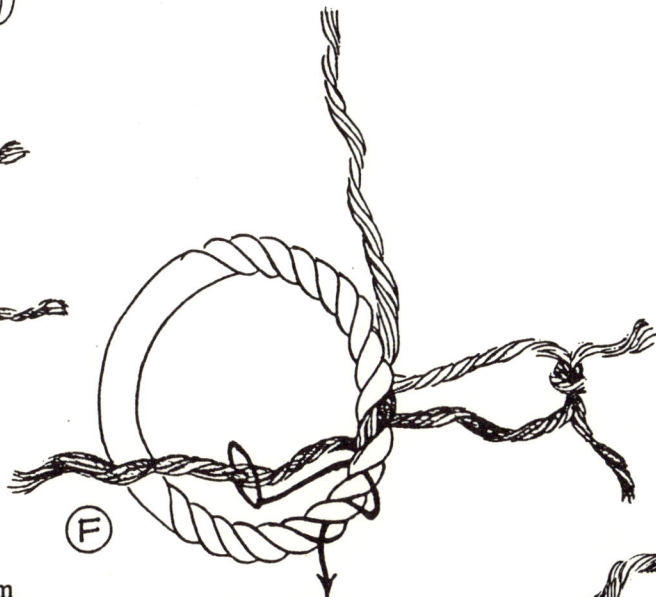

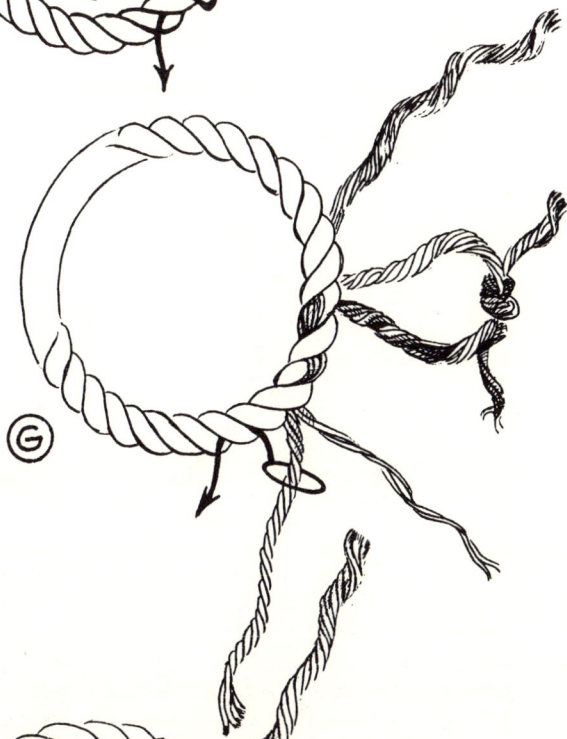

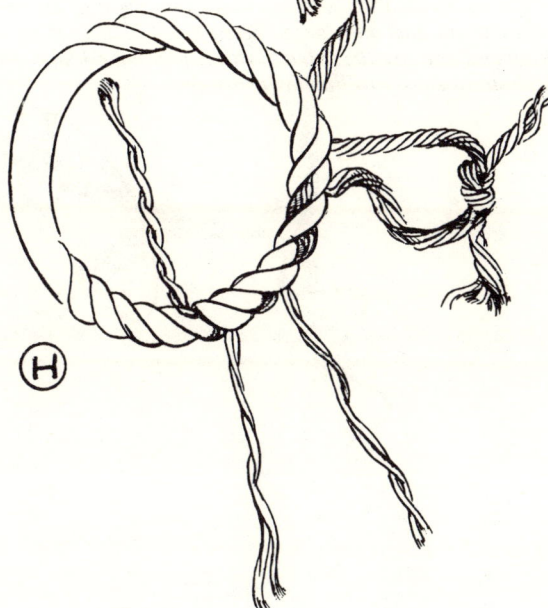

Back at the starting point, lay out the last form strand, replacing it with the other end of the working strand (Figure 154-D). You'll wind up inordinately pleased with yourself, with all three form strands gone and the two ends of the working strand meeting in the same score.

Grommets finish with a type of splice that provides security without bulk—no sense needlessly distorting that perfect circularity. Start by splitting the two strands in half down to where they emerge from the grommet. Make an Overhand Knot, *left over right*, with the two halves that are closest to each other (Figure 154-E). When you draw this knot down it should look just like a whole strand. If it bulges or flattens, the halves you chose were either too close together or too far apart. Untie the knot and experiment with different ends until you find the two that are just right. With a little practice, it's easy to choose the proper pair.

The other two halves are not employed further; tie them together for now so that you don't confuse them with the others. Then take one of the working halves and tuck it against the lay, over one and under one (Figure 154-F). As with any splice, flatten each strand by untwisting it a little as you tuck, and be sure to pull any slack out of individual yarns; a fair splice is a strong splice. Tuck both strands whole twice, lay out one-third of each and tuck again, then lay out another third and tuck once more, *with the lay,* to finish (Figure 154-G,H).

Roll the splice underfoot for a final fairing and trim the ends about ¼ inch from the rope; they will draw back flush or wear off in use. In very slick synthetics it may be necessary to whip or fuse the ends to keep them from pulling out.

107

155-B. *Jump the gap with both ends and continue to lay out form strands.*

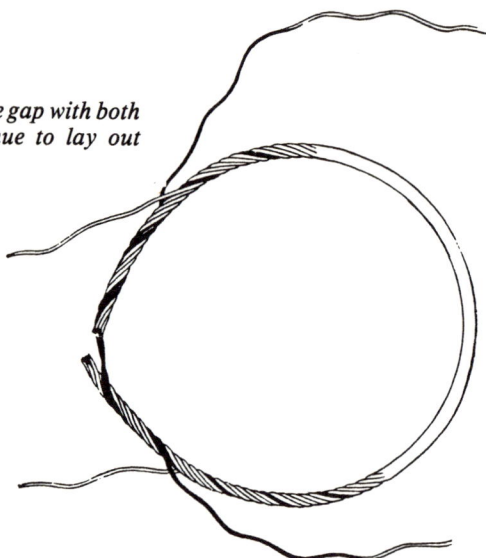

155-C. *Keep laying in and out, taking care to remove consecutive form strands each time around; it's easy to get crossed.*

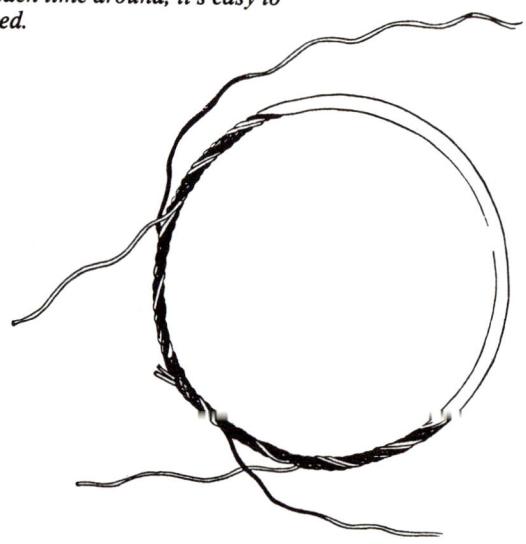

155-D. *The working end is completely laid up around the form heart, with the ends meeting. Wrap one working strand end around the grommet several times to keep it from shifting, then enter a spike under three strands, just to the right of the other working strand end and the adjacent heart end. Pull on the working end and use the spike to roll it into the middle of the wire, simultaneously rolling the heart out.*

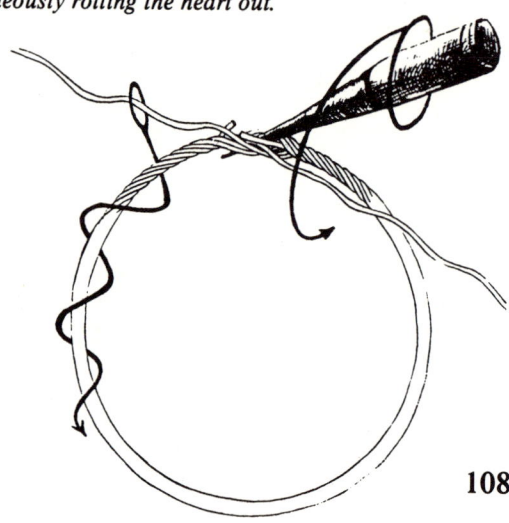

FIGURE 155-A. *Making the wire rope grommet. This grommet also starts with a form equal in length to the circumference of the desired grommet, but has a working strand end measuring exactly seven times that circumference.*

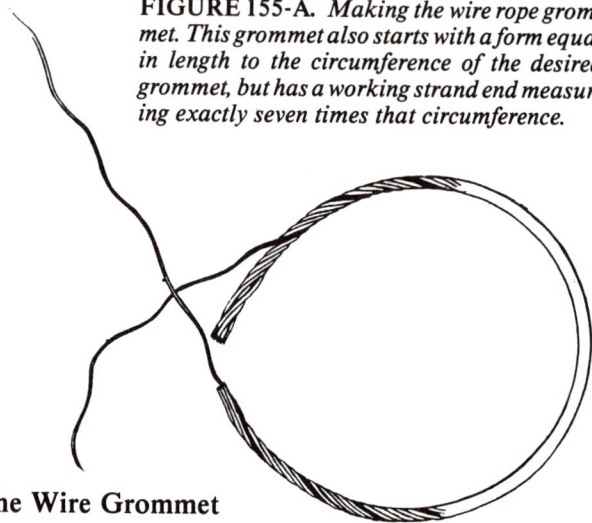

The Wire Grommet

The working-strand-and-form technique can also be used to produce the heavier-duty, longer-lived wire rope grommet. Here, lay loss is not a problem, since nearly all wire rope these days is "preformed." That is, each strand is permanently set into its spiral shape before the rope is laid up. But here we are dealing not with three but with six strands; if the working strand shifts at all as you are laying up the grommet, it becomes very difficult to make the fifth and sixth passes fit. So again, use a form.

A "perfect grommet" in wire begins with a form the length of the finished grommet's circumference and a working strand exactly seven times that length. Lay the strand into the form as with rope, but this time start with the middle of the strand at the end of the form. Bring the ends together and jump across with both ends for a firm start. The lay of the wire might not come out exactly at the length you want, in which case you should enlarge the circle a bit until the lays match (Figure 155-A). If the grommet is small and the wire springy, the remaining form strands might jump apart. Holding them temporarily in place with a bit of electrical tape should cure this, although heavy wire might need the clamping apparatus shown as #2866 in *The Ashley Book of Knots*. In any event, be very careful as you pass the end that it doesn't whip around and smack you.

Every time you cross the gap, be sure you lay in alongside the previous turn—it's easy to get out of sequence. Keep going until all six form strands are on the floor and the working strand is completely laid up around the heart, ends meeting in the same score (Figure 155-B,C,D).

Now for the hard part. Instead of tucking the ends as with rope, we're going to make them dive into the

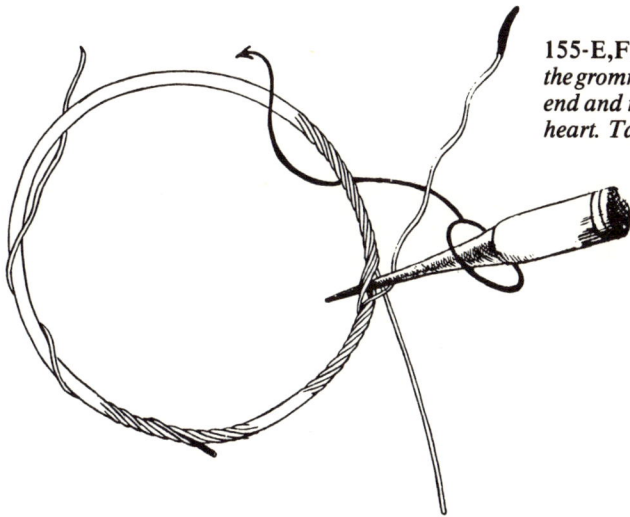

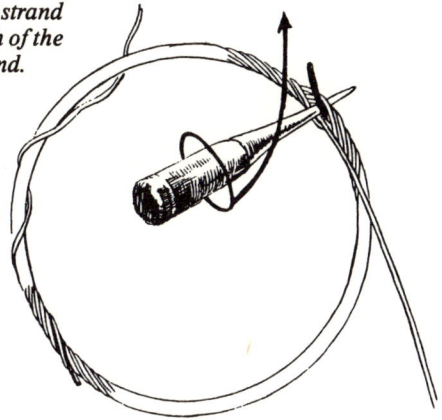

middle of the wire and run them along until they completely replace the heart. Set things up by clamping the grommet securely in a vise, then pry both ends of the heart a short distance out of the wire. Wrap one end of the working strand around the grommet a few times to keep it from shifting while you deal with the other end (Figure 155-D).

Enter a spike under the three strands immediately to the right of the end you are going to roll in. Pry the three strands a little to the right and you'll be able to pull the standing part of the end down into the middle of the wire (Figure 155-E). Rotating the spike counterclockwise will make it travel down one side of the grommet, burying the end and pushing the heart out as it goes (Figure 155-F). Experiment with the angle at which you hold the spike until you can roll the end in without distorting the strands. When you're halfway around, the taped end will disappear inside. Go back to the start for one last bit of finesse.

The second strand is more difficult to submerge than the first. To get it started I use two spikes, a slightly involved method but one that works every time. Turn the grommet (or yourself) around and insert a spike under the three strands to the right of where the other end dove in. Insert the other spike, from left to right, under three strands so that it emerges in the same space that the first spike went into. Place the new working end between the spikes and lever it down with the first spike (Figure 155-G). Then rotate the first spike as before, pushing the strand in ahead of it and pushing the heart out. Remove the second spike once you're well started.

If you measured well, the heart will fall out just as you run out of end, and the two ends will nearly meet inside the wire (Figure 155-H). Ah, perfect. A smooth, steel-strong beauty, and all from a single strand.

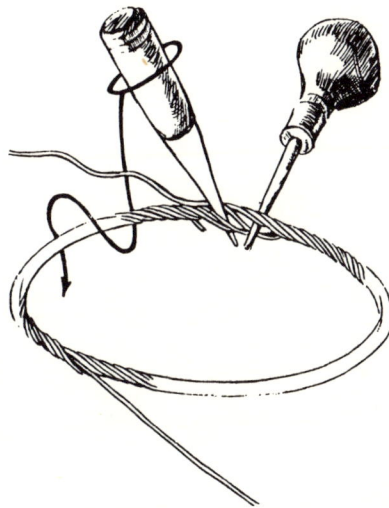

155-G. *To roll the more stubborn other end in, trap it between two spikes, one going into the wire on its left, the other emerging from the wire on its right. Wedge the strand into the middle, then roll it along as above. When it's well started, remove the right-hand spike. Note: The two ends should not cross each other at this juncture, but go into the wire after passing by each other.*

155-H. *Roll the second end completely into the wire; the heart will fall free as the end goes in, butted against the other end. Tap lightly with the mallet to fair all turns.*

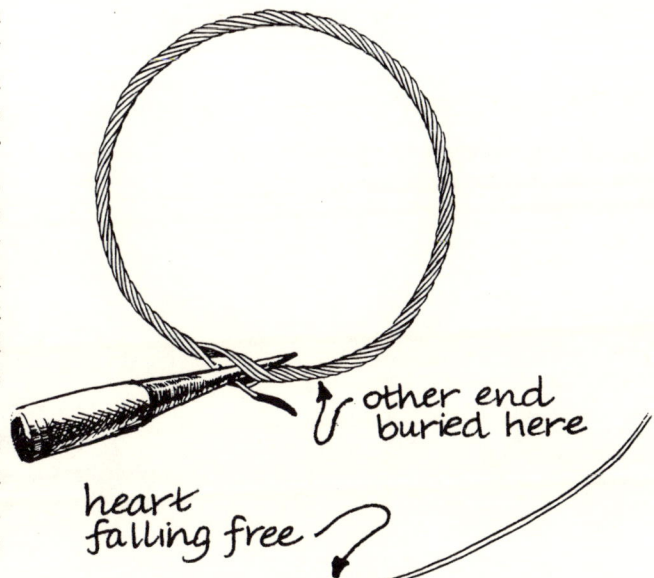

other end buried here

heart falling free

FIGURE 156. *Some sample grommet locations, including blocks, yard, painter, sling, bucket, thole pin, and neck, head, and smoke gear.*

Now, getting back to those Expensive Fittings, Figure 156 shows a few of the places where your handiwork can be put to use. Wire grommets are usually served and sometimes leathered where they bear on mast or boom, to waterproof and to better distribute strain. Thimbles are held in place with wire throat seizings. With the softer rope grommets, service is optional, and seizings are made with marline or nylon seine twine. Even an ardent Fittingist would have to concede that knowing how to grommet is a useful skill, especially in an emergency. And for those who like to fit out in the traditional manner, the possibilities are endless.

110

THE COMFORTS OF SERVICE

Service, hah! I can't think of a sillier waste of time than wrapping rope with little-bitty pieces of string. It's an absurd, archaic, ridiculously labor-intensive exercise in drudgery that you, a contemporary sailor, could never conceivably have a use for.

Unless maybe you're looking for a cheap, easy way to hang your boathook from a shroud. A few turns of marline at the appropriate height make a firm base to seize a round sail thimble to, to hold the hook. Seize another thimble aloft to slide the handle into (Figure 157). A seizing put onto bare wire would be prone to slip.

A layer of friction tape parceling comes first, to keep moisture from settling in the wire's interior (plastic electrical tape grows brittle with age and should be avoided). Put this waterproof "bedding" on from the bottom up, with the lay, so the turns shed water, shingle-like. Next put the service on good and tight with no spaces between the turns. Apply it from the top down so that (a) it disturbs the parceling the least, and (b) the slight untwisting of the wire under load will tighten the service. The simplest way to serve is by pulling each turn taught with a marlingspike (see Figures 10 and 11), although the job will go faster and more smoothly if you take the time to make up a serving board like the one shown in Figure 158. This

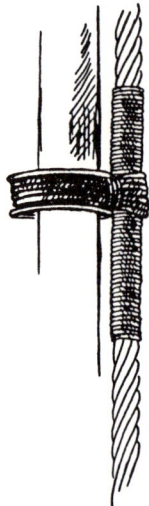

FIGURE 157. *To secure a boathook on a shroud, serve two short streches, 2 feet or so closer together than the length of the handle. Lash sail thimbles in place.*

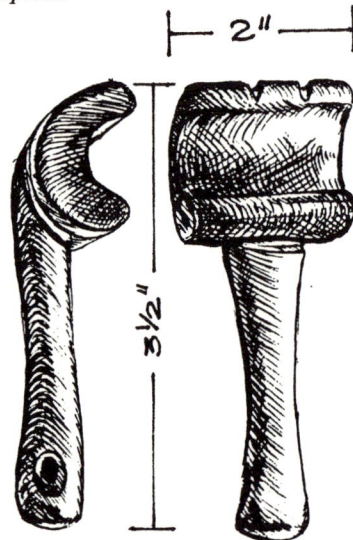

FIGURE 158. *"Lil' Bub," a typical serving board.*

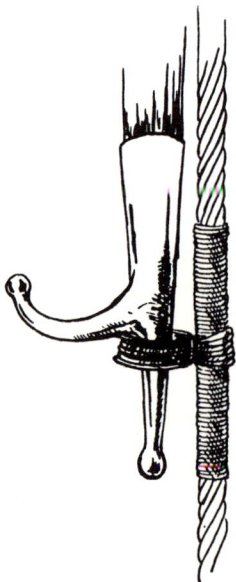

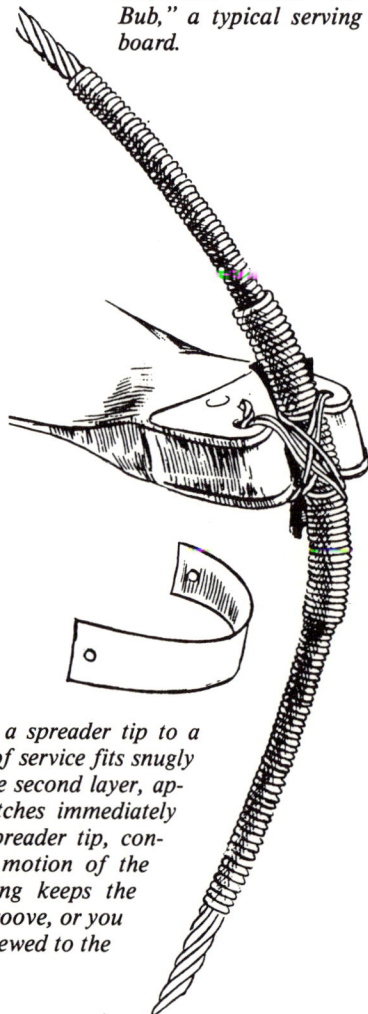

FIGURE 159. *Securing a spreader tip to a shroud. The first layer of service fits snugly into the spreader tip; the second layer, applied in two short stretches immediately above and below the spreader tip, contains the up-and-down motion of the spreader. A light lashing keeps the shroud in the spreader groove, or you can use a metal band screwed to the spreader.*

board is "threaded" onto the marline in the same way that "Runaround Sue" is threaded (Figure 168). The marline will sometimes make a creaking sound as it passes over the board; this is generally taken as an indication that the service is tight enough. But I've found that creaking is also related to how much tar is in the marline, how big and smooth the head of the serving board is, and how fast it's moving. For my money, the only sure indication of tension is in the finished product; service should feel *hard*, with all the turns jammed right up against each other. If the marline breaks frequently, it's too tight.

There are two ways to stop service: If you're using a spike, make the last three or four turns loosely around both it and the wire. Pass the end under the turns, then tighten the turns by working them around with the spike. Hitch onto the end and pull all slack out, then give a few sharp jerks to snug things completely down before trimming.

The serving board's tidier finish involves stopping at the same point, but making the three or four turns *on the other side of the board* from the end of the service, quite loosely. Then tuck the end of the marline under the last turn of service and begin serving over it, thus undoing the turns you made and ending up with a large bight at the end of a smooth, tight service. Remove the serving board and hold onto the service with one hand, hitch onto the end with a spike and pull with the other hand, and guide the slack out, keeping the twine from twisting, with your third hand. Be careful, as you pull, to keep the spike away from face and body; twine has been known to break. This procedure is the same when made with seizing wire, as in Figures 164 and 165.

Come to think of it, little stretches of service are great for lashing hammocks, lightboards, fairleads, ratlines, or cleats to, or just as a comfortable handhold on backstay or shrouds (title illustration). And I don't recall ever seeing a better way of holding spreaders in place than the one L. Francis Herreshoff used to recommend (Figure 159, reproduced from construction drawings for *Araminta*). As you can see, the first layer of service fits snugly into the spreader tip, easing the bend and providing a foundation for the little bits of service that go on above and below the spreader, holding it from traveling up or down and making reinstallation easy after a haulout. Leather backing is optional. A metal strap will keep the wire from jumping out, but a light seizing (shown) will do the trick, too.

112

FIGURE 160. *"U.P.I.," a serving iron, with suggested dimensions.*

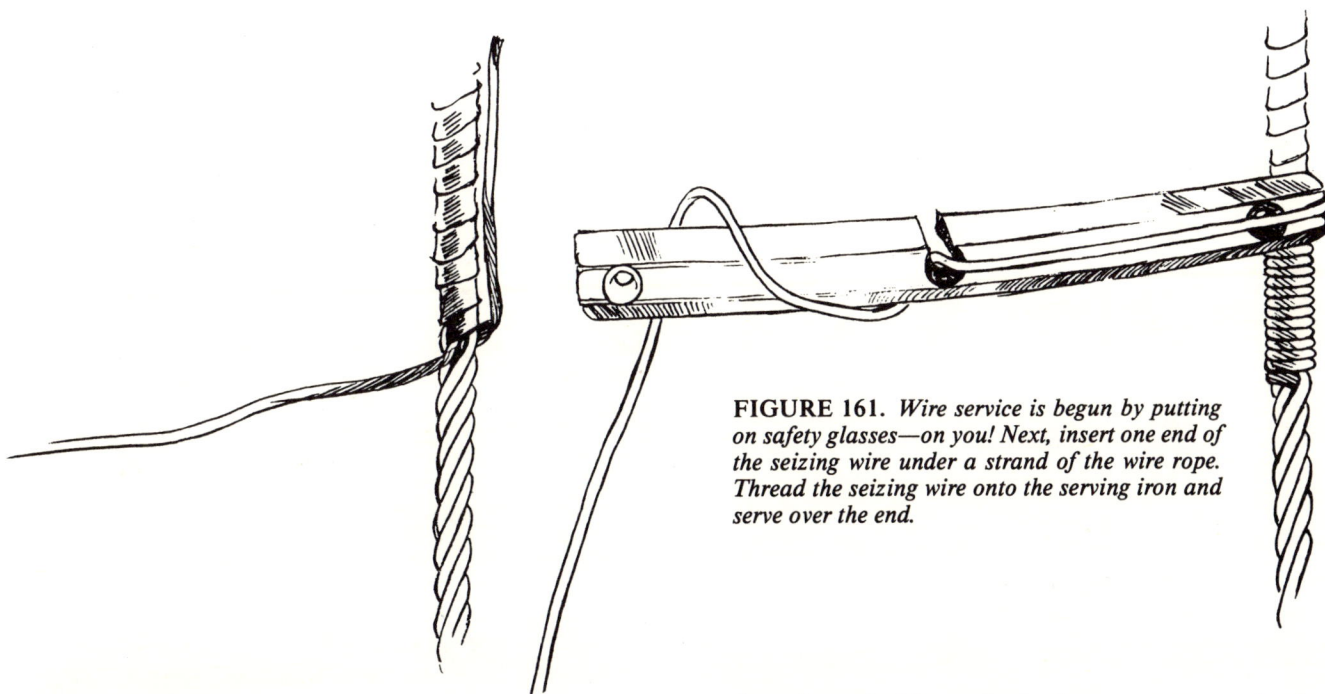

FIGURE 161. *Wire service is begun by putting on safety glasses—on you! Next, insert one end of the seizing wire under a strand of the wire rope. Thread the seizing wire onto the serving iron and serve over the end.*

Wire Service

If you have a wire halyard, the best thing to end it with is a splice, which is less liable than a mechanical fitting to jam or break if it gets run into the masthead sheave. And splices should be served to cover and protect the ends, either with marline or with seizing wire. Marline service is easier and cheaper to apply but can chafe through, so use wire service on halyard splices, the lower ends of shrouds if sheets and sails ride on them, and on stays that have sails set on them.

Wire and marline service are the same in principle, but differ in tools and technique. At the start of wire service, raise a strand of the piece you're serving and slip the end of the seizing wire under to anchor it, then serve over the end as with marline, but using a serving iron instead of a too-soft-for-wire serving board. Figure 161 shows wire service being applied with my serving iron "U.P.I.," which I made from the broken stempiece of a Wianno Sr. If your local chandlery

doesn't stock this particular item, any scrap chunk of bronze roughly matching the proportions shown will do just fine.

To finish wire service, come within five or six turns of the thimble (wire is slicker than marline, thus the greater number of turns), make and undo the turns as with marline, pull the slack out with a pair of pliers (Figure 165), and get out your heaving mallet. Figure 166 shows "Mallet de Mer" with the seizing wire belayed to its head and handle, ready to pull the last turn taut—too much of a job for a marlingspike. Apply just enough tension to bring the turn down snug, then put the mallet over on the other side so that the strand will be pulled to that side, wedging itself permanently between the rope and the turns of service. If the service is very tight the strand will shear off cleanly at its exit point with a good haul on the mallet.

If it won't shear, but you're sure the fit is snug, just bend the seizing wire sharply back and forth repeatedly until it breaks off at the exit point.

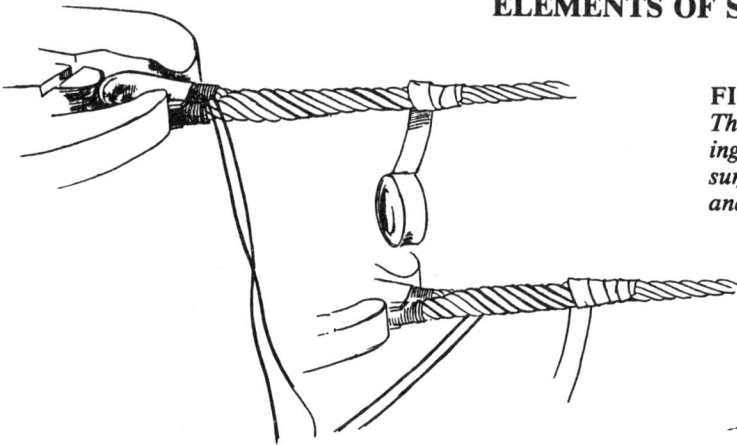

FIGURE 162. *The eye of the splice is served before splicing. The finished splice is tarred, then wormed and parceled. Worming material should be just large enough to provide a smooth surface over which to parcel. Carefully seal the join between eye and splice with parceling.*

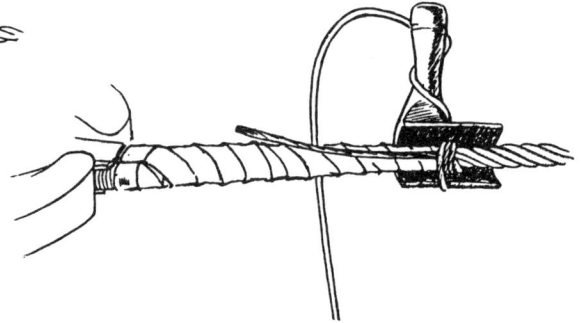

FIGURE 163. *Marline service being applied with another type of serving board—one with a very wide groove suited to splices. Note that marline is threaded through the hole in the handle to gain tension and to prevent accidentally dropping the board overboard.*

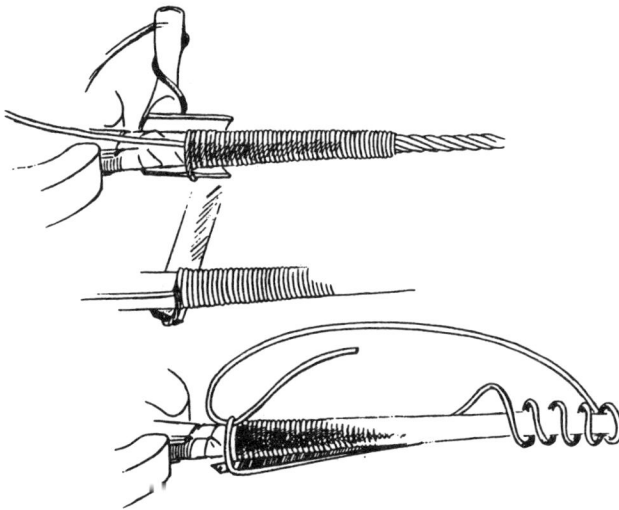

FIGURE 164. *Marline-to-seizing-wire transition: When you're 15 turns from the thimble, begin serving over the end of a 6-foot length of seizing wire. At seven turns from the thimble, bend the wire over the marline and begin serving over marline with seizing wire (got your safety glasses on?). After two turns with seizing wire, stop and pass five turns around the standing part of the wire rope, then slip the seizing wire end under its second turn of service. Continue serving until all five turns are undone.*

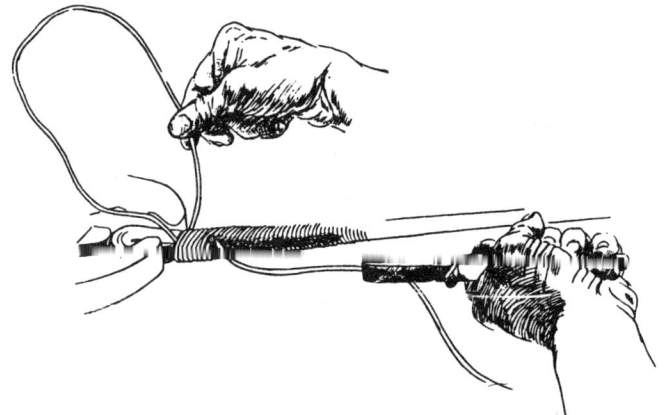

FIGURE 165. *Holding tension with one hand, use pliers to pull slack out.*

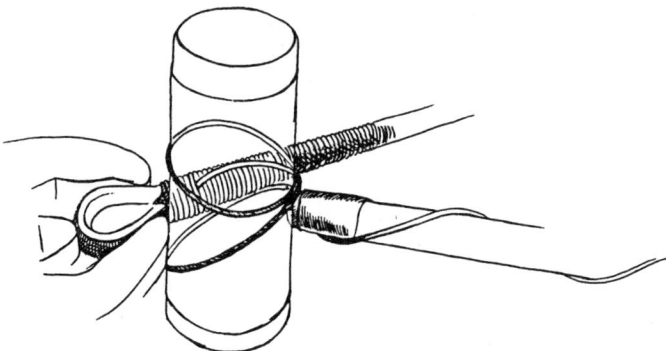

FIGURE 166. *To finish the seizing, use a heaving mallet to pull first left (facing vise), then right. The wire should snap at the exit point during the pull to the right.*

114

One Highly Evolved Splice Service

Figure 167 shows a spliced eye that is oversized and served for its entire circumference. And the splice is served with marline, except up at the thimble, where there's a short bit of wire service. Why the complication? Two reasons: (1) The splice and its eye are completely waterproofed. (2) If the thimble or the eye service is ever damaged, cutting away the seizing wire will allow replacement or repair. The regular snug-up-to-the-thimble splice means that you'll either have to shorten up drastically or replace the piece in case of thimble damage.

To produce this ultimate in eyesplice protection, serve the circumference of the eye before splicing, then tar, worm, and parcel the splice (Figures 162 through 166). Run your marline service up to within 15 turns from the thimble, then make five or six turns with the marline over one end of a 6-foot length of similar-diameter seizing wire (Figure 164).

Continue marline service until you're seven turns from the thimble (use a ruler or caliper gauge to judge the distance), then bend the wire over the marline and begin serving with wire. Make two turns, then make and unmake the last five turns as with the straight wire service to finish.

Full Service

As long as we've come this far, I might as well acquaint you with the ultimate service absurdity: covering your shrouds full length. That's right, there are crazies out there who think it a reasonable practice to completely encase their galvanized standing rigging in marline. The wire, which costs about one-third as much as stainless, is thus indefinitely preserved, assuming an annual coat of "slush" to keep the service sealed. Although the payoff is ageless wire as well as less chafe on sails and running rigging, the amount of time and effort that full-length service requires makes low-maintenance stainless the choice for all but a lunatic fringe. But for those of us who care to indulge ourselves, here's how it's done.

To start, stretch the spliced wire between two posts, trees, or walls using a come-along for tension. This will exert extreme strain on the attachment points, so be certain they are very solid. Apply a coat of pine tar as an anticorrosive—liberally, but not so that it's going to drip out. Then parcel toward the upper end with

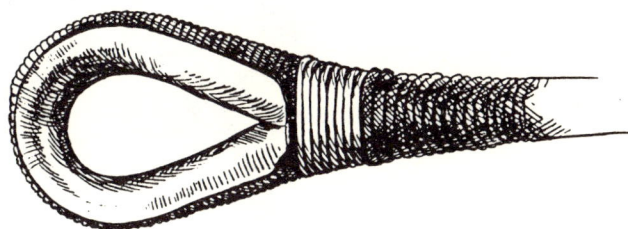

FIGURE 167. *A finished oversized eye. Note that the seizing wire diameter matches the marline. Most often, $^{3}/_{32}$-inch wire will suit.*

friction tape or tarred cloth. Worm both splices; if the wire is ⅞ inch or larger, you might want to worm the entire length, because water could collect in the large spaces between the strands.

Runaround Sue

Sue's a relatively high-tech, spool-fed, self-tensioning, air-cooled, semiautomatic serving board who literally flies through her job. In the old days, service was put on by a rigger and an apprentice, the former passing a spool-less mallet, the latter passing a ball of marline around to match, and both of them inching along with the slo-o-o-wly progressing work. But with Sue, one person just leans back and oscillates the wire to make the mallet move along all by itself, thus bearing witness to the old saying, "They also serve who only stand and wait."

For the best job, start with a not-quite-bar-taut wire, thread the mallet as shown (Figure 168) and use an oscillation technique that swings the mallet around and down on the pull stroke, then eases off to let it swing up and over before the next pull. With a little practice you can time the push-and-pull to maximum effect (that is, minimum effort). Always lean back slightly to dampen jerking motions of the wire. Tricing lines can be tied on every 20 feet or so to further control the wire's motion. With this setup, you can parcel and serve 20 to 30 feet an hour. Not exactly a blistering rate by track and field standards, but fast enough to get the job done while you're still young enough to go sailing.

So I guess marline is good for more than keeping your ditty bag smelling nice. Its applications are handsome, simple, and cost-effective, so it can free you up for other silly wastes of time. Like going sailing.

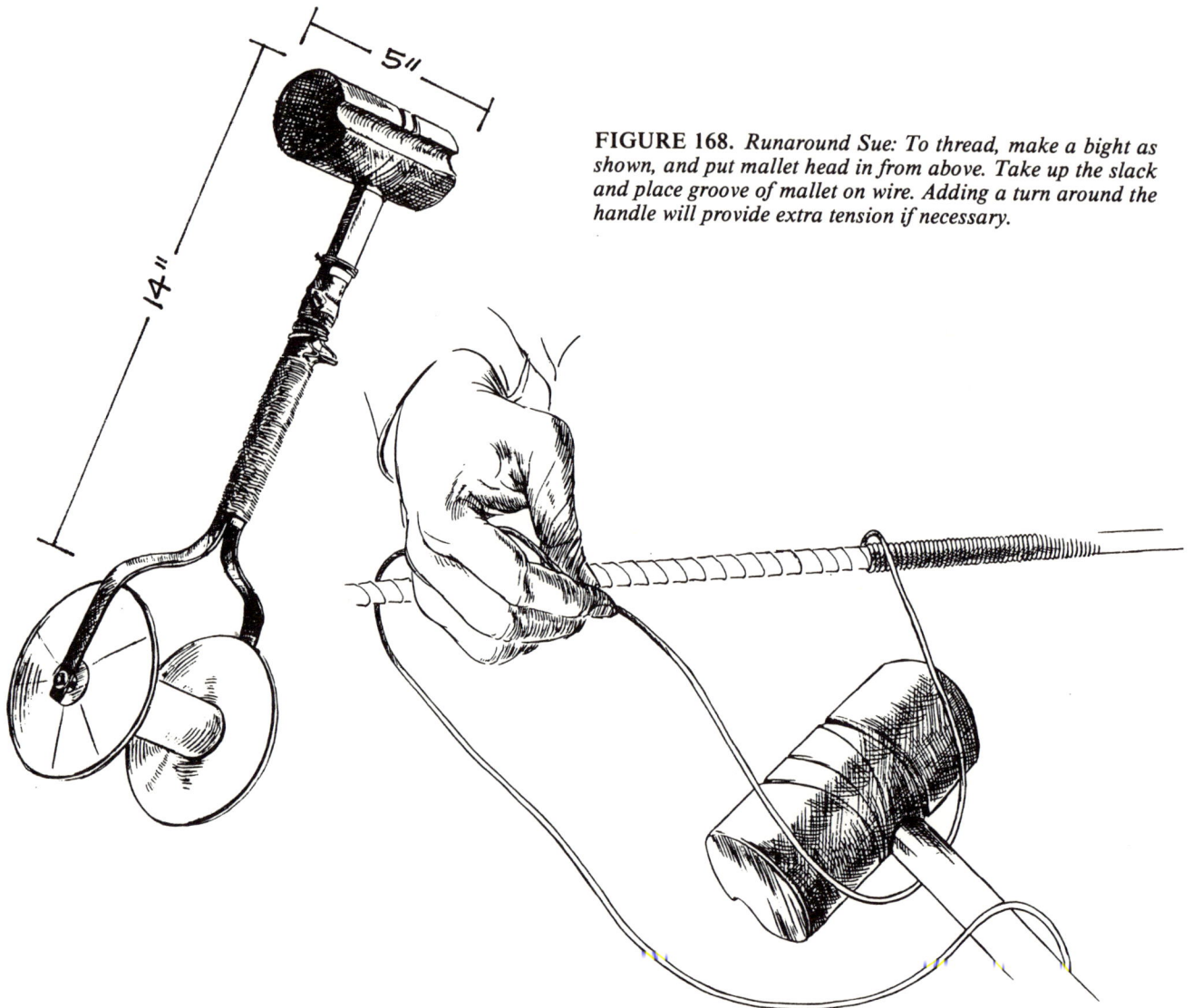

FIGURE 168. *Runaround Sue: To thread, make a bight as shown, and put mallet head in from above. Take up the slack and place groove of mallet on wire. Adding a turn around the handle will provide extra tension if necessary.*

FIGURE 169. *Flying Service: Stretch wire rope out taut, but be sure your anchor points can take the strain. Tar and worm the splices, and parcel the wire full length. Thread mallet on and "fly" by oscillating wire with rhythmic pull-and-release motion. If the marline breaks, retrieve mallet and bend in new piece as for marline-to-wire transition.*

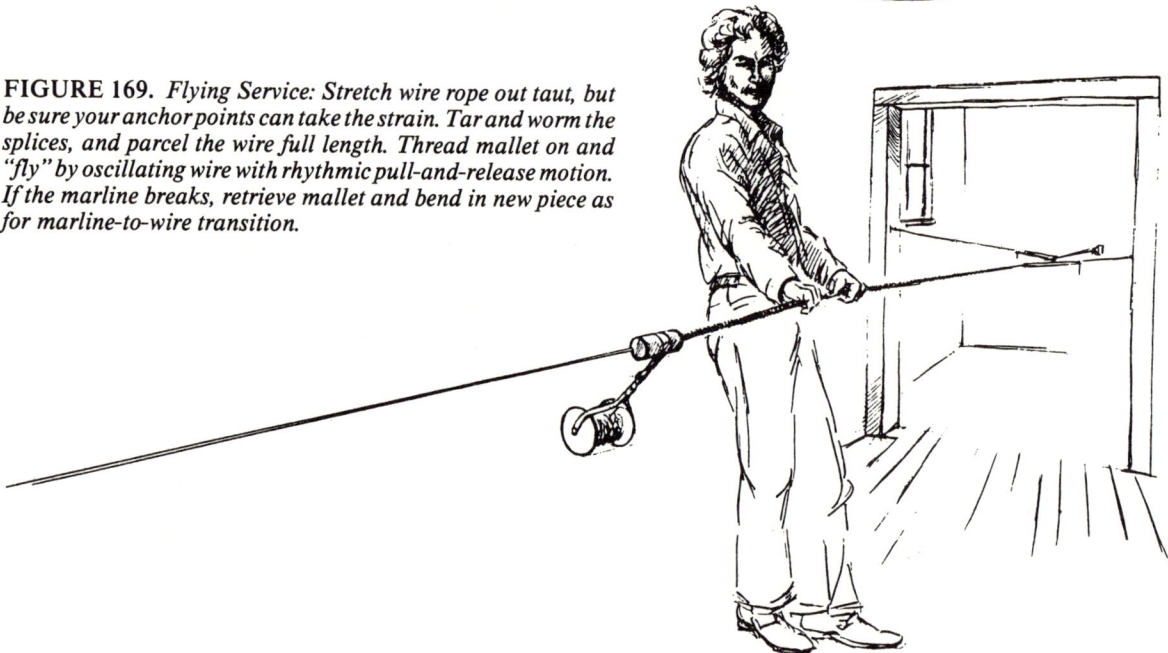

FIGURE 170-A. *Leathering a stretch of wire. To determine circumference, wrap a piece of leather around the wire.*

170-B. *The Baseball Stitch, a double-needle technique, requires a fathom of waxed twine per foot of leathering on each needle. The twine is middled on the needle, making a 3-foot working length per foot of leathering. To start the stitch, pass the needles in opposite directions, in complete round turns, through both end holes in the leather.*

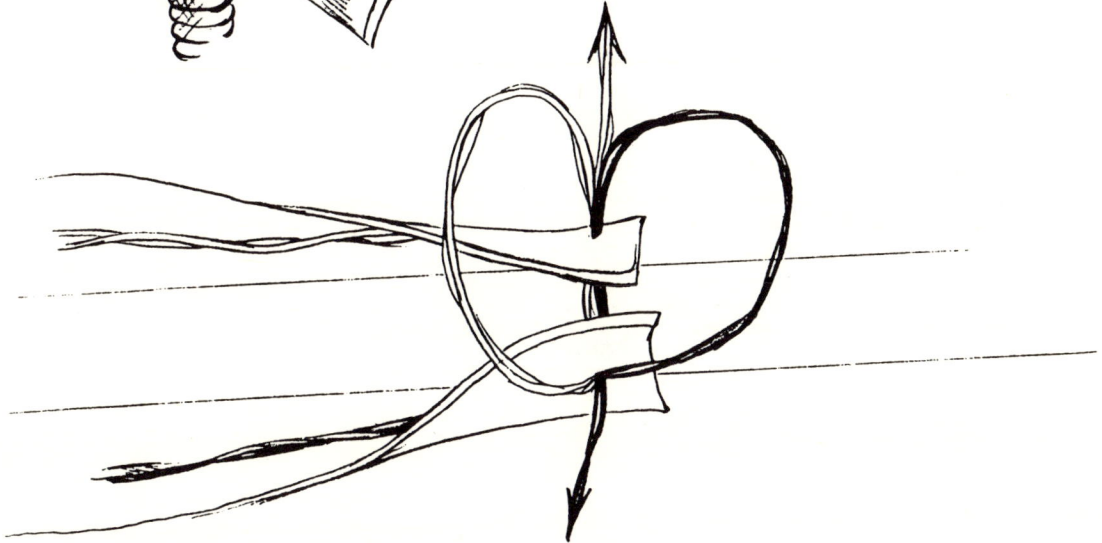

INTO LEATHER

Leather is a cushion, an insulator, that keeps your standing rigging from damaging your mast and sails. A layer of leather over one or two layers of service is standard procedure for soft eyes, and a stretch of leather over service is a tidy alternative to baggy-wrinkle for chafe-prone stretches of wire. There's nothing terribly complicated about applying leather, so it makes sense to keep a split hide of oiled shoulder or Latigo around for the above uses as well as for oar leathers, gaff jaws, chafing gear on sail eyelets, sheaths, handles, and all the other places you'll find use for it once you have it around and know how to work it.

A number of stitch patterns are in general use; I like the Baseball Stitch for its neat appearance, its diagonal pull, which draws seams tight without being inclined to rip the leather, and its use of two independent threads for redundant security from chafe. Two people with needles can make this stitch go very quickly indeed: Set the work up at waist level, one of you on either side, and commence stitching, hauling tight after each pass (use a roping palm or heavy gloves to prevent sliced hands from hauling). With a bit of practice you'll work into a pleasant little choreography.

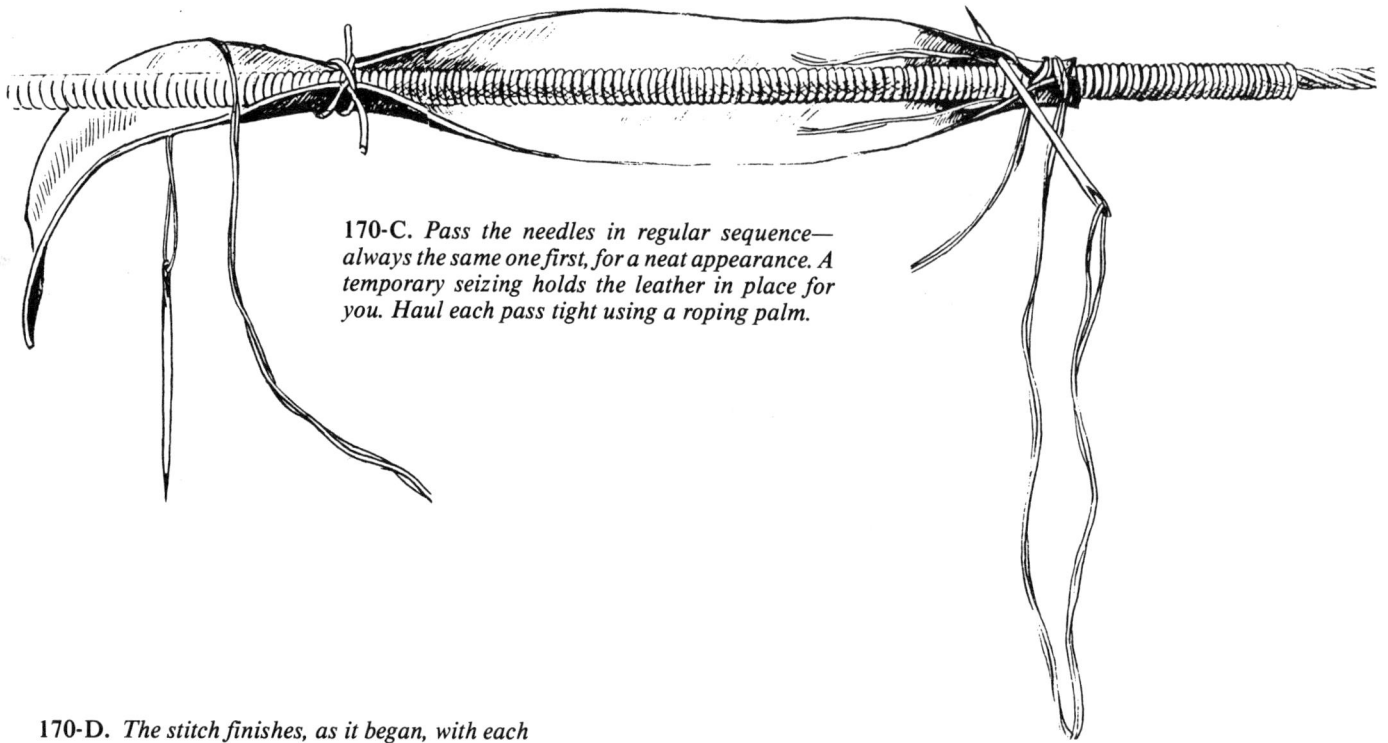

170-C. *Pass the needles in regular sequence— always the same one first, for a neat appearance. A temporary seizing holds the leather in place for you. Haul each pass tight using a roping palm.*

170-D. *The stitch finishes, as it began, with each needle making a complete round turn. Reef-knot the ends together and cut off flush with the leather.*

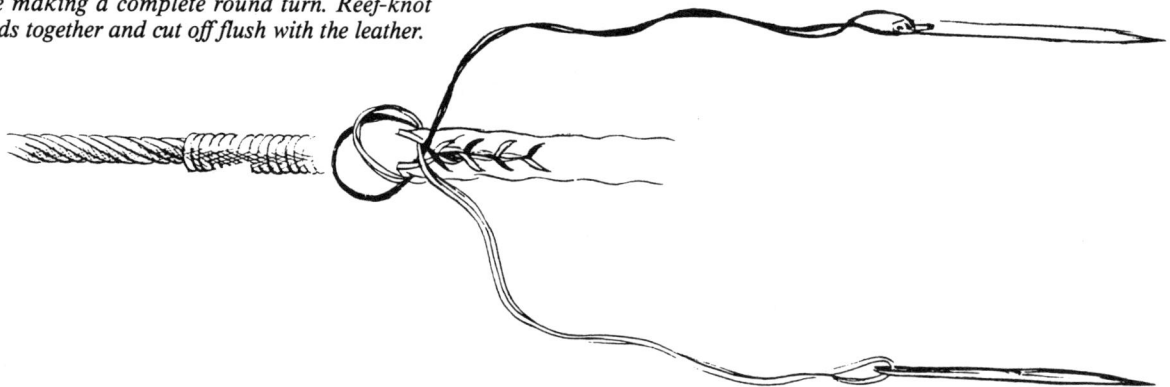

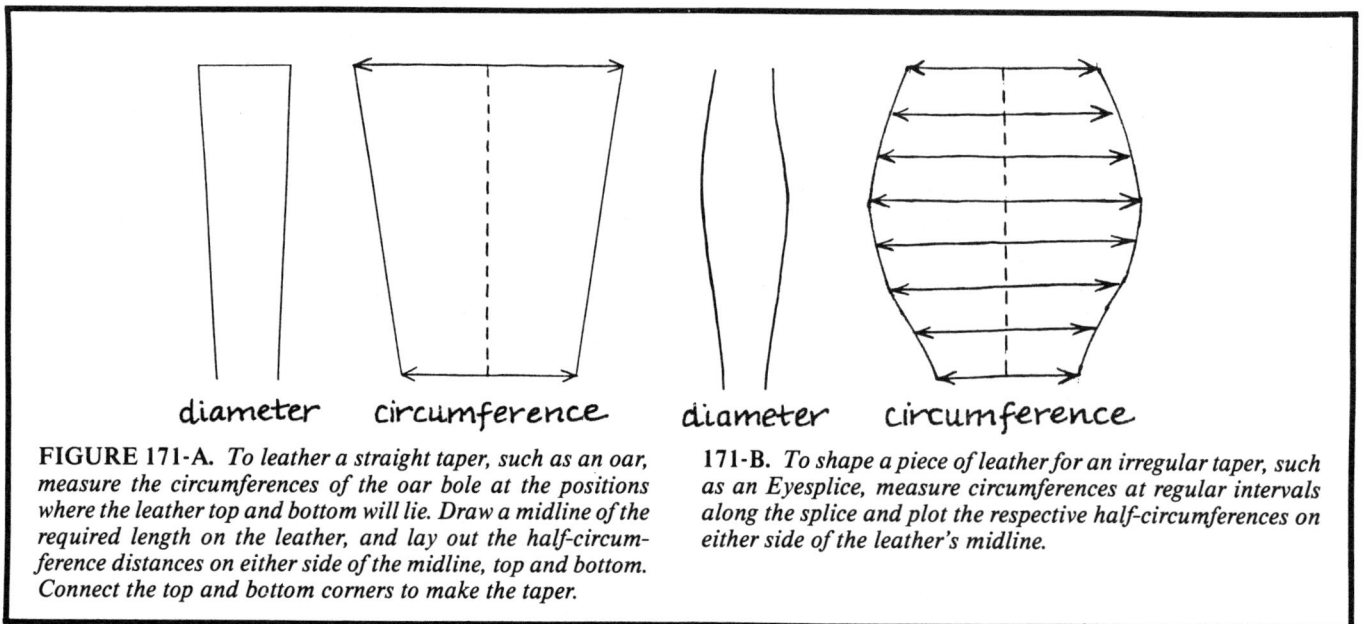

diameter   circumference   diameter   circumference

FIGURE 171-A. *To leather a straight taper, such as an oar, measure the circumferences of the oar bole at the positions where the leather top and bottom will lie. Draw a midline of the required length on the leather, and lay out the half-circumference distances on either side of the midline, top and bottom. Connect the top and bottom corners to make the taper.*

171-B. *To shape a piece of leather for an irregular taper, such as an Eyesplice, measure circumferences at regular intervals along the splice and plot the respective half-circumferences on either side of the leather's midline.*

FIGURE 172. *A double-served, leathered soft eye is shown in A. This heavy leather was prepared by pre-punching holes ⅜ inch apart and ⅜ inch from the edges (B). The holes were marked with a jogging wheel for regular spacing (C), and the stitches were smoothed down with a seam rubber (D).*

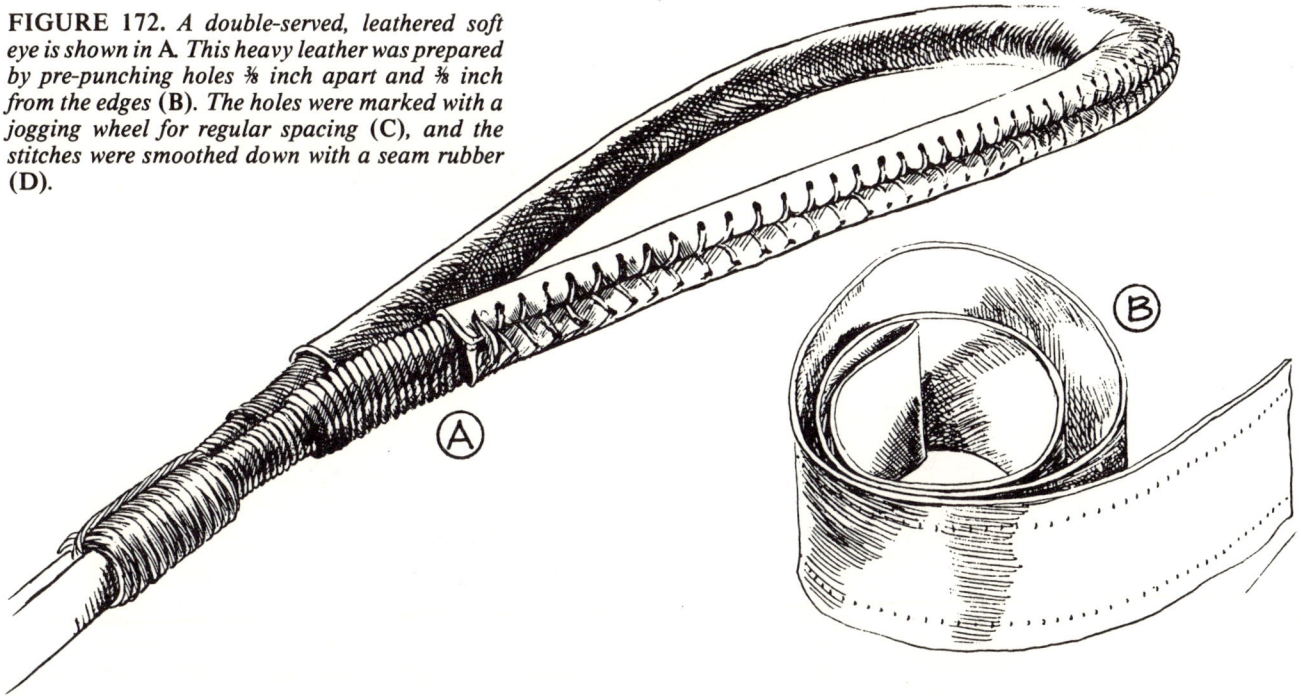

For the neatest job, bevel the meeting edges back from the finished face of the leather and make the piece slightly (1/16 to ⅛ inch, depending on the elasticity of the leather you're using) undersized so that the leather will stretch to fill the gap.

Rub liberal amounts of neats-foot oil or other conditioner into both sides of the leather before sewing, and renew the coating periodically on the outside.

Always leather soft eyes *before* splicing; it is so much easier to leather in a straight line. To leather grommets or to re-leather old eyes, straighten and cover a section of the piece at a time.

Stitch with sail needles threaded with stout waxed Dacron sail twine. Push the needle through with a roping palm or, if the leather is too dense, pre-punch holes. Pull the twine tight enough for a good fit, but not so tight that there's a danger of ripping the material. Go over the finished job with a seam rubber (use the back of your rigger's knife if you don't have a specialized seam-rubbing tool); this improves appearance while bedding down the stitching so it is less susceptible to chafe.

When I go aloft and find a neatly sewn piece of Latigo following an eye around the mast, I think, "Ah, here's beauty, and evidence of care." Riggers are into leather.

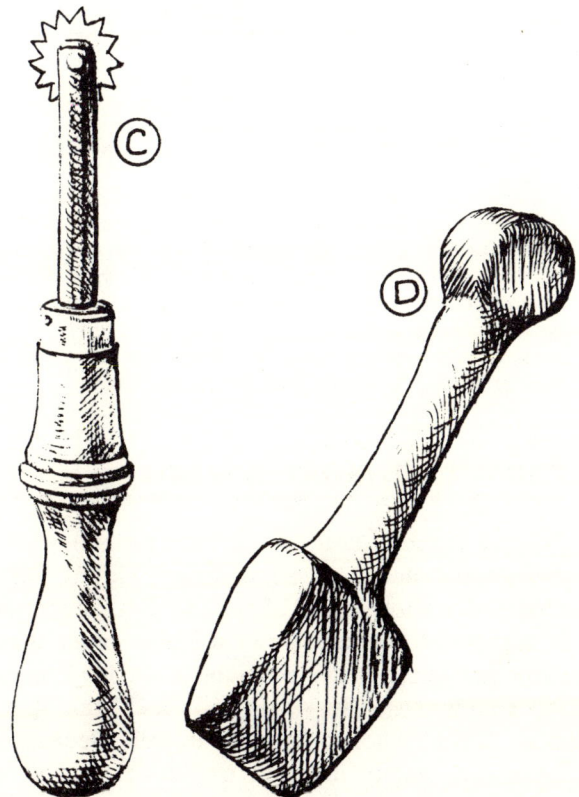

119

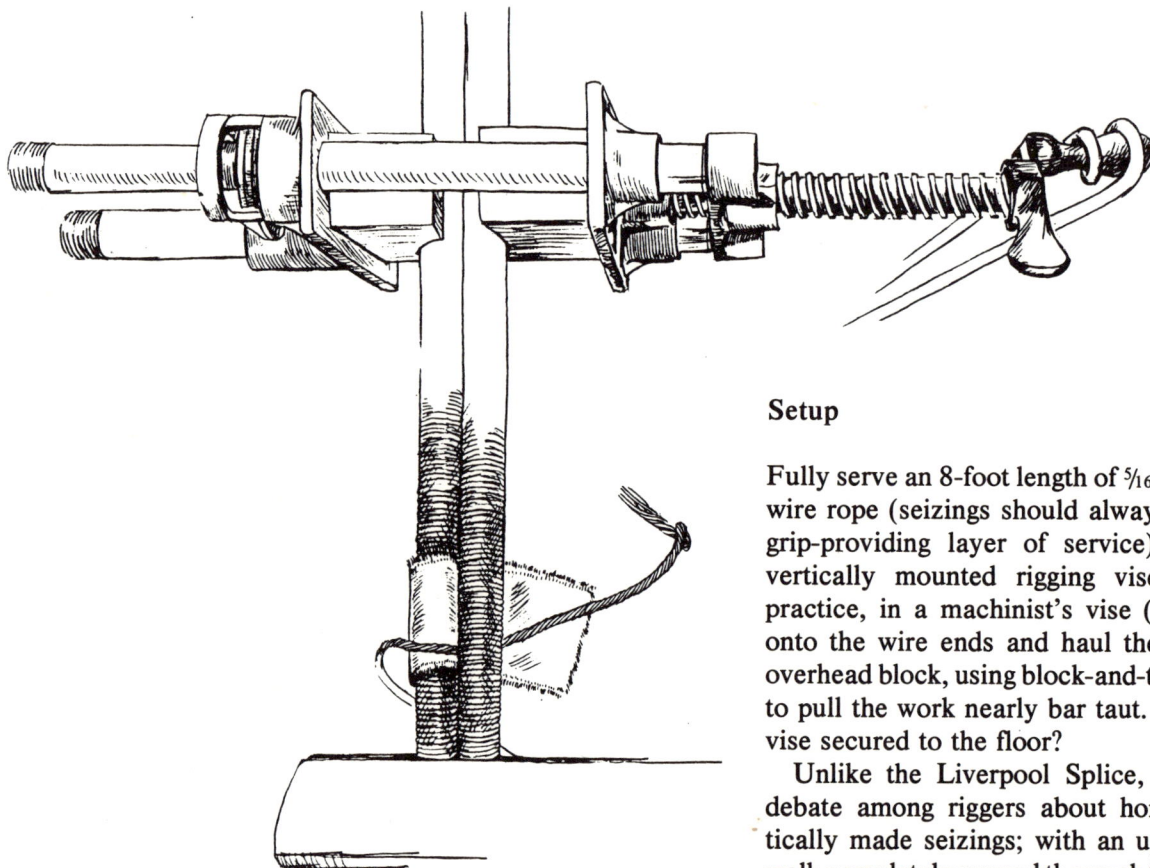

FIGURE 173. *Wire throat seizing set-up. The served wires have been clamped in place at their lower ends, and the upper ends have been pulled taut overhead. The rigger's screw is in position, with a line led from its handle to torque the wire a quarter-turn counterclockwise. This will provide resistance for the clockwise torque that the seizing stick will apply. A strip of canvas and a length of seizing wire have been inserted between the legs at the seizing site, as the text describes.*

THE WIRE THROAT SEIZING

There is no more subtle knot than this one. In structure and appearance it is an ordinary Throat Seizing, rendered in wire instead of marline. But the stresses it is designed to endure are of a higher order than its twine cousin's, and the technique of making it properly relies so much on fussiness and "feel" that it is the most difficult knot to learn to do well. Because it is intrinsic to many items of traditional rigging, particularly shroud pairs, wire rope grommets, and deadeyes, I'm going to attempt a description of it here. But understand that practice and something I can only describe as utilitarian intuition will do you a lot more good than words and pictures will.

Setup

Fully serve an 8-foot length of 5/16-inch 7 x 7 or 7 x 19 wire rope (seizings should always be applied over a grip-providing layer of service). Clamp this in a vertically mounted rigging vise or, just for this practice, in a machinist's vise (Figure 173). Hitch onto the wire ends and haul them up snugly to an overhead block, using block-and-tackle or come-along to pull the work nearly bar taut. How firmly is your vise secured to the floor?

Unlike the Liverpool Splice, there is almost no debate among riggers about horizontal versus vertically made seizings; with an upright wire one can walk completely around the work for greater speed and better-controlled "tracking."

Six to 8 inches above the vise jaws, apply a homemade rigger's screw (made from a double-bar clamp with shaped wood jaws screwed to it), and snug it up to pinch the legs firmly together. Hitch a light line to the clamp's handle and lead it out horizontally under sufficient strain to put a slight right-hand twist into the wire. This is to counteract the left-hand twist that applying the seizing will cause.

Drive in a small spike below the rigger's screw and insert one end of a 1½-inch by 2¼-inch strip of medium-weight canvas and one end of a 10-foot-long piece of 1/16-inch galvanized or stainless 1 x 7 seizing wire (Figure 173). Work a little stopper crimp into the end of the wire and position the wire down near the bottom of the canvas. Remove the spike. Pull on the seizing wire until the knot fetches up against the wire rope. Wrap the canvas strip tightly around, against the lay, and fix it in place with a layer of friction tape.

Now step over to the bandsaw and cut yourself a seizing stick (Figure 174) out of the toughest, orneriest wood you can find: Lignum vitae, some of the oaks, or hickory, among others, will do. Round off the rough edges and get back to the vise.

120

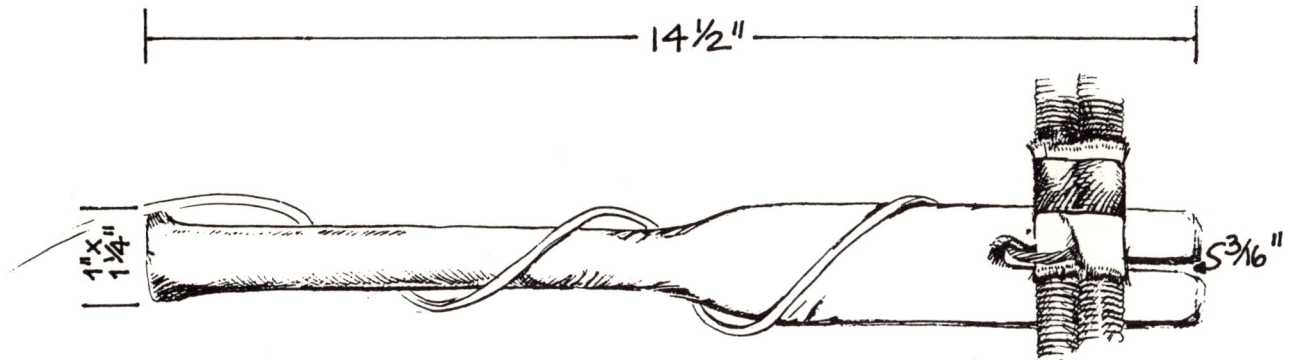

14½"

1" x 1¼"

5 3/16"

Start

From here on, an extra pair of hands is a big help, so try to talk someone into reading all this and working with you. I'll assume in the instructions that you were successful.

Coil and lightly seize the seizing wire, then pull on and bend it at its beginning so that it leads slightly downward from where it emerges between the two parts of the wire rope. Then veer it off horizontally to the left. Thread the wire onto the stick and take up the slack.

Essaying to keep the seizing wire absolutely horizontal, move the stick around, easing up just a bit on friction as you round the first corner, then clamping down tightly and stre-e-e-tching it across the face. If the end pulls out or if the wire rope starts to twist, stop, redo things more tightly, and then start again. The first revolution should finish at the level at which it began. At this point, against all instincts of tidiness, you must raise the lead a little so that the wire crosses this face crookedly and lays in directly above its start. In making the turn and wrapping around the other face the lead will be horizontal.

Continue wrapping, moderate tension on the corners, heavy on the faces. Allow no gaps between the turns. Faithfully follow that crooked lead in front.

FIGURE 174-A. *Bend the seizing wire down slightly where it emerges from the wire, then lead it horizontally clockwise (to the left). Thread it onto the seizing stick as shown and take up the slack.*

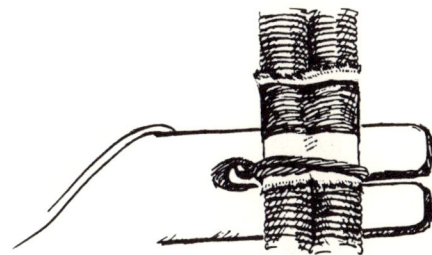

174-B. *Make the first half turn perfectly horizontal. You'll need to angle the second half turn upward to clear the start, but that's okay. Apply tight turns, stretching the wire across the flat faces, easing up a bit at the rounded sides.*

174-C. *After completing the round turns, angle the lead back down to begin riding turns.*

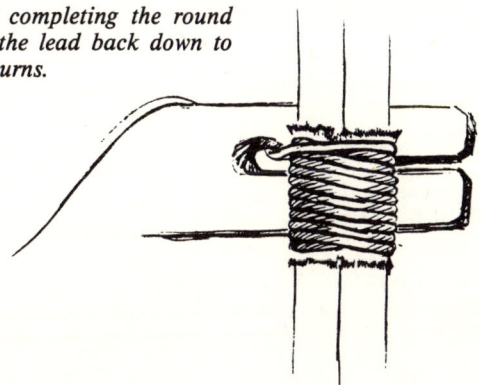

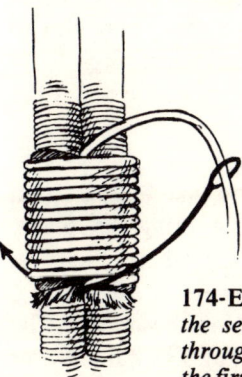

174-E. *Poke a hole at the top of the seizing and pass the end through this, then back through the first hole. Snap the turn into place.*

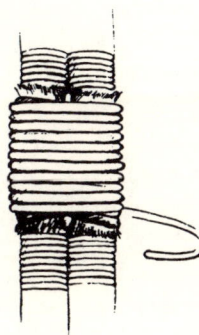

174-D. *The last riding turn should cleanly cover the first round turn. Begin frapping turns by poking a hole with an awl or small spike just as close to the bottom of the seizing as you can get. Don't snag anything with the awl. Pass the end through the hole, being careful not to lose any slack, and snap it into place, being careful not to lose any fingers.*

FIGURE 175. *Heave the first frapping turn taut with your Mallet de Mer (see Figure 166). A bit of tallow or shortening applied under the turn at its top left and bottom right corners (as seen in the drawing) will help the wire slide around. "Massage" the slack toward the mallet with a marlingspike.*

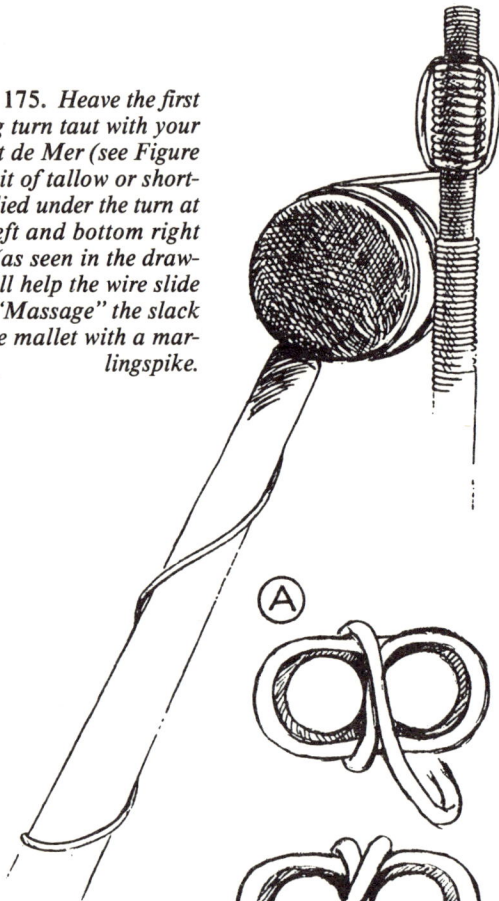

FIGURE 177-A. *After two frapping turns, the end will emerge at the point where the seizing started. Make a space with your spike or awl under the frapping turns on that side and pass the end behind those turns, right to left. Pull smartly to set the wire behind the turns. Enlarge the hole between the legs at the bottom of the seizing if necessary, and pass the end back through, creating a hitch in the seizing wire.*

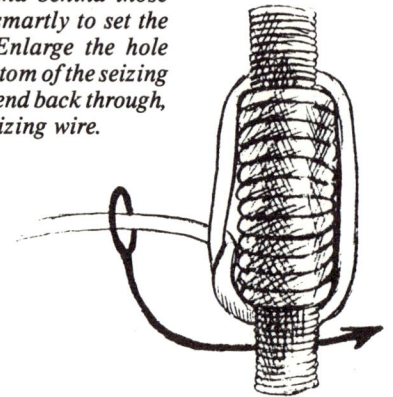

FIGURE 176. *The second frapping turn crosses over the first at the bottom of the seizing (A). The end then recrosses its own part at the end of the second frapping turn (the top of the seizing). Haul this turn taut with the mallet also, again massaging slack toward the mallet as you haul.*

Riding Turns

After you've made enough full turns (12 for this diameter wire) so that the seizing is longer than it is wide, angle the stick down so that the wire eases onto the first layer to begin a series of riding turns. Apply the riding turns snugly too, but not so much that they displace the round turns beneath. As you progress, you will note that the crooked face underneath makes the riding turns lie horizontal on both faces. Elegant.

The wire should continue to feed smoothly right to the bottom of the seizing. When you run out of turns to cover, pinch the bottom turn tightly with one hand to keep it from slipping, and remove the seizing stick with the other while your assistant removes the rigger's

screw. From this point on you will have a loose end of seizing wire inclined to whip around. Caution and safety goggles, as with wire splicing and service, are a very good idea.

Frapping Turns

Next, one of you hefts a scratch-awl spike and pushes it between the two parts of the wire rope, immediately above then immediately below the seizing. It may be necessary to pound it through with a mallet in order to make holes large enough to pass the seizing wire through. Be sure the flat tip of the spike is horizontal so that it will not cut the service as it goes through.

Pull the spike out and thread the end of the wire into the lower hole (Figure 174). When there's just a small bight of wire left on the front face of the seizing, fair carefully and take up the rest of the slack sharply to set the wire. Keeping tension on the standing part, thread the wire end through the upper hole and once more through the lower hole, snapping each time to set the wire. Watch your fingers.

Pinching the seizing so that slack can't work back, bend on your "Mallet de Mer" and take a light strain (Figure 175), just enough to hold things in place. Apply a little tallow or shortening where this first frapping turn goes around the corners of the seizing, then gradually increase the strain on the mallet. The wire will flatten and start to move, and as it does your assistant should lightly tap the last riding turn to work

122

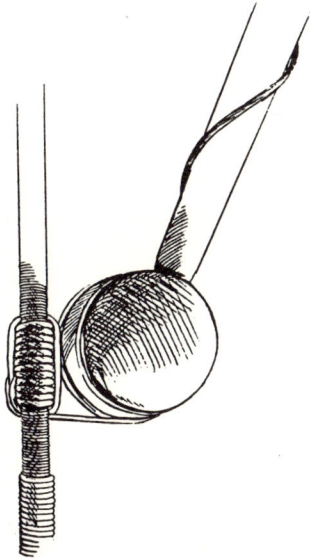

177-B. *Set the mallet against the side of the seizing opposite the hitch and thread the wire on. Smear a little tallow into the hitch and take a strain. The hitch will slide around the corner and fetch up between the legs of the wire rope. Don't force it, just set it in there firmly. The frapping turns should remain undisturbed.*

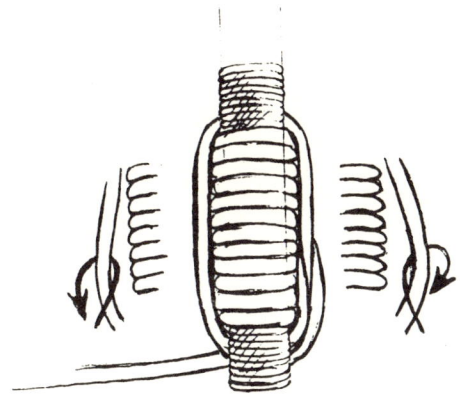

FIGURE 178. *Make a second hitch on the side opposite the first one,* in the same direction *as the first one (see arrows). Set this hitch as before, and pass the end through again.*

FIGURE 179. *To finish, move the mallet over to the side of the seizing to sharpen the end's exit from the second hitch, and pull hard. The seizing wire should break cleanly inside.*

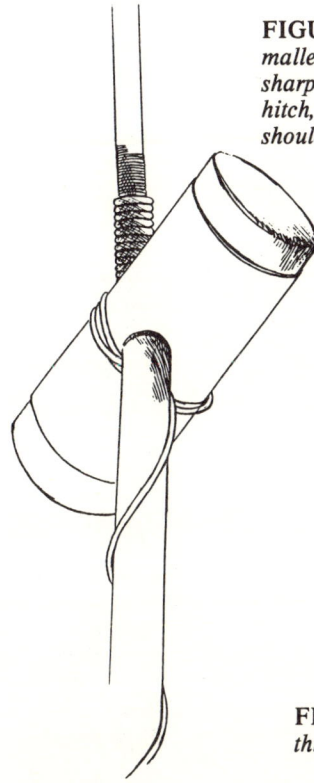

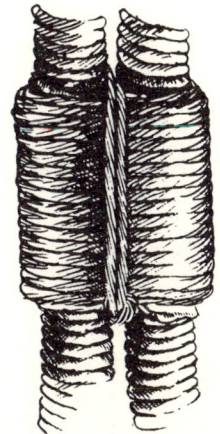

any slack in it toward the mallet, then use a spike handle or other rounded tool to "massage" slack in the frapping turn toward the mallet. Just press down and slide it along the seizing.

How hard do you haul on the mallet? Hard enough to slightly stretch the wire, but not hard enough to be in danger of wasting all your work by breaking the wire. This happens. You just have to get to know your own strength and that of the wire.

Pinch the seizing again with your hand to hold what you've gained, widen the holes a little with the little spike if necessary, and pass the end around again. Cross over the first frapping turn to bind it top and bottom (Figure 176), then apply a bit more tallow and heave and massage this second frapping turn taut.

Finishing

Work the tip of your spike under the frapping turns below the seizing wire end. Remove the spike and thread the wire through the space it made (Figure 177-A), from right to left. Pull the slack out, being careful not to distort the frapping turns or let any slack escape under them, then thread the end back into the hole from whence it came and snap it tight by hand. Smear a little tallow onto the hitch it forms, hook up your Mallet de Mer to the standing part, and pull the hitch gently out of sight, letting up when it is right between the two parts of the wire rope (Figure 177-B).

Raise another space under the frapping turns on this side and thread the seizing wire through, again from right to left; if this hitch is not made in the same direction as the first one they'll untie each other. Pull out the slack and thread the seizing wire back through

FIGURE 180. *A finished wire throat seizing.*

as before, snap it down, apply a little more tallow, and haul the hitch in against the first one. Pull square to the seizing until this hitch renders itself around the corner and down into the middle (Figure 178); then set the head of the mallet onto the right-hand leg of the wire rope (Figure 179) for the coup de grace. If all the turns are in good snug order, you can just haul tighter and tighter until the seizing wire breaks off cleanly, right where it exits the second hitch. Just the sweetest seizing finish you'll ever see (Figure 180).

123

FIGURE 181-A. *By splicing and then seizing in a deadeye, one gains a splice with no lateral strain on its legs, a tightly secured deadeye, and the ability to remove the deadeye for repair to it or to the eye's service.*

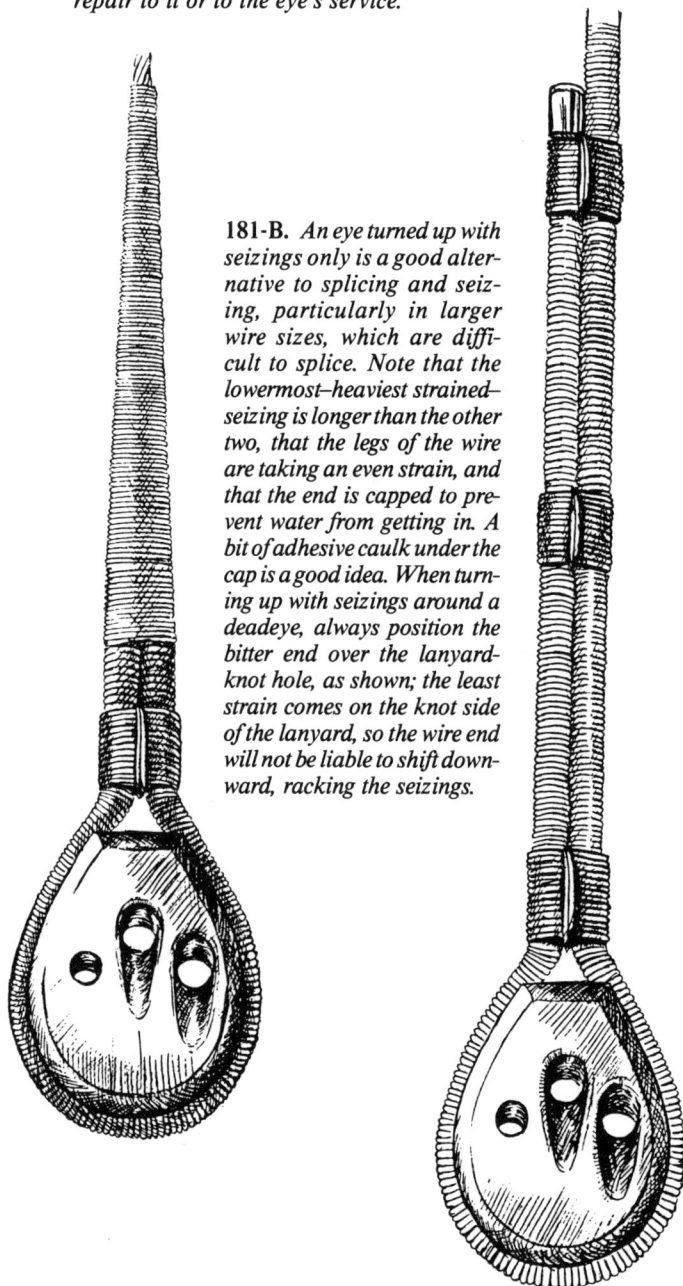

181-B. *An eye turned up with seizings only is a good alternative to splicing and seizing, particularly in larger wire sizes, which are difficult to splice. Note that the lowermost–heaviest strained-seizing is longer than the other two, that the legs of the wire are taking an even strain, and that the end is capped to prevent water from getting in. A bit of adhesive caulk under the cap is a good idea. When turning up with seizings around a deadeye, always position the bitter end over the lanyard-knot hole, as shown; the least strain comes on the knot side of the lanyard, so the wire end will not be liable to shift downward, racking the seizings.*

Living with Seizings

Some knots, like the Bowline or half hitch, inspire feelings of familiarity, even friendship. Some, like the Granny, arouse only contempt. But the Tail Splice is considered a mystery; it is treated with awe, spoken of in hushed tones, and is generally considered beyond the capabilities of mere sailors.

alternatives. At boatyards that store old and new traditional craft, one can tour the spar sheds and see Herreshoff and Concordia seizings that are still dependable works of art after 30 years. But next to them you'll find examples that have about as much structural significance as a neckerchief slide. These are dangerous and unattractive. They give seizings a bad name.

Throat Seizing Details

A spliced-and-seized-in deadeye eliminates lateral strain on the legs of the splice, holds the deadeye most firmly in place, and allows for deadeye removal in the event of damage to it or to the wire service.

A series of seizings in place of a splice is a good terminal alternative, especially on large vessels, whose standing rigging is also large and thus difficult to splice. Three seizings are applied for wire up to ⅝-inch diameter, four seizings on wire ¾-inch diameter and up.

When turning up seized ends, leave the bitter end 2 feet or more longer than it will be when finished, in order to be able to take a strain on both parts while seizing. When you're done, trim this end by (1) backing off the service to within ½ inch of the top seizing, (2) driving a thin hardwood wedge between end and standing part, (3) using the edge of an abrasive disc on an electric grinder to cut the end 1 to 1½ inches above the top seizing (the wedge protects the standing part), (4) re-serving to the end of the nub, and (5) capping off with a copper plumbing cap of appropriate diameter. Be sure that it is the end you are cutting—it is frighteningly easy to mistake the standing part for it—and cut in two or three stages, resting a few seconds between each so that the grinder doesn't heat the tar in the wire to the flash point. One can work from the top down or the bottom up; either way it is extremely important that the legs of the wire rope bear an even strain. A little slack in one leg will distort the seizings.

When seizing around deadeyes, *always* lead the bitter end of the wire rope so that it is above the lanyard-knot side of the deadeye (Figure 181). This side invariably receives less strain than the other, since when deadeyes are set up one tightens away from the lanyard knot. With the configuration shown, the majority of the lanyard strain will bear on the standing part of the wire, lessening the tendency of the seizings to "rack" (shift) under load.

124

MYSTERIES OF THE TAIL SPLICE REVEALED

Some knots, like the Bowline or half hitch, inspire feelings of familiarity, even friendship. Some, like the Granny, arouse only contempt. But the Tail Splice is considered a mystery; it is treated with awe, spoken of in hushed tones, and is generally considered beyond the capabilities of mere sailors.

This attitude is understandable. In the Tail Splice's finished form a double-braided, many-stranded rope of cordage gradually and elegantly fades into a six-stranded rope of wire. There's something alchemical about this, an aura of magic that has been played up by generations of sailmakers and riggers. But the Sacred Secret is not a mantra, a series of planetary conjunctions, a brew of lengthy formulas, nor even a lot of expensive tools. It's just this: you *pretend*. That's right; the instructions that follow just offer a way to take two complex, dissimilar pieces of line and connect them by pretending that they are a couple of pieces of ordinary three-strand rope.

FIGURE 182. *Double-braided rope. The braided cover contains a braided core.*

FIGURE 183. *In 7 x 19 wire, standard for halyards, six strands are laid up around a wire core that is the seventh strand. Each strand is composed of 19 yarns.*

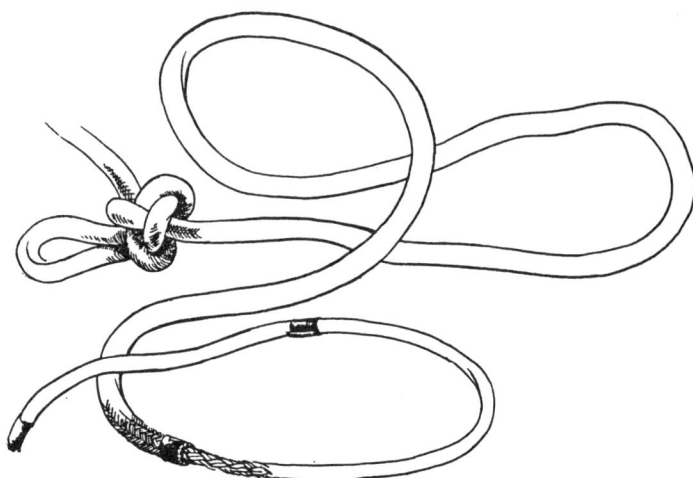

FIGURE 184. *To prepare the rope for a Tail Splice, make a knot in its standing part, then pull the cover back, exposing the core. Tape the core about 1 foot from its end and cut at the tape.*

Materials

For each practice splice, you'll need 8 feet of ³/₁₆-inch 7 x 19 wire rope and 8 feet of ⅜-inch double-braided Dacron. Double-braided rope consists of a pair of concentric woven tubes, the inner one called the core and the outer one called the cover. The core has fewer strands than the cover, but otherwise the two are structurally the same (Figure 182).

Wire halyard rope, usually stainless steel, is formed of six strands laid up (twisted helically) around a wire core. Each strand is composed of 19 yarns. In wire rope nomenclature, this construction is called 7 x 19.

For any Tail Splice, make the rope within an eighth inch of being twice the diameter of the wire; a larger difference results in distortion and a weaker splice.

Preparation

Make a knot in the double-braid about 5 feet from its end. A Farmer's Loop or Lineman's Rider (Figures 58 and 59) is perfect. Wrap the end of the cover lightly with electrical tape and cut off the whipped or fused end (Figure 184). Slide the cover back, exposing the core; the knot keeps this move from disturbing core-to-cover evenness in the rest of the rope. Cut 1 foot off the core and put a light wrapping of electrical tape on the core 10 inches from its end.

With a pair of nippers, unlay and cut the wire strands one at a time to form a tapered end (Figure 185). If the yarns of each strand spring apart when cut, carefully twist them back into place. Wrap the tapered end tightly with two layers of good-quality electrical tape.

Clamp a 6-inch Swedish fid firmly in place at waist height (Figure 186). Don't break the fid.

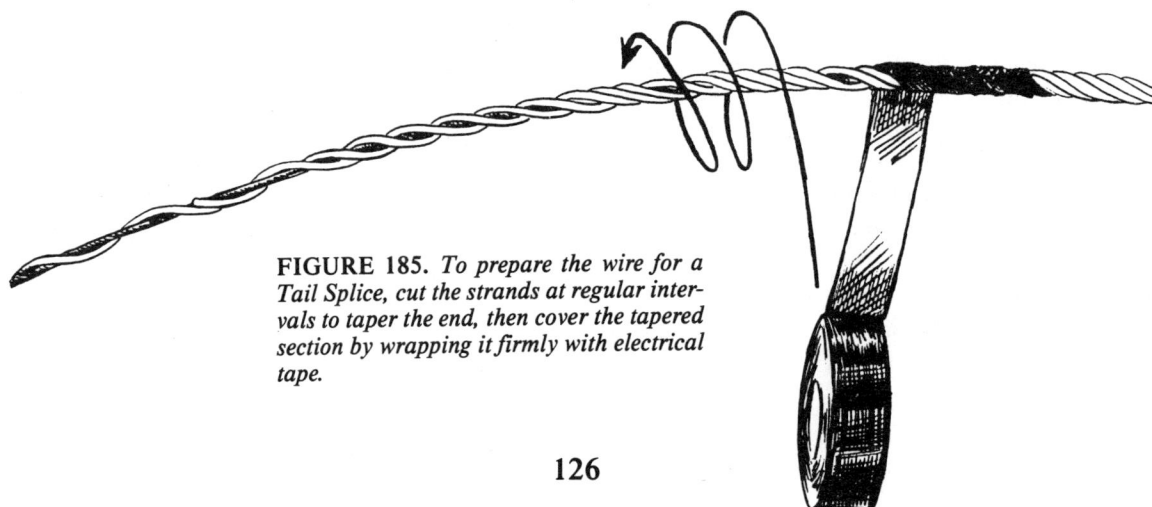

FIGURE 185. *To prepare the wire for a Tail Splice, cut the strands at regular intervals to taper the end, then cover the tapered section by wrapping it firmly with electrical tape.*

126

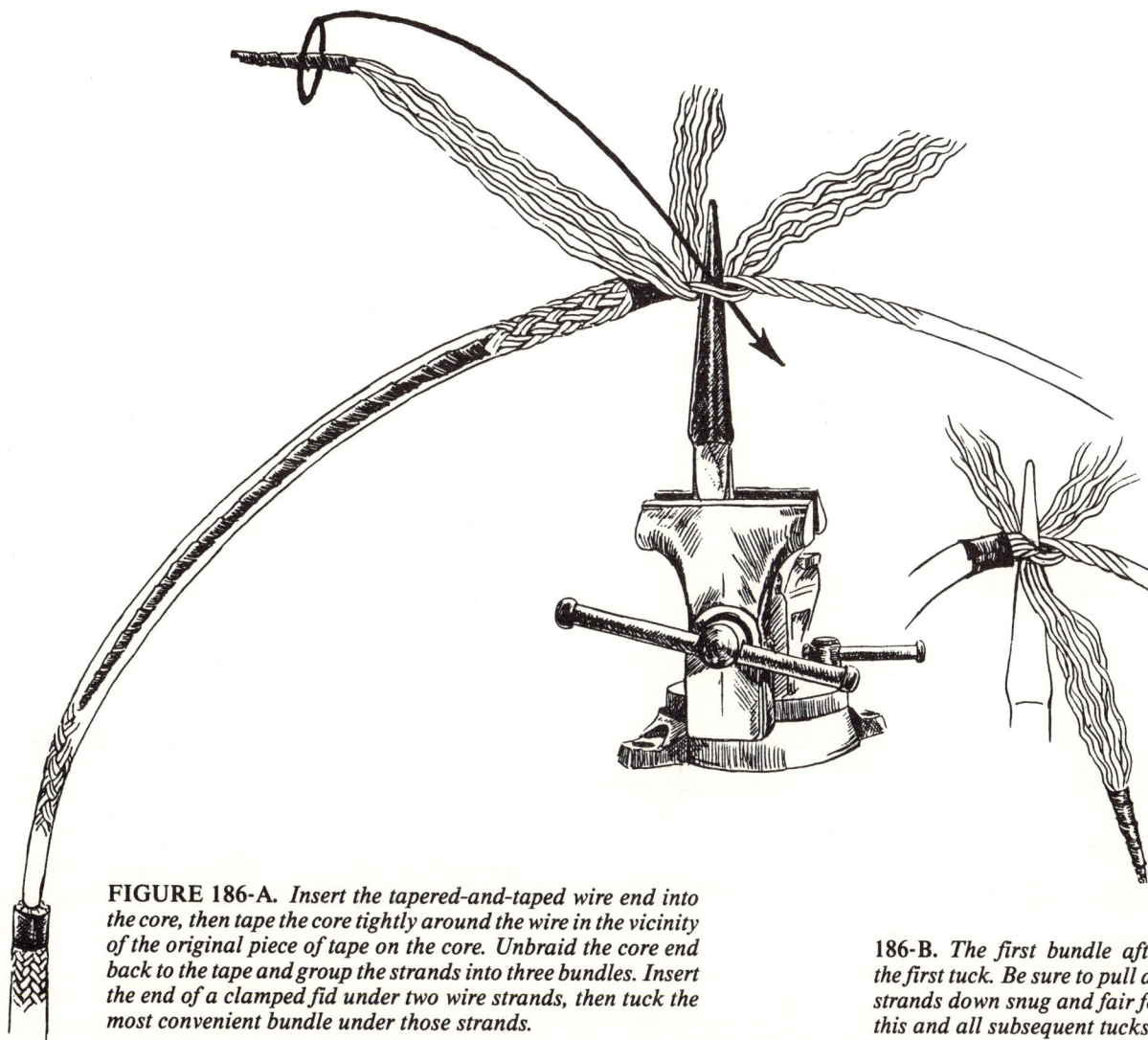

FIGURE 186-A. *Insert the tapered-and-taped wire end into the core, then tape the core tightly around the wire in the vicinity of the original piece of tape on the core. Unbraid the core end back to the tape and group the strands into three bundles. Insert the end of a clamped fid under two wire strands, then tuck the most convenient bundle under those strands.*

186-B. *The first bundle after the first tuck. Be sure to pull all strands down snug and fair for this and all subsequent tucks.*

Transformation

Insert the tapered wire end into the core until the tape on the wire is past the tape on the core, then wrap the core very tightly with more electrical tape to keep the wire from moving inside (Figure 186). Wrap over but not past the original bit of tape on the core.

Now comb the 10 inches of loose braid out until all the strands are straight, then divide the strands into three even bundles with tightly taped ends. There's one of your three-strand ropes.

Look at the wire where it emerges from the tape. Six strands? No, three *pairs* of strands; there's your other three-strand rope.

Splicing the Core

Take your taped-together jumble of line over to the fid, lay the wire on it right next to the tape, and gently push down on the wire to force the fid under a pair of strands. Be careful not to pick up any of the wire's heart yarns or to leave any of the pair's yarns behind. Work the wire down over the fid until you have a big enough space to tuck the most convenient rope bundle through, with the lay. If the rope is on your left and the wire on your right, tucking down will be tucking with the lay. Adjust the bundle until all its yarns are snugged down evenly, then pull the wire up off the fid.

127

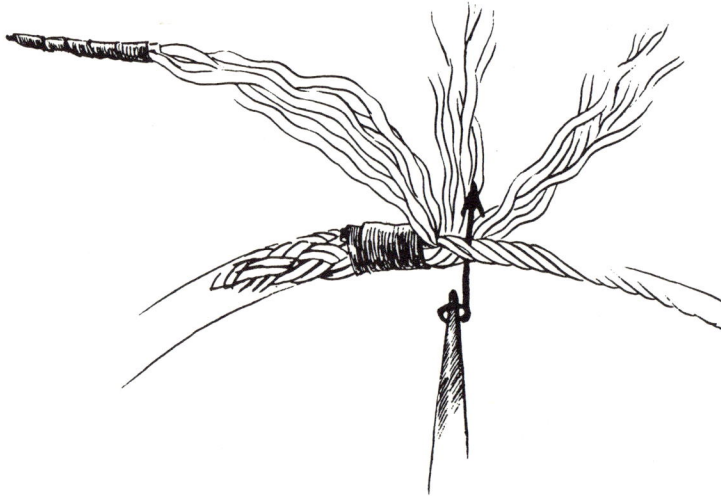

FIGURE 187. *Preparing to tuck the second bundle: Enter the fid under the two strands above the first bundle.*

FIGURE 188. *Tapering the core splice: Make three full tucks with each bundle, then drop one-third of the strands from the wire side of each bundle and tuck again. Drop another one-third, tuck again, trim the ends close, and fuse lightly.*

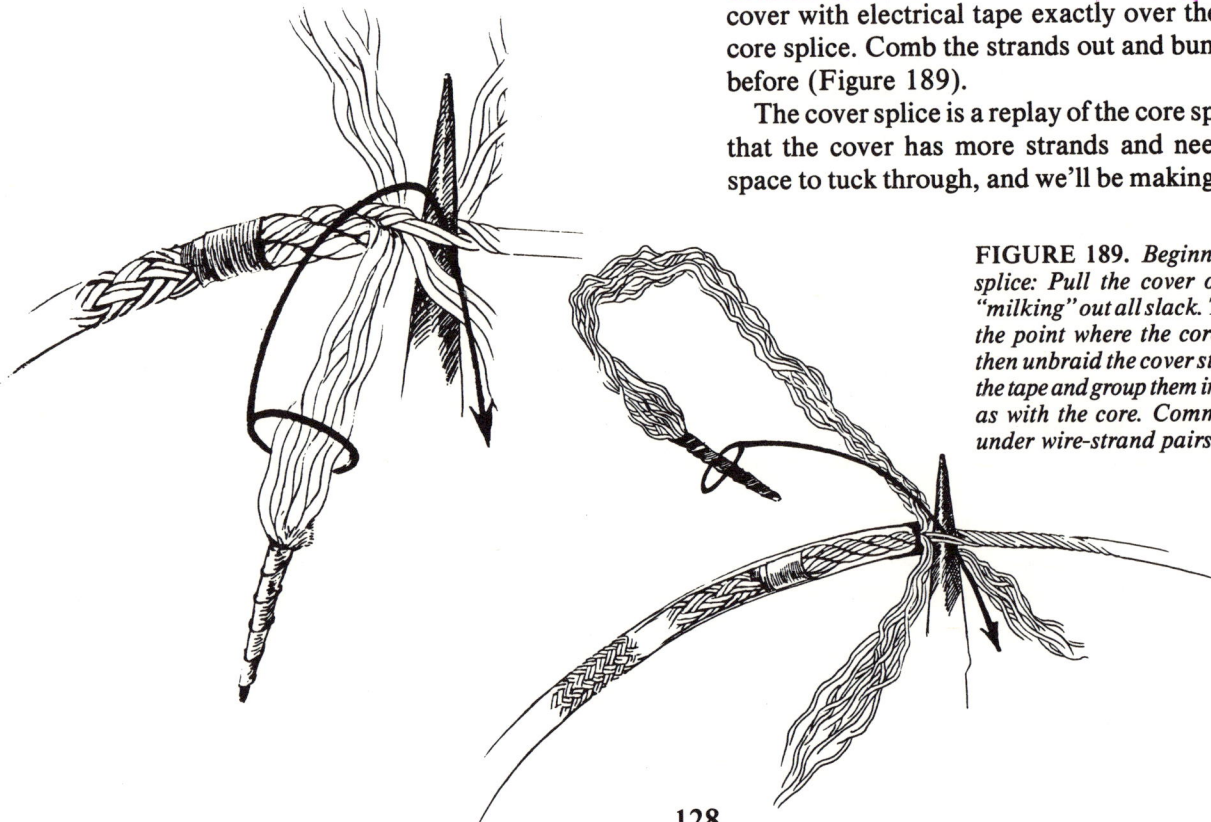

Enter the fid under another pair of wire strands and tuck another bundle (Figure 187). You'll probably find it easiest to enter into the same space where the previous bundle entered, but in the opposite direction.

Repeat with the third bundle under the last pair of wires. All bundles should now be exiting at the same level, or "a-tier."

Tuck all three bundles twice more, spiraling each one around and around its own pair of wire strands. Then taper by cutting one-third of the yarns from the right-hand side of each bundle, tucking them again, removing another one-third, and tucking the remainder once more (Figure 188). Trim the ends to within ⅛ inch of the wire and fuse them *lightly* with a match, to keep them from slipping out during the next step.

If the core splice isn't smooth, it isn't strong; cut it off and throw it away. If it looks good, say goodbye and slide the cover back over it.

Splicing the Cover

Pull every possible bit of slack out of the cover; when strain comes on the splice, you want core and cover to share the load evenly. It's good practice to belay the rope behind the knot so you can pull on the cover with both hands. When all the slack is out, tightly wrap the cover with electrical tape exactly over the end of the core splice. Comb the strands out and bundle them as before (Figure 189).

The cover splice is a replay of the core splice, except that the cover has more strands and needs a bigger space to tuck through, and we'll be making more tucks

FIGURE 189. *Beginning the cover splice: Pull the cover over the core, "milking" out all slack. Tape firmly at the point where the core splice ends, then unbraid the cover strands back to the tape and group them in three bundles as with the core. Commence tucking under wire-strand pairs as before.*

and a longer taper to ensure that the splice will run smoothly through the masthead sheave.

Make four full tucks, then taper by cutting away two yarns at a time (Figure 190). With the greater number of strands, even more attention must be paid to seeing that the splice is fair. Little if any wire should be visible under the tucks. Stop when you get down to six or eight strands, trim the ends, and serve over the wire-to-rope juncture with waxed sail twine (Figure 191), to prevent chafe on the strands. Remove the tape on the beginning of the splice and you're done.

Location

After you've made a few practice splices and feel ready to put one into an actual halyard, you'll need to figure how to position it properly along the length of that halyard; the splice should be just above the winch when the sail is fully hoisted.

If you're replacing a properly fitted old halyard, just send it down and reproduce the wire and rope lengths in the new halyard. If the old one doesn't fit right, hoist the sail, measure how far off it is, then send it down and adjust accordingly when you take measurements off it for the new one. If the mast is new, measure while it's out of the boat. For a headsail halyard on a new mast, be sure to "loft" the angle and length of the stay or you'll come up short. You'll also get a misfit if you cleverly reeve a rope to measure with, marking it "for an exact fit"; when you later stretch it out as a pattern for the new halyard, you'll almost certainly stretch it more or less than you did on the mast. Use a tape measure.

FIGURE 190. *Tapering the cover splice: After four full tucks, begin dropping two strands with each tuck until just six or eight strands remain. Trim the ends close and serve the splice end with sail twine.*

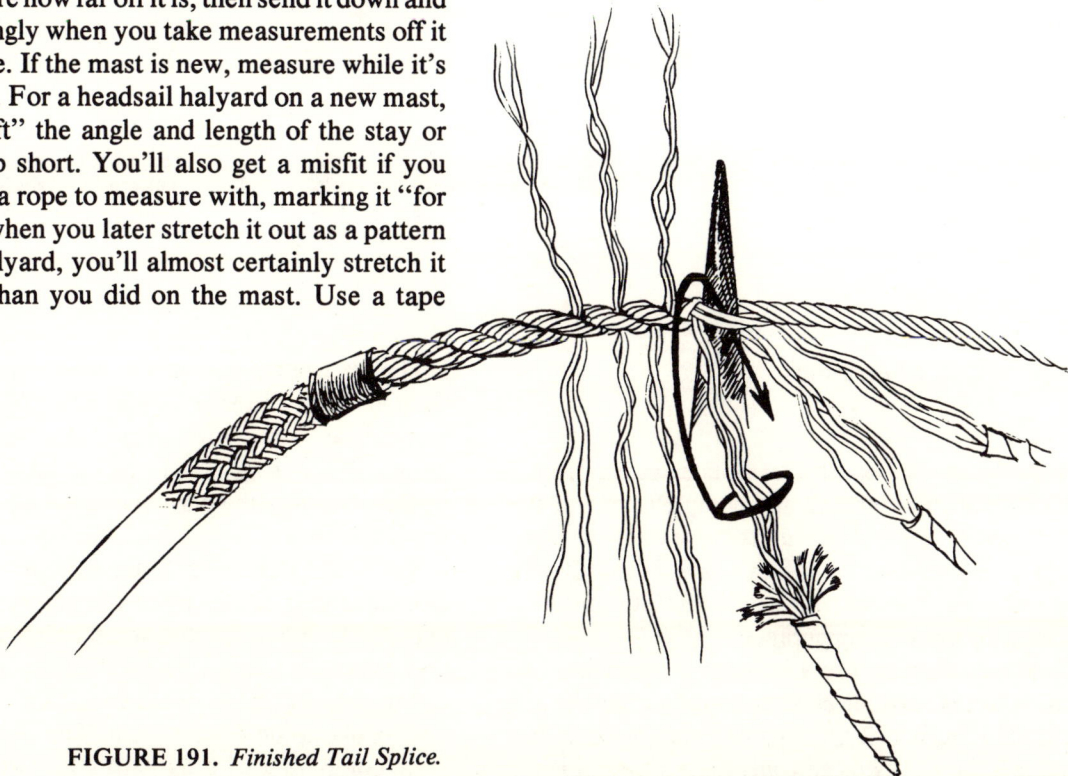

FIGURE 191. *Finished Tail Splice.*

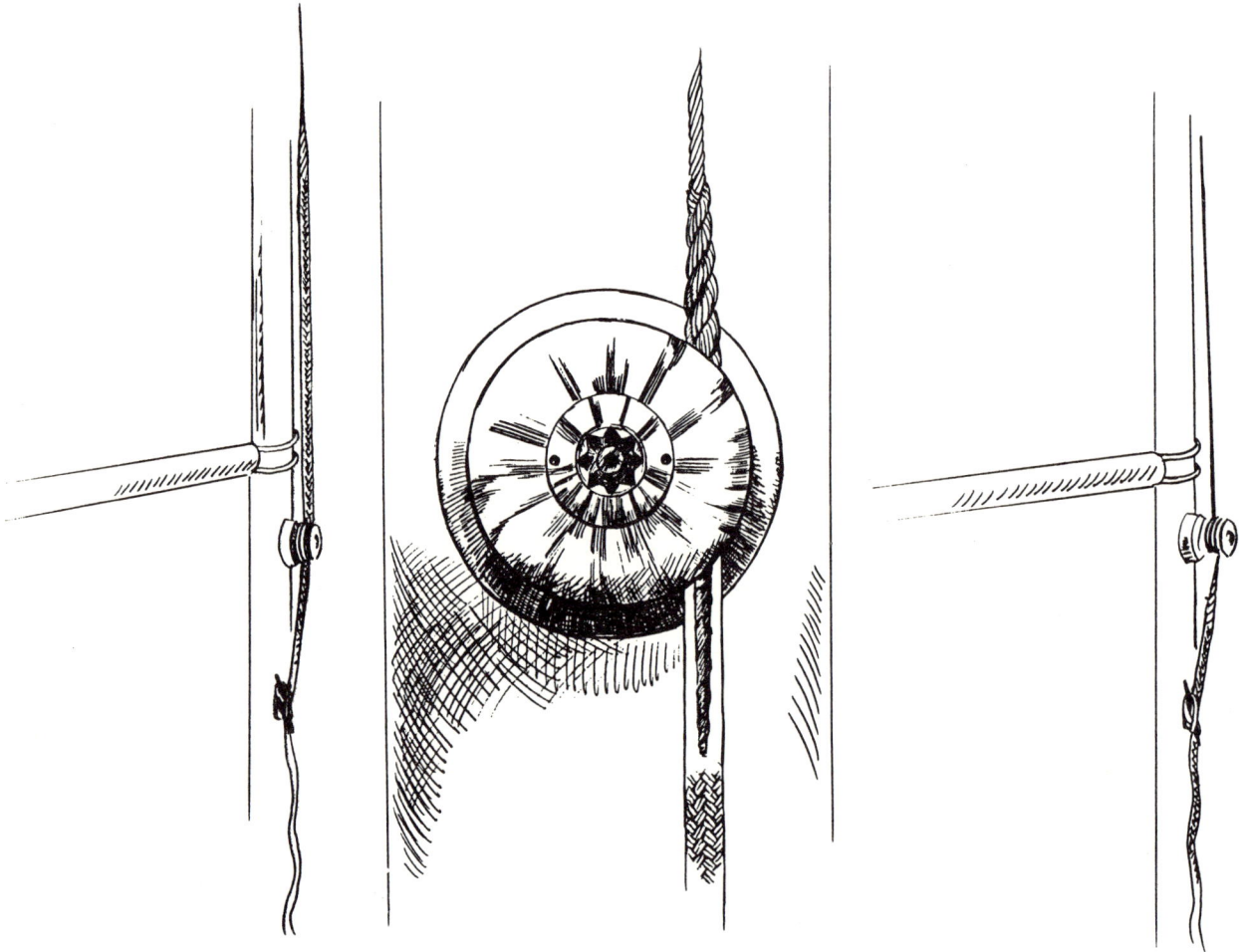

FIGURE 192-A. *Having the Tail Splice too far above the winch defeats the purpose of using wire.*

192-B. *A rope-and-wire "sandwich" around the winch results in crushed wire and chafed-through rope, shortening halyard life.*

192-C. *The splice positioned between winch and cleat: another to-be-avoided variation.*

Variations and Aberrations

There are many styles of Tail Splice, as one might expect with such an arcane and complex knot. If the style you use or buy is different from the one described here, just be sure that it, like this one, is thoroughly tested and proven. Avoid those with abrupt shoulders, few tucks, or uneven appearance.

You'll occasionally see a halyard proportioned so that the splice is between cleat and winch when the sail is hoisted (Figure 192-C). The rationale here is that the splice is the weak link and only the wire should take a full strain. A variation on this involves inserting the wire far enough into the rope at the beginning of the splice that a wire-and-rope "sandwich" will be wrapped around the winch when the sail is fully hoisted. Both of these techniques subject the wire to unnecessary abuse by wrapping it around a winch designed for rope, and the sandwich version, in addition, causes the wire to chafe the rope away from the inside out.

But with either of these techniques the worst moment surely comes when you go to put a reef or two in the sail. The splice that you didn't trust in light air is now exposed, along with weakened rope and wire on either side of it, to conditions that can make you uneasy about the stoutest gear. The Tail Splice allows us to combine a wire halyard's low weight, windage, elasticity, and cost with a rope halyard's speed and ease of handling. Properly made in the right size materials, it's a strong link, not a weak one.

CHAPTER 6

Installation and Maintenance

•

Installation transforms your work from a series of specialized tasks into an integral part of a sailing entity. When a mast goes in, the boat is changed; it acquires wholeness, intent, life. You, too, must be transformed now, in order to take part in this life. It's a romantic-seeming notion, but one consistent with the complexity and depth of the relationship that begins here.

When everything is in its place, your attention naturally shifts to maintenance. This involves a whole new series of tasks, but much more is involved than a "you-take-care-of-it, it-takes-care-of-you" philosophy; ideally, distinctions will blur until the most painstaking labors become a happy matter of course, part of sailing. Writing about this, Joseph Conrad said, "A ship is not a slave. You must make her easy in a seaway, you must never forget that you owe her the fullest share of your thoughts, of your skill, of your self

love. If you remember that obligation naturally, and without effort, as if it were an instinctive feeling of your inner life, she will sail, stay, run for as long as she is able, or like a seabird going to rest upon the angry waves, she will lay out the heaviest gale that ever made you doubt living enough to see another sunrise."

This chapter is a run-through of the procedures that put the rigger out of work. The times it is concerned with are always exciting and usually chaotic—thus the emphasis on forethought and preparation. What follows describes preparations for the launching of a good-sized new boat, but the annual outfittings of similar craft, or the launchings of smaller ones, require no less care, even though the operation might be simpler or more familiar. Given the consequences of dropping the stick through the hull, for example, it makes sense always to proceed with studied skill and near-paranoid caution.

131

FIGURE 193. Hoist signals. (A) *Raise boom.* (B) *Lower boom.* (C) *Lower boom slowly. (Palm facing any signal qualifies it as "slowly.")* (D) *Slew (travel) boom.* (E) *Lower load.* (F) *Raise load.* (G) *Hold that; take a turn.* (H) *Make fast.*

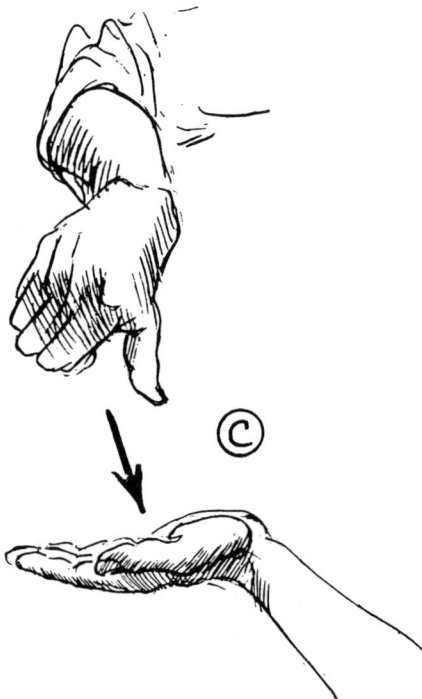

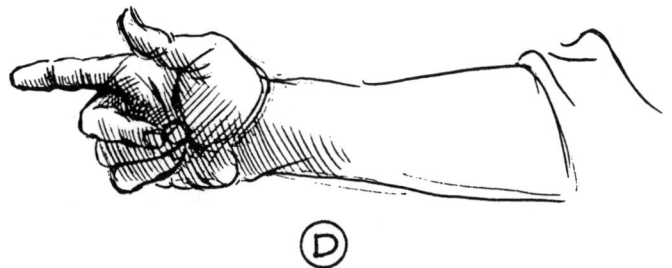

INSTALLATION

Getting Ready

Set up a workspace out of the traffic and gather together the fewest possible assistants necessary for the job (two or three is usually enough, though you may need some unskilled line-holders later). Improve the chances of an efficient operation by discouraging onlookers and unsolicited help.

Do you have all the pieces? Check them off your lists, port and starboard, fore and aft. All turnbuckles, toggles, pins, shackles, lanyards, pieces of standing rigging, and spools of cordage for running rigging should be sorted and clearly labeled. Have spare pins and shackles on hand.

Is the mast ready? See that all hardware and fittings are in place, their locations checked against the sail plan and common sense. Check all bolts for tightness, cotter pins for security, and in-mast sheaves for smooth running. If there are mast hoops, are they on? Are there enough? Count sail eyelets. Imagine the mast in place and check the lead and location of everything against that image. Take a few minutes at this; things sometimes get inexplicably out of place and it's much easier to fix them now than later.

Stand on deck and imagine everything working. Will it work? Cast a critical eye on deck leads, winch locations, and fitting clearances.

Get together tools and items such as marline, seizing wire, and slush, to name a few. (More will be mentioned in the section on installing a topmast.) Keep any tools you're not wearing in your rigging bucket or toolbox. Sharpen your knife.

Go over hoist signals (Figure 193) with the crane operator or, if you're using a block and tackle, with the person tailing the fall. Some people use different signals than the ones shown; make sure you're in agreement.

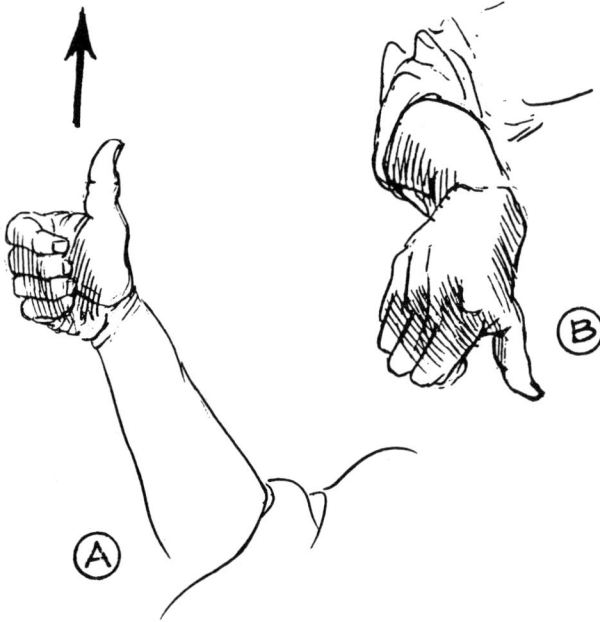

Dressing the Mast

Whenever possible, put all rigging on the mast before stepping it. First, get everything over next to the boat and put the mast on sawhorses. If the mast has a sail track, be sure the track faces upward so the mast won't bear on it. With no track, either side can be up, although the stepping of a rig with pronounced rake will be easier if you dress the mast backside-down and pick it up from the front side (Figure 194).

Lay the standing-rigging coils on the ground at appropriate points along the mast, port and starboard. With a copy of the standing rigging list to hand, begin attaching the pieces starting with the lowers and working up, checking each piece off the list as you go. If the mast is tanged, see that the thimbles are set well down on the pin or shackle, with no foul leads. Seize and cotter as you go. With a soft-eye rig, remember to put on the starboard eye of any pair first and to seat and lead the eyes as well as you can on the ground. Attach any spreaders or struts and seize in their wires, lightly, so you can adjust angle and tension later. Uncoil the pieces, either after they're all attached or as you go, pull them out so they're not sagging too much, and lash them to the mast at gooseneck height. See that all pieces will lead fair. It's easy, for example, to thread a backstay between an upper shroud and a spreader, necessitating a trip aloft to clear it before it can be set up. Is everything checked off? Good. Examine all attachments once more, remove the tags, and proceed to the running rigging.

Running Rigging

Get out the appropriate list along with all the blocks and their shackles. Lay these out in a rigger's smorgasbord, then prepare the rope for reeving by slinging spools on rod or pipe to pay out toilet-paper fashion. When coils are used, place these at convenient points and start them by pulling the end *up from the bottom* of the coil, to avoid kinks.

Let's say your list starts with a throat halyard. Attach the upper block to the mast and have an assistant hold the lower block close to it. Reeve the

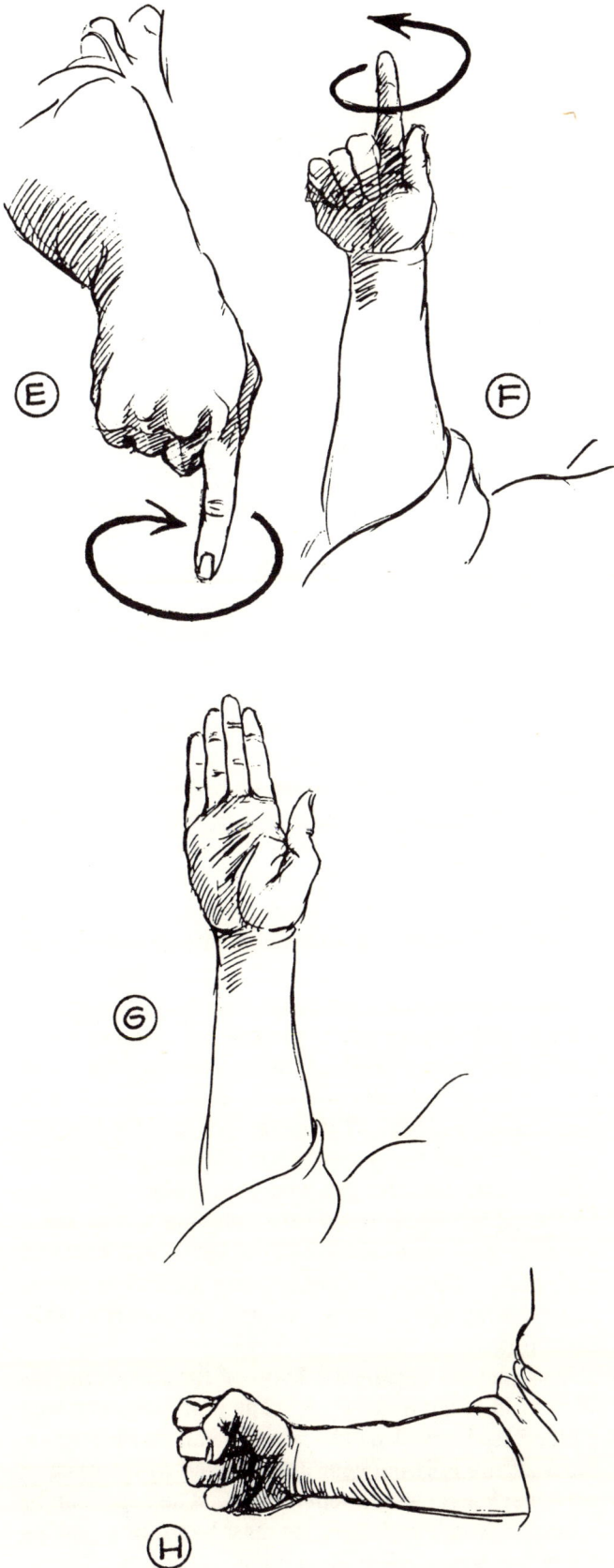

133

blocks and hitch the standing end temporarily to its becket, or, in the case of a double-ended halyard, to the gooseneck or boom saddle. Walk the lower block down to about the level of the boom, pulling rope off the spool or out of the coil as you go. Lead the hauling part down to about the height it will belay, add enough for three turns around a winch, if any, plus four to six feet for belaying, plus a like amount for shortening up due to chafe. Constrictor the end, cut, hitch the end around the tackle to keep things from fouling, and go to the next line.

If you're rigging with Manila, which shrinks when wet, allow enough length for shrinkage. Lines that see an extraordinary amount of chafe, such as the foresail vang on a gaff schooner, can do with extra length for shortening up. If a line leads to the cockpit or to the end of the bowsprit, pace off the distance away from the mast to get the required length. On a topping lift for a 14-foot boom, for instance, reeve the end through the block on the mast and walk with the end to a point 14 feet out from the gooseneck or boom saddle. Lead the standing part to its belay point and cut.

Keep leads from fouling with other pieces of running or standing rigging. See that the right diameter rope gets into the right blocks. Leave the sheets and other low lines until the stepping is done. When everything else is rove, it's time to splice and whip all ends. Because this is so time consuming, it's best done the day before the launching. Splicing parties are great places to teach and learn different techniques, to socialize, and to become familiar with the gear. Unfortunately, most mast dressings seem to take place with the crane operator impatiently tapping his feet, the tide cresting, and an expectant crowd looking over your shoulder. And no matter how fast you splice or whip, to others you will look slow and contemplative. So if time is short, have good help on hand, assign them specific tasks, and keep them out of each other's way. If time is very short, just do the ends you won't be able to reach from deck. If there's no time, reconcile yourself to the prospect of some time in the bosun's chair.

With a second lashing, make the running rig off to the mast. If there are many pieces threatening to flap around and tangle, you might want to contain them with some Swedish Furling (see Figure 21).

You're nearly ready for the pick now, but before everyone gets geared up, take note of the wind: More than 10 to 15 knots of it can make a mast very difficult to handle in transit.

Stepping the Keel-Stepped Mast

For anything bigger than a Whitehall, use hoisting gear to step the mast. A raising-of-the-flag-at-Iwo-Jima routine is dramatic and emotionally satisfying when it works, but presents too many opportunities for things to go wrong (picture the butt skidding across your pristine foredeck, or the mast falling onto hapless guests), and at any rate is always harder than letting pulleys do the work.

The size of the mast and the availability of equipment and personnel will determine the exact form and size of the gear you use. Block and tackle of three to seven parts can be hung from beams, yards, bridges, docks, etc. Given strong attachment and tailing points, all but the largest masts can be hoisted. On the other hand, this system only works if the boat is directly under the gear or can be moved under it after the mast is in the air. Building a derrick on deck or alongside solves this problem, but unless you plan to use it more than once—say for annual steppings and unsteppings at your own yard—it is more like an emergency fix, something you might lash up if you were dismasted in Faroffistan. So unless you can easily get the boat under the mast, get a crane. This is not as difficult or expensive as you might think. Any boatyard worth the name will have a crane and someone to operate it. If you're launching in some secluded cove, call the phone, power, or cable TV company in your area and make an appointment for one of their boom trucks to come over next time they're in the neighborhood. Schedule your stepping around their schedule and you'll get the job done quickly, easily, and inexpensively. Finally, you can always call up your local building contractor and arrange to rent a crane and operator. Whomever you get for the job, remember that the better prepared you are, the less time it takes and the less you pay. Before the crane arrives take a look around the stepping site to see if there are any power lines that you have even a remote chance of fouling. If so, either move the hull or get the power company to come out and temporarily take them down.

The best arrangement I know of for a mast pick is shown in Figure 194. A rope collar, preferably padded, is hooked or shackled to the padded lower block of the hoisting gear and belayed to the mast at gooseneck level with a separate line. The belay can be around a winch and cleat, or mast band, or a lashing below the boom saddle, depending on the type of mast.

FIGURE 194. *A mast ready for stepping is in the foreground, running rigging omitted for simplicity. The standing rigging is led down and bundled against the mast at the gooseneck. The padded crane pulley and padded mast collar provide mar-free strength. The downhaul on the collar is made off securely to a mast winch and cleat. In the background, the same mast is shown being stepped. Tag lines control movement of the butt as the crane carries it toward the boat. Time to get on deck and guide it home.*

Just make sure it's very strong. The beauty of this arrangement aside from its simplicity is that you don't have to go aloft to cast off hitches and seizings once the mast is stepped; just slack away on the tackle and pull the collar down to the deck.

Position the collar just above the balance point—usually just below the spreaders—so that the mast will hang fairly plumb yet be angled enough to allow the collar to take some strain off the heel line. Never allow any lifting gear to bear on the spreaders; they're not designed to take strain from that direction.

It's a good idea at this time to wrap some padding around the bury of a keel-stepped mast. This section will be completely exposed below, dominating the cabin, and people will tend to stare at it, clucking over any scratches it might have received on the way down.

Hitch on a couple of tag lines and have some volunteers tail them. Explain to them that they are not

to hoist or hold back, just to follow the mast to the boat, keeping the butt from swinging.

Take a look around. Any stray dogs or children nearby? Anything you or the tailers might trip over? Anything likely to snag the mast between where it is and where it's going? Think things through. If necessary, get some help to keep the area clear.

When everyone's ready, signal to hoist and let the top end come off its sawhorse a foot or so. Give the stop signal and check the gear again. All in order? Stand from under and continue the pick. Have your tailers take a strain as the head goes up, to keep the butt from sliding forward too fast. Once the mast is clear, signal to lift and travel. Watch the mast, the crane operator, the tailers, and yourself. When the mast is over the boat and 4 to 5 feet above the deck, give the stop signal and get aboard along with some helpers.

Send a good hand below to guide the mast into the step, and have one or two other helpers on deck to help

135

you guide it into the hole. On large craft, station a reliable, clear-voiced person in the companionway or next to a porthole to relay information between step and deck.

Make sure the mast is oriented properly (it's amazing how easy it is to put a mast in backward), and signal to lower away, adjusting to center over the hole as you go. When it's well in, it is up to the person at the step to begin giving you directions for final adjustments. Properly, these are in terms of the direction of the butt's travel: "Two inches to port" means you signal the crane to move the head to starboard; "Two inches aft" means you signal to move the head forward. When the tenon is right at the step, you and your helpers can help it along by pushing on the mast. It's almost in the hole now.... Wait! Did they put the lucky coin in? Come up a couple of inches, deposit the talisman (after swinging the butt off to one side) and let it down again. Tchunnngk. Stepped.

Is the tenon firmly seated? All the wires lead properly? Good. Set some temporary wedges, cast off the standing rigging lashing, and lead the wires out to their homes. What with the relief of tension at this moment, people tend to get a little crazy, grabbing at everything and falling over each other. So send all but one or two helpers away, calm your own giddy heart, and proceed methodically. First the shrouds, then the fore-and-aft stays—just hand tight, enough to stabilize the mast. If the crane is in the way of the fore or backstay, the shrouds will hold the stick for now. If the rig design does not include shrouds with the necessary lead, rig a temporary stay to a winch or cleat, low enough or at a steep enough angle to clear the crane's boom.

Have the crane operator let some slack into the lift, and see that everything is holding well. Then cast off the heel line and bring the collar down. Detach it and carefully send the lifting gear away; don't let it bash into the stick or your crew. Attach anything that wouldn't lead properly before.

If your meticulous preparations and measurements result in a perfect fit for all pieces, you deserve congratulations—but I know from sad experience that this is not always so. On those unlucky occasions the rigger may rue the fact that his first opportunity to see a rig in place is often a very public viewing, and any failure will be immediately, glaringly evident to the most untrained observer. I hope that the first time you read this is long before the launching. Go back over your figures, recheck measurements, and reread the layout instructions in the Loft Procedures chapter. Help your luck.

DECK-STEPPED MASTS

Given a choice, I like to treat a deck-stepped mast like a keel-stepped one, using a crane to set it in place. It's so much easier and, I believe, safer. But the reason people have these masts is so they can get them up and down *without* a crane, so here's the routine.

Carry, parbuckle, hoist, or slide the bare mast aboard and position it longitudinally over the vessel's centerline. These masts are heavier for their size than keel-stepped ones (deck mounting means that the mast must take thrust that the partners would otherwise bear), so proceed carefully, padding points of contact with the hull, tailing hauling parts, and rigging preventer gear to keep the thing from getting away if somebody slips.

Dress as for a keel-stepped mast, but leave one stout line out of the bundle, rove through a masthead sheave. Use a halyard for an aft-hinging mast or the topping lift for a forward-hinging mast. Slide the butt aft or forward, depending on which way the mast hinges, until it can bolt into its tabernacle or plate, and run the line forward to the anchor windlass or aft to a tackle. Since the line is now just about parallel with the mast, cranking in on it will do you no good; you need a strut to widen the angle between mast and hauling line. There are different ways of doing this, but the most convenient for an aft-hinging mast is to set up a spinnaker pole with its butt locked in place on the mast and its other end seized or fed to the halyard (Figure 195). For a forward-hinger, lead the topping lift to the end of the boom and haul with the mainsheet. Failing that, make up shear legs, fastening the butt ends securely on deck. Before hoisting, attach tag lines near the masthead to prevent it from swinging laterally. Either run these through turning blocks and tail them to cleats or winches, or tail them to secure objects on the ground on either side of the boat.

Take up the slack with the mast end of the halyard or topping lift and belay it on the mast. Clear the area, check all connections, then start cranking away cautiously on the windlass or sheet to raise the mast. The people on the tag lines should take a slight strain against the pull of the halyard or sheet, just enough so there's no slack, and then pay out evenly as the mast goes up. When the butt swings into place, belay hauling and tag lines as temporary stays and go about getting the standing rigging secured.

If your vessel is multiple masted, step the one farthest forward, then use it to hoist the next one aft. For example:

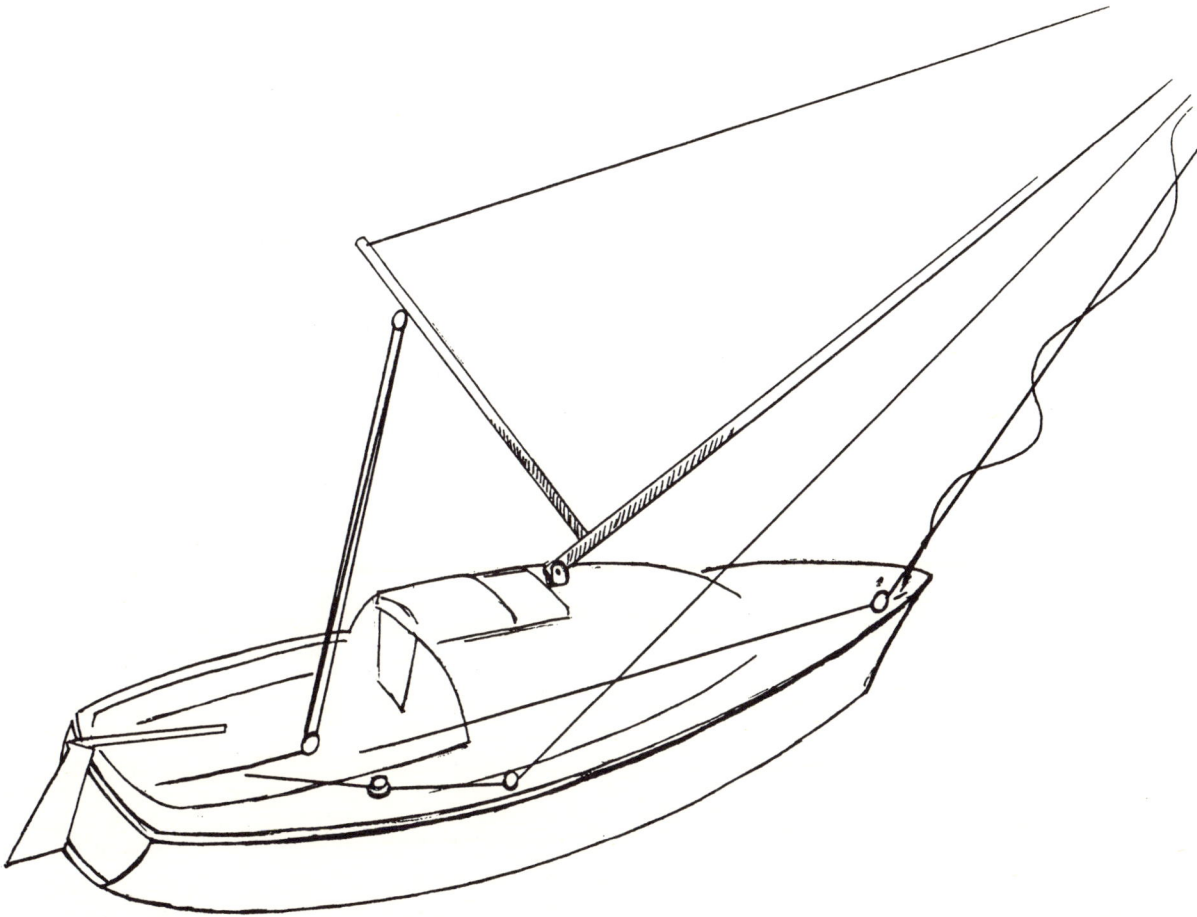

FIGURE 195. *A deck- or tabernacle-stepped mast (forward hinging). Carry the mast on board and secure its butt in the tabernacle. Affix the boom, with sheet and topping lift attached. Belay one end of the jibstay halyard on the mast and lead the other end through a block at the stem and aft to the cockpit. Attach forestay to masthead and stem. Lead two other belayed halyards to turning blocks and thence aft for lateral control. Take up on the sheet, pay out on the jib halyard, and keep tension on the lateral guys as you raise the mast. Attach remaining standing rigging when mast is in fully upright position.*

The foremast is in place on your junk-rigged schooner and all the standing rigging and tabernacle fittings are secured. You'll be using the foresail halyard to pull the mainmast up, but first you have to get the mainmast into position. The procedure is pretty much as it was for the foremast except that this mast is much heavier, so requires greater care, and is much longer; its balance point might be out over the stern before the butt is at the tabernacle. To prevent having to deal with a 50-foot steel seesaw, make a heavy lashing to arc over the mast, keeping the butt from coming up while still allowing you to slide the mast aft. Tie the ends of the lashing through scuppers, hawse-holes, or other structures capable of taking a heavy

vertical load. As you approach the tabernacle and friction against the lashing increases, a come-along or handy-billy can help to move the last few feet.

Lash the foresail halyard lower block to the main at the point where it rests on the padded taffrail (you did pad the taffrail, didn't you?). If the bulk of the mast is out over the rail, you'll have lashed the halyard on earlier at a point higher up on the mast, to help keep the masthead from dropping. Take up on your tag lines, which lead from the same spot, and hoist away. As the mast gets within 30 degrees of the vertical, lead the tag lines well aft to serve as backstays. Secure all shrouds and fittings and settle down for a nice, cold.... What? This is a *three*-masted schooner?

137

to lower masthead

heel rope

two standing parts
of heel rope
seized together

hitches

standing parts
lashed to mast

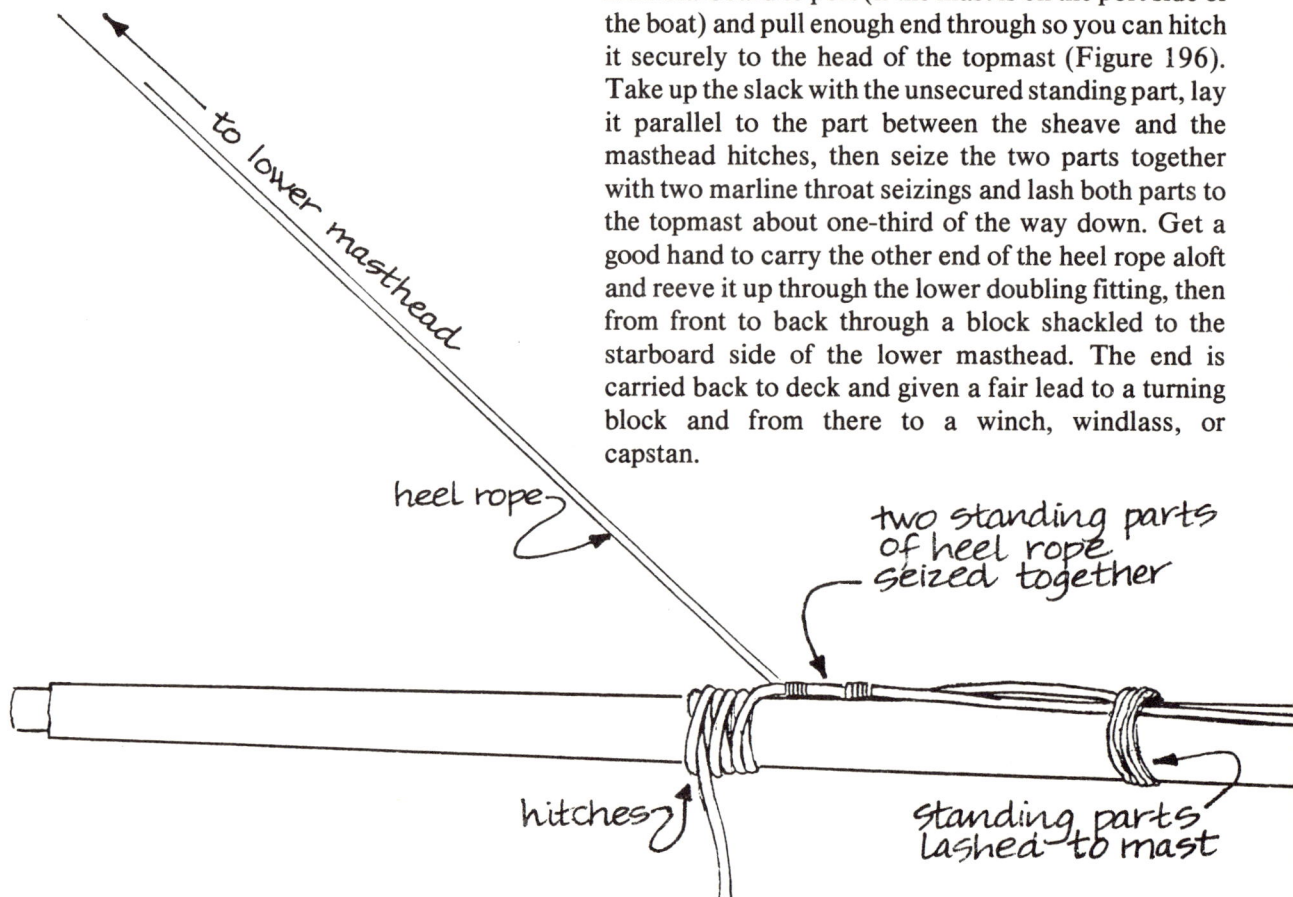

newest, strongest piece of rope you have that will fit the heel sheave. Reeve this rope through the sheave from starboard to port (if the mast is on the port side of the boat) and pull enough end through so you can hitch it securely to the head of the topmast (Figure 196). Take up the slack with the unsecured standing part, lay it parallel to the part between the sheave and the masthead hitches, then seize the two parts together with two marline throat seizings and lash both parts to the topmast about one-third of the way down. Get a good hand to carry the other end of the heel rope aloft and reeve it up through the lower doubling fitting, then from front to back through a block shackled to the starboard side of the lower masthead. The end is carried back to deck and given a fair lead to a turning block and from there to a winch, windlass, or capstan.

Installing Topmasts and Working Aloft

To most sailors these days, a topmast is a hopelessly archaic piece of gear; modern materials and sail plans have obviated its use. But "character boats" and historical reproductions need them, and they can be justified in practical terms since they allow you to use one big and one little tree instead of one huge one to set the same amount of sail. Beyond that, they give me an excellent opportunity to describe proper procedures for working aloft.

So. Your lower is in and well set up, the running rigging is neatly belayed and coiled, and the gear you've been spreading around has been collected and put away; you're ready to send up the topmast. If it's light enough, carry it on deck. Otherwise, set it on sawhorses alongside, abeam of the lower. Because it must pass through the tight confines of the "doubling," the only piece of gear you put on it now is the heel rope, with which the mast will be hoisted. This should be the

Lay out the rigging in two piles, port and starboard of the mast, with the pieces that will go on first uppermost in the piles. Attach a tag line to the topmast butt, tail the line securely, and haul away on the heel rope. As the strain comes on, the topmast will want to shoot ahead from its horizontal position. Restrain with the tag line, paying out slack gradually until the topmast hangs plumb below the doubling. Time to go aloft.

With complete disregard for the little voice telling you that only fools would voluntarily leave a nice, safe deck, you are about to climb wa-a-ay up in the air and fiddle around with large, heavy objects. No amount of care and skill can make this act absolutely safe, so every precautionary measure is justified. When you climb ratlines, always hold onto the shrouds, not the ratline itself, in case a seizing lets go. When you go up in a bosun's chair, check the halyard, cleat, winch, and the chair itself to make sure that all of them are *far* stronger than they have to be to hoist you.

Making the hauling line off to two cleats is painless insurance, and if you have an extra crewmember, going up on two halyards is comforting. Always take up the slack, then bounce vigorously in the chair a couple of times to prove the gear before leaving deck.

Wear a safety line when going aloft by either method, and shackle or tie it to something strong at every opportunity. Especially when underway, pass it around the mast as you go up in the chair, pausing to detach it below and reattach it above the spreaders. A tag line attached to the bottom of the chair can be kept under tension to keep you from swinging wildly, too, and can also be used to haul things up once you reach your destination.

The moment you're off the deck, very powerful instincts will come to your aid, helping you to move faster and hang on tighter than you've ever believed possible. Combined with some good sense, they'll help you to get the job done and arrive back on deck whole and hearty.

Back to the topmast. Let's say you've made your way to the lower masthead via ratlines, tied yourself

Or Frank might not have heard the whole thing, and since he didn't repeat it back you won't know until he starts sending up the topmast rigging. ("Oh, rigging *bucket*. Speak up!") Worse yet, Frank doesn't know by what means the bucket is supposed to travel. He might come clambering up with it in his hand, spilling tools en route. Or he might cast off the wrong gantline, one that you or some other important piece of gear is hanging from. No, a precise, graceful deck/aloft litany is much to be preferred.

So your rigging bucket is coming up. Brake its ascent slightly with one hand, in case it and the shortening end become outweighed by the standing part. It can easily happen on a long hoist, the bucket zipping upward the last few feet, launching tools when it fetches against the block.

The bucket reaches you and you call, "Hold that!" then, "Belay!"

When the line is belayed, deck calls out "Fast!" (made fast).

In your bucket you should have a spike, hammer, wrench, marline, seizing wire, knife, screwdrivers, nippers, and maybe some tallow—plus whatever else

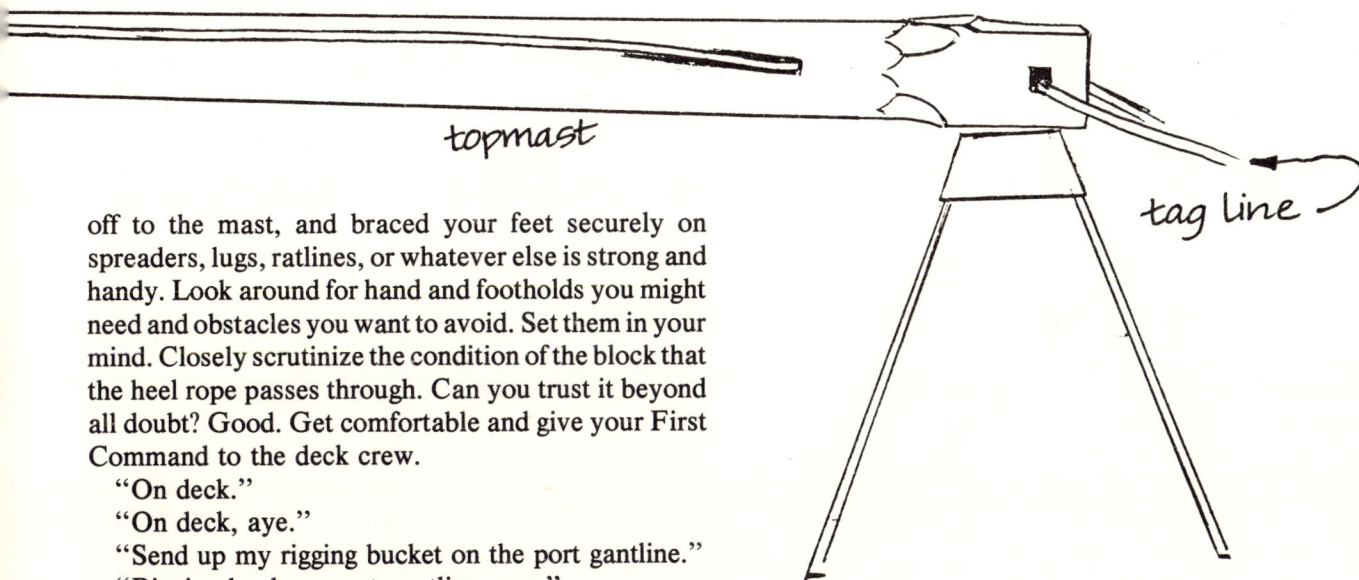

off to the mast, and braced your feet securely on spreaders, lugs, ratlines, or whatever else is strong and handy. Look around for hand and footholds you might need and obstacles you want to avoid. Set them in your mind. Closely scrutinize the condition of the block that the heel rope passes through. Can you trust it beyond all doubt? Good. Get comfortable and give your First Command to the deck crew.

"On deck."

"On deck, aye."

"Send up my rigging bucket on the port gantline."

"Rigging buck on port gantline, aye."

Now that's a rather formal exchange, maybe too formal for some tastes. Contrast it with a more relaxed version:

"Hey, Frank! Send up my rigging bucket!"

"Okay!"

Much simpler, true, but it allows of too many misunderstandings. By not getting Frank's attention first, the caller is likely to have to repeat the message.

FIGURE 196. *A topmast prepared for hoisting.*

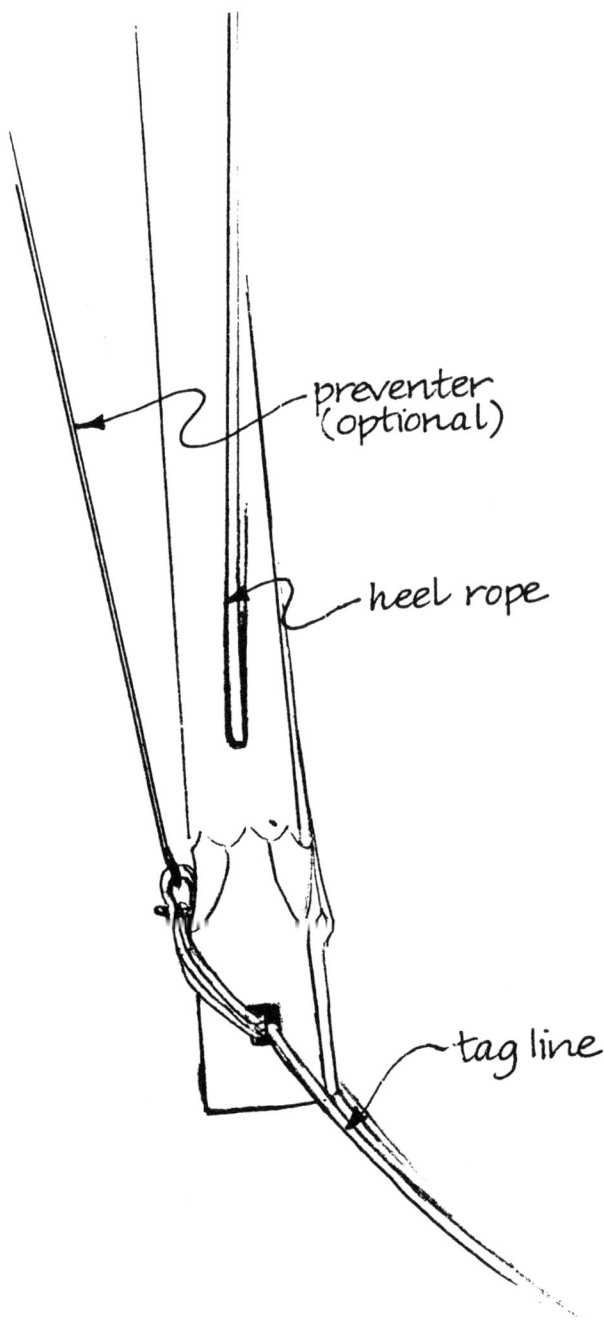

FIGURE 197. *As an option, lash a safety line to the fid hole and masthead hole to back up the heel rope as the mast goes up. The safety line is lead through another masthead block and is tailed on deck.*

this particular topmast calls for. You packed these items on deck, attaching lanyards to the tools, and mentally went through the procedure you were about to follow to make sure you had everything you needed. It's awful to have to shout down the name and size of a particular tool that you think is in the cabinet next to the chart table but there might be a spare in the lazarette, etc. For any given job, you can easily forget something crucial, but always taking the items mentioned above will lessen this likelihood.

You and your tools are up and ready, an assistant is perhaps made off on the other side of the mast, and the deck crew is standing by the hoisting gear. The topmast can now come up. Give the signal to haul, and guide the head through the lower doubling. When it's just short of the upper one, give the signal to belay. Now Camel Hitch a short, stout piece of line anywhere on the bitter-end part of the heel rope; tie the other end of that short line to the lower masthead. Cast off the hitches holding the end of the heel rope to the topmast head. Even with those stout marline seizings holding, this can be a tense moment, but that short, stout line is insurance in case the seizings slip. Try to ease off slowly to make sure all is well. Wasting no time, make the end off to a lug or other fitting on the port side of the lower masthead. The topmast is now suspended between the two parts of the heel rope, a configuration made necessary by its need to be hoisted well above the tackle's point of attachment. You've also just formed a two-part purchase, something the deck crew will have no objection to.

With the end belayed, carefully cut the seizings, remove the insurance line, and give the signal to resume hauling. Guide the masthead through the upper doubling and get it two feet or so through, then again signal to hold and make fast. Time to send the rigging up.

Unless you have a surfeit of gantlines, you'll probably want to tie the bucket onto the mast with its lanyard, then cast off its gantline. In that order. Tie the gantline around its own standing part with a Bowline so it doesn't get tangled on anything on the way down, then have the deck crew slack away and send it to them.

The standing rigging comes up one piece at a time, first starboard, then port. Check each tag as you get it, then drop the eye over the stick. If the eyes are tight you'll need to smear the wood with tallow. When everything's on, check the order once more, then cut the tags off. Give the signal to hoist, and slide the eyes

140

down to their stops as the mast comes up. Pause when the stops are level with you to seat and lead the eyes, then hoist again.

A long score cut on either side of the heel sheave keeps the heel rope from chafing on the lower doubling as it comes through, but check now to make sure the lead is fair in the score. As the sheave passes through the doubling, pause to cast off the tag line, then continue until the fid hole in the mast lines up with the ones in the doubling. Drive the fid in and lock it in place. Done.

More Likely Aloft

As I said before, there's not much call for topmasts these days, but installing one is an operation calling for most of the procedures you're ever likely to need aloft, whether you're re-reeving a parted halyard, inspecting the spreaders, or sending up a new radar. Just remember the need for clear communication, failsafe gear, and personal security. Insofar as possible, keep people away from the area of deck directly below you; if they wander in, call out "Stand from under!" in your most stentorian tone. A remarkably effective command.

On a small boat, you might need to go aloft singlehanded. One way to do this is to reeve a handybilly with an extra-long line, send the upper block up to the masthead on a halyard, make the lower block off to your chair, and hoist yourself aloft. (Incidentally, you can haul yourself up more easily than someone else can haul you; being your own load makes the handybilly into a four- rather than a three-part purchase.) Even a dependable child can tail the fall for you, but if none is available, make your safety belt to the standing part with a Rolling Hitch and slide it up as you go. A related procedure can be used if for some godawful reason you have no handy-billy available: Use a Rolling Hitch or Camel Hitch to make two 4- to 5-foot lines to a belayed halyard or even to a stay, and attach their other ends to your safety belt or bosun's chair. Slide one up as far as you comfortably can, then reach down and slide the other one up to knee level (you can use your feet to do this). Stand in the bight of the lower line and you find yourself two feet higher than you were. Slide the upper knot up again, then the lower one, working yourself aloft by your proverbial bootstraps. Slow but sure.

For block-less, winch-less, ratline-less methods of getting aloft, see the Emergency Procedures chapter.

TUNING

The rig you've just installed exists to distribute strain from the sails in such a way that the boat moves through the water to optimum effect. But without careful tuning, all you've got is a bunch of wires hanging off the mast. This business of bringing the vessel to life involves knitting everything together so that, as nearly as possible, all strains are shared and no single member takes a disproportionate load.

For rough tuning at the dock or on the ways, use the lower shrouds to plumb the mast in the thwartships plane and to induce any desired rake in the fore-and-aft plane. Take up a little bit at a time on each turnbuckle, and when you think things are about right, take a look from some distance away for perspective. Ignore the other shrouds and stays while you're doing this, except to ensure that they remain slack enough not to pull the mast out of line.

When you're satisfied with the lowers, take up a little on the forestay, just so it's straining some against the aftermost lower shroud. Now go to the intermediates, if any, then to the uppers, the jibstay, and finally the backstay. Don't go to the next wires until the slack is gone from the ones you're working on and the related section of mast is straight in both planes. If you don't "tighten upward" like this, it is easy to put assorted bows into the stick without knowing which wires have caused them.

With the slack out of everything, go around again, tightening by proportion. That is, since longer wires stretch more than shorter ones, tighten the longer ones more. This way, when the boat heels under a press of wind, the mast will stay straight; the masthead will not fall off to leeward, hurting sail shape and straining the mast. Start with the lowers. I like to get them so I can strum a low musical note on them. The intermediates get a little more tension, and the uppers still more. Just how much tension you start and finish with depends on the condition and construction of the hull, height and type of rig, type of wire, and personal preference.

Fine tuning the mast is done during and between the first few sails. If the wire is new, initial elasticity will have to be taken out. After that, minute adjustments are made based on observation of the rig's behavior on different points of sail. The idea is the same as for rough tuning: Keep the mast straight (or in the case of a bendy mast, make it bend when and where you want).

Beware overtuning. Taking all the slack out of lee

shrouds on successive tacks can literally drive a mast right through the keel, or stretch the wire beyond its elastic limit. Make only the most minor adjustments when actually sailing, and check their effects before adjusting further.

MAINTENANCE

Here's where the distinction between rigger and sailor should become blurred; a rig's longevity has as much to do with efficient sailing practices as it does with particular maintenance chores.

Keeping the standing rigging tuned is a form of maintenance, as is "feathering" into a puff of wind, or using large-sheaved blocks, or reefing as soon as you think of it. Of course, all of these things can also be classed as "good boat handling," since they make sailing easier and safer. Regardless of what you call it, boats appreciate every little attention you give them and will reward you in kind. Here are a few specific chores to keep in mind.

Rinse standing rigging with fresh water after a sail; otherwise salt accumulates and hastens corrosion, even of so-called stainless steel. If the wire gets dirty, wash it with a mild soap and a plastic or natural-bristle scrubber; steel wool leaves behind little fragments that quickly rust.

Chafe covers on shrouds should be slid up out of the way so you can clean underneath them.

If served rigging is slushed whenever it gets to looking dry, it will last a century or more. Very cost effective. As I write this, the 40-or-more-year-old standing rigging of the Arctic exploration schooner *Bowdoin* is sitting in my loft. The foundation that owns this boat wanted me to replace the gang, but stripping the service off a few splices revealed wire that is as good as new. I had to ace myself out of a big job and talk them into a little renovation instead.

Slush, also known as tar varnish or blacking compound, is a tar-based paint applied periodically to standing rigging to protect it from decay. Recipes vary, but here's a good basic one for served rigging:

> 6 parts Stockholm tar
> 3 parts boiled linseed oil
> 1 part Japan drier
> 1 part spar varnish

Mix the ingredients together and apply to marline or seizing wire in thin coats until the material is "full" but not overflowing. When dry, slush is hard enough to resist scuffing but resilient and durable enough to maintain a waterproof seal over the wire rope.

The type of tar you use makes a considerable difference; most commercially available pine tars are chemically processed and may contain impurities. Stockholm tar is produced by simple distillation and cooking. It smells sweet, doesn't irritate skin the way other tars do, and holds up much better in the weather.

Be sure the drier you use is fresh and still volatile; it makes the slush "go off" and harden. Mix up small batches and seal containers securely between uses.

When slushing nylon-served rigging, "Net Dip," an asphalt tar available from fishery supply houses, is a good choice for slush.

Using less tar and adding some thinner (Solvex or Xylol is good) makes a good bare-wire slush. Straight-boiled linseed oil or mineral oil is less effective but tidier, anhydrous lanolin thinned with mineral oil is also good, and I've recently found that Marvel Mystery Oil applied generously and allowed to soak in is an excellent wire preservative. There are also some extremely expensive wire preservatives developed for industry, which, if you can find them in small amounts at bargain prices, are very effective. Wear gloves and a respirator when working with them. All preservative coatings can be applied with a paintbrush.

It's most convenient, of course, to slush the rigging when the sticks are out; if they're in place and you have to work aloft you will find on your return that your deck is spattered with hundreds of droplets of slush. To avoid this, bend a springline onto the anchor rode while at anchor and pay out on the rode to form a bridle. This will put you at right angles to the wind, so that as you slush the lee rigging, those spatters will hit the water instead. Turn the boat around to slush the other side. And don't do this bridling procedure in a crowded harbor unless your neighbors to leeward don't mind a tarred bootstripe.

Bare wire is not as long-lived as served wire, but a little attention will keep it from dying prematurely. Any one of the various slush recipes will do for galvanized wire. I recently replaced a couple of 40-year-old shrouds that had been treated exclusively with zinc chromate; they were just about worn out, but a little tar or anhydrous lanolin a few years ago would have gotten them to the half-century mark with ease. Stainless wire will fatigue eventually, so putting a little mineral oil on it once in a while might seem a futile gesture—it'll break before it rusts. But adverse climatic conditions or air pollution can accelerate deterioration, so go ahead and treat the wire—the stuff is expensive and you want it to last as long as possible.

Inspection takes two forms: the formal once- or twice-a-year going over that leaves nothing unscrutinized, and the reflexive glance-at-things-as-you-go-about-your-business inspection that is probably more valuable. A rig goes a little bit here, a little bit there, and the redundancy inherent in its design means you get a chance to spot problems before the integrity of the whole is seriously affected. Rust stains, cracked fittings, and wire with kinks or broken strands or a slight unlaying due to heavy strain are all things that are possible to spot if you habitually look for them but easy to miss if you don't. Cotter pins, shackle mousings, swages, and seizings don't require much effort on your part to examine. If one of these is not healthy and you spot it soon enough, it is easy to fix or replace; if six months elapse between looks, serious trouble can develop.

Rigs with swaged terminals are among the most susceptible to failures; very frequent inspections are necessary to ensure their integrity. If the strands of a wire rope do not lead fairly into a swaged terminal; if there is evidence of corrosion, especially at the top of the terminal; or if the terminal is cracked or warped, no matter how slightly, it is of uncertain integrity and should be replaced at once. Swages are the overwhelmingly favorite choice for sailboat terminals because of their low cost, neat, compact appearance, and high initial tensile strength. But they are not to be trusted.

For your formal scrutiny, consider the following procedure:

Select a couple of shrouds and go over every inch of them, either on the ground or from a bosun's chair. Look closely for signs of corrosion or broken strands, paying particular attention to the terminals. Sight down the length of the wire to see that all the strands run smoothly, none being distorted or sucked down due to uneven strain. Slack off on each shroud in turn, enough to enter a spike so you can see how things look inside. Use a very small spike; no sense hurting the wire you're helping.

If it's a spliced rig over 10 years old, or new to you no matter how old, strip a couple of lower end splices and have a look. Are all strands bearing evenly at the entry? Have any of the ends pulled? Is there corrosion in there? Is the splice fair? If you have any doubts, send the pieces off to a testing outfit and have them run their machine up to 50 percent of the wire's rated breaking strength. This should be more of a load than your boat will ever impose, so passing will do wonders for your peace of mind. If the wire fails, on the other hand, you can congratulate yourself on your good judgment. Just about every major city has at least one testing facility, and you can find them through industrial rigging suppliers or contractors.

When you are satisfied that a wire is in good shape, turn your attention to its points of attachment. Chainplates, tangs, turnbuckles, and toggles are all susceptible to failure and will usually give warning. Proof-testing is a good idea here, too, though it might be practicable only for the turnbuckles and toggles. One frequent cause of gear failure, easy to overlook, is a toggle or shackle wearing away against its tang or eye, so disconnect things occasionally for a good look.

Running rigging, ground tackle, and the miscellany of seizings and whippings that populate most boats are no less in need of inspection, though their decay is usually more obvious (fraying, stiffening line, rusted chain, slack marline). Changing leads, fairing sheave cheeks, and padding unavoidable chafe points with leather, service, garden hose, or such (let your imagination be your guide) will prolong rope life greatly, as will proper coiling and stowage; inspect running rigging not just to determine if a line needs replacing, but to isolate the perhaps avoidable causes of its deterioration.

Just how frayed or rusty must a piece be for it to be condemned? There are plenty of people out there who can point to a battered but still-functioning wreck and tell you that it's held up fine and they'd still trust it in a gale. Gear will sometimes hold together far longer than anyone could reasonably expect. But the point is to have, not a long-lived rig, but a *safe* long-lived rig. Why incorporate a safety factor in a rig design, only to erode it away? In view of the possible consequences of gear failure, it seems foolhardy to go out with anything but the strongest, best-conditioned rig that is compatible with performance and your purse. Watch, understand, and respond as if it were an instinctive feeling of your inner life.

143

CHAPTER 7

Emergency Procedures

•

Problem: When the 55-foot ketch *Nabob* was a thousand miles off the west coast of Africa, her ½-inch stainless steel 7 x 7 bobstay suddenly parted.

The vessel was off the wind at the time, but the strain on the ½-inch wire was sufficient that the sound of its breaking could be heard and felt back in the cockpit. With a healthy redundancy of shrouds and stays,

Nabob did not depend on the bobstay for rig integrity to the extent that some craft do, but the accident rendered the jibstay useless and threatened the mainmast above the spreaders. Had the vessel been on the wind this portion of the mast would probably have broken off, falling aft toward the crew, taking the radio antenna—integral with the backstay—with it.

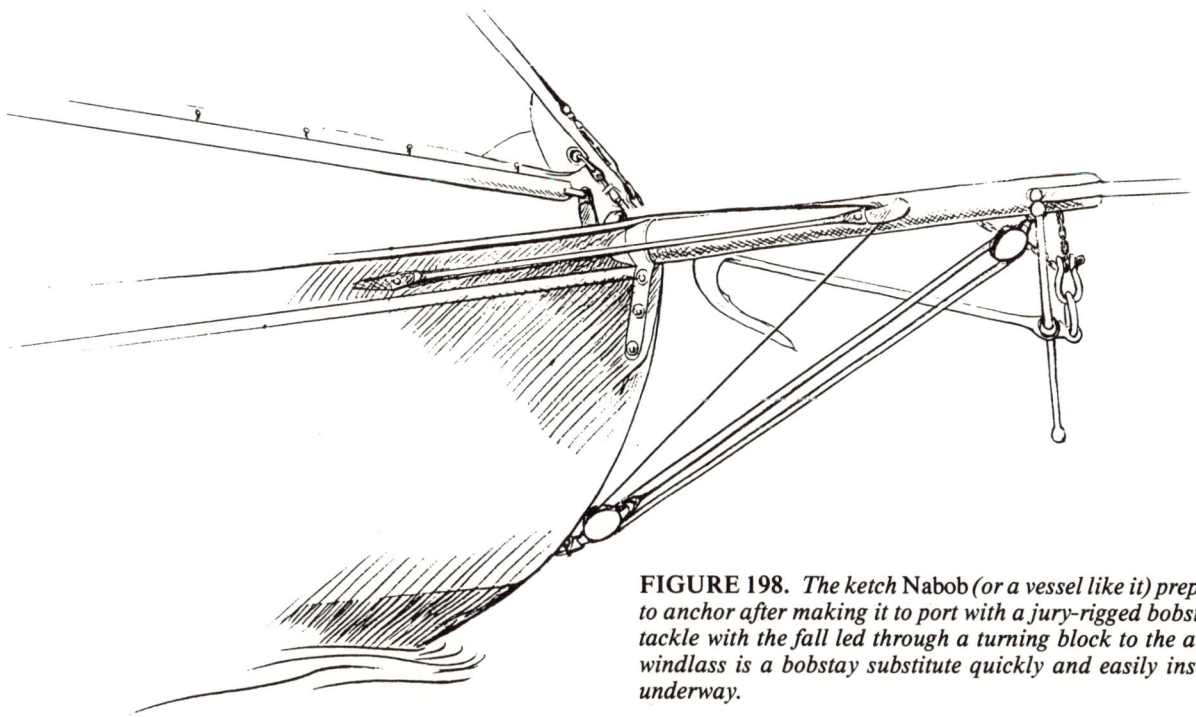

FIGURE 198. *The ketch* Nabob *(or a vessel like it) preparing to anchor after making it to port with a jury-rigged bobstay. A tackle with the fall led through a turning block to the anchor windlass is a bobstay substitute quickly and easily installed underway.*

Response: Even off the wind the situation was serious, since wave action (there was an appreciable sea running) and the aft-directed pull of the mainsail could unduly strain the mast, so the first steps were to lower the main, start the engine, and steer to ease motion. Next some way had to be found of temporarily replacing the bobstay, bringing the rig back into balance. This was done by attaching a block and tackle to the bobstay fittings, slacking the jibstay turnbuckle, gaining as much tension as possible with the purchase, and then retightening the jibstay. Additional power was gained by leading the hauling part of the tackle through a turning block and aft to the windlass. When conditions moderated a measured length of chain was shackled to the old turnbuckle to replace the temporary rig.

Good design, the presence of useful gear, the alacrity of the crew, and a bit of luck all contributed to a happy ending when the *Nabob*'s bobstay broke. But next we must ask, "How could the accident have been avoided?" It turns out that the lower end of the bobstay had been eaten away by severe electrolytic action over the course of years and was just waiting to break. Wire is the best material for a bobstay because, unlike chain or rod, it usually gives advance warning of failure; not inspecting it throws this advantage away. The electrol-

ysis problem was compounded by the bobstay's being slightly undersized relative to the jibstay. This is a common flaw; for some reason many riggers and builders feel that a properly scaled bobstay "looks too big" and opt for a smaller one. So headstay strain, corrosion, and the likelihood of occasionally striking other objects all conspire to abuse a bobstay. I know I replace a disproportionate number of them in my shop.

What happend to *Nabob* was classic rig trauma, the rig-as-strain-distribution system suddenly jeopardized by the failure of one of its parts. But for the rigger and sailor, there's more to the situation than equations involving consequences of strain; people and their skills are part of the system, adding immeasurably to its complexity and strength and giving it the ability to avoid trauma or to respond to it if it does occur. The more prepared and aware we are, the richer the system is.

When people talk about effective responses to emergencies, much is made of preparedness—having the right tools, duplicate parts, and rehearsed procedures. These things are very important, but from a traditional perspective, too much emphasis is placed on specific items and actions. Since things do not always break down when and how one expects, specific practices must be complemented by broad

145

knowledge and a resilient attitude that fosters the associative thinking that can put broad knowledge to work. When I read or hear accounts of sailors who have pulled the fat out of notably fierce fires, these attributes are usually evident; in accounts of fiascoes they are likely absent. In my own small brushes with misfortune, luck has made a difference more often than I'd care to admit, but basic precautions backed up by odd inspirations usually made the difference.

In an era when pleasure craft have gained aerodynamic efficiency at the expense of systems redundancy, the crew's skills at keeping things working can be severely taxed by incidents that, on "old-fashioned" craft, would be inconveniences or at worst easily addressed problems. It's easier to jury-rig a block than a winch, or a shroud than an unstayed carbon-fiber mast, or reefing gear than a roll-away mainsail. I'm not saying that the old ways were better—only that increased efficiency and convenience, with sailboats no less than kitchen appliances, carry with them increased consequences of malfunction; traditional skills can be of *greater* value on a modern boat than on a traditional one.

Problem: The 160-foot barque *Elissa* was on her way in from the last of four daysails celebrating her complete restoration when the tug that was accompanying her somehow wandered in under the head gear. *Elissa*'s dolphin striker speared the tug's house and was broken off; jibboom guys were carried away, the jibboom was cracked, and strain on the foreroyal and topgallant stays pulled the fore topgallant mast forward at a frightening angle, threatening to bring it crashing down, yards and all. It was *Nabob* again only worse, with many more people in much greater jeopardy from a larger, more complex, more heavily damaged rig.

Response: The foredeck was cleared in an instant. Instinct took care of that. As the tug was working clear, staysails were lowered and squaresails clewed up; riggers dove into the forepeak to get come-alongs, blocks, and tackle; qualified crew went cautiously aloft to check for mast damage; and passengers were moved well aft. The key was teamwork—skills in concert, with a minimum of noise and motion. There was no opportunity to take stock and plan a formal procedure, and given the crew's familiarity with the boat and each other, none was needed. *Elissa* got home safely with temporary gear guying and supporting her injured jibboom.

Problem: The 45-foot triple-spreader racing sloop *Pendragon* was en route to San Francisco, nine days out of Honolulu, when the starboard D-2 shroud broke at its upper terminal. The vessel was close-hauled on the starboard tack in 10 knots of wind, and the suddenly unsupported section of mast bent sharply, obviously close to breaking until the crew got her over onto port tack. The situation wasn't dangerous, at least not immediately, but California was too far to go under engine alone, and part of the course would have to be sailed with the injured starboard side to windward. The crew had to come up with some form of jury rig.

Response: One can imagine them going through a checklist of possible remedies:

Repair the shroud?

No, it was rod rigging, and it had broken at its very end. Had the break occurred somewhere along the length, it might have been possible to notch the broken ends, fasten them together with cable clamps, make up for the shortened length with a heavy lashing above the turnbuckle, and proceed cautiously (Figure 199).

FIGURE 199. *Filing notches in rod rigging and clamping overlapped pieces together for an emergency repair.*

Replace it with a spare?

No spares aboard. Because rod terminals cannot be fabricated aboard ship, the usual practice of carrying a spare length at least as long as the longest piece in the rig would have been no use; rod failure insurance means carrying a complete side of shrouds plus spare stays. This would mean a heavy, 6-foot diameter coil of vulnerable, expensive metal that would have to find a safe home somewhere aboard a relatively small boat.

Carrying a spare piece of 7 x 7 or 1 x 19 wire and some compatible terminals might be a good idea for some boats, but this is not usually done because not just ends but also spreader fittings are highly specialized with rod rigging; improvising a reliable spreader connection could be a major task. Add to this the exaggerated "failsafe" claims of some rigging salespersons, and the fact that chandleries are usually nearby anyway, and it's easy to see why this delivery crew found themselves with no spares aboard.

Switch rigging pieces?

On a more moderate rig, it would be conceivable in moderate weather to take a shroud from the port side and install it temporarily on the starboard side. But this rig was so fragile that the crew couldn't even lower the mainsail lest the boat's rolling break the mast; they had to stay on port tack, and so couldn't remove a rigging piece from the port side.

It was as though circumstances had conspired with rig design to produce the least repairable problem possible. An innovative solution was called for. Figure 200 shows the fix that the crew came up with: a spinnaker pole as spreader, quadrupled halyard above and winched-tight fore and afterguys below, with a spare halyard, assorted blocks, lashings, eyes, and no fewer than five winches called into play before it seemed safe to put the starboard side back to work. The makeshift rig had some elasticity and its components were heavily strained, but everything held together. *Pendragon* was able to make San Francisco in good time (16 days for 2,600 miles, with seven days under jury rig and three of those days in fresh winds on starboard tack).

Upon first reading an account of this repair in the February 1983 issue of *Sail* magazine, I was impressed with the use of diverse materials in unlikely combination to mimic a shroud. The configuration was of a different order entirely than, say, simply using a halyard to mimic a broken jibstay. I later realized that this configuration was not a repair but a piece of extemporaneous design superimposed on an unrepairable rig. I do not know who else was in the crew, but the skipper and author of the *Sail* article was Warwick Tompkins, Jr., who races as well as delivers boats and who supervised the operation of Jabba the Hut's sailing barge during the filming of the movie *Return of the Jedi*, taught millions of people the mechanical principles of sailing on Public Broadcasting's "Under Sail" series, and, at the age of nine, rounded Cape Horn aboard his father's 95-foot pilot schooner

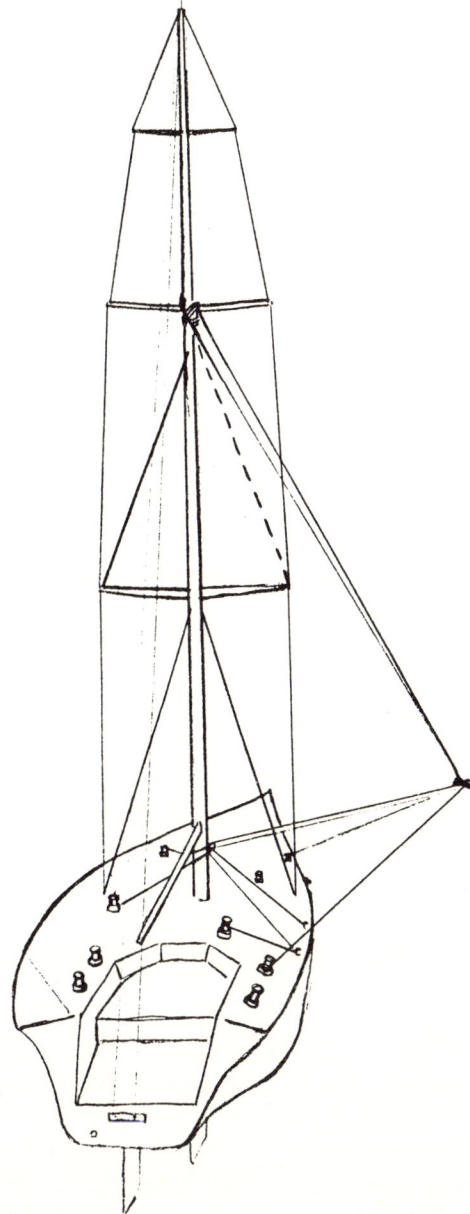

FIGURE 200. *The crew of the racing yacht* Pendragon *used a spinnaker pole, five winches, and assorted blocks, tackle, and lashings to replace the starboard D-2 (second lowest diagonal) shroud on their rod-rigged mast. The spinnaker pole provided a healthy staying angle and was reinforced with lashings at its base to relieve the heavy compression loads there. The rope and wire rope used as shroud, fore guy, and after guy were far more elastic than rod rigging, but inelastic enough to keep the mast up.*

Wander Bird. He personifies the benefits of wildly diverse experience. A deep, intuitive understanding of rigs and rigging is the most valuable component of any emergency procedure.

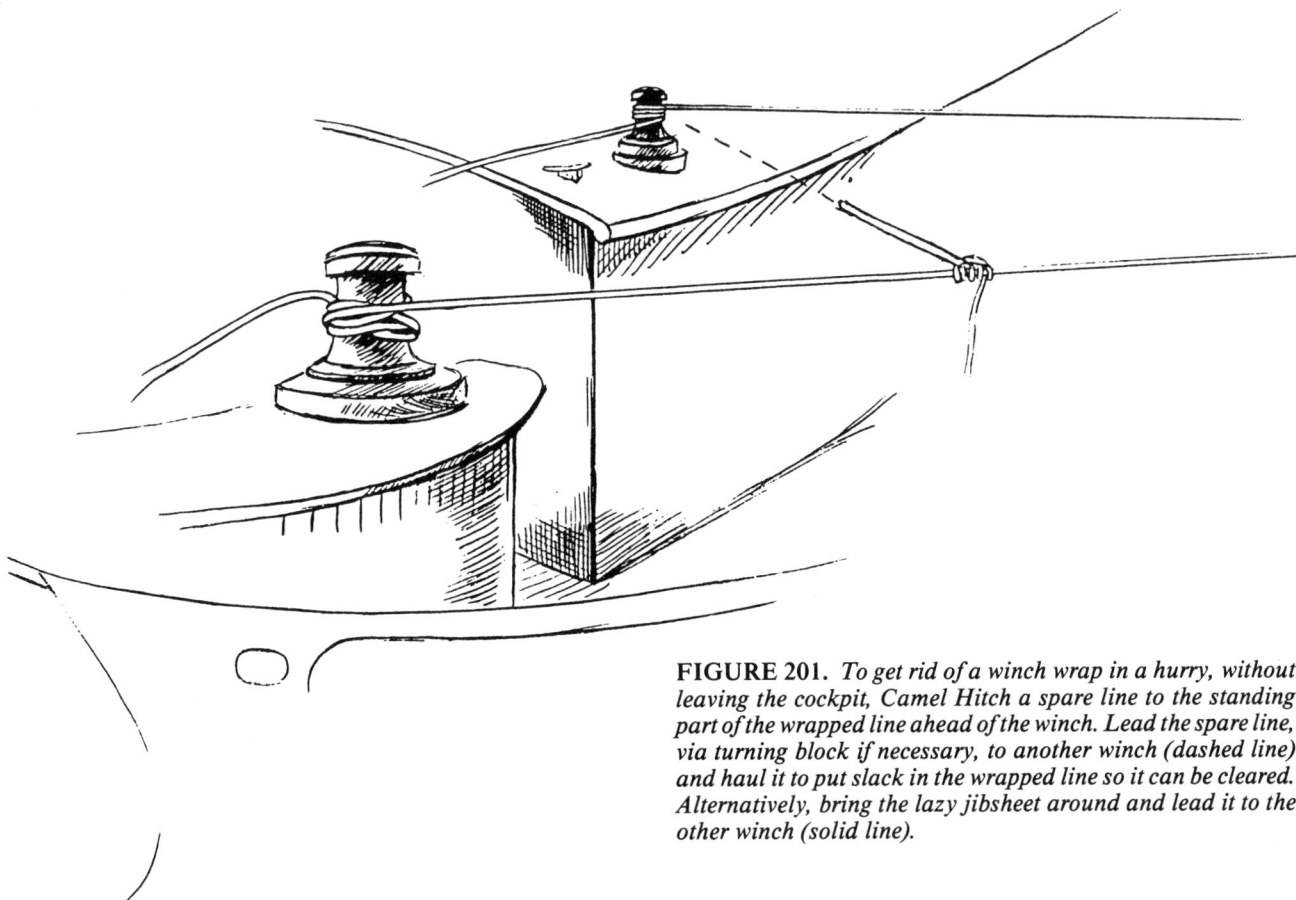

FIGURE 201. *To get rid of a winch wrap in a hurry, without leaving the cockpit, Camel Hitch a spare line to the standing part of the wrapped line ahead of the winch. Lead the spare line, via turning block if necessary, to another winch (dashed line) and haul it to put slack in the wrapped line so it can be cleared. Alternatively, bring the lazy jibsheet around and lead it to the other winch (solid line).*

Some emergencies are even more involved than *Pendragon*'s. What could have been done, for example, had the mast collapsed? But most sudden problems are smaller and simpler though not necessarily any more obvious of solution. Whatever the level of complexity, your road to intuitive understanding begins with a basic idea: restore appropriate tension. As you sail, consider what pieces are under how much tension, and why; study design to see the logical beauty of a resolution of forces; look at and sail many different boats to see how differently and with what varying degrees of success forces can be resolved. Ask yourself, "If that halyard jams now, what could I do? If a crack appears in the mast...there... what could I do? If that roller-furling headsail jams, what could I do?" This line of questioning leads to interesting conversations, encourages design comprehension, occupies the mind, and most important, helps you avoid emergencies by making you aware of potential trouble. Here are a few examples of tension restoration.

Problem: Through inattentive tailing, the turns on a headsail sheet winch become thoroughly, profoundly "wrapped" under heavy tension, so that you cannot cast them off to tack. You're in the midst of a closely contested race (not all emergencies are life threatening), and it's unthinkable that you should create slack in the sheet by bearing off to let the main blanket the headsail. A stiff breeze is blowing, so that even if you were willing to head into the wind, the flogging of the sail would keep you from clearing the line.

Response: Pull the lazy sheet around to the lee side and lead it via snatch block, stanchion, cleat, or what-have-you to another winch. Take a strain to put slack in the jammed sheet. Clear turns and reset properly. Return lazy sheet and prepare to come about. Alternatively, for a quicker, don't-leave-the-cockpit fix, Rolling Hitch or Camel Hitch a spare line to the standing part of the fouled sheet and lead this line to a spare winch.

148

Problem: Preparing to reef, you take up smartly on the main topping lift not realizing that the pin on the boom-end shackle has been gradually working loose and has chosen this precise moment to fall out. Braced for appreciable tension, you appear to dive for the deck when there isn't any. A physical gag worthy of Buster Keaton. With the bail of the shackle still hanging in the eye splice and giving it carrying weight, the loose end soars up and out, wrapping itself a few times around the leeward shrouds. You have to suddenly dodge when the bail finally slips loose and comes hurtling directly at you. Hilarious.

Response: Since you are a prudent sailor and were prepared to reef as soon as you thought of it, there's no reason to panic. Lead a spare halyard aft, set it up as a temporary topping lift, and proceed to reduce sail. Or sheet the main into the gallows, drop the sail, and put in the reef while it's down. Now ask yourself, "Do I really need that loose topping lift?" Sometimes the safest, most appropriate procedure is to do nothing. If it isn't fouling any other lines or sails, let the damn thing be. Maybe it'll shake loose and you can at least haul on it until the end fetches up against the block aloft so it stays out of the way. The wind is picking up, so why leave the deck if you don't have to?

But if it's wrapped around not only the shrouds but also vital halyards made off to a sheer-pole pinrail, it's a different situation. Sure you can't reach it with the boathook? That it won't come loose by itself? Then get into a safety harness and get out the bosun's chair. No bosun's chair? Put a Bowline on the Bight or Double Rider into the halyard end and sit in that. Tie yourself to one or more of the shrouds on a short tether, have the person at the helm steer the course that imparts the least motion to the boat, and go aloft. Just two people aboard, so no one to winch you up? Heave-to to free the other hand. If this isn't possible, reeve a long spare line into a handy-billy and haul yourself aloft. When you get up to the work, belay the hauling part by passing a bight of it through and under the chair as shown in Figure 202, or hitch a bight to the chair just as securely as you can. If you have no handy-billy, curse yourself soundly, do a few limbering-up exercises (no kidding), and shinny up a pair of shrouds as shown in Figure 203. This little-known technique is strenuous at best, and on vessels with small diameter wires it's downright painful. But it's the fastest way aloft and it might be your only alternative.

Get a bosun's chair. Get a handy-billy. And above all, get around to seizing shackles.

FIGURE 202. *A bosun's chair can be belayed by the person sitting in it when there's no one available on deck to do it. Hold the halyard with one hand to keep the chair at the desired height; with the other hand, pull a bight of the halyard fall through the chair and over your head. Let the bight extend down far enough so you can catch it with your foot, and bring it forward and up. Take out the slack and the bight will form a hitch at the chair's becket. The chair can be gradually lowered by feeding slack through the hitch.*

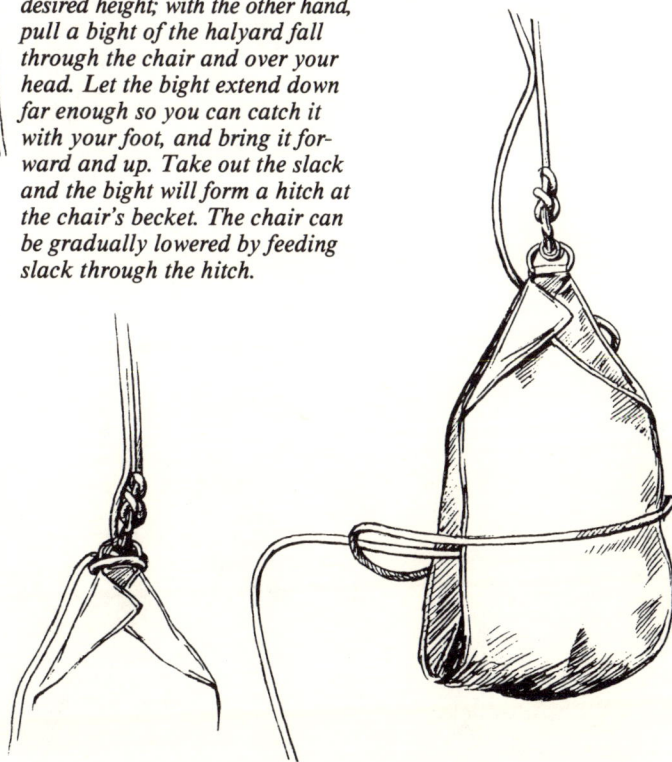

It is natural to think immediately of dismastings when we think of rig failures. What if, despite all precautions, your mast does collapse far from help? Here is a scenario based on reports of actual jury rigs, a little disaster sampler for your consideration.

149

FIGURE 203. *A ratline-less emergency climbing technique: Wrap feet and hands around adjacent shrouds and monkey your way up. Stretching beforehand to limber knee and ankle joints is a good idea.*

Problem: A weak spot in the mast at the spreaders causes a failure far from land, in 20 to 25 knots of wind. The mast doesn't teeter and fall; it's under tons of compression load so it comes down Bang! in the blink of an eye and bounces over the leeward side before it fetches up in a tangle of rigging. The boom crumples at its outer end when it hits a corner of the gallows, and shears away at the gooseneck. Some of the shrouds and stays carry away and go whipping through the air, the leeward lifeline stanchions collapse and add to the tangle, and sections of the smashed dinghy fly into the cockpit. Deprived of the rig's stabilizing effect the hull begins pitching and lurching sharply, so footing is none too sure. From belowdecks comes the sound of cascading gear and shouts of alarm. Someone fights his way to the wheel, shoulders the dazed helmsman aside, and starts the engine to get the boat under control, only to have a stray piece of running rigging immediately foul the prop.

Then things stop going wrong, and it's time to jury rig.

Response: You attend to any crewmembers who might have been injured, send a distress call if possible, check the condition of the hull, and set a sea anchor to ease the motion. Then you very carefully begin to clean up the mess in the water, getting everything close and secure alongside. All that tangle is really working against you, so you have at it with your wire cutters—not an ax or hacksaw—using spare line to keep it all from drifting away as you work. If conditions were calmer and you had more time, you could disconnect the wires by unscrewing their turnbuckles.

Soon things are under enough control that you can remove the sails, cut away or unreeve the running rigging, and even remove the upper ends of most of the standing rigging pieces. All of these salvaged items you stow out of the way for the moment, then take time to do a little housekeeping, clearing the decks of broken gear, splintered wood, and such. Then it's time to return to those two mast sections.

Hmmm. The lower one is buckled badly, with jagged edges at both ends. The spreaders are gone, the tangs are useless, and there are no sheaves in this section. Let it go—just untie it and let it go.

The upper section is longer and fairly straight, but its top is smashed, ruining sheaves and tangs. No matter, get some hands on the lashing lines at either end and time the roll of the boat for the best moment to

150

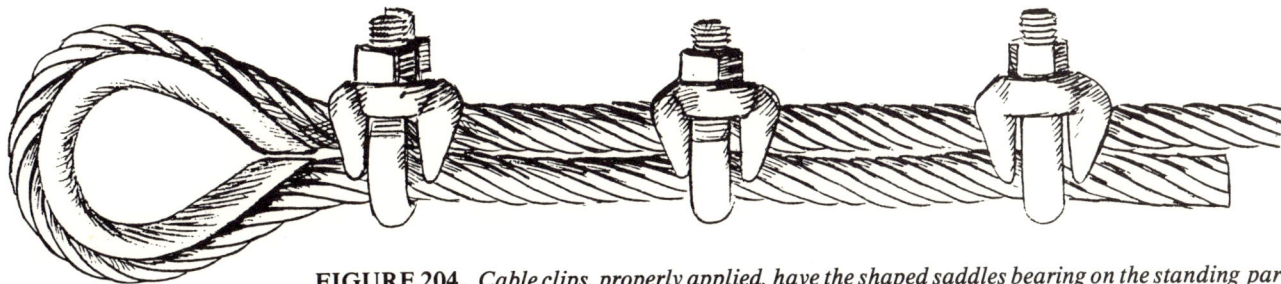

FIGURE 204. *Cable clips, properly applied, have the shaped saddles bearing on the standing part.*

FIGURE 205. *A Molly Hogan splice is made by unlaying three adjacent strands of a 7 x 7 or 7 x 19 wire rope for a distance equal to about 2¼ times the circumference of the desired eye. Overhand Knot the resulting two bundles together—left over right—to form the eye (A), then lay the two bundles into each other's vacant spaces, right down to the standing part (B). At this point, cut the heart out of the bundle it's in (C), helix the six strands smoothly down onto the standing part, and tape them down (D).*

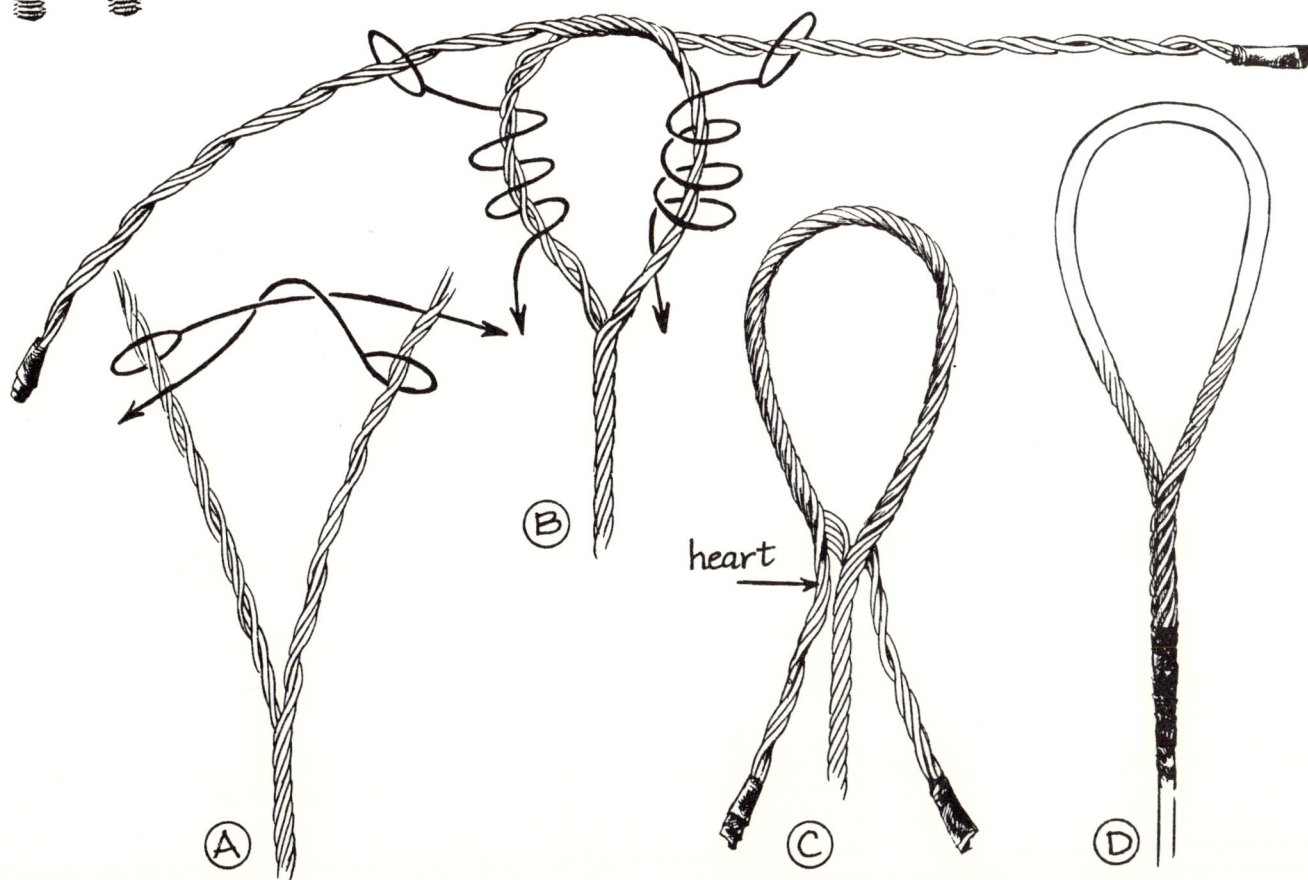

heart

Ⓐ Ⓑ Ⓒ Ⓓ

haul the thing aboard. Secure it on deck and set hands to squaring and filing the ends while you work up some shroud attachments. A simple, strong procedure is to unbolt a pair of cleats from the deck and throughbolt them together near the top of the stick. It's a good idea to shape a reinforcing wood plug to insert in the mast at this point.

Next you get out four pieces of wire rope, each about 6 feet longer than your jury mast, and turn in an eye at either end of each. The upper eye is big enough to slip over the mast, and the lower is maybe 8 inches in circumference. If your wire is 1 x 19, you make the eyes with cable clips properly applied (Figure 204). With 7 x 7 wire you can "splice with your bare hands" by turning in a Molly Hogan at each end (Figure 205). This is a very fast and easy method, nearly as strong as cable clips*, and it imposes no chance of dropping tools or nuts overboard.

*Tensile strengths (as percent of rated wire strengths): Molly Hogan 70%, clips 80%.

The four pieces are your forestay, backstay, and two shrouds. Seat them securely on the cleats, and on top of them add some rope grommets for halyard blocks. Seize the assorted eyes and grommets in place. Tie spare lines through the lower eyes so you'll have something to hold onto to stabilize the mast as you raise it. It's going to be a deck-stepped mast, sans tabernacle, so get it up on the cabintop, brace its butt against the stump of the old mast, and lash it down so that it will pivot but not shift. Put a hatchcover, breadboard, or other stout object underneath the butt as a pad, and reinforce the cabin beams at this point with heavy bracing salvaged from the boom, whisker pole, or bowsprit. Run the backstay line through a turning block to a winch and horse the mast up by main force until the angle is high enough for the winch to take over. The hands on the shrouds will have a tough time of keeping the mast from falling sideways; go slowly so they can pay their lines evenly. You'll have to go forward to tend the forestay as the mast goes up, so the backstay, turning block, winch, and winchers had all better be first-rate. Take a turn around the capstan with the forestay line and snub it to keep the mast from going over backward.

When it's plumb, pass the attached ropes through shackles on the chainplates and the lower ends of the shrouds several times to form lanyards, and tighten them moderately. Now get out some more spare lines and a come-along and lash the base of the mast very tightly to the stump. Take up some more on the shrouds and stays, check all attachment points, and you're ready to hoist a sail or two.

Most boats do not carry spare rigging, cable clips, wire rope cutters, or much else that might be of use in an emergency. Worse yet, they do not carry crew who can splice barehanded, use cleats as tangs, or raise an impromptu mast. There's no excuse for this; emergency gear costs little and takes up little space, while knowledge is absolutely free and goes with you everywhere. Consider the possibility of accidents, speculate on various courses of action, and stock and learn accordingly. Stress versatility—accidents are never exactly as you imagine and there are always surprising complications. The result of your wide-ranging preparations will be a greatly reduced chance of ever having to use them. As Stewart Brand's fine-grain philosophy puts it, "Take care of the big problems and the little problems will defeat you; take care of the little problems and the big problems will take care of themselves."

Smooth Sailing.

152

CHAPTER 8
Fancy Work

•

What with the years-long voyages that used to be the rule in olden days, sailors would find themselves with a lot of time on their hands, and lines in them. Given patience, trial and error, and that peculiarly human urge to create semi-useful frippery, hundreds of beautiful, intricate complications came into being: fancy work. It's an art form like scrimshaw or woodcarving, but unlike these pursuits, its artfulness is intrinsic to its use; what's right for a bellrope is wrong for a thump mat.

Today fancy work is too often mere decoration made with no concern for proportion or appropriate intricacy. I know, I know—picky, picky, picky. But as long as we have the fruit of thousands of hours of boredom (the Mother of Invention?), why not take a little time and make good use of it?

For instance, there's decorative hitching, a way to cover cylindrical objects with twine to provide chafing gear or a more comfortable handhold. The simplest form is French Hitching (Figure 206), a series of half hitches laid up in mind-numbing sequence. The finished product is functional and nearly attractive. But use two lines, hitch them alternately in opposite directions, and you have Moku Hitching (Figure 207), downright eye-catching and involved enough to keep the mind alive. It's important to draw each hitch up snugly and see that the two spirals proceed at the same pace. When the spirals cross, jump by with whichever side is closest for a neat crossing. Many patterns can be made with Moku Hitching by reversing hitch direction at different points in the spiral.

Why the name "Moku Hitching?" Because the first place I saw it was on the gangplank of an old Sacramento River sugar hauler of that name. Who tied the knot or what they called it I do not know, but it hasn't appeared in any other knot book, so it was probably originated by some unknown marlingspike artist. Inspired by that individual I set about develop-

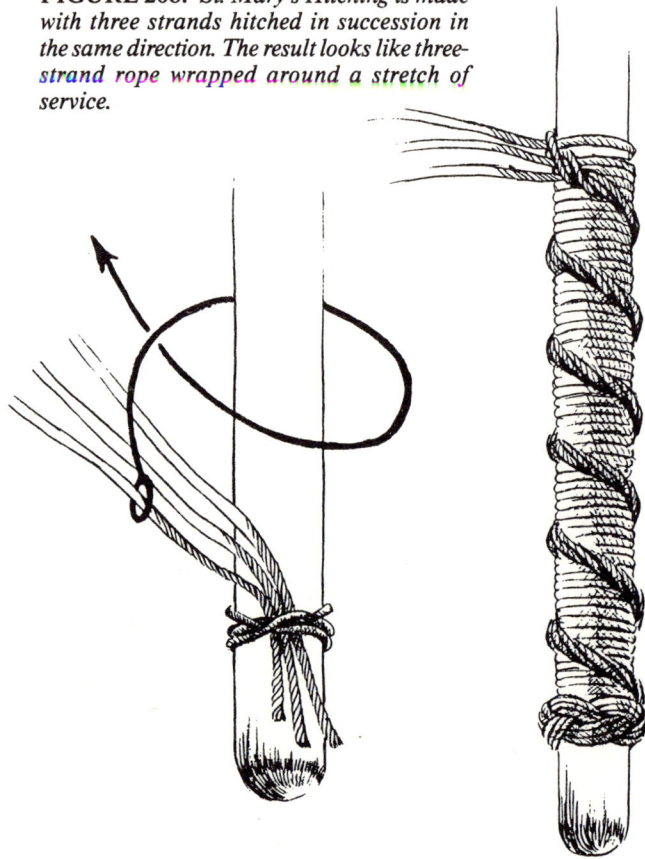

FIGURE 206. *French Hitching is a series of half hitches made one upon the other. Snug the hitches firmly against each other and they'll form a smooth spiral.*

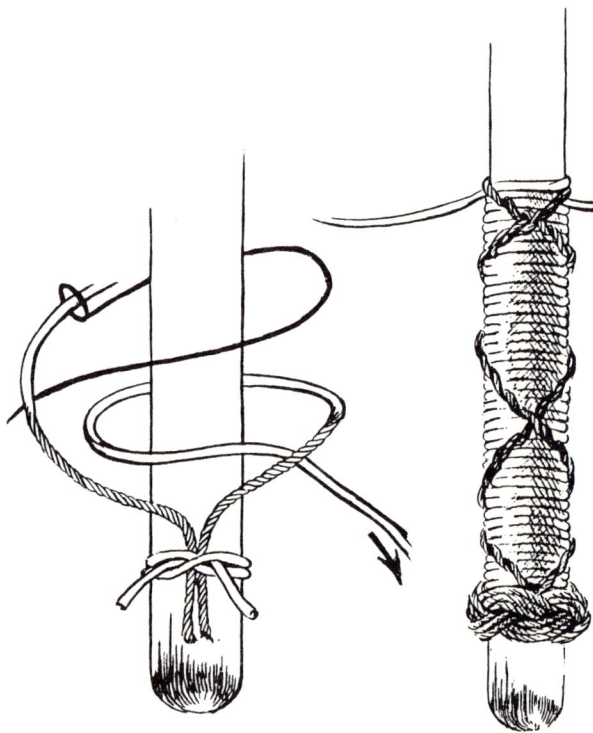

FIGURE 207. *Moku Hitching involves two lines half-hitched alternately in opposite directions. Tighten both spirals with identical, consistent tension. Cover the ends with Turk's Heads.*

FIGURE 208. *St. Mary's Hitching is made with three strands hitched in succession in the same direction. The result looks like three-strand rope wrapped around a stretch of service.*

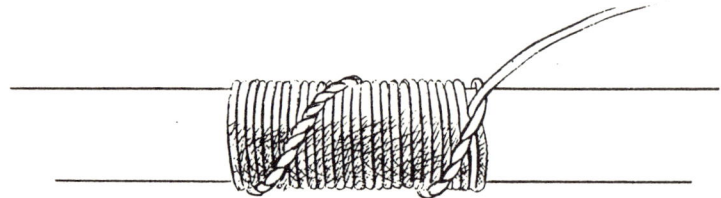

ing an original hitch and came up with the one shown in Figure 208, St. Mary's Hitching. As you can see, it is made with three strands, the lowermost one always being hitched in the same direction over the other two. The result looks a lot like a three-strand rope laid over service, a gratifyingly pretty knot to make.

Why "St. Mary's Hitching?" False modesty; I could have called it "Brion's Spiral" or some such, but instead named it after a fine little church in Anacortes, Washington. Knots should have names.

Both of these knots are new, and there are certainly many more out there waiting to be discovered; play around some, improvise, and you just might find one.

Next in order of complexity is Ringbolt Hitching, always involving three or more strands tucked in different directions. In the basic form, the first strand is hitched left, the next right, next left, and so on, so that the hitches form a ridge along one side of the object being covered. Keep the ridge straight (Figure 209). A variation involves tucking all three left, then all three right.

For a big jump in complexity try a five-strand Ringbolt Hitching (Figure 210), a lovely, infuriatingly complicated production that is just the thing for a tiller, companionway rail, or other special place.

Ringbolt Hitching is particularly suited to covering arced cylinders such as the rim of a wheel. It was developed as chafing gear on the deck ringbolts to which hemp anchor cables were stopped in the days before chain. Nowadays one sees it on chest beckets, lanyards, rail corners, and tire fenders, as well as ship's wheels. And it isn't limited to arcs; by hauling back on the hitches and slightly spreading the underside turns, it works for straight cylinders, too.

Once you've got hitching figured out and have covered the object of your choice, you'll want to hide the hitching ends; they're just hanging out there. This is best done with a Turk's Head at either end (see below), of whatever complexity you feel up to.

154

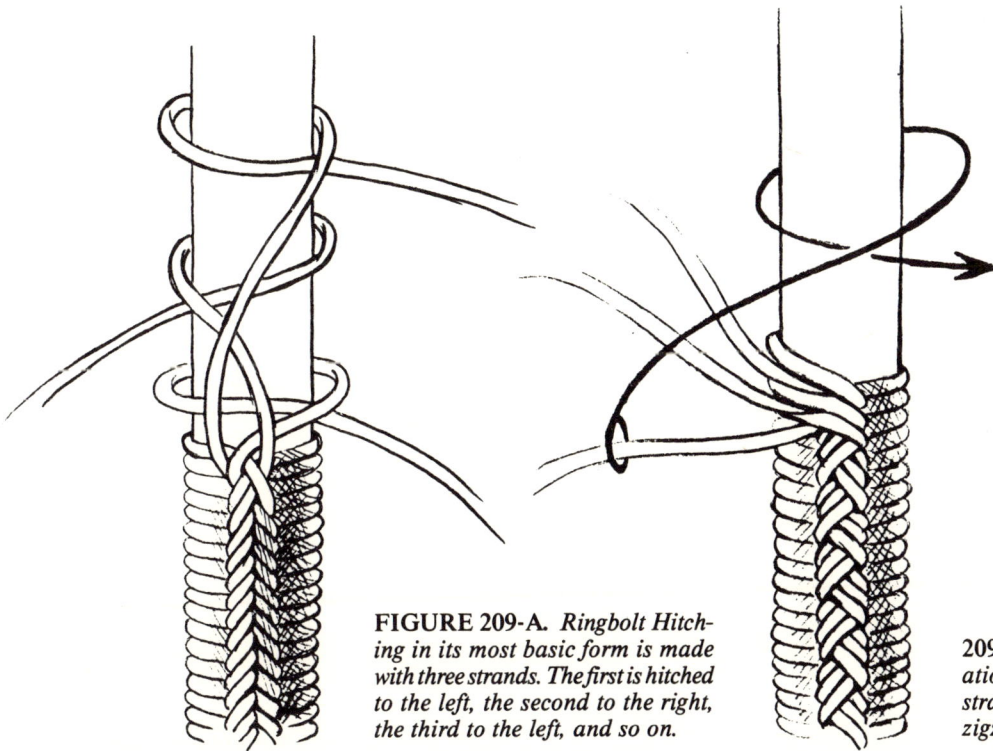

FIGURE 209-A. *Ringbolt Hitching in its most basic form is made with three strands. The first is hitched to the left, the second to the right, the third to the left, and so on.*

209-B. *A Ringbolt Hitching variation involves hitching all three strands first left, then right, for a zigzag pattern.*

Some Practical Details

Whatever form of knot you use, the surface you're covering should be clean and well sealed. If the surface is slippery, parcel with adhesive tape or, on wood, work over tacky shellac.

Cord size is important: too large, and you'll get clumsy looking, lumpy hitches that are uncomfortable to hold; too small, and you'll have a lovely little antimacassar. But by then you'll be old and blind. Linen twine or cotton cod line of 32 to 60 thread is right for most fancy work. Match the size to the project at hand. Avoid synthetic twines, for they do not finish well and are unpleasant to work with.

To find how much twine you need to cover a given length and diameter, make a practice run—a good idea anyway—using a known length of twine. Measure how far this length gets, then multiply it to get enough to cover the whole project. Before you start, make the lengths up into "foxes," figure-eight turns made around the thumb and pinky and seized with a Constrictor Knot. Pull a working length out as you go and draw up the Constrictor occasionally to keep the foxes intact.

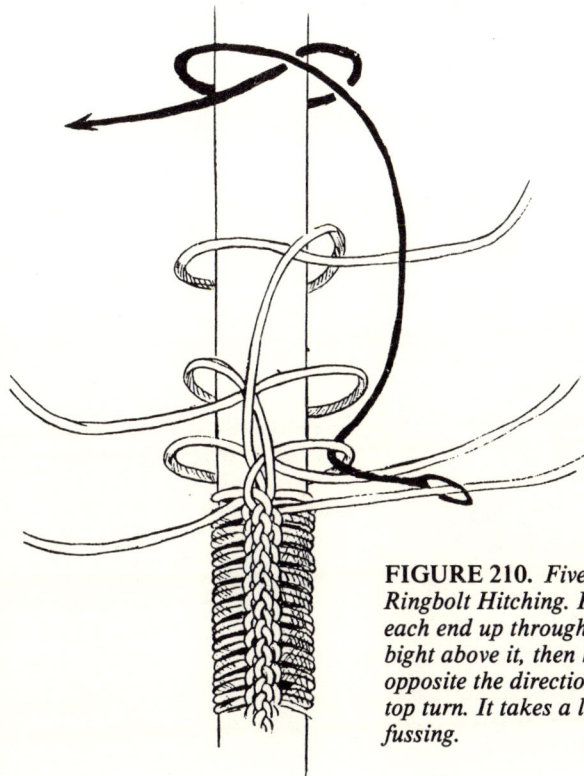

FIGURE 210. *Five-strand Ringbolt Hitching. Pass each end up through the bight above it, then hitch opposite the direction of the top turn. It takes a lot of fussing.*

155

FIGURE 212. *Beginning a Star Knot. Middle two 18-inch pieces of twine, lay alongside a 9-inch piece of twine, and bundle all together with a Constrictor Knot about ¼ inch from the bight end (A). Arrange the ends petal-like and hitch one around its neighbor to the right, passing the end over to the right and back under to the left (B). Spill the hitch just made into the other strand (C), and the result will look like (D). Hitch the strand with the hitch in it around its neighbor, and spill this new hitch into the neighbor's strand. Continue with the other ends. Since there's no end hanging down, it can be difficult to spot strand #1, which strand #5 hitches around. Trace it up from the stem and pull a little slack into it for easier spilling (E).*

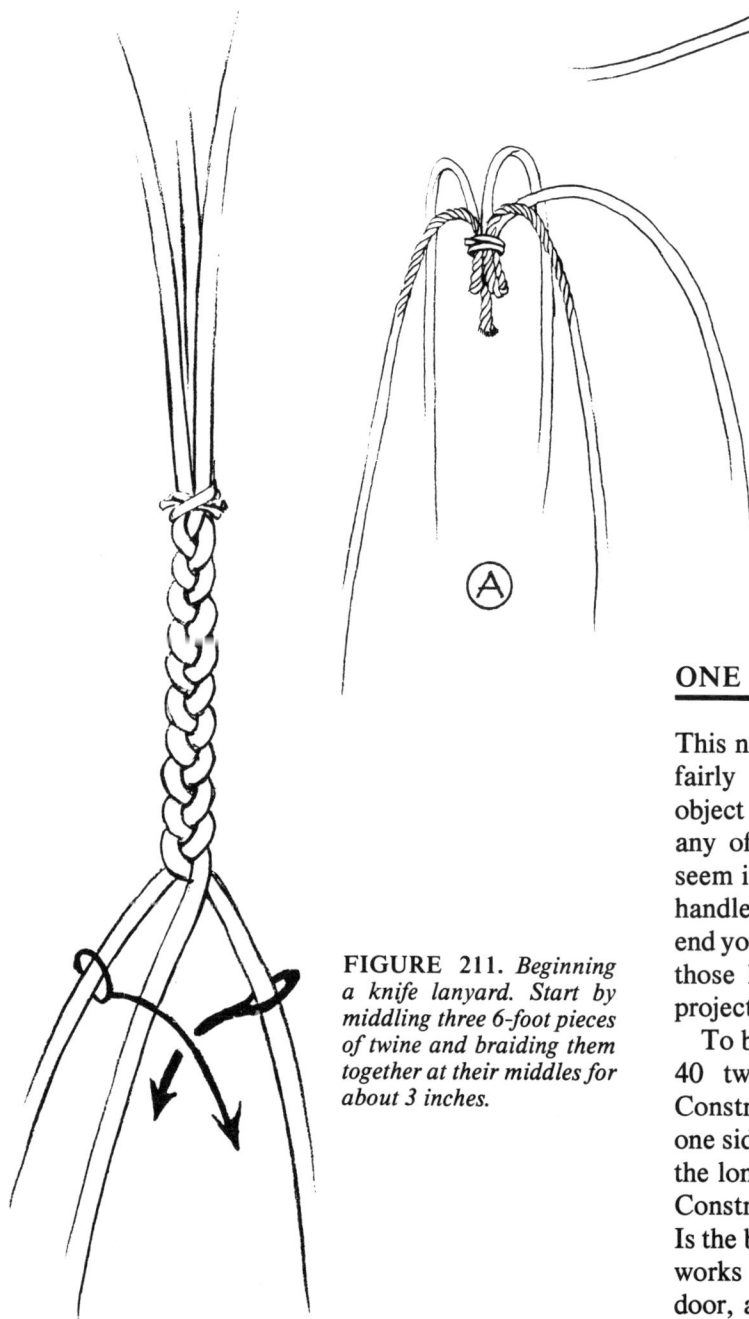

FIGURE 211. *Beginning a knife lanyard. Start by middling three 6-foot pieces of twine and braiding them together at their middles for about 3 inches.*

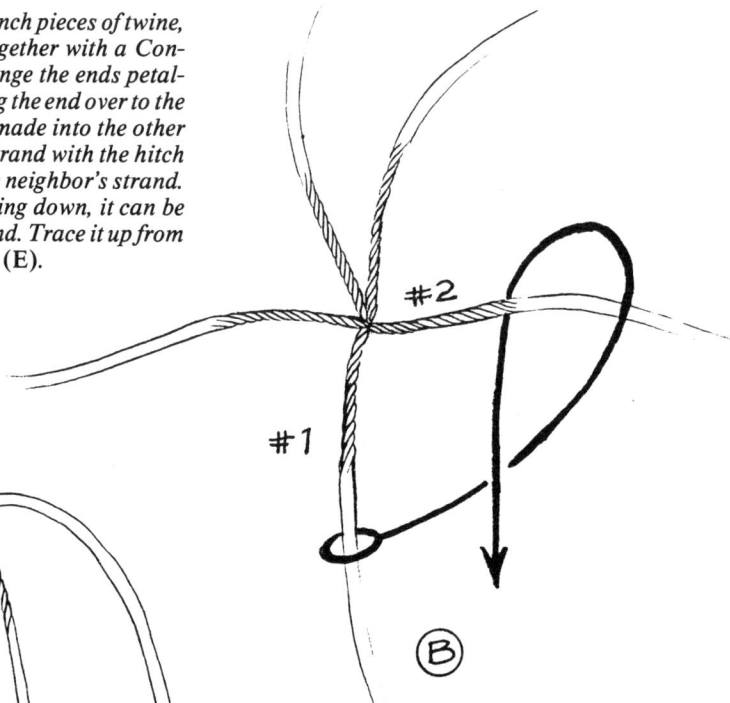

ONE HIGH-CLASS KNIFE LANYARD

This next project is a fancy work sampler, a series of fairly involved knots blended together to form an object of graceful utility. You may never have made any of these knots, but though the diagrams might seem involved, there's nothing going on that can't be handled if you just take things one step at a time. At the end you'll have a useful object plus the ability to use all those knots in any combination for whatever other projects you desire.

To begin, take three 6-foot lengths of number 32 to 40 twine, middle them together, and put on a Constrictor Knot with stout sail twine, 2 to 3 inches to one side of the middle, around all three strands. Braid the longer half of the bundle, working away from the Constrictor, until you have a braid about 3 inches long. Is the braid good and tight? Even? Fine, put the whole works down, take the phone off the hook, close the door, and prepare to tie a Star Knot.

Measure off two 18-inch pieces and one 9-inch

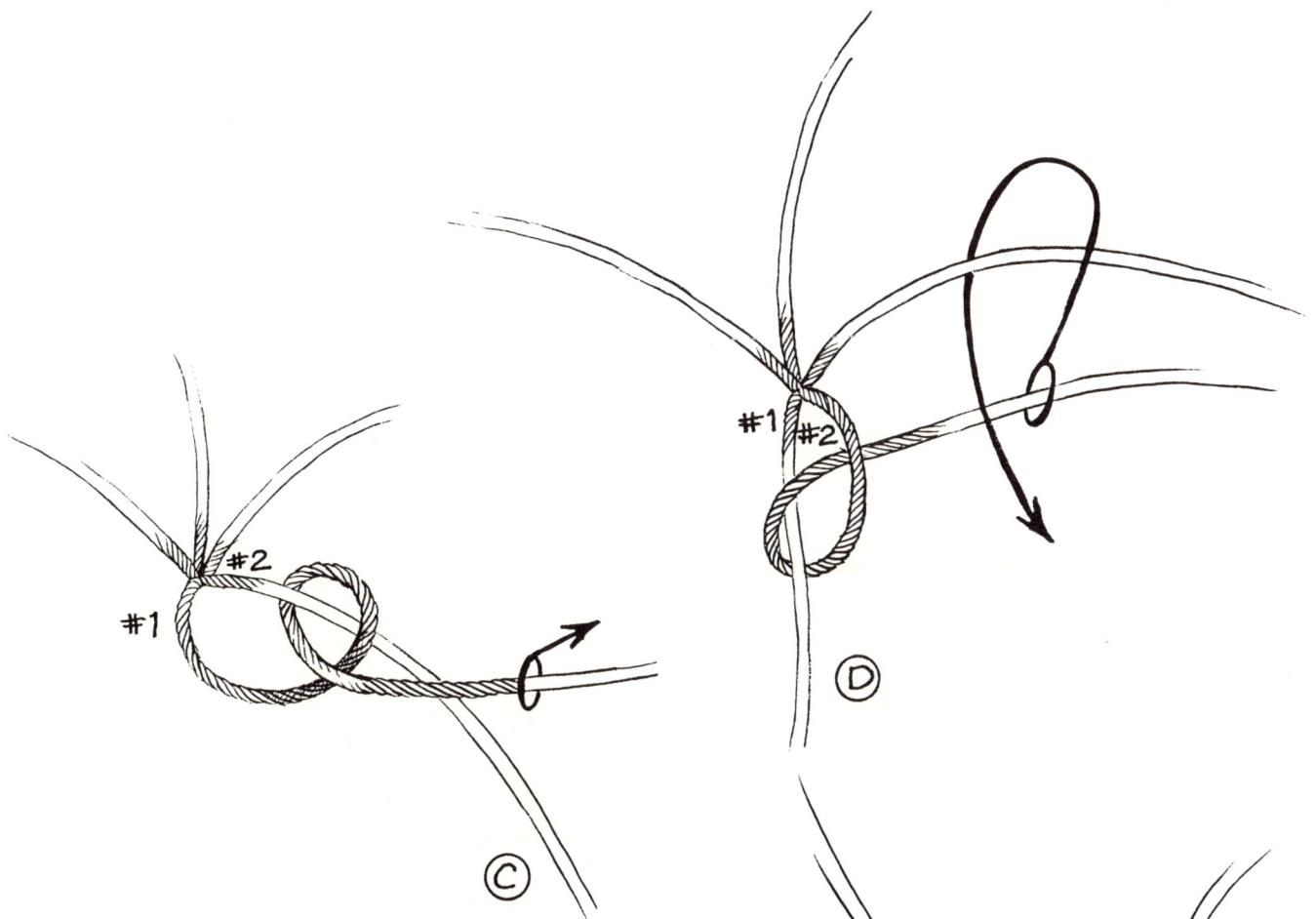

piece of the same cord you used for the braid. Double the longer pieces, lay the short one alongside them, and Constrictor all together about ¼ inch from the bight end (Figure 212-A). Hold the doubled bights in one hand and open up the ends like the petals of a flower. Start with any strand and hitch it around its neighbor to the right (counterclockwise), passing the end over to the right, back under to the left. Now spill the hitch into the other strand by pulling on the one that made the hitch, just as for the Spilled Hitch Bowline (Figure 63), to get Figure 212-D. Now take the strand into which the hitch was just spilled and hitch it around its neighbor to the right and likewise spill that hitch. Continue with all the strands. Because there's no end hanging down, figuring out where to hitch the fifth strand can be difficult. But if you look close to the stem on the right of number 5's beginning, you'll see number 1 (Figure 212-E). Pull a little slack into it to give you room, and hitch around it. Fair everything up so it is compact and symmetrical; fuss with it or you'll get hopelessly lost later.

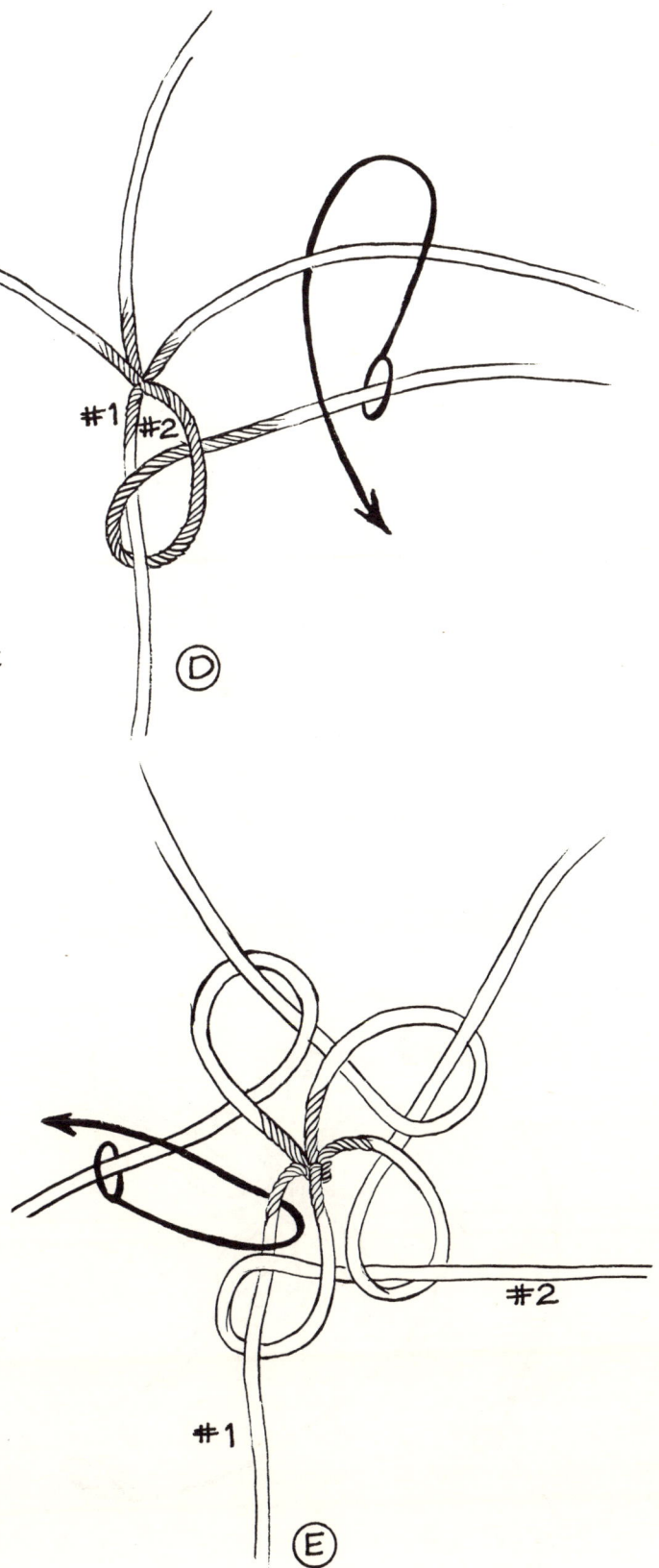

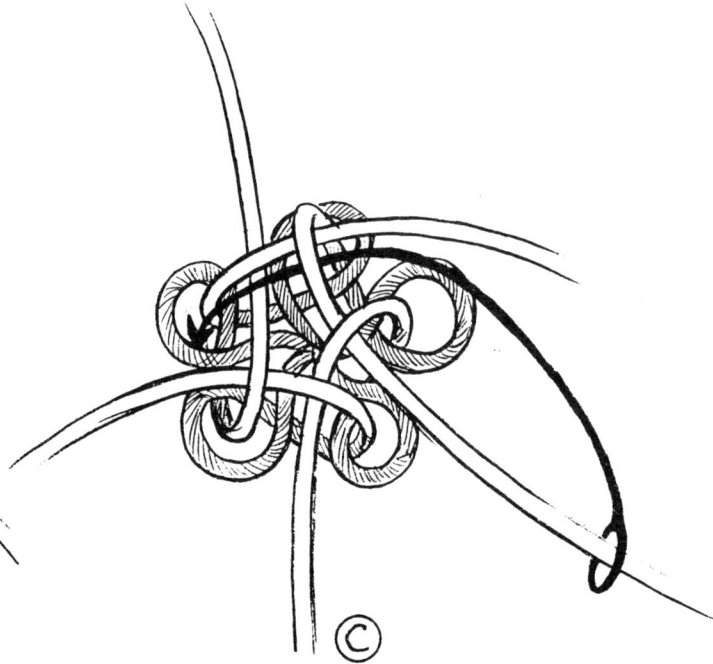

Next, crown all the strands clockwise (Figures 213-A,B). This is just like crowning for a Backsplice (Figure 87), but in the other direction. Fair the crown.

Moderately tricky: Take an end, lead it counterclockwise, and follow the course of the strand on the right into the knot (Figure 213-C) going first under the working strand's own part then down through the loop. Repeat this procedure with the other four strands, taking care that the working strand always stays inside the strand it parallels. Again the fifth strand can be confusing, but since you've kept everything fair you'll see how one of the crown parts remains undoubled. That's the one you parallel (Figure 213-D).

Turn the knot over, take a strand, and continue following its neighbor to completely double it, then tuck the working strand directly through the middle of the knot, inboard of everything else (Figure 213-E). Repeat with each strand, taking care that each one goes into a subsequent space at the stem when it is tucked.

Turn the knot back over. The ends should all be coming out of the center. As you can see (Figure 213-F), the face of the knot is doubled; we'll now use the strands to triple it, finishing the knot. As Figure 213-G shows, you don't follow the closest face but the one next to it; otherwise you don't get a fair run. So lay each strand alongside the appropriate face and tuck it to the stem, under four parts. A carpet-hooking tool or bent piece of wire is a great help here.

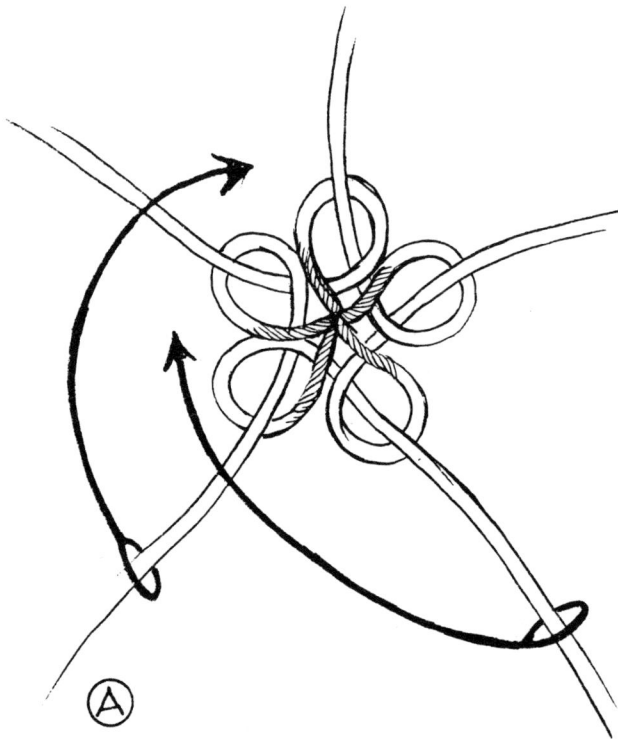

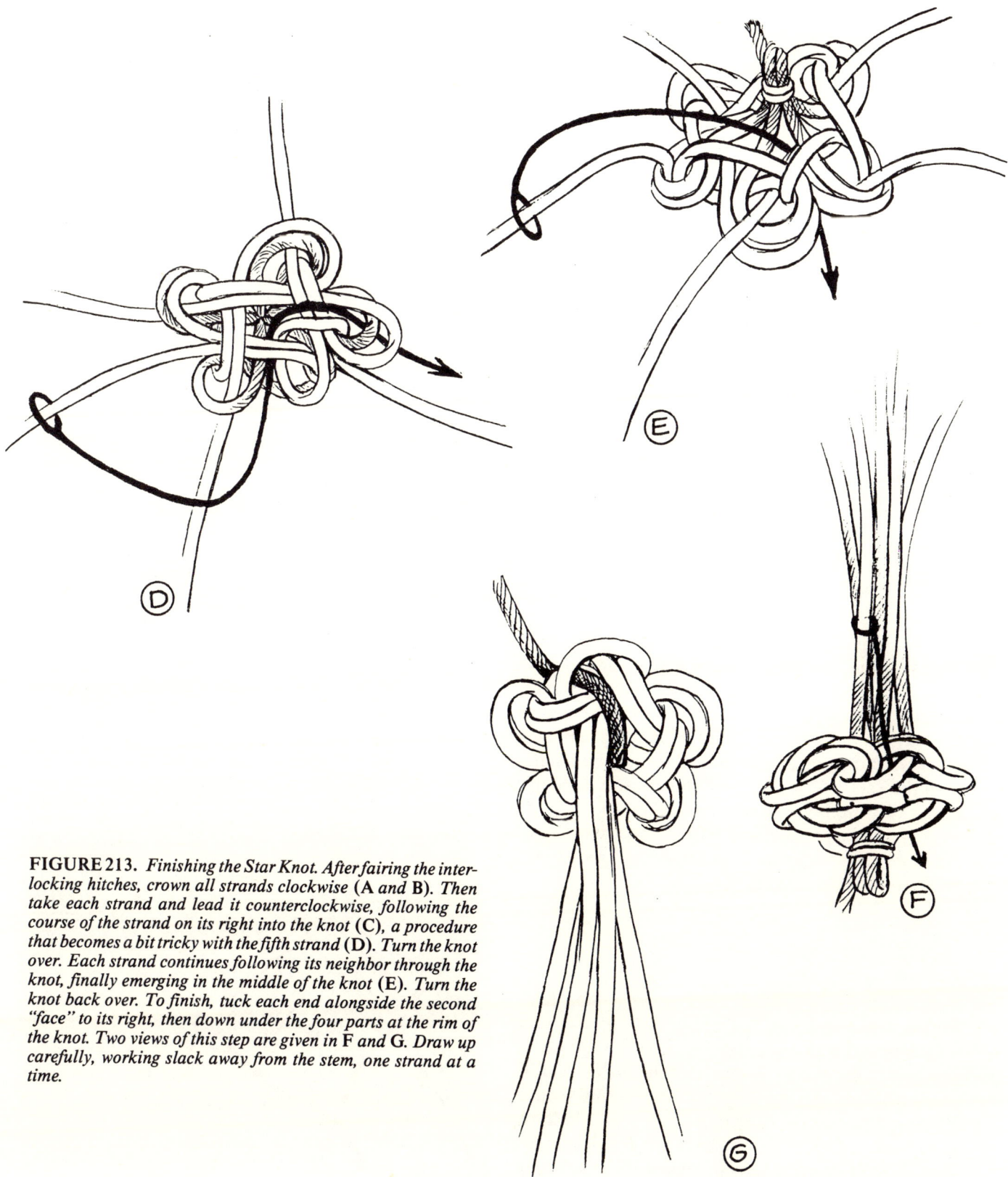

FIGURE 213. *Finishing the Star Knot. After fairing the interlocking hitches, crown all strands clockwise (A and B). Then
take each strand and lead it counterclockwise, following the
course of the strand on its right into the knot (C), a procedure
that becomes a bit tricky with the fifth strand (D). Turn the knot
over. Each strand continues following its neighbor through the
knot, finally emerging in the middle of the knot (E). Turn the
knot back over. To finish, tuck each end alongside the second
"face" to its right, then down under the four parts at the rim of
the knot. Two views of this step are given in F and G. Draw up
carefully, working slack away from the stem, one strand at a
time.*

159

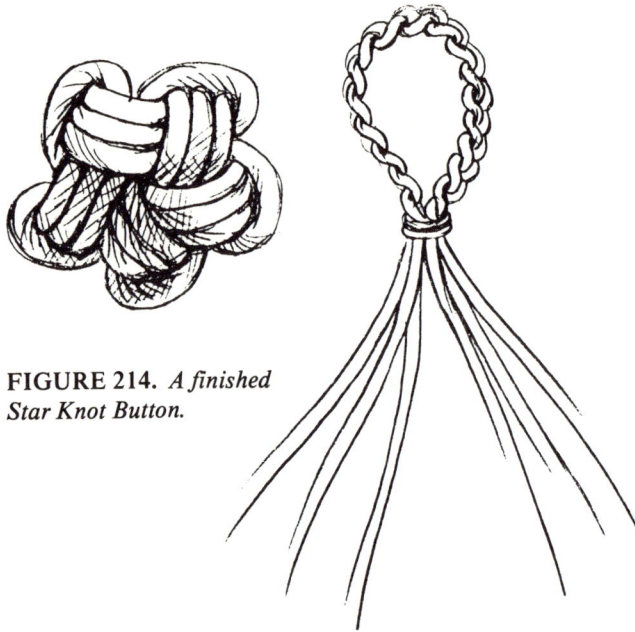

FIGURE 214. *A finished Star Knot Button.*

FIGURE 215. *Continuing the knife lanyard. After fitting the three-strand braid around the Star Knot Button, put a loose Contrictor at the appropriate spot on the legs of the braid.*

Drawing Up and Trimming

Use your small, blunted spike to draw the knot up. Start with the lower half of a horizontal pair and work your way around, taking out slack as you go. Leave that last, tripling pass standing up a little. Pulling it all the way down now will distort things. Tighten each strand in turn, going over them all two or three times until the knot is firm, then pull those last turns down flush. To trim, lay a small, sharp blade at the point where an end emerges, press lightly, and *work the end back and forth under the knife;* slicing with the knife is liable to result in severed button loops.

Back to the Lanyard

You are the proud owner of a genuine Star Knot Button, which can now be fitted to the button loop of your lanyard. Remember the lanyard? We're making one here. Take that little stretch of three-strand braid and pass it around the circumference of the button. Pinch it down so the fit is tight, then put on a loose Constrictor (Figure 215). Check the fit; the button should just fit through the loop. Tighten the Constrictor and lay the button aside for now.

A Six-Strand Double Matthew Walker Knot

Matthew Walker, for a long time "the only man to have a knot named after him," was possibly a master rigger in a British naval dockyard, circa 1800, according to Ashley. Whoever he was, he certainly came up with an elegant, wide-range-of-usefulness knot. I described the three-strand version in the Friction chapter (see Figure 91); the one we'll do here is tied in the same manner but with twice as many strands, which is to say it's five times more difficult. But this is a fancy-work chapter, so have at it. As with the Star Knot, success is largely determined by keeping all the turns compact and fair. Draw up carefully, slowly.

Figure 216 shows the finished knot at the base of the button loop braid. Pull that little Constrictor up to the base of the knot when drawing up. You can pry the thread off later.

Before going to the next knot, pound the Matthew Walker into a flattish oval shape, the faces of the oval being perpendicular to the faces of the three-strand braid.

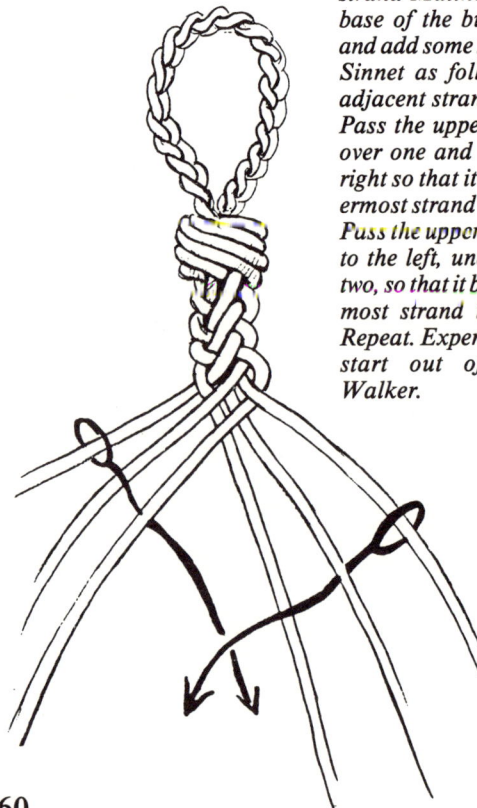

FIGURE 216. *Make a six-strand Matthew Walker at the base of the button loop braid, and add some six-strand French Sinnet as follows: Take three adjacent strands in each hand. Pass the uppermost left strand over one and under one to the right so that it becomes the lowermost strand in the right hand. Pass the uppermost right strand to the left, under one and over two, so that it becomes the lowermost strand in the left hand. Repeat. Experiment to get a fair start out of the Matthew Walker.*

Six-Strand French Sinnet

Hang the braided eye over a nail or peg at chest height and proceed to make some flat sinnet as shown in Figure 216. It is very important to get a fair start, so experiment with leading different ends first until all six strands travel the shortest possible distance before entering the braid, and the braid is parallel with the faces of the oval. Work the strands up snug and fair.

Make a 2¾-inch length of sinnet and Constrictor it ¼ inch from its end for a fair finish. Unlay the strands back to the Constrictor and put in another six-strand Matthew Walker.

Attaching the Button

Flatten the second Matthew Walker and make up two ¾-inch bits of three-strand braid, one behind the other, as shown in Figure 217. Thread the Star Knot onto the front one and Constrictor the two braids together just below the Star. Make and flatten another six-strand Matthew Walker (Figure 218-A).

FIGURE 217. *Make another six-strand Matthew Walker at the end of about 2¾ inches of French Sinnet, flatten the Matthew Walker with a mallet, and make two three-strand braids below it. Thread the Star Knot onto the front braid and make another six-strand Matthew Walker (not shown) below the Star Knot.*

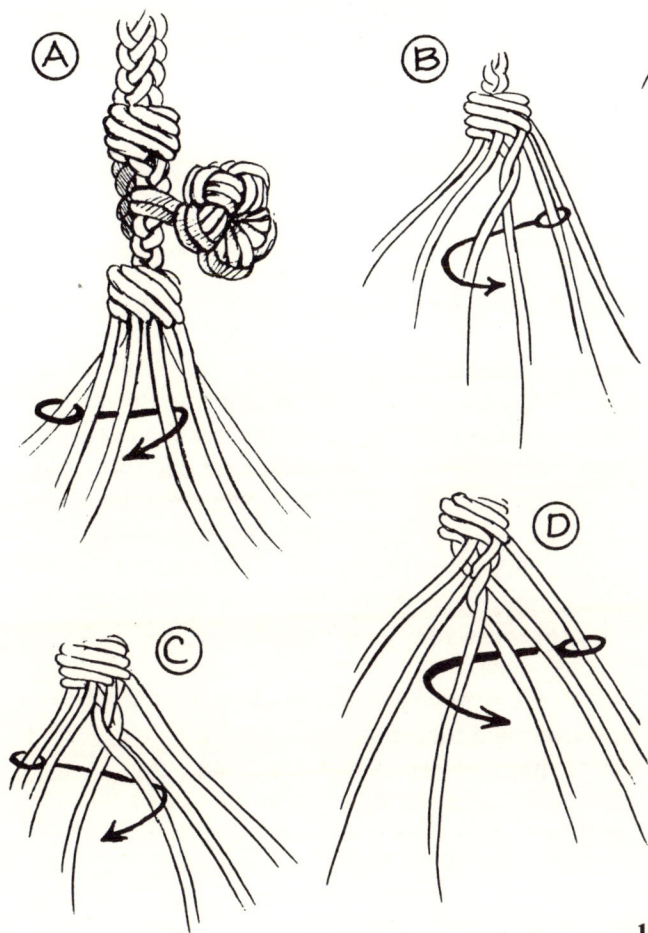

FIGURE 218. *Make some six-strand Half-Round Sinnet: With the strands divided three and three, pass the upper left strand behind to the right and out between the lowest and middle right-hand strands, then over to the left to become the lower left-hand strand. Repeat from the right. Figures B through D show how this pattern can be altered for a fair start out of the Matthew Walker.*

Six-Strand Half-Round Sinnet

This handsome sinnet, which will make up the greater part of the lanyard's length, is begun as in Figure 218. Again, experiment to get a fair entry with your braid. This knot proceeds with the upper left strand going behind three strands to the right and over one strand to the left; then the upper right strand goes behind three strands to the left and over one strand to the right. Keep everything symmetrical with even tension on all strands. Continue braiding until the lanyard thus far will encircle your wrist 1½ times. Custom tailoring.

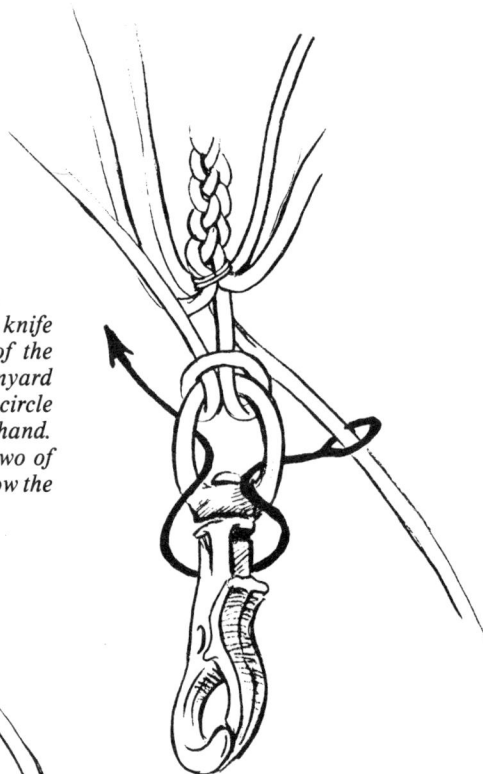

FIGURE 219. *Finishing the knife lanyard. Constrictor the end of the Half-Round Sinnet when the lanyard is long enough to completely encircle your wrist and lead up into your hand. Ring Hitch a snap shackle to two of the strands about 1¼ inches below the end of the sinnet....*

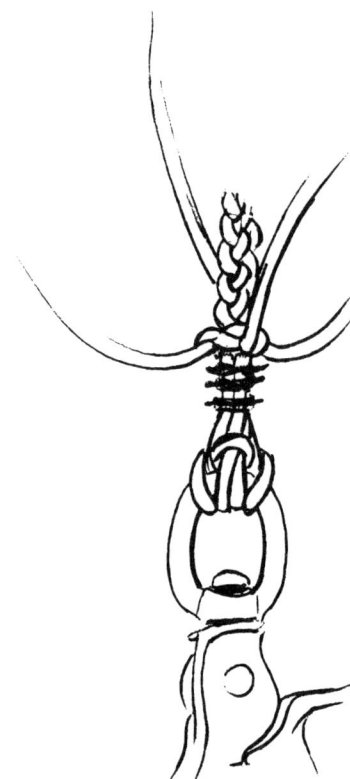

FIGURE 220. *....Then cut off the Ring Hitch ends and Constrictor them together between the shackle and the end of the sinnet. Wall Knot the remaining four strands.*

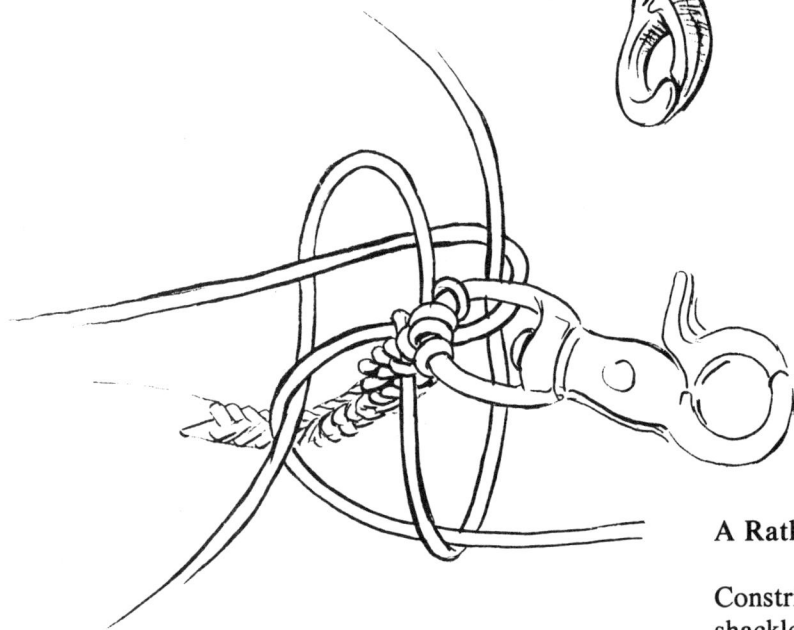

FIGURE 221. *Make a series of four-strand Crown Knots, one on top of the other, to cover the Constrictored ends. Stop when you're just short of the Ring Hitches, and make a Wall Knot as shown.*

A Rather Involved Finish

Constrictor the end of your sinnet and get a small snap-shackle. My favorite is the kind shown in Figure 219. Take two ends and Ring Hitch them to the eye of the shackle as shown in the same illustration. Shorten up the hitches until the eye is 1¼ inches from the end of the sinnet, then cut them so that their ends are just shy of the Constrictor (Figure 220). With strong, waxed thread, apply several Constrictors to the ends, so that they are securely fastened to each other and their own standing parts.

With the remaining four strands make a Wall Knot as shown, and then a series of Crown Knots, one on top of the other, right over the bound ends (Figure 221). Proceed for about an inch, until you're almost at the Ring Hitches, then make a four-strand Wall and

162

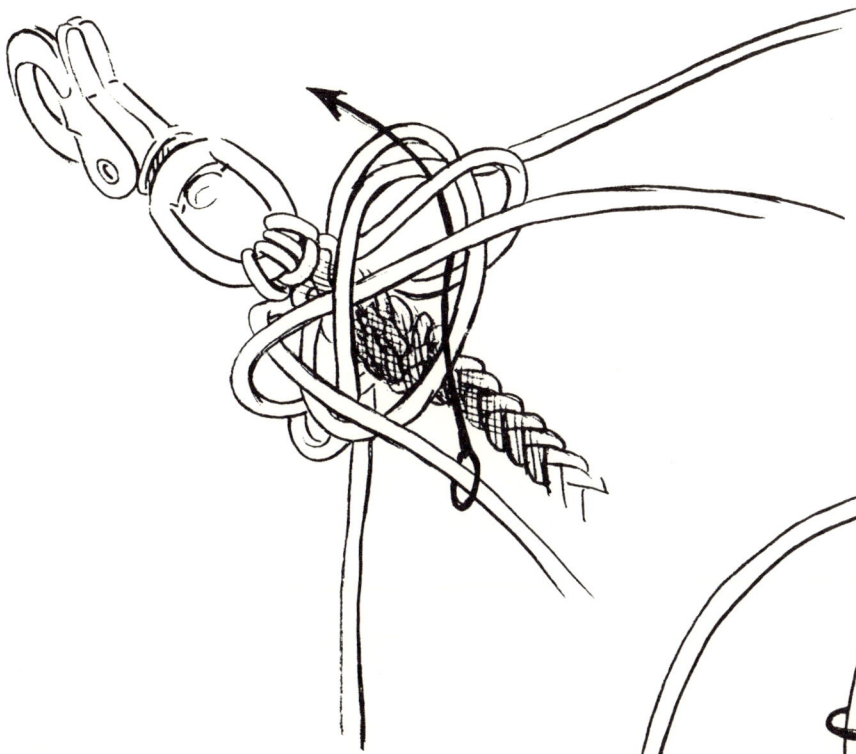

FIGURE 222-A. *Finally, make a Crown Knot over the Wall Knot, as shown, to get a Wall and Crown button. Fair up but do not tighten this arrangement. Double the knot by following above the original lead with each strand (as shown by the arrow)...*

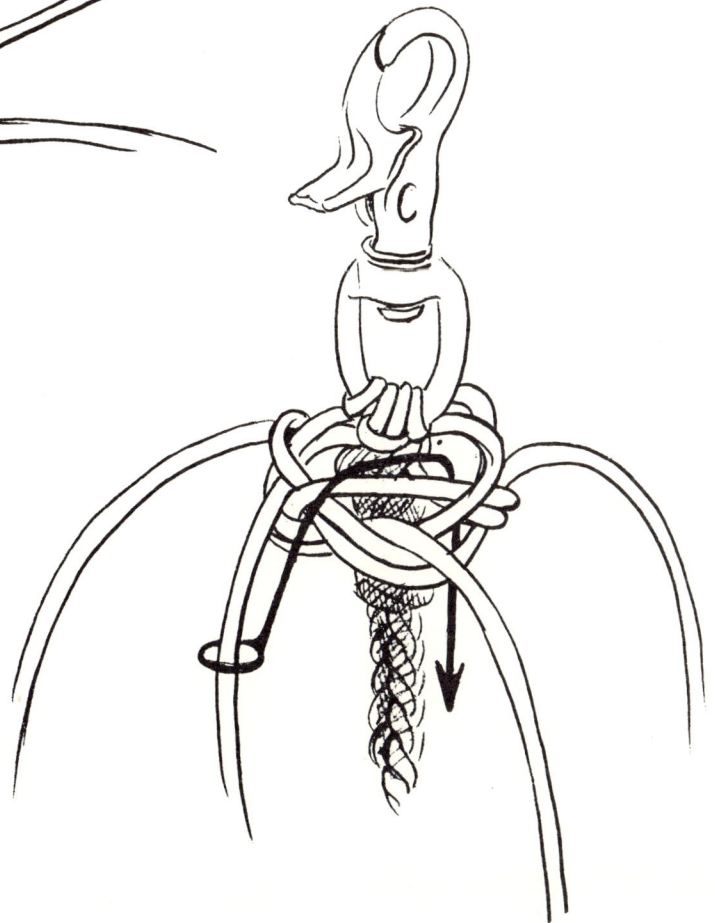

222-B. *...then tuck all four ends down between the knot and the braid, into adjacent spaces.*

Crown button as shown in Figure 222. Draw this knot up as snugly as you can, trim the ends, and you're done.

You should now have a lanyard that is perfect for carrying keys, knife, or other gear in a pocket, and which also can be worn around the hand as a tool lanyard when working aloft (Figure 223). If your finished product does not closely resemble mine, do not despair; this is a fairly involved, difficult sampler, and you may have to make several before all the knots come easily.

Once you feel comfortable with this arrangement, try altering proportions or substituting other knots. Remember that it isn't just the intricacy of a knot that makes it valuable, but its appropriateness. Some of the best fancy work is structurally simple, and even makes use of stretches of unknotted line. Always consider proportion, and the job the knots must do.

FIGURE 223. *A finished high-class knife lanyard.*

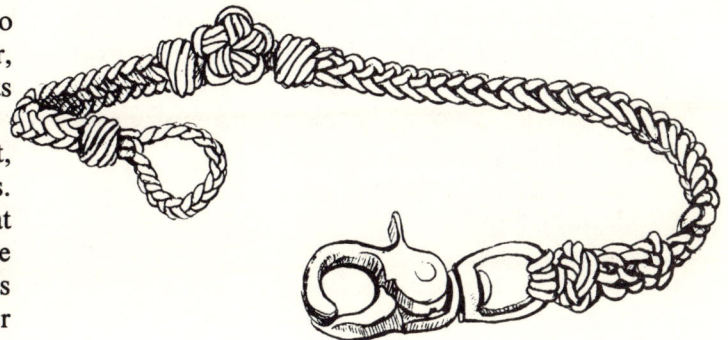

163

FIGURE 224. *A tripled 3-lead-by-5-bight Turk's Head. The ends finish under the same turn and will be trimmed flush.*

THE TURK'S HEAD: HARMONIC SEQUENCE AND THE SAILOR

Maybe I'm just easily stupified, but I've always thought that the Turk's Head's beauty, range of usefulness, and elegant mathematical underpinnings qualified it as a miraculous knot. I've made different forms of it for ditty bags, bellropes, bottles, wrists, and oars, and when I was almost making a living at fancy work, I used to turn out simple ones by the hundred as candleholders; the knots never failed to fascinate me. In this section, I hope to share this fascination with you by explaining the Turk's Head structure, showing some basic as well as little-known sizes of the knot, and introducing a new system by which any size knot can be built up into a more complex one.

For starters, take a look at Figure 224, which shows a "3 lead by 5 bight" knot, tripled. "Leads" are the number of parts that make up the width of the braid, and "bights" are the scalloped edges formed when the leads change direction. Because the type of Turk's Head we'll be dealing with here is made with a single

strand, only certain combinations of leads and bights will result in a symmetrical knot; the pattern has to match up with itself to form a circular braid with a regular over-and-under sequence. For an example of this, look at Figure 225, which shows how to make a 3 lead by 5 bight knot. Three turns are taken around the hand and the end and two bights are braided together. Pass the end four times, as shown, and you can lead it alongside the standing part to form an endless braid. But pass the end five times and the braids don't match up. So a harmonic sequence—the end traveling in a certain pattern so that it comes back into sync with itself—is what makes a Turk's Head work. This harmonic sequence will occur whenever the number of leads and the number of bights have no common divisor; a 3L x 4B or 3L x 5B knot is possible; 3L x 6B or 3L x 9B knot isn't. Understanding this mathematical hoo-haw is valuable when you want to make a knot of certain proportions.

But let's return to finish up that 3L x 5B knot. The end lays in alongside the standing part to complete the knot, and if it continues to parallel the standing part, going under where the standing part goes under, over where it goes over, and never crossing it, then the knot will be doubled (Figure 225-E). Go around once more and the knot is tripled, which is the usual procedure with Turk's Heads. The knot can now be drawn up around a suitable object and the ends trimmed flush after having been led under the same part (Figure 224).

Next trick: Although passing the end five times while forming the knot gave us a mess, passing it six times gives us a 3L x 8B knot; making the braid longer gives us Turk's Heads with more and more bights, the exact size of each finished knot being dictated by the Law of the Common Divisor.

Ah, but wait, you say, we skipped 3L x 7B—that fits the Law. And so it does, which brings up another wrinkle: The Law of You Can't Get There from Here. In order to make a knot of 3 leads and 7 bights, one must have a different "start" than 3 leads and 5 bights. In this case it's a knot of 3 leads and *4* bights, shown being made in Figure 226. As you can see, the technique is a slight variation on the 3L x 5B knot.

So whenever we want to build up to a knot of a particular size, we must know what the correct starting knot is. There are relatively few starts, and you've already learned two of them, which puts you ahead of most of the world. Learn a couple more and you'll almost be an expert.

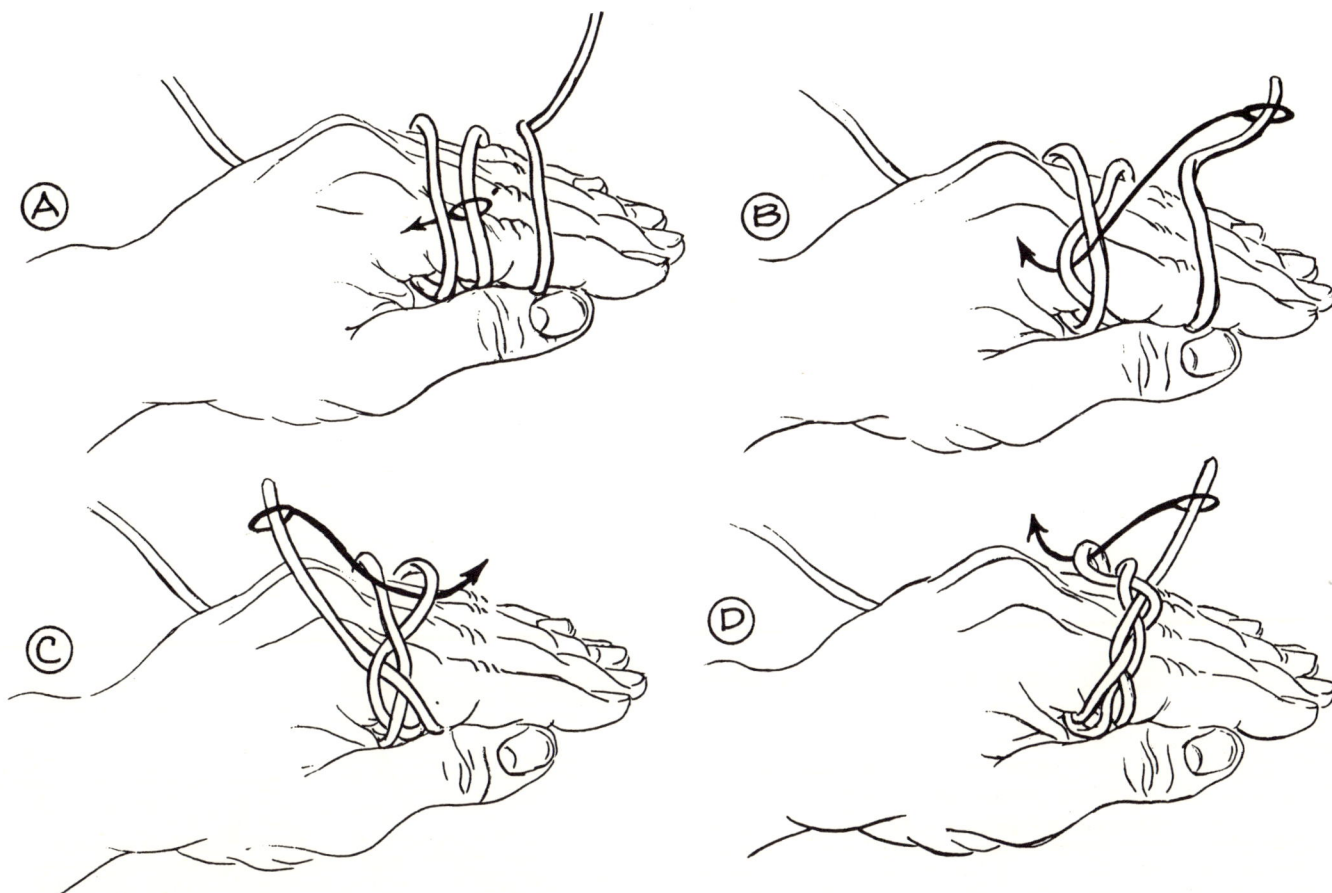

FIGURE 225. *To make a 3L x 5B knot, make three turns around a hand, push the middle turn under the left one (A), pass the end over and under (B), push the middle turn under the right one and pass the end over and under (C), and once more push the middle turn under the left one and pass the end over and under (D). Lead the end back into the knot parallel to the standing part and follow all the way around to double and triple the knot (E).*

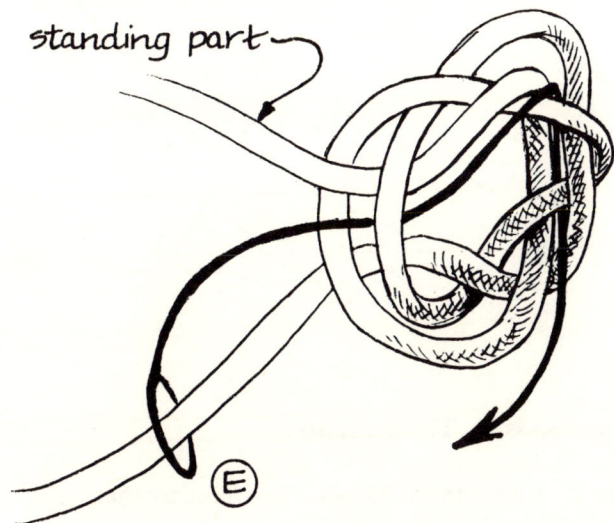

standing part

FIGURE 226. *A 3L x 4B knot is made by first moving the end under the left turn, then proceeding as with the 3L x 5B knot by moving the middle turn to the right, passing the end, etc.*

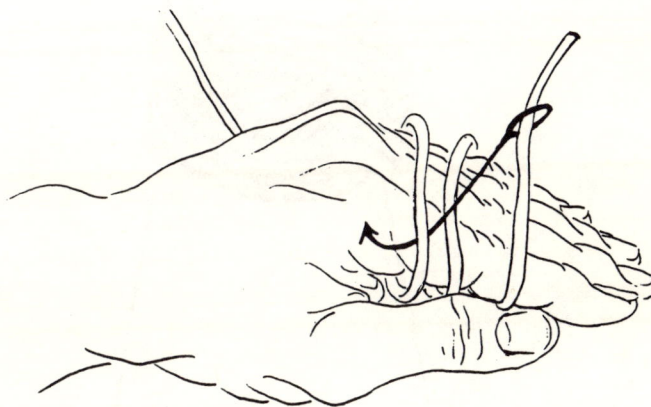

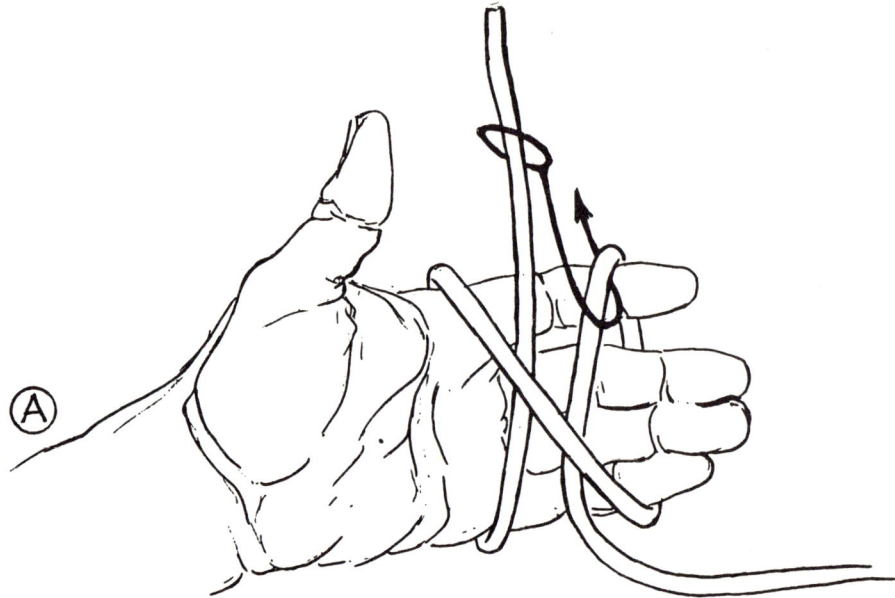

FIGURE 227. *A 4L x 3B knot. Begin with a Clove Hitch and tuck the end under the right-hand turn from right to left* (A). *Pass the end behind the hand, bring it up on the left side of the standing part, and tuck it under, over, and under as shown* (B). *Lead the end back into the knot alongside the standing part. Double and triple to finish* (C).

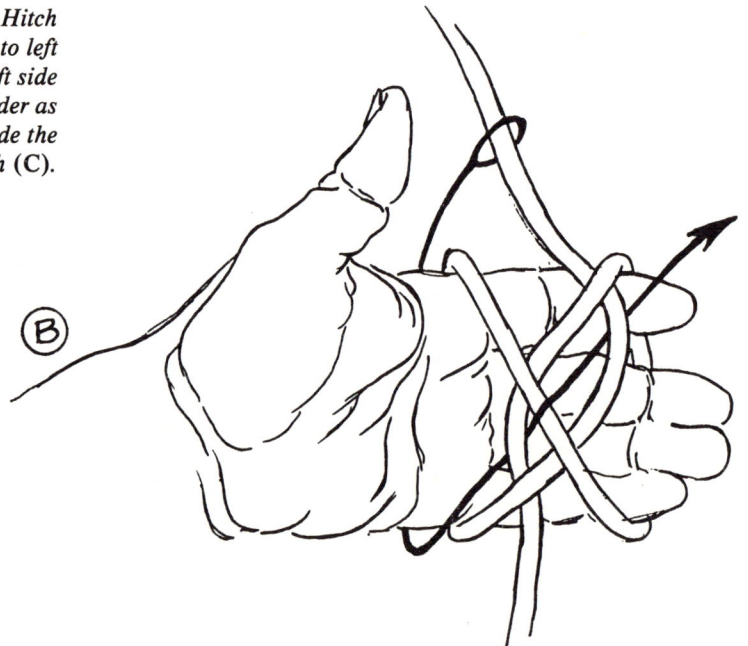

Four Leads by Three Bights

This is a simple knot, but rare. Notice that it is proportionately wider than the previous examples (Figure 227), an attribute that looks especially pleasing on narrow cylinders such as tool handles and lanyards. It starts with an ordinary Clove Hitch, then the end is passed first over then under the part on its right, led behind the hand, and brought up in front again on the left side of the standing part. Finally it is led under, over, and under as shown, then led in alongside the standing part to double and triple.

166

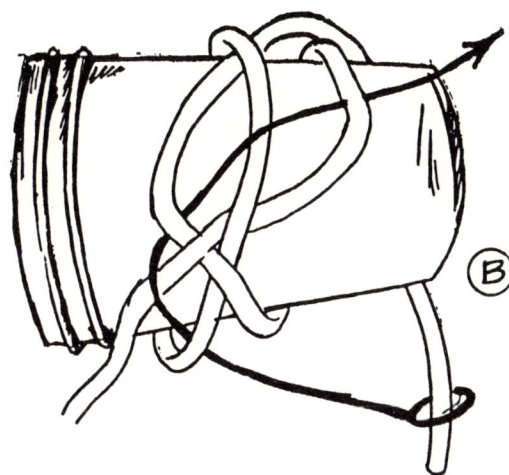

FIGURE 228. *A 4L x 5B Turk's Head. Make an Overhand Knot with the working end leading off to the right. Pass the end down, behind the standing part, then up through the eye of the Overhand Knot and out to the right* (**A**). *Slip the evolving knot onto a jar or your hand. Pass the end down behind the jar, back up over the first bight encountered, under the second, and over the standing part to the left. Then pass the end upward to the right, under, over, and under successive sections* (**B**). Important: Note that these sections do not have a regular weave, but pass under or over two parts at a time. By weaving through them as shown you produce a symmetrical weave. *Now rotate the knot toward you and you will find one more series of "bars" (sections that go over and under two at a time). Pass the end over, under, and over as shown* (**C**) *to complete the knot. A finished 4L x 5B knot, tripled, is shown in* **D.**

Four Leads by Five Bights

A handsome knot, complicated enough to keep the mind alive (Figure 228). Start with an Overhand Knot with the end leading off to the right. Pass the end behind the hand, bring it up on the left side of the standing part, and tuck it up to the right, through the center of the Overhand Knot. Rotate the works toward you and tuck the end over and under to the left. Rotate back to where you were, pass the end behind your hand, again on the left side, but this time pass it over the standing part, then under, over, and under as shown. Rotate things toward you again and pass the end over, under, and over to finish.

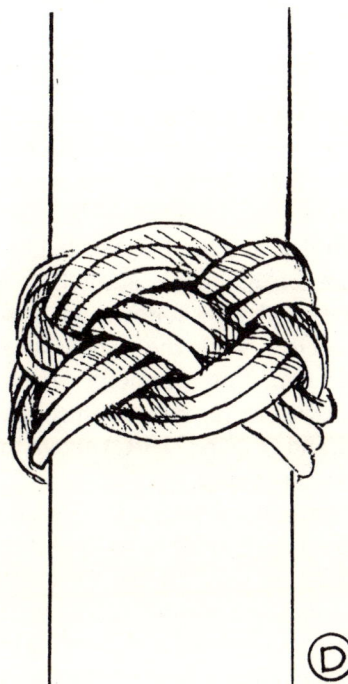

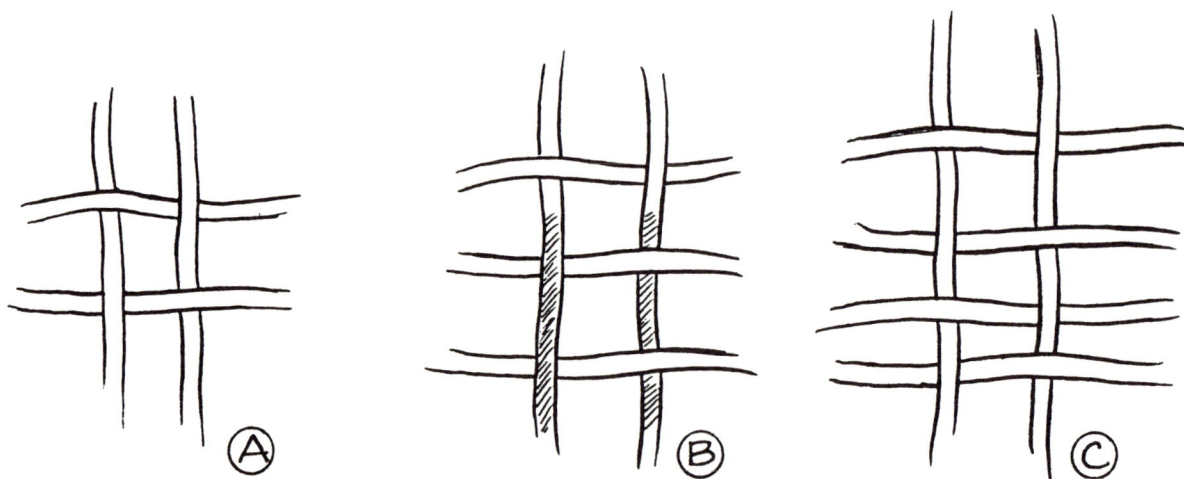

FIGURE 229. *A weaving comparison. Four pieces of twine can be arranged in a regular under-and-over weave* (**A**), *but introducing a fifth strand between the original horizontal strands makes the weave asymmetrical; the left-hand vertical strand now goes under one and over two, while the right-hand vertical strand goes over one and under two* (**B**). *The symmetry of the weave is restored by introducing a sixth strand whose course is opposite that of the fifth strand; once again all strands follow a regular under-and-over sequence* (**C**).

Building Up

One of the most interesting and least understood features of the Turk's Head is that one can increase the number of leads and bights in a given knot, building it up to make a more complex knot. We've seen how to increase the number of bights alone, using a 3 x 4 or 3 x 5 knot, but what we're about to do is more involved and results in a much more impressive finished product.

Let's start with a comparison to weaving. Figure 229-A shows two vertical strands with two horizontal strands woven into them. All the strands follow a regular under-and-over sequence. In Figure 229-B, a third horizontal strand has been added, but its course duplicates that of the middle strand. As a result, the left vertical strand now follows an under-one-and-over-two sequence, while the right strand goes under two and over one. The symmetry of the weave has been lost. But we can regain it by introducing a fourth horizontal strand (Figure 229-C) above the third one, in an opposing sequence.

This is essentially the process followed in enlarging Turk's Heads. It's referred to as "splitting the lead"; first you create an asymmetry by leading the end parallel to an existing lead, then you go around again and restore order. The trick is in knowing which lead to parallel, no small matter since the niceties of harmonic sequence must be attended to here as well as in the formation of the knot you enlarge. Up till now, writers have given specific sets of instructions for enlarging specific starts. This works fine unless they don't describe the one you want to enlarge, or unless you mislaid the damn book. But there is a lead-splitting procedure applicable to any start. To build up any Turk's Head to a larger size:

(1) Weave the working end parallel to the previously established lead, but in an opposite over-and-under sequence.

(2) Keep the working end either "ahead of" or "behind" (that is, to one side or the other of) the previously established lead. Which one you do depends on the structure of the particular knot and is determined when you begin to split the lead.

For an example, return to the 4L x 3B knot (Figure 230). If you trace backward from the working end one full circuit, you will have traced the previously established lead—the last circuit made (shaded line). To split the lead we'll orient to the circuit, going under where it goes over, and vice versa. You'll find that the lead will go under or over two parts at the edges of the knot in order to continue following opposite to the previous lead.

When you get back where you started from, you'll see ahead of you a series of "bar" sections that travel either over or under two parts (Figure 230-C). By

168

continuing to travel as you have, you split these bars, restoring a symmetrical weave. If the bars don't march along in regular sequence, you've distorted the knot while passing the end; fair things up to make the bars appear. If this doesn't work, retie the knot and be more finicky about preserving the pattern.

When you've threaded through all the bars and brought the end in alongside the standing part, you'll have a 6L x 5B knot, ready to be doubled and tripled to finish (Figure 230-E). Or you can split the lead again and build the knot up even further.

Depending on the dimensions of the Turk's Head, the end can travel on either side of the previous lead, so don't be thrown off by the variation between one knot and another. As you begin to split the lead, you will notice that the working end is traveling parallel to the standing part, in the same over-and-under sequence. Pay no attention to this, and resist the temptation to follow the standing part into the knot. Rather, chart your course by the previous lead, keeping to the opposite over-and-under sequence.

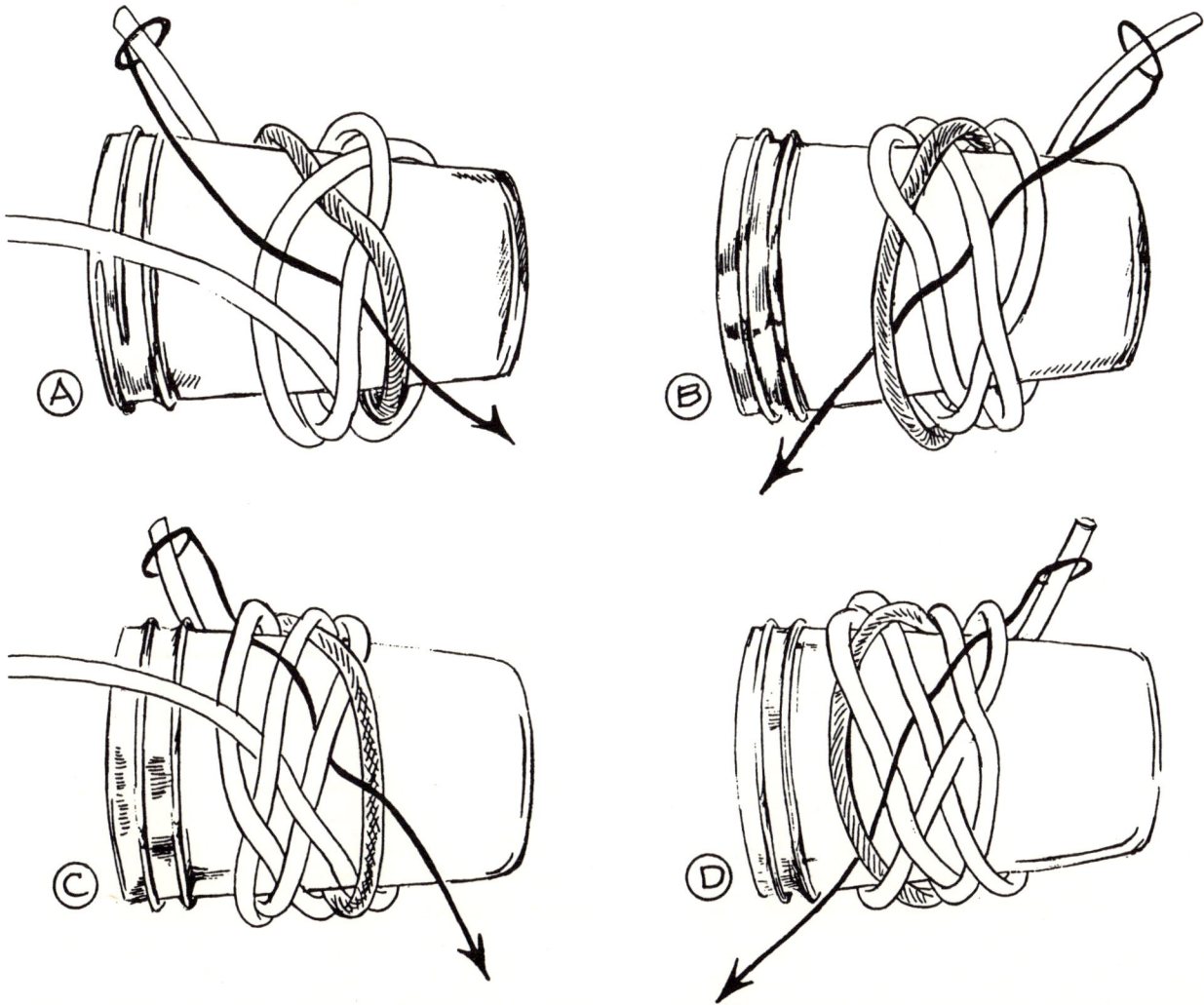

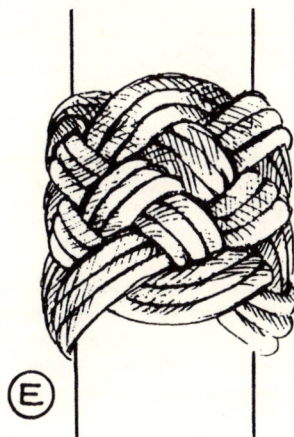

FIGURE 230. *To split the lead of a 4L x 3B knot, pass the working end (arrow) in an opposite pattern to the previous lead (shaded), going over where it goes under and vice versa. Continue following opposite to the previous lead until the end once again meets up with the standing part (C). You'll have a series of "bars"—sections going under two or over two—facing you. Restore symmetry by passing the end under the bars that go under two and over the bars that go over two (C and D). By doing so you're also continuing to travel opposite the previous lead. Double and triple to get the finished knot (E).*

169

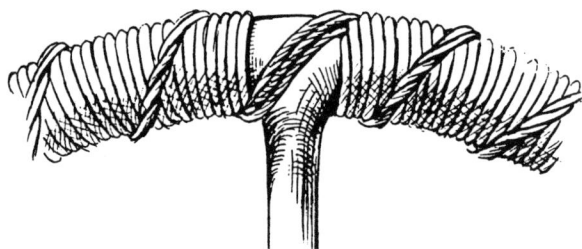

Jumping the Gap

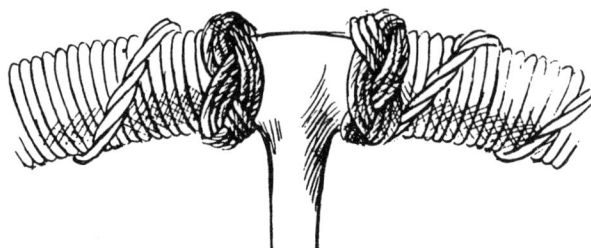

Turk's Head Either Side

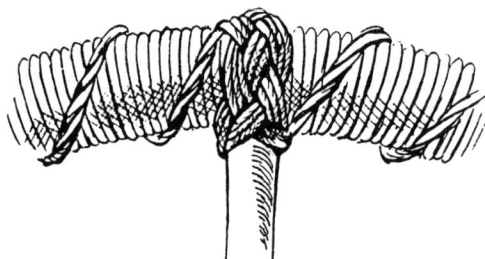

Three-Legged Turk's Head

FIGURE 231. *Three answers to the question, "What do you do when you're hitching and reach an intersection of rim and spoke or rail and stanchion?" You can just hitch right by, jumping past the gap, but as Clifford Ashley said, this is "lubberly and not to be countenanced." It looks sloppy, leaves a bare spot, and is an opportunity for slack and snag. Seizing the ends and covering with simple Turk's Heads either side is a satisfactory solution, but for real flair, why not make a Three-Legged Turk's Head? Figure 232 shows how.*

The Three-Legged Turk's Head

Here's an odd one to round out your fancy work vocabulary: a Turk's Head to put at the junction of wheel and spoke (Figure 231). It's a 4L x 5B knot made to be three-legged, and it's worth the bother of learning just on the chance that some marlingspike artists will come aboard some day, stare at it in amazement and say, "How did you do that?" That question can gladden the heart, can make you feel as though the eyestrain and tedium were worth the effort. Come to think of it, there's one question that's even better: Someone looks at a Turk's Head, button, lanyard, or whatever you've been slaving over and asks, "But what did you do with the ends?" To which the only reasonable reply is, "I cut them off and threw them away." Never give boring details, however informative, when a smart-ass answer will do just as well.

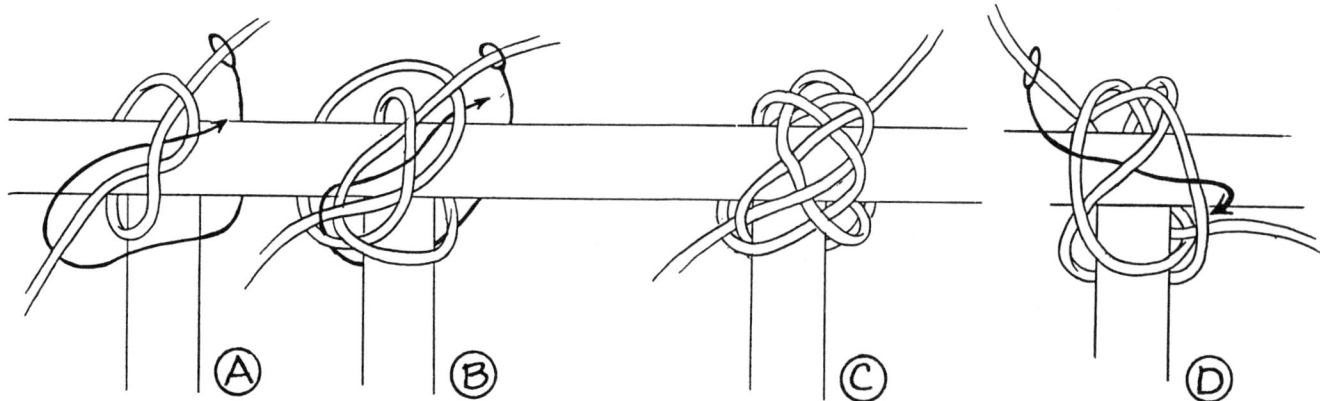

FIGURE 232. *To tie a Three-Legged Turk's Head (4L x 5B), make an Overhand Knot that angles across the T, the end coming out at top right. Pass the end behind the right-hand bar of the T, over the vertical bar from right to left, behind the standing part, then up through the eye of the Overhand Knot (A). Pass the end behind the right-hand bar of the T again, then behind the upright to the left. Pass it up under, over, under, over, under as shown (B) to arrive at C. To finish, turn the T around and tuck over, under, over (D), and lead the end alongside the standing part for doubling and tripling.*

CHAPTER 9

Tricks
and Puzzles

•

Study these until you can fool yourself in a mirror.

Show them with joy to willing audiences.

Serenely ignore bimbos who say, "*I* know how you did *that*"; by trampling on magic's essential ingredient—a sense of wonder—they clearly show that they have no idea whatsoever of "how you did *that*."

By disclosing techniques, the magician tramples on that sense of wonder; people who are really interested in figuring it out, will.

You take a piece of line, oh, about 8 feet long. It's ⅛- to ¼-inch three-strand or braided line, not too stiff, a supple, clean, white tool for magic.

You start talking about the mysteries and profundities of knots, about their vast profusion and universal presence, luring your listeners into a world where knots are so self-evidently magical that you need employ no deceptions to do magic.

As you speak, you casually throw hitches 2 to 3 feet through the air, catching them on your outstretched

index finger, hitch after hitch. The effect is mesmerizing, surprising.

And then you work into the grand Theme: We don't understand knots; we use them every day, trust our lives and property to them, know them by reflex, but we do not understand them, no not even the absurdly simple, elemental Overhand Knot. You tie one, draw it up. It just gets tighter and can't be undone unless you loosen it and pull an end out. You make another, very slowly, explaining in self-evident detail that once the end is passed through, that knot is there to stay until it is pulled out. You take this second knot apart and make a third one—those watching will swear it was made just like the others. But this time, after you've drawn it up, you cover it with your hand, apply a little gumption, a dash of mojo, open your hand, and it's *gone*. No, we don't even understand the simplest knots.

Then you lay the line over your hand, and note that the same knot which disappears mysteriously can

171

FIGURE 233. Throwing Hitches. *With your right hand grasp one end of a line, standing part emerging between thumb and forefinger. Grasp the standing part about 3 feet away with your left hand, index finger extended. Move your hands apart so the line is just slack, and turn your right hand palm up (A). By flipping your right hand over and moving it slightly to the left, you will form a loop that travels along the standing part (B). Properly aimed, it will land and form a hitch on your extended index finger. Keep throwing hitches until the standing part becomes too short.*

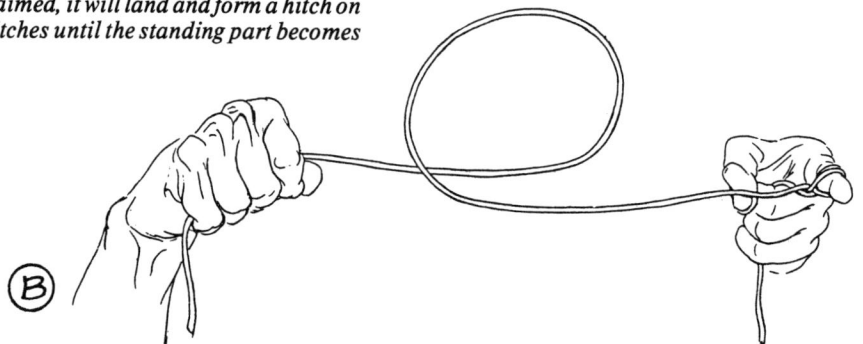

FIGURE 234. A Vanishing Overhand Knot. *Hold the end between your left thumb and forefinger and grasp the standing part a few inches away with your right thumb and forefinger. Both palms face you. Move the hands together, turning the right hand over as you do, and grasp the standing part with your left thumb and forefinger to form a loop (A). If you now reach away from you through the loop with your right hand, grab the end, and pull it out, you'll form an Overhand Knot (B). Keep the two parts pinched in your left hand as you draw up the knot, then display it. If you reach instead through the loop toward you and grasp the end with your right hand, no knot will result, but as you pull the slack out it will look exactly as the Overhand Knot did when it was being drawn up. Cover the "drawn-up" non-knot with your hand and pull theatrically on the end to make it "disappear."*

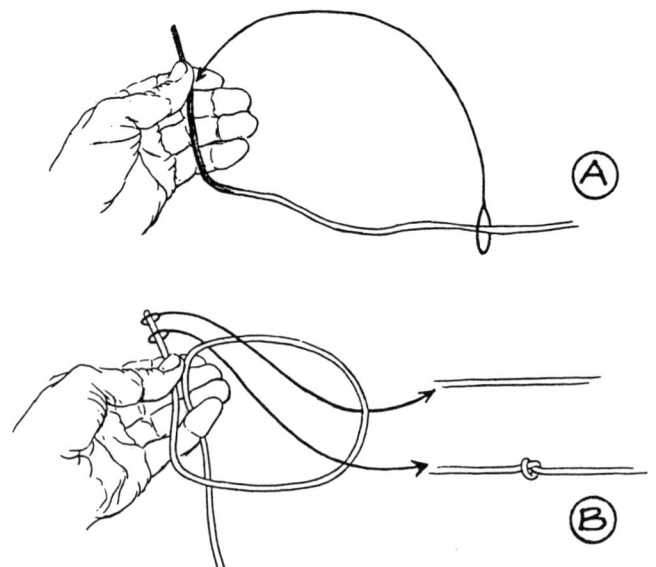

(flourish of motion) be made to reappear in an instant in the middle of a string. You remove that knot, then with another flourish produce a slipknot. These things can come out of nowhere. With equal facility you produce a Clove Hitch (see the Four Hitches section of Chapter 3), a Figure-Eight Knot, and then a Bowline made out of a slipknot (see the Seven Bowlines section of Chapter 3). That's right, the quintessentially utilitarian must-be-counted-on King of Knots plays tricks with us too! Or seen another way,

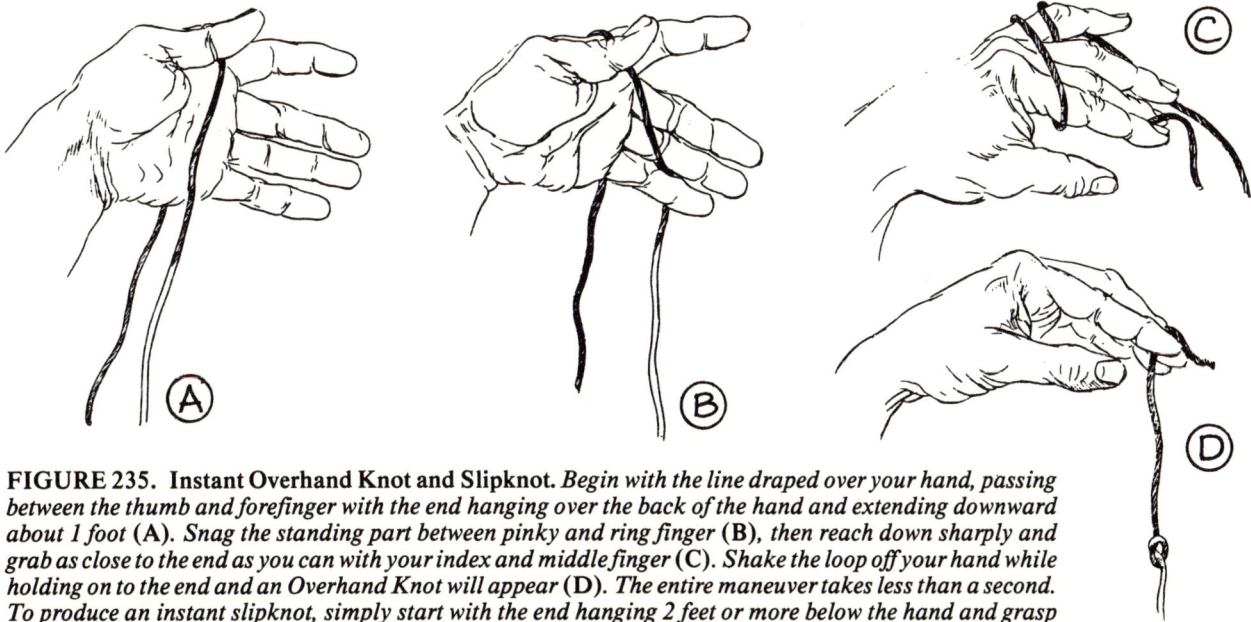

FIGURE 235. Instant Overhand Knot and Slipknot. *Begin with the line draped over your hand, passing between the thumb and forefinger with the end hanging over the back of the hand and extending downward about 1 foot (A). Snag the standing part between pinky and ring finger (B), then reach down sharply and grab as close to the end as you can with your index and middle finger (C). Shake the loop off your hand while holding on to the end and an Overhand Knot will appear (D). The entire maneuver takes less than a second. To produce an instant slipknot, simply start with the end hanging 2 feet or more below the hand and grasp midway toward it.*

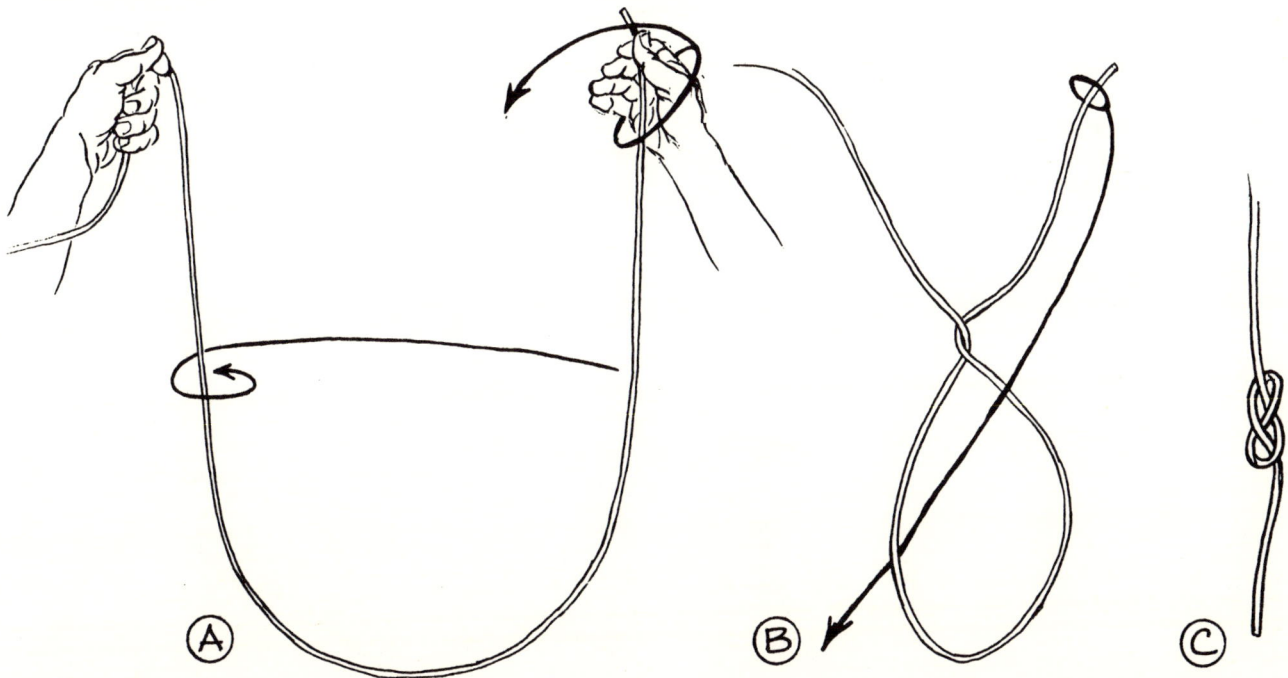

the speed and freshness of magic can breathe life and a range of usefulness into the simplest forms of knotting. Ah, practical magic.

But then, lest your audience begin to feel that rope tricks are Logical and Useful, tell them (a) that it is absolutely positively impossible to tie an Overhand Knot without letting go of an end, and (b) that there are three different ways of doing this, one of which is ingenious, the second cheating, and the third is by-God-actual-inexplicable Magic.

FIGURE 236. Instant Figure Eight. *Hold the end between the thumb and forefinger of your right hand and grasp the standing part with your left hand so that a long bight hangs between the hands. Drape the rest of the standing part over your left arm or shoulder to keep it out of the way. Move your right hand sharply to the left, causing the bight to twist around into a loop (A). The loop will be held in place by momentum for an instant; throw the end through it with your right hand (B), and a Figure Eight Knot will appear (C).*

173

FIGURE 237. An Overhand Knot Without Letting Go, First Method. *Cross your arms, grasp an end in each hand, and uncross your arms. Presto! An Overhand Knot.*

First, demonstrate that one must indeed let go the end in order to reach around to pass it through the loop; not letting go means, by definition, that a slipknot will result. But have someone else hold the ends, fold your arms, pick up the ends, then unfold your arms and an Overhand Knot appears in the middle of the line.

That was the ingenious solution. Now explain you're going to use the second method, the one in which you cheat. Be very clear on this point, then immediately explain that you are bound by sacred oath as a member of the F.S.A. (Future Saints of America) to never, ever, cheat, so to preclude any possibility of deception you are going to move very slowly, holding the ends in plain view in your fingertips at all times.

FIGURE 238-A. An Overhand Knot Without Letting Go, Second Method. *Hold an end between the thumb and index fingertips of each hand. A couple of inches of end should be showing, "So you can see the ends," you tell your audience, "at all times." Actually, the arrangement helps you with the trick. Drape the right side of the standing part over your left wrist and move your right hand off to the right side. You'll have a long bight (the longer the better) with a diagonal crossing it.*

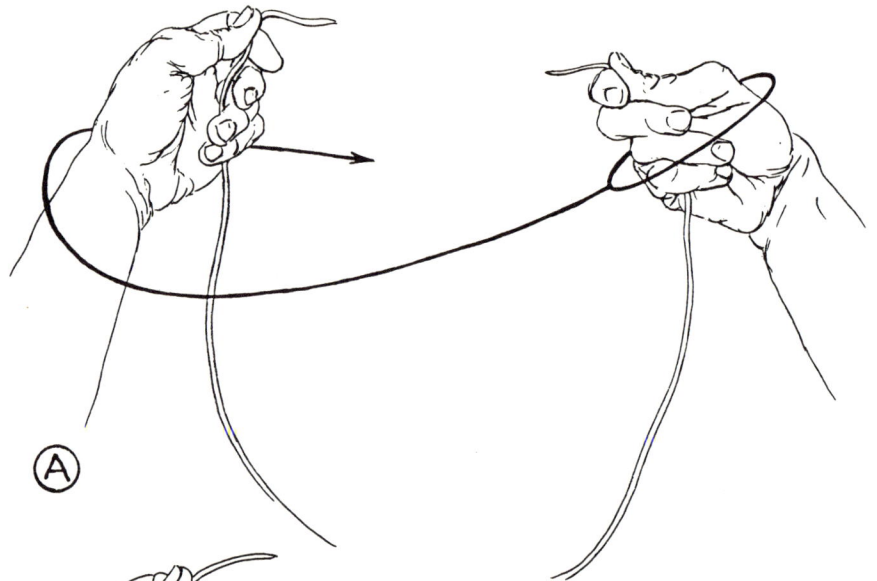

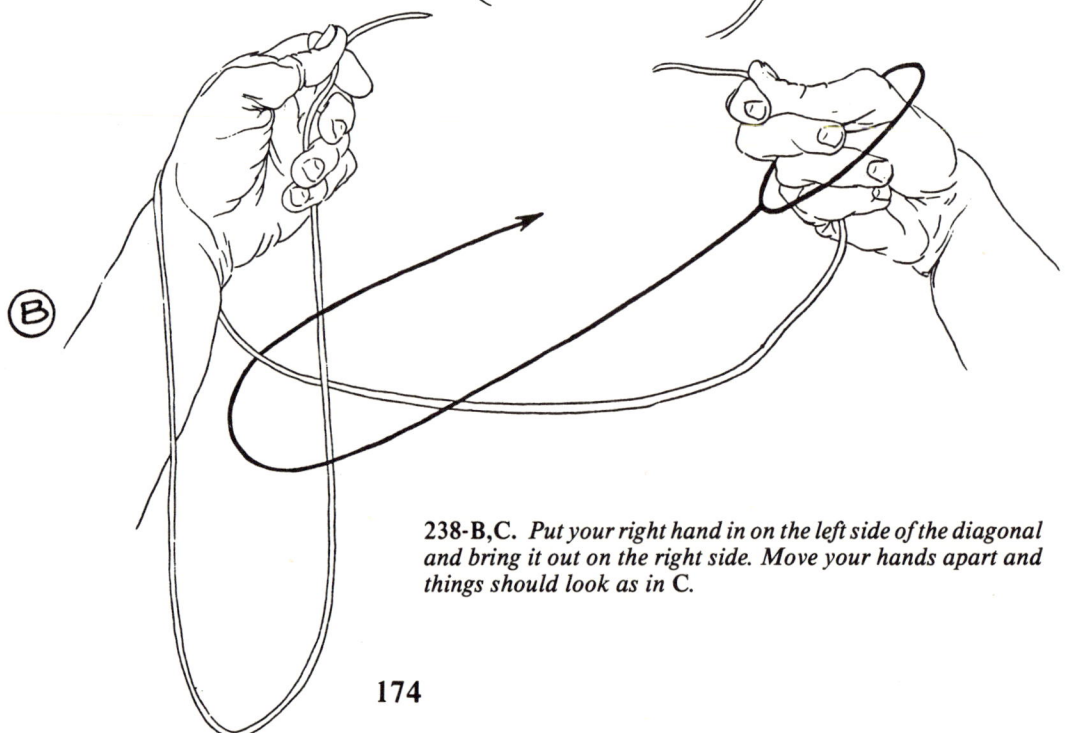

238-B,C. *Put your right hand in on the left side of the diagonal and bring it out on the right side. Move your hands apart and things should look as in C.*

After a simple, easily followed series of moves, during which you reiterate that what you are about to do is impossible, you gently lower your hands, and the knot appears mid-string. You repeat, invite volunteers to try, even tie along with them simultaneously. It only works for you. "One of us is cheating and it certainly isn't me," you note, "so you should just be ashamed of yourself." While they are apologizing for their dishonest behavior, you prepare for the third method, getting out a 3-foot by 4-inch piece of paper—newspaper is handy—twisting an end 1½ times, then taping the two ends together to form a circle. You can have someone else do this if you like, so that everyone is sure there is no trickery.

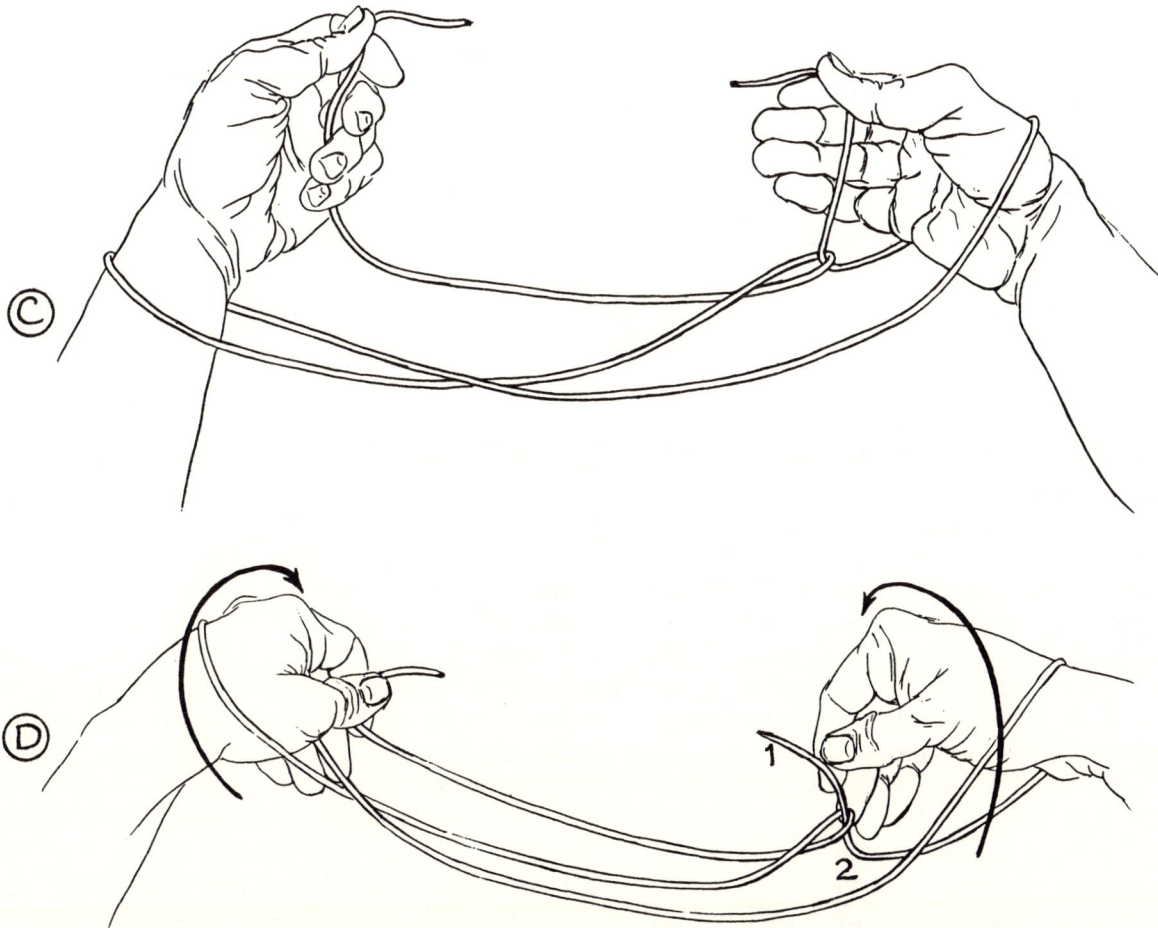

238-D. *Drop your hands down while simultaneously turning them inward. As the line falls from your hands the right end (1) will approach the loop at the right side. Let go of the end on one side of the loop and catch it on the other (2). Practice this until the movement is very smooth. An Overhand Knot will appear in the middle of the standing part as you move your hands apart. There'll be a little more end sticking out of your right hand than your left, but since you started with a little end showing, a little extra won't be noticed.*

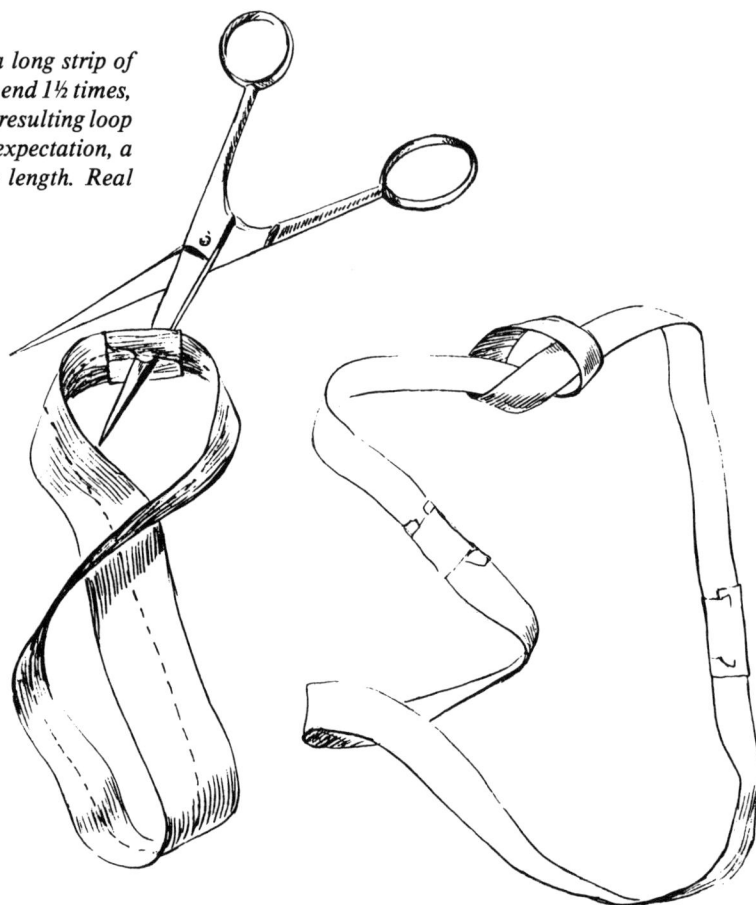

FIGURE 239. The Mobius Overhand. *Take a long strip of paper or cloth—about 3 feet by 4 inches. Twist one end 1½ times, then tape the two ends together. If you now cut the resulting loop lengthwise, you will get, contrary to all rational expectation, a single loop with an Overhand Knot tied in its length. Real magic.*

Now produce a pair of scissors and ask rhetorically what would happen if you were to cut lengthwise along the entire circle; it's obvious that you'll end up with two separate circles. But when you—or someone else—makes the cut, something entirely unexpected and inexplicable happens: you get a single, large circle, with (*Twilight Zone* theme music) an Overhand Knot tied in its length. This Mobius strip variant is real magic, a jolt to the mind and somewhat unnerving, so put it away and return to silliness.

Note that the best-known rope trick is the cut-and-restored string. This is old hat for you, so you're a little bored as you demonstrate how one can cut a line in the middle and restore it to a single piece. It's simple mechanics, you say: Cutting the string in half produces four ends, which necessarily means two pieces, right? So by cutting off one end and throwing the other away you're back to two ends, thus one piece. It's simple. You, of course, do not do simple cut-and-restored tricks, but you did once learn how to splice with your tongue.

It all started when you were sailing off the coast of

(your preference) in company with a wise old salt and a few other friends. You were sitting a little to windward as the old man declaimed upon the necessity for resourcefulness at sea. "Every finger a marlingspike," he intoned, "and every hair a rope yarn." A classic saying that, due to the noise of the wind, came to your ears as, "Every tongue a marlingspike to repair a rope yarn." It made no sense, but everyone else was nodding sagely, so you nodded sagely too, suddenly convinced that any *real* sailor could make a splice using tongue for spike.

People do silly things out of pride and you were no exception. You began furtively to practice this impossible feat, sitting in darkened closets with string in your mouth. Accidentally discovered, you explained that you were using a very large dental floss because your teeth are widely spaced. Your tongue became calloused, you grew depressed, certain that you'd never be a real sailor.

And then one day you heard of Swami Seezanahta, the world's leading exponent of Knot Yoga. You asked spiritually inclined friends who had seen him what

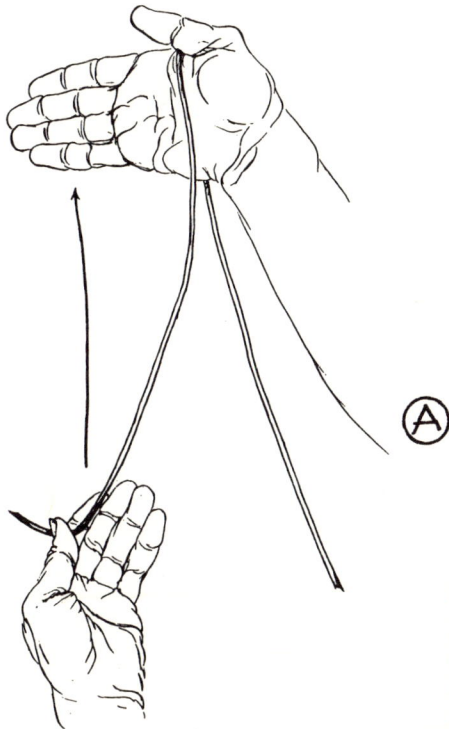

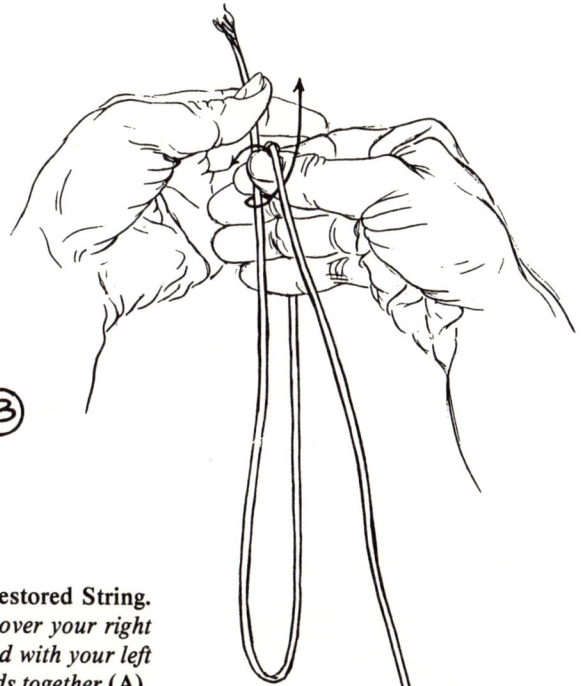

FIGURE 240. Cut-and-Restored String.
Middle a line and hang it over your right hand. Pick up the nearer end with your left hand and move the two hands together (A). Seeming to place the middle bight of the line alongside the end in your left hand, you actually let the bight slip off your right hand as you raise a "false middle"—a bight brought up from the left end (B). Cut this bight at its middle (C), drop the right end down, and you will appear to have two equal-length pieces of line (D). With scissors, cut the right upper end close to your fingers, then "throw the other end away." Before, you had four ends, thus two pieces; now you have only two ends, thus one piece, or so the patter goes as you show the one whole piece.

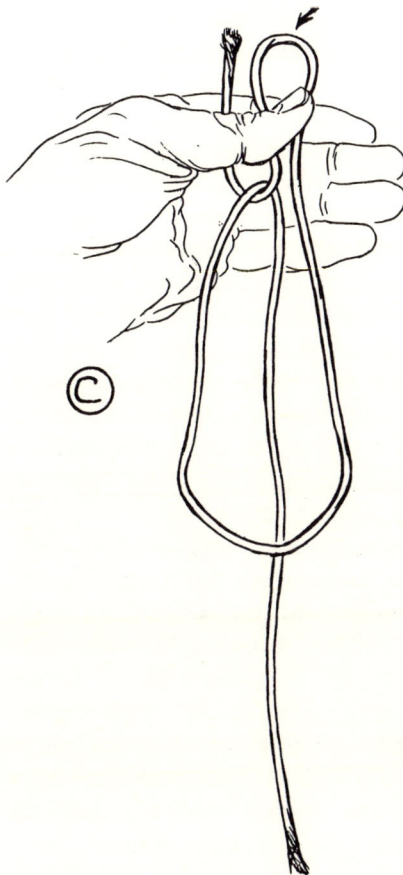

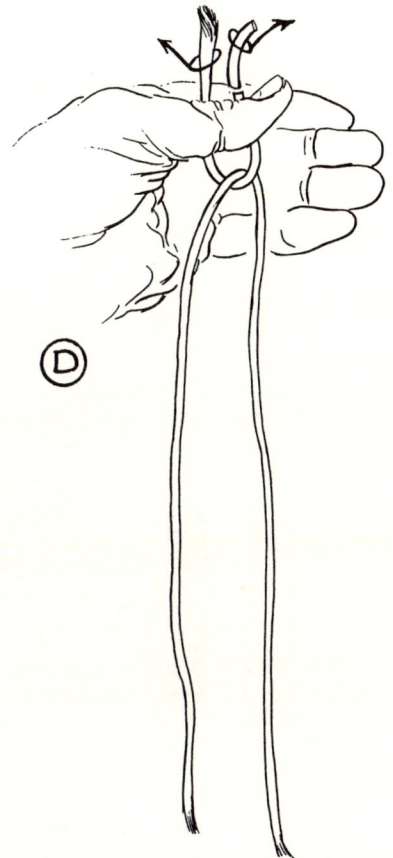

177

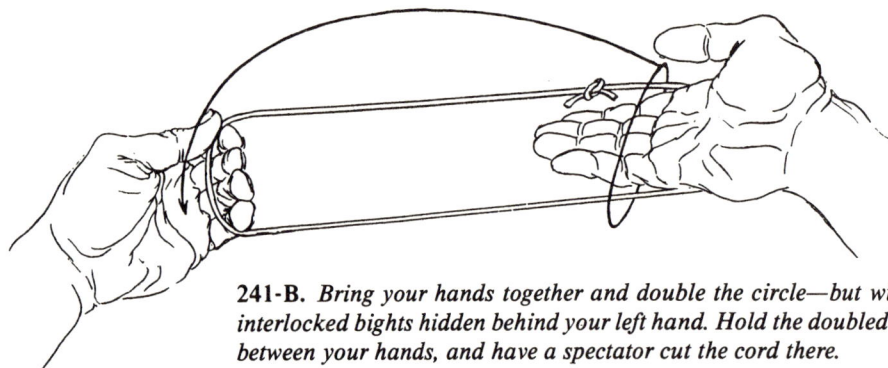

241-B. *Bring your hands together and double the circle—but with a twist, which results in a couple of interlocked bights hidden behind your left hand. Hold the doubled line with an unsuspiciously small space between your hands, and have a spectator cut the cord there.*

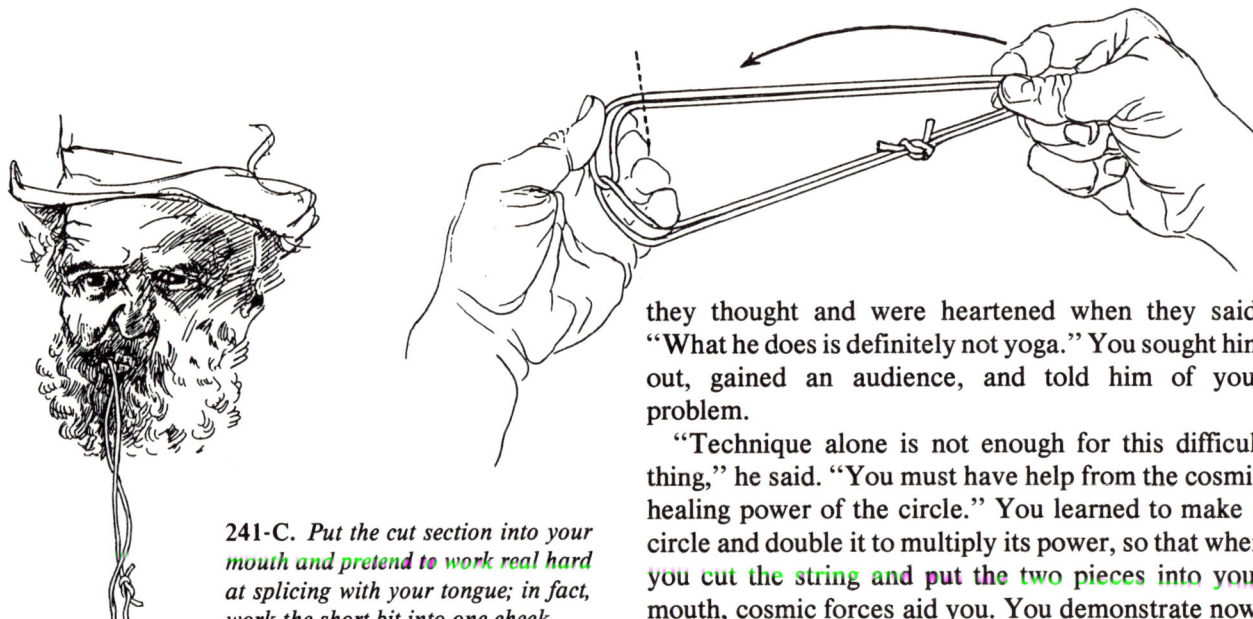

241-C. *Put the cut section into your mouth and pretend to work real hard at splicing with your tongue; in fact, work the short bit into one cheek.*

they thought and were heartened when they said, "What he does is definitely not yoga." You sought him out, gained an audience, and told him of your problem.

"Technique alone is not enough for this difficult thing," he said. "You must have help from the cosmic healing power of the circle." You learned to make a circle and double it to multiply its power, so that when you cut the string and put the two pieces into your mouth, cosmic forces aid you. You demonstrate now, making a tapered Long Splice no less, carefully trimming the ends off flush, a real sailor at last.

But enough of mysticism. Get a couple of volunteers to join you to figure out a little puzzle. Ideally they are slightly drunk, easily embarrassed, and of opposite sex. Tell them that the name of this puzzle is Topographical Bondage. Restrain them from leaving. Tie the hands of each together with a 3-foot length of line, the two lines crossing. Use loose Bowlines around the wrists so that they can get out if they need or want to. ("Now remember, if at any time this gets to be too much for you, you can slip the loops off, bury your face in your hands, and run weeping out of the room. Fair enough?") Their arms and lines now form two interlocked circles. The challenge is to get separated without untying the knots, removing the loops from their wrists, or severing either the line or their limbs. Anything else is legal and there is a solution. Explain that if they succeed, everyone watching will be filled with awe and admiration, but if they fail they will be laughed at, not with. Having thus reassured them, you tell them to begin.

241-D. *After suitable patter and facial gymnastics, pull out the miraculously restored string.*

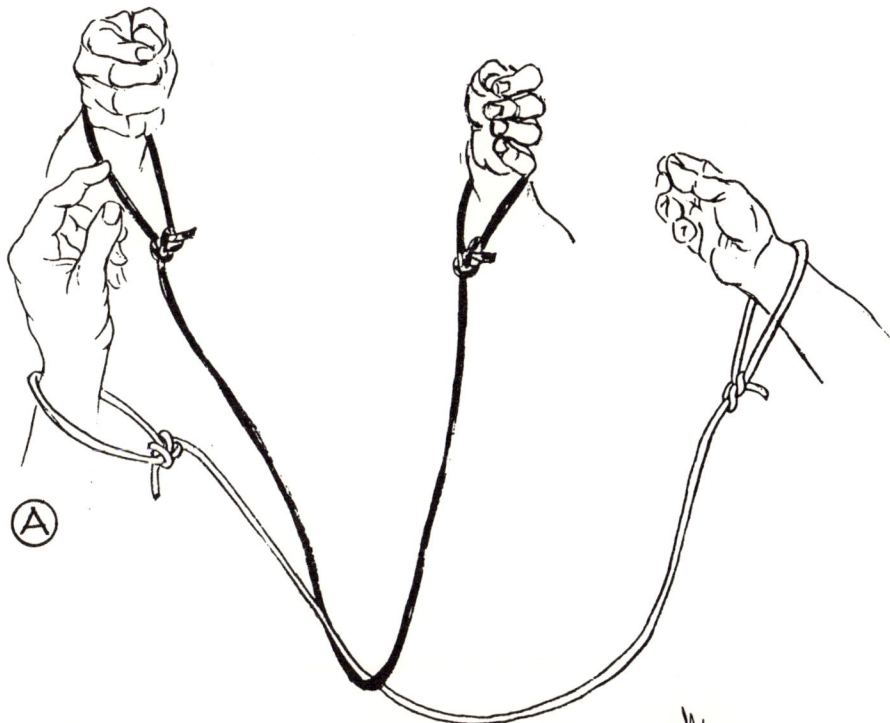

FIGURE 242. **Topographical Bondage.** *Two interlocked ropes bind two volunteers together. The puzzle is to get separated without untying the Bowlines, removing them from wrists, or cutting the cords (or arms). The search for a solution can lead to some creative contortions, but the solution is topo-(not porno-) graphical: Pass a bight from one side out through a wrist loop of the other side, over the hand, and back under the wrist loop (C). Sweet.*

If you've chosen your volunteers well, and if those in the audience help by suggesting techniques, you will now be treated to a randy acrobatic spectacle, a series of contortions and intertwinings that look like the Kama Sutra according to Woody Allen. It may be necessary to disentangle the subjects from time to time before you mercifully step in and pass a bight through one of the wrist loops. I call the trick Topographical Bondage because it's a perfect example of the main reason knots aren't understood: We assume we understand them, so we limit their range of expression. This particular trick, by the way, has an application in the real world when you want to drop a mooring eye over a piling or bit that is already occupied by another eye. With yours on too, the other eye, which might belong to another vessel, can't be removed without first removing yours. But if you thread your eye up through the other before putting it over the piling, either one can be removed without disturbing the other. This works for any number of eyes.

But we're sneaking back into practicality here; time for an entertaining finale.

Once upon a time there was a sailor, and a girl who loved him, and he her, and they knew their love would stay. But her father only wished he would stay away. Couldn't see *his* daughter paired up with someone who couldn't keep his feet on solid ground. The haberdasher's clerk down to the village was the father's sensible choice for a spouse-to-be. The clerk was dull, bony, and his nose tended to drip, but he was steady, moderate, and agreed with the father's political views.

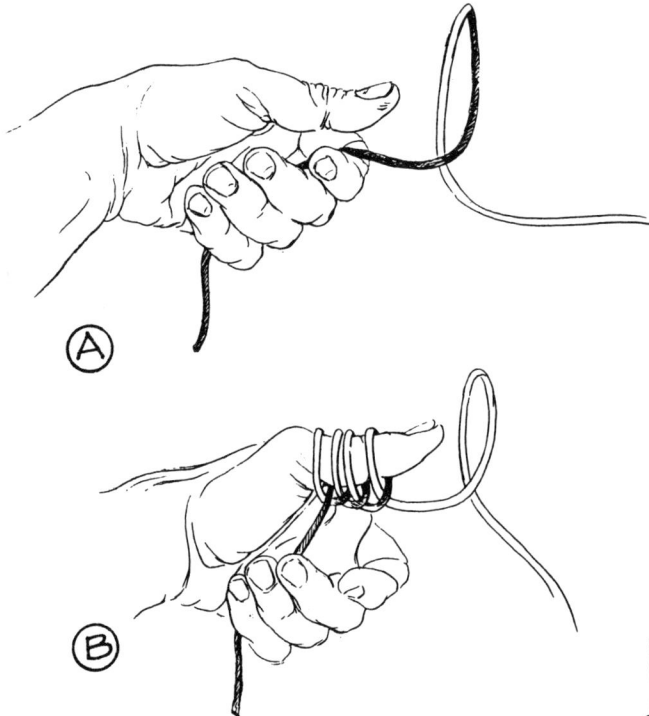

FIGURE 243. How the Sailor Made Many Knots in Little Time. *He made many half hitches on his thumb (A,B), passed the left end through all the half hitches (C), gently cradled the hitches in one hand, and pulled handsomely on the end with his other hand (D). End of contest, end of book.*

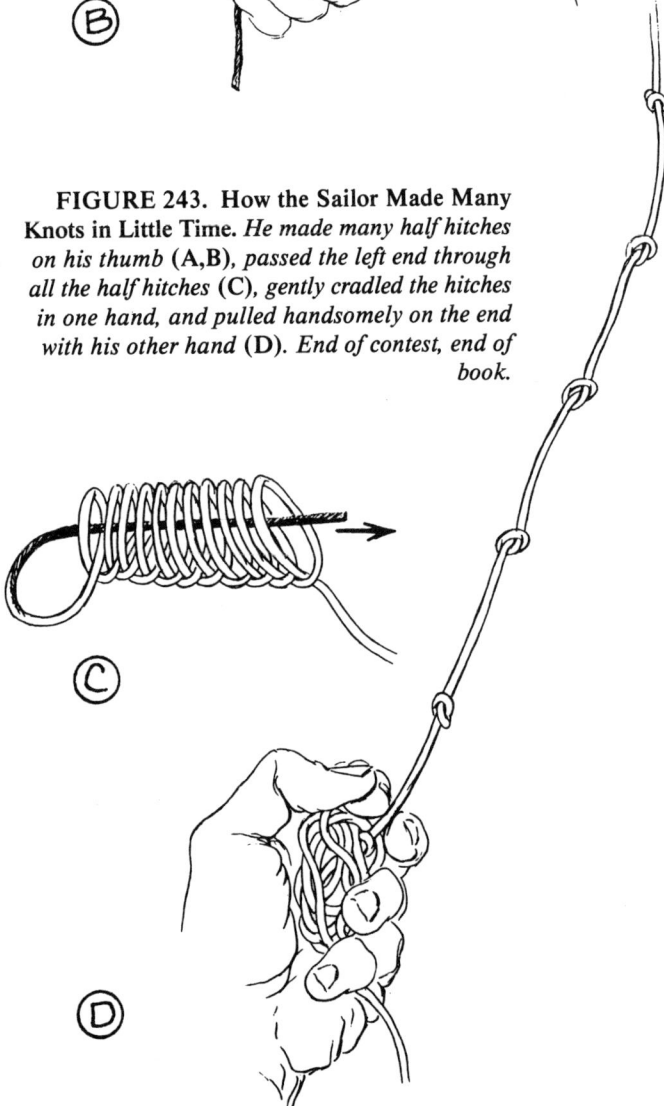

Neither father nor clerk was particularly bright, but synergy plays no favorites and between them they came up with a clever plan to remove the sailor from the scene: A contest would be held to win the girl's hand. The winner would be the one who could tie the most Overhand Knots while the father counted to 60. The sailor, who like all sailors prided himself to vain excess on proficiency in ropework, would surely accept. But the clerk, whose package-wrapping duties involved a very few simple knots, had been motivated by brisk business and impatient customers to learn to tie those knots very, very fast, and in string, which sailors rarely touch. Sure enough, the sailor promptly accepted the challenge and the girl, confident in her Jack's ability, agreed to abide by the results.

The day of the contest came, half the town it seemed turned out to watch, the two contestants were each given a length of string, and the father began to count.

The clerk began tying Overhand Knot after Overhand Knot with such celerity that it was thought he might run out of string before the time was up. Flying fingers.

The sailor, meanwhile, began methodically looping half hitches around one thumb. Now a half hitch is a fine knot with many uses, but it is not an Overhand Knot and never will be. The count went past 30 and he still hadn't tied anything but a lot of hitches (he had a long piece of string and great large thumbs). The count went past 40 without a single Overhand Knot and his girlfriend can be forgiven for tearfully wondering if this was a particularly inelegant way of skipping out on her.

There was an exultant tone in the father's voice as the count neared 50, and the clerk had just about given off trying to make any more knots, when the sailor gently removed the hitches from his thumb, threaded the end through them, pulled on it handsomely, which at sea means slowly and carefully, and a plentitude of Overhand Knots emerged like pearls from his hand. He tied the string around his sweetheart's throat as a necklace, they tied the archetypal knot the very next day, and they both lived happily ever after.

180

Appendix
Additional Tables

•

TABLE 7. Fiber Cordage — Typical Weights and Minimum Breaking Strengths in Pounds
(From Chapman, Charles F., et al. *Piloting, Seamanship and Small Boat Handling*. 54th ed. New York: Hearst, 1979)

The figures on synthetics presented here are an average of those available from four large cordage manufacturers. Those for the rope you buy should be available at your dealers. Check them carefully. Also check the rope. In general a soft, sleazy rope may be somewhat stronger and easier to splice but it will not wear as well and is more apt to hockle or unlay than a firm, well "locked-up" rope. Blended ropes, part polyolefins and part other fibers, may be found. Multifilament (fine filament) polypropylene looks like nylon—don't expect it to be as strong or do the job of nylon. (It floats, nylon doesn't.) Spun, or stapled, nylon and Dacron are not as strong as ropes made from continuous filaments but are less slippery and easier to grasp. Sometimes used for sheets on sailing craft.

NOMINAL SIZE (inches)		MANILA Fed. Spec. TR 605			NYLON (High Tenacity–H.T.)			DUPONT DACRON or H.T. POLYESTER			POLYOLEFINS (H.T.) (Polypropylene and/or Polyethylene)			DOUBLE NYLON BRAID			POLYESTER/ POLYOLEFIN DOUBLE BRAID		
Dia.	Circ.	Net Wt. 100'	Ft. per lb.	Breaking Strength	Net Wt. 100'	Ft. per lb.	Breaking Strength	Net Wt. 100'	Ft. per lb.	Breaking Strength	Net Wt. 100'	Ft. per lb.	Breaking Strength	Net Wt. 100'	Ft. per lb.	Breaking Strength	Net Wt. 100'	Ft. per lb.	Breaking Strength
³⁄₁₆	⅝	1.47	68.	450	1.	100	1,000	1.3	77.	1,000	.73	137	750	NA	NA	NA	.75	133	900
¼	¾	1.96	51.	600	1.5	66.6	1,700	2.1	47.5	1,700	1.24	80.	1,250	1.66	60.3	2,100	1.7	60.2	1,700
⁵⁄₁₆	1	2.84	35.	1,000	2.5	40.	2,650	3.3	30.	2,550	1.88	53.	1,850	2.78	36.	3,500	2.6	38.4	2,600
⅜	1⅛	4.02	24.	1,350	3.6	28.	3,650	4.7	21.3	3,500	2.9	34.5	2,600	3.33	30.	4,200	3.5	28.5	3,500
⁷⁄₁₆	1¼	5.15	19.4	1,750	5.	20.	5,100	6.3	15.9	4,800	3.9	25.5	3,400	5.	20.	6,000	5.1	20.	5,100
½	1½	7.35	13.6	2,650	6.6	15.	6,650	8.2	12.2	6,100	4.9	20.4	4,150	6.67	14.9	7,500	6.8	15.	6,800
⁹⁄₁₆	1¾	10.2	9.8	3,450	8.4	11.9	8,500	10.2	9.8	7,700	6.2	16.	4,900	8.33	12.	9,500	NA	NA	NA
⅝	2	13.1	7.6	4,400	10.5	9.5	10,300	13.2	7.6	9,500	7.8	12.8	5,900	11.1	9.	12,000	11.	9.	11,000
¾	2¼	16.3	6.1	5,400	14.5	6.9	14,600	17.9	5.6	13,200	11.1	9.	7,900	15.	6.7	17,000	15.	6.7	15,000
⅞	2¾	22.	4.55	7,700	20.	5.	19,600	24.9	4.	17,500	15.4	6.5	11,000	20.8	4.8	23,700	20.	5.	20,000
1	3	26.5	3.77	9,000	26.	3.84	25,000	30.4	3.3	22,000	18.6	5.4	13,000	25.	4.	28,500	28.	3.6	28,000
1⅛	3½	35.2	2.84	12,000	34.	2.94	33,250	40.5	2.5	26,500	24.2	4.1	17,500	35.	2.8	39,000	35.	2.8	35,000
1¼	3¾	40.8	2.45	13,500	39.	2.56	37,800	46.2	2.16	30,500	27.5	3.6	20,000	40.	2.5	44,000	40.	2.5	40,000
1⁵⁄₁₆	4	46.9	2.13	15,000	45.	2.22	44,500	53.4	1.87	34,500	31.3	3.2	23,000	45.	2.2	49,500	45.	2.2	45,000
1½	4½	58.8	1.7	18,500	55.	1.8	55,000	67.	1.5	43,000	39.5	2.5	29,000	60.	1.6	65,000	60.	1.6	60,000

181

TABLE 8. Fiber Rope Characteristics
(From Chapman's *Piloting, Seamanship and Small Boat Handling.* 54th ed.)

	MANILA	NYLON	DACRON	POLY-OLEFINS
Relative Strength	1	4	3	2
Relative Weight	3	2	4	1
Elongation	1	4	2	3
Relative Resistance to Impact or Shock Loads	1	4	2	3
Mildew and Rot Resistance	Poor	Excellent	Excellent	Excellent
Acid Resistance	Poor	Fair	Fair	Excellent
Alkali Resistance	Poor	Excellent	Excellent	Excellent
Sunlight Resistance	Fair	Fair	Good	Fair
Organic Solvent Resistance	Good	Good	Good	Fair
Melting Point	711° F. (Burns)	410° F.	410° F.	about 300° F.
Floatability	Only when new	None	None	Indefinite
*Relative Abrasion Resistance	2	3	4	1

*Depends on many factors—whether wet or dry, etc.
KEY TO RATINGS: 1=Lowest 4=Highest

TABLE 9. Weights and Tensile Strengths of Wire Ropes

Diam.	1x7 galv. iron seizing strand		1x7 annealed s.s. seiz. strand		7x7 galv. improved plow steel		7x19 galv. improved plow steel		7x7 s.s. 302/304		7x19 s.s. 302/304		1x19 s.s. 302/304	
	strength [lbs]	wt/1000 ft	strength [lbs]	wt/1000 ft	strength [lbs]	wt/1000 ft	strength [lbs]	wt/1000 ft	strength [lbs]	wt/1000 ft	strength [lbs]	wt/1000 ft	strength [lbs]	wt/1000 ft
1/16	140	10	230	8.5	480	7.5			480	7.5			500	8.5
3/32	300	20	500	20	920	16	1,000	16	920	16	920	16	1,200	20
1/8	540	33	900	33	1,700	28.5	2,000	29	1,700	28.5	1,760	29	2,100	35
5/32	870	50	1,350	50	2,600	43	2,800	45	2,400	43	2,400	45	3,300	55
3/16	1,150	73			3,700	62	4,200	65	3,700	62	3,700	65	4,700	77
7/32					4,800	83	5,600	86	4,800	83	5,000	86	6,300	102
1/4					6,100	106	7,000	110	6,100	106	6,400	110	8,200	135
9/32					7,400	134	8,000	139	7,600	134	7,800	139	10,300	170
5/16					9,200	167	9,800	173	9,000	167	9,000	173	12,500	210
3/8					13,300	236	14,400	243	12,000	236	12,000	243	17,500	300
7/16*					NA		17,600	356	15,600	342	16,300	356	22,500	410
1/2*					NA		22,800	458	21,300	440	22,800	458	30,000	521
9/16*									26,600	550	28,500	590	36,200	670
5/8*									32,500	680	35,000	715	47,000	855

*IWRC in 7x19

182

TABLE 10. Working Elongation Three-Strand and Braided Ropes

Data presented in this chart represent percentage working elongation of New England Ropes' products under various loads and are results obtained from tests conducted under Cordage Institute Standard Test Methods. *(Courtesy New England Ropes, Inc.)*

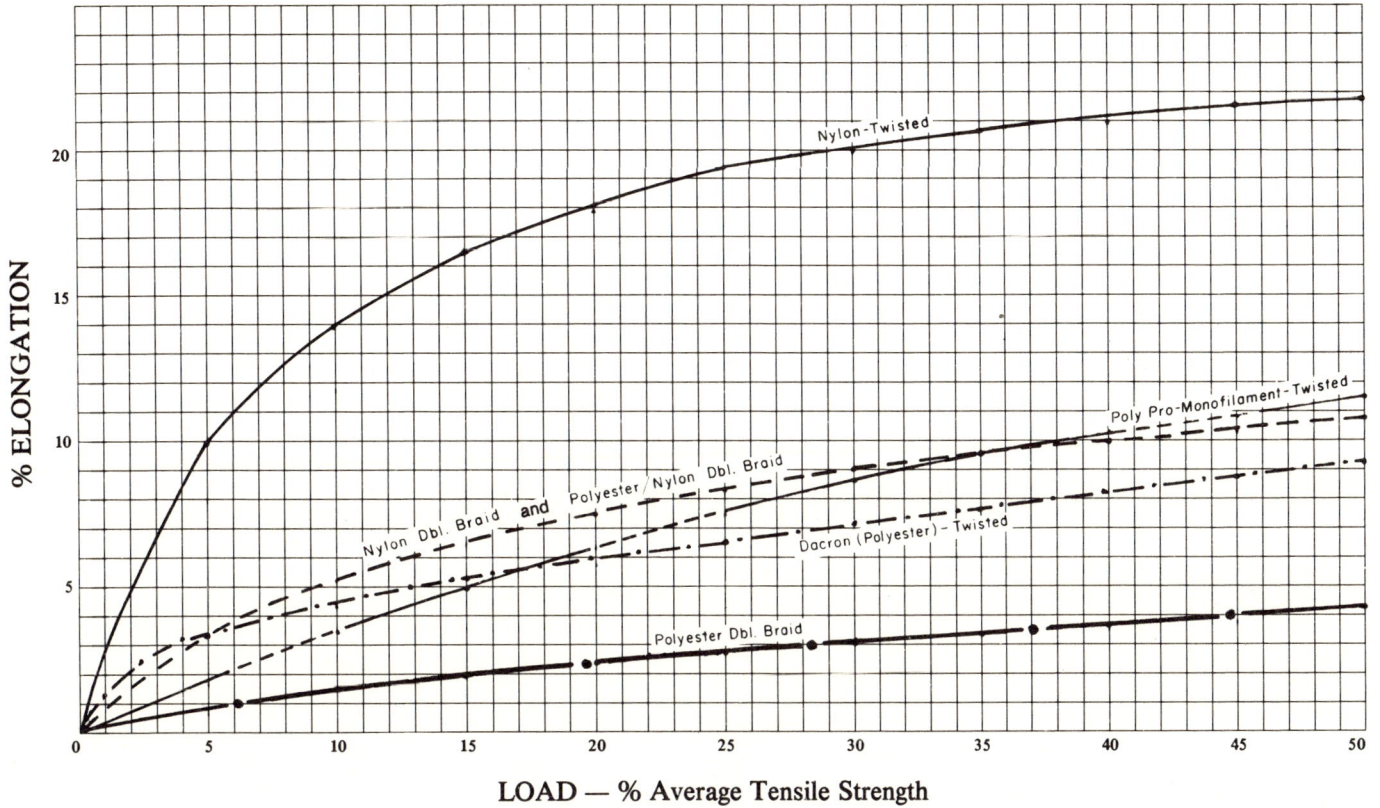

TABLE 11. Metric Equivalents of Standard Rope Sizes

DIAMETER		CIRCUMFERENCE		DIAMETER		CIRCUMFERENCE	
Inches	Millimeters	Inches	Millimeters	Inches	Millimeters	Inches	Millimeters
⅛	3.2	⅜	10.0	¹⁵⁄₁₆	23.8	3	76.2
⁵⁄₃₂	4.0	¹⁵⁄₃₂	12.0	1	25.4	3⅛	79.4
³⁄₁₆	4.8	⁹⁄₁₆	15.0	1¹⁄₁₆	27.0	3⅜	85.7
⁷⁄₃₂	5.6	¹¹⁄₁₆	17.0	1⅛	28.6	3½	88.9
¼	6.3	¾	20.0	1³⁄₁₆	30.2	3¾	95.2
⁵⁄₁₆	7.9	1	25.4	1¼	31.7	3⅞	98.4
⅜	9.5	1⅛	28.6	1⅜	34.9	4⅜	111.0
⁷⁄₁₆	11.1	1⅜	34.9	1⁷⁄₁₆	36.5	4½	114.0
½	12.7	1⅝	41.3	1½	38.1	4¾	121.0
⁹⁄₁₆	14.3	1¾	44.4	1⅝	41.3	5⅛	130.0
⅝	15.9	2	50.8	1¹¹⁄₁₆	42.9	5¼	133.0
¹¹⁄₁₆	17.5	2¼	57.1	1¾	44.4	5½	140.0
¾	19.0	2⅜	60.3	1¹³⁄₁₆	46.0	5¾	146.0
¹³⁄₁₆	20.6	2½	63.5	1⅞	47.6	5⅞	149.0
⅞	22.2	2¾	69.8	1¹⁵⁄₁₆	49.2	6⅛	156.0
				2	50.8	6¼	159.0

TABLE 12. Converting from Inches and Fractions of an Inch to Decimals of a Foot

Inches	1	2	3	4	5	6	7	8	9	10	11
Feet	0.0833	0.1667	0.2500	0.3333	0.4167	0.5000	0.5833	0.6667	0.7500	0.8333	0.9167
Inches	⅛	¼	⅜	½	⅝	¾	⅞				
Feet	0.0104	0.0208	0.0313	0.0417	0.0521	0.0625	0.0729				

Example: 5 ft. 7⅜ in. = 5.0 + 0.5833 + 0.0313 = 5.6146 ft.

TABLE 13. Decimal Equivalents of Common Fractions

8ths	16ths	32nds	64ths	Exact decimal values	8ths	16ths	32nds	64ths	Exact decimal values
					4	8	16	32	0.50
			1	0.01 5625				33	.51 5625
		1	2	.03 125			17	34	.53 125
			3	.04 6875				35	.54 6875
	1	2	4	.06 25			9	18	36	.56 25
			5	.07 8125				37	.57 8125
		3	6	.09 375			19	38	.59 375
			7	.10 9375				39	.60 9375
1	2	4	8	.12 5	5	10	20	40	.62 5
			9	.14 0625				41	.64 0625
		5	10	.15 625			21	42	.65 625
			11	.17 1875				43	.67 1875
	3	6	12	.18 75		11	22	44	.68 75
			13	.20 3125				45	.70 3125
		7	14	.21 875			23	46	.71 875
			15	.23 4375				47	.73 4375
2	4	8	16	.25	6	12	24	48	.75
			17	.26 5625				49	.76 5625
		9	18	.28 125			25	50	.78 125
			19	.29 6875				51	.79 6875
	5	10	20	.31 25		13	26	52	.81 25
			21	.32 8125				53	.82 8125
		11	22	.34 375			27	54	.84 375
			23	.35 9375				55	.85 9375
3	6	12	24	.37 5	7	14	28	56	.87 5
			25	.39 0625				57	.89 0625
		13	26	.40 625			29	58	.90 625
			27	.42 1875				59	.92 1875
	7	14	28	.43 75		15	30	60	.93 75
			29	.45 3125				61	.95 3125
		15	30	.46 875			31	62	.96 875
			31	.48 4375				63	.98 4375

Glossary

•

Abrasion: Chafe or surface wear on a rope or wire rope.

Aircraft cable: Strands, cords, and wire ropes made of very strong wire intended originally for aircraft controls and now widely used as standing rigging in traditional vessels.

Area, metallic: The sum of the cross-sectional areas of the individual wires in a wire rope; that is, the amount of "meat" in a wire, which varies with construction.

Back a strand, to: In a Long Splice or Grommet, to fill the score vacated by one strand with one of the opposite strands.

Backsplice: An end-of-the-rope knot in which the strands are first crowned, then spliced back into their own standing part.

Becket: 1. A rope handle. 2. The eye or hook of a block or block strop. 3. A short rope with an eye at one end and a button at the other, used for securing spars, oars, etc.

Belay, to: To secure a rope with round and figure-eight turns around a belaying pin, cleat, or bitts.

Belaying pin: A wood or metal pin inserted through a hole in a rail, to which running rigging is belayed.

Bend: A knot that ties two ropes' ends together.

Bight: A slack section in a rope's standing part.

Bitts: Upright timbers, usually in pairs, for making fast mooring and towing lines.

Block: A device with grooved wheels for changing the lead of a line, or, when compounded, for increasing the power of a tackle.

Bollards: Posts, commonly of iron, suitable for mooring. Like bitts, they are usually found in pairs, but they are more often round, while bitts are usually square.

Breaking strength: The measured load required to break a rope in tension. See *Nominal strength*.

By the run: To let go or cast off instantly instead of slacking gradually.

*Thanks to Doubleday & Co. for permission to take many of these definitions from *The Ashley Book of Knots*. Clifford Ashley's precise and painstaking definitions can hardly be improved on.

Cable: A term loosely applied to wire ropes, wire strands, fiber ropes, and electrical conductors.

Capsize: When applied to knots, this means to change the form under stress; to pervert.

Carry away, to: To break and go adrift. Applied to both sails and rigging. "The main topmast *carried away* in the storm."

Chafe, to: To fray, fret, gall, or rub. See *Abrasion*.

Circumference: The perimeter of a cross section through a rope or wire rope; the girth.

Cleat: A wooden or metal object with two horns, secured to deck, mast, dock, or rigging, to which ropes are belayed.

Clevis pin: A transverse pin in a shackle, tang, turnbuckle, or toggle, to which standing rigging attaches.

Coil: A bundle of rope or wire rope, usually circular, arranged for convenience of handling and storing. See *Reel*.

Come-along: A ratchet winch with wire pendant used to stretch cable for service, to set up lanyards, to effect emergency repairs, etc.

Construction: The design of a wire rope, including its number of strands, the number of wires per strand, and the arrangement of wires in each strand.

Cordage: Fiber rope of any material or size.

Corrosion: Chemical decomposition of a wire rope by exposure to moisture, acids, alkalines, or other destructive agents.

Cotter pin: A split pin used in rigging to prevent clevis pins from backing out of position.

Cuntlines: The surface seams between the strands of a rope.

Design factor: See *Safety factor*.

Diameter: The thickness of a strand, a rope, or a wire rope.

Dog-leg: A permanent, short bend in a wire rope caused by carelessness, especially while stepping or unstepping a mast, or by improper use, especially from running the wire over a sheave or winch of insufficient size.

Double, to: To continue the lead of a decorative knot around an additional circuit, as in a Turk's Head or Button Knot.

Ease or ease off: To slacken.

Elastic limit: The limit of stress above which a permanent deformation takes place within the material. This limit is approximately 55 to 65 percent of the breaking strength of steel wire rope.

Eye or Eyesplice: A spliced, seized, swaged, or knotted loop, with or without a thimble.

Fair, to: To smooth out or to even a knot, splice, or sinnet, in order to improve its appearance and ensure an even strain on all strands.

Fall: The hauling end of a tackle.

Fast: Secure. "The throat halyard is fast."

Fatigue: Denotes the progressive fracturing of the wires in a rope due to a loss of resiliency with age and use; work hardening. Alloyed steels are particularly susceptible to fatigue.

Fiber heart or core: A twisted rope or strand employed as a core in wire rope.

Filler wire: Small auxiliary wires in a wire rope strand for spacing and positioning other wires.

Fox: Yarns wound or twisted together to shorten their working length, especially for fancy work.

Frapping turns: A number of crossing turns in a lashing or seizing or in the leads of a tackle, which serve both to tighten and secure the piece.

Galvanized wire: Wire coated with zinc to retard corrosion.

Gang: A set of rigging for a mast or yard.

Grades, wire rope: Classification of wire rope by its breaking strength. In order of their increasing breaking strengths the unalloyed steels are: iron, traction, mild plow steel, plow steel, improved plow steel, and extra improved plow steel. Alloyed steels vary widely in breaking strength depending on their composition, but most of the alloys used in yacht rigging have approximately the strength of improved plow steel.

Grommet: An endless wire or fiber rope made from one continuous strand.

Ground tackle: A general term for all hawsers, chains, cables, buoy ropes, and warps employed in anchoring, mooring, and sometimes in towing a vessel.

Halyard: Rope for hoisting a sail or yard.

Handsomely: Slowly, carefully, gently; as, "to lower away handsomely."

Handy-billy: A small tackle kept handy for small jobs.

Haul, to: To pull by hand on a rope or tackle.

Hitch: A knot that secures a rope to another object, such as a piling, rail, ring, etc., or to its own standing part, or to the standing part of another rope.

Hoist, to: To lift by means of a tackle.

Independent wire rope core (I.W.R.C.): A type of wire heart for a wire rope, the heart constructed so that it is itself a miniature wire rope. The I.W.R.C. is stronger and more resistant to crushing and is stronger than fiber hearts and other wire hearts.

Irish Pennants: Cordage ends that are frayed or raveled due to neglect.

Jute: A material of low breaking strength, sometimes used for cheap rope and sometimes as a heart for four-stranded fiber ropes and wire ropes.

Kink: A sharp bend in a rope or wire rope that permanently distorts and thus weakens the rope.

Knot: Any complication in a rope except for accidental ones such as snarls and kinks.

Lanyard: 1. A small rope for making fast the end of a piece of standing rigging. 2. Handles, frequently ornamentally decorated, for tools, bags, watches, or any other small item you don't want to lose overboard.

Lash: To secure or contain an object or objects by binding them with rope.

Lay: 1. The direction of the strand twist or lead in a rope. 2. The firmness or angle of that twist.

Lead: The direction of a rope, or the direction of a strand in a knot.

Leads: The parts of a tackle between the two blocks, as opposed to the standing part and the fall.

Let go, to: To cast off.

Line: In general parlance, a length of rope put to a specific use.

Long-jawed rope: Old rope that has stretched and lost much of its twist.

Make fast: 1. To secure a rope with a hitch or hitches. 2. To finish off a belay with a single hitch.

Marl, to: To secure or contain with a series of Marling Hitches.

Marlingspike: A conical, metal tool employed in just about every procedure of traditional rigging, especially for tightening, loosening, separating, pounding, and toggling.

Marry, to: To intermesh the strands of two rope ends preparatory to splicing.

Modulus of elasticity: A mathematical quantity giving the ratio, within the elastic limit, of a defined stress on a rope or wire rope to the corresponding elongation.

Nominal strength: The published or advertised design stength of a rope or wire rope. This is usually though not always less than the actual breaking strength of the rope.

Overhaul: 1. To separate the blocks of a tackle preparatory to another haul. 2. To eliminate kinks in a line by recoiling, stretching, or flaking.

Palm: A narrow leather strap with thumb hole and, affixed next to the thumb hole, a dimpled "iron." The palm is worn around the palm of the hand as an aid to pushing needles through heavy cloth or leather, the blunt end of the needle being braced against the iron.

Parcel: To wrap with canvas or tape the length of a rope or wire rope, in order to produce a waterproof base for service.

Part, to: To break.

Pendant: A standing rope or wire rope to which a tackle is hooked, seized, or shackled.

Preformed: Said of a wire rope in which the strands are shaped to a permanent helix. The strands of preformed wire will not spring apart when cut.

Prestressing: Stressing a rope or wire rope before use in order to remove constructional stretch.

Purchase: A mechanical advantage gained with block and tackle or winch.

Ravel: To fray. "Unravel" is a redundant term.

Reel: The flanged spool on which rope or wire rope is wound for storage and shipment.

Reeve: To pass the end of a rope or wire rope through any hole or opening.

Reeve off: To reeve through blocks for running rigging.

Riding turns: In seizings, whippings, and lashings, a second tier of turns over the base or round turns.

Rigging: The art of using knots and lines either to move things or keep them from moving.

Rope: Any cordage stouter than one inch in circumference.

Running rigging: All rigging that is rove through blocks.

Safety factor: The ratio of breaking strength to maximum expected stress.

Seizing: A means of binding two or more ropes together with cordage or seizing wire.

Seizing strand or wire: A small strand, usually of seven wires, made of soft annealed iron or stainless steel.

Service: Marline, small stuff, or seizing wire wrapped around standing rigging for protection against wear and weather.

Serving board: A small serving mallet.

Serving mallet: A tool for applying marline service.

Set up, to: To tune rigging by tightening lanyards or turnbuckles.

Shears: Two spars lashed together at the top and guyed; used for raising masts and hoisting heavy weights.

Sheave: A grooved pulley that rotates on a pin and constitutes the moving part of a block. Nonrotating sheaves, as found in topmast heels, are called "dumb sheaves."

Shock loading: The sudden impact that results when a load comes rapidly onto a slack rope. The measured strain of a shock load can far exceed the load that produced it.

Shroud: A standing-rig piece that stays a mast laterally. The lateral stays that extend from a topmast or topgallant to the chainplates, however, are called "backstays" rather than shrouds.

Sinnet: Braided cordage.

Slack away: To pay out or let out slack.

Sling: Any of numerous configurations of rope or wire rope attached to an object, by means of which that object is to be hoisted.

Slushing: Protecting standing rigging from deterioration by coating it with a waterproofing agent that usually contains pine tar, linseed oil, varnish, or other ingredients in various combinations. Slush applications should congeal to a hard finish that will not scuff off on sails, running rigging, or crew.

Small stuff: Rope that is less than one inch in circumference.

Smartly: Together, with precision and alacrity.

Snarl: An entanglement of cordage.

Span: A length of rope or wire rope, fast at both ends, to be hauled on at the center; a bridle; a form of sling.

Splice, to: To interweave two ends of ropes or wire ropes so as to make a continuous length. Also, to make a loop or eye in the end of a rope or wire rope by tucking the strand ends into the standing part.

Stainless steel rope: Wire rope made of alloyed steel having great resistance to corrosion.

Stand by, to: To take hold of a rope and stand ready to haul, slacken, or belay.

Standing part: The inactive part, as opposed to the end, bight, or loop.

Stay: A piece of fore-and-aft standing rigging.

Strand: A component piece of a rope, itself composed of two or more yarns twisted together.

Strop: A grommet or short pendant seized around a block, mast, or boom, by means of which a purchase is applied.

Surge, to: To slack away on a line under strain by allowing it to slide in controlled fashion over the surface of a pin, winch, windlass, etc.

Swage: A fitting into which a wire-rope end is inserted. The rope is secured there by the application of tremendous pressure to the sides of the fitting.

Sweat up, to: To pull on a taut rope at right angles to its length, feeding the slack so gained to the tailer.

Tackle: A mechanism of blocks and rope for increasing power. The ancient pronunciation "tay'-ckle" is still preferred.

Tag line: A rope used to prevent the rotation or swinging of a load.

Tail: To take up slack in a load-bearing line and subsequently maintain the advantage with the aid of one or more round turns on a pin or winch. The slack is usually fed to the tailer by another crewmember.

Tail on: An order to grasp and haul.

Taper: To diminish the diameter of a rope or a splice in a rope by removing yarns at staggered intervals over a given length.

Thimble: A grooved metal fitting to protect the eye of a rope or wire rope.

Thoroughfoot: A tangle in a tackle due to a block's upsetting.

Turn: One round of a rope on a pin, cleat, or rail; one round of a coil.

Turnbuckle: A device attached to a wire rope for applying tension. It consists of a barrel and right- and left-threaded bolts.

Two-blocked: Said of an exhausted purchase, the blocks of which are jammed against one another.

Weed, to: To clear rigging of stops, rope yarns, etc.

Whip, to: To bind the end of a rope to prevent fraying.

Wire rope: A plurality of wire strands helically laid about a longitudinal axis.

With the lay: To the right or clockwise with right-laid rope; to the left or counterclockwise with left-laid rope.

Worm, to: To fill the seams of a rope with spun yarns or marline.

Yarn: A number of fibers twisted together.

Bibliography

•

Ashley, Clifford W. *The Ashley Book of Knots*. New York: Doubleday, 1944. Illustrates, explains, and analyzes knots, sets them in their historical context, and encourages their contemporary application. And it does all this with warmth, thoroughgoing professionalism, and unfailing humor. The one indispensable book for the marlingspike artist.

Day, Cyrus L. *The Art of Knotting and Splicing*. Third Edition. Annapolis, Maryland: United States Naval Institute, 1970. A great introduction, clear photographs, intelligent layout, and concise text make this the best basic ropework text.

Kinney, Francis S. *Skene's Elements of Yacht Design*. Eighth Edition. New York: Dodd, Mead, and Co., 1973. A compendium of the principles and procedures of yacht design. Read it to put your rigging in the context of the entire vessel.

Nares, George S. *Seamanship*. Henley, England: Gresham Books, 1979. A reprint of the 1862 edition of a book first published in 1860 as an instruction manual for naval cadets. The procedures it describes are unquestionably archaic, but its principles can inform the most modern rig. Exceptional illustrations and a helpful question-and-answer format.

Norgrove, Ross. *Cruising Rigs and Rigging*. Camden, Maine: International Marine Publishing Co., 1982. The wisdom distilled from years of paying attention to what makes rigs live longer. Norgrove emphasizes good design and maintenance procedures with stories that are variously amusing and hair-raising.

Rigging Handbooks. Available from wire rope manufacturers. Every manufacturer prints a list of its products detailing wire materials, constructions, and designed uses. These specifications are supplemented by reference tables, charts, essays on manufacture and use, explanations of inspection procedures, instructions for splicing and seizing, and a few words about slings, lubrication, and sling tolerances. Presto! You've got a little technical manual. Most of the information refers to industrial applications but is easily extrapolated to boat rigging.

Rossnagel, W.E. *Handbook of Rigging: In Construction and Industrial Operations*. Third Edition. New York: McGraw-Hill, 1964. The industrial rigger's bible, and great-granddaddy to the manufacturers' handbooks. Gives safe loads for everything from crane guys to nailed joists; instructions for making a life nest; finding the center of gravity of odd-shaped objects; the proper use of steel scaffolding; and just about anything else you'll ever need to know about other-than-strictly-nautical rigging.

Steel, David. *The Elements of Mastmaking, Sailmaking, and Rigging*. New York: Edward W. Sweetman, 1978. A reprint of the 1932 edition of a book first published in 1794 under the title, *The Elements and Practice of Rigging and Seamanship*. Helpful in the sense that Nares's *Seamanship* is helpful, but more archaic.

Taylor, Roger C. *The Elements of Seamanship*. Camden, Maine: International Marine Publishing Co., 1982. This little book is to seamanship what Strunk and White's *Elements of Style* is to writing. If you would learn to rig, you must learn to sail.

Texas Instruments, Inc. *Understanding Calculator Math*. Ft. Worth, Texas: Radio Shack, 1978. Arithmetic, algebra, and trigonometry are of great value to the rigger. You get a kindly introduction to these and many other subjects here, to enable you to better employ the traditional electronic calculator.

Index

•